THE
LIFE PROGRESSION
SYSTEM

Author/Editor: Rev. Darryl Bass

Electronic ISBN: 978-1-972115-00-8 (EPUB)
                  978-1-972115-29-9 (Kindle)
Paperback ISBN: 978-1-972115-01-5
Hardcover ISBN: 978-1-972115-02-2
Printed in the United States

The Library of Congress Control Number: 2026905391

Bass Publishing, LLC
Maywood, IL 60153

Disclaimer

The information contained in this book is for educational and informational purposes only. It is not intended as financial, legal, tax, medical, psychological, or professional advice. The author and publisher make no guarantees regarding the results that may be obtained from the use of this material.

All examples provided are illustrative and are not intended to represent or guarantee that any individual will achieve similar results. Personal growth, financial improvement, and life progression outcomes depend on individual effort, discipline, decisions, and circumstances.

Readers are encouraged to seek qualified professional advice regarding financial planning, legal matters, mental health, or other specialized areas before making decisions based on the information provided in this book.

The author and publisher disclaim any liability for any loss, risk, or damages, direct or indirect, that may arise from the use or application of the information contained herein.

By reading this book, you acknowledge that you are responsible for your own decisions, actions, and results.

Details in any stories and anecdotes have been changed to protect the identities of the person(s) involved.

Scripture quotations are taken from the King James Version of the Bible.

Table of Contents

FOREWORD

Welcome to a transformative journey within the pages of this book. In the pursuit of a stronger, more resilient self, we often find ourselves grappling with obstacles, fears, and the weight of our own habits. Throughout this remarkable journey, you will unlock the depths of your potential and ignite the fire of your determination. Within these pages lies a progression system designed to shape not only your actions but your very mindset—a system that will empower you to cultivate an unyielding will and foster unwavering beliefs. This unique progression system is your guide, helping you build a robust foundation—a strong will—that propels you forward, unearths your true potential, and paves the way to conquering challenges.

With each turn of the page, you'll uncover the power of solid belief—the art of shedding what holds you back. This isn't just a manual for change; it's a blueprint for empowerment. It's about breaking free from the chains of self-doubt and uncertainty and forging ahead with the tools and strategies meticulously laid out. Life's challenges often seem insurmountable, fears loom large, and habits can hold us captive. But fear not, for this book is your steadfast companion on the path to greatness. With the power of solid belief, you'll learn how to overcome adversity, dismantle obstacles, and shatter the chains of bad habits hindering your progress.

Throughout this journey, you'll be equipped with step-by-step instructions, offering a clear path to the pursuit of your aspirations. Remember, growth is not a linear process, and change is rarely instantaneous. But as you delve into these pages, you'll find the guidance you need to navigate the twists and turns of personal evolution. In the chapters ahead, you'll discover the art of setting audacious goals and pursuing them with unrelenting fervor. Every step of the way, meticulously outlined instructions will guide you towards success. Remember, the journey might be arduous at times, but it's in those moments that your spirit strengthens, and your will solidifies.

As you absorb the wisdom within, envision the life you aspire to lead and embrace the power you hold within yourself. The pursuit of your dreams is not just a desire; it's a birthright. So, let this book be your beacon, lighting the way through doubt and uncertainty, and steering you towards the achievements that are rightfully yours.

Your transformation begins now, and the victory that awaits is a testament to the strength of your will, the depth of your belief, and the power of your unwavering pursuit. Onward, intrepid seeker, for your journey towards a stronger will and a life well-lived starts with these pages. Remember, the possibilities that lie ahead are as boundless as your willingness to embrace them.

Read the mantra on the following page each day; it will help you continue on your journey.

ABOUT THE AUTHOR

Meet the visionary behind "The Life Progression System," Reverend Darryl Bass. From his tenure at Citibank to his current role as Assistant Pastor at Impact Church in Maywood, IL, Darryl's journey as a life, financial, and spiritual coach epitomizes determination and unwavering faith.

For more than two decades, Darryl has been joined in marriage to his steadfast partner, Patricia. Their enduring union stands as a testament to the values he cherishes. As a devoted father to nine children—Darnisha, Darryl Jr., Wardell, Darrell, Candance, Tyanne, Cierra, Cayleen, and John—he imparts his wisdom to future generations, leaving behind a legacy of love, strength, and commitment.

Darryl's entrepreneurial spirit shines through his various ventures. Founding Divine and Righteous Solutions, Divine Debt Solutions, Righteous Rewards, Savings Solutions, 4MyDebt Solutions, Divine and Righteous Realty, and collaborating with his wife in Divine Delights and Clara's Kitchen, he paints a picture of success across diverse domains.

Always forward-thinking, Darryl is pioneering a transformative course to liberate individuals from the burdens of debt. His holistic approach encompasses credit building, income growth, robust savings, and secure retirement planning—while also nurturing families and building legacies for generations. His commitment to giving back is evident through his emphasis on tithing, a cornerstone of his belief in abundance.

With steadfast dedication, Reverend Darryl Bass answers the divine call to create abundance for all who seek it and to lead an Exodus from the bondage of debt, freeing individuals from the chains of indebtedness. He stands as a beacon of possibility. His life's work, encapsulated within the pages of "The Life Progression System," illuminates a path toward personal, financial, and spiritual elevation. Join us in honoring a journey fueled by purpose, perseverance, and an unwavering commitment to enrich lives.

ACKNOWLEDGEMENT

I express my deepest gratitude to God for granting me the vision, inspiration, and insight to bring this book to life. Without His divine guidance, this project would not have been possible. Through His grace, I aim to convey the message that God desires us to lead abundant lives, free from the chaos of this world and the burdens of debt.

I am profoundly thankful to my wife, Patricia, for her unwavering patience and support throughout the research and writing process. I also extend my gratitude to my children, Cayleen and John, for their understanding and sacrifice during this time of dedication. Special thanks to Annie Smolucha for her outstanding work in helping to create the cover for this book.

I extend my heartfelt appreciation to my Pastor, Anthony Pelegrino, the members of Impact Church, and my beloved family and friends for their unwavering encouragement and support. A special acknowledgment goes to my cousin, Angela, for her meticulous proofreading and invaluable contributions to my writing.

your contributions have greatly enriched the content of this book and have been instrumental in its completion. Thank you for your valuable input and support. I extend my heartfelt gratitude to each of you for your invaluable contributions and unwavering faith in this endeavor. Without your support, this book would never have come to fruition. I also want to express my sincere appreciation to those who preordered the book, for your belief and trust in me. Lastly, I want to express my deepest thanks to you, the purchaser and reader of this book. Your trust in me to lead and guide you on this journey of personal growth is truly humbling. Thank you for embarking on this transformative journey with me.

THE LPS MANTRA

"I Embrace Progress, I Embrace Life: With every step, I grow, I thrive, and I become the best version of myself."

Every day presents a fresh opportunity for growth, and I am dedicated to seizing it fully. I choose to integrate progress into the fabric of my life's journey.

My personal evolution stands as evidence of my commitment to self-improvement. I recognize that growth often accompanies challenges, and I confront them directly, understanding they propel me toward self-betterment.

I place my trust in the Life Progression System as an invaluable resource on my voyage of self-discovery. It furnishes me with the guidance and framework necessary to navigate life's intricacies.

Each goal I set serves as a pledge to myself—a commitment to labor diligently, learn continuously, and strive for excellence in all facets of my existence.

I acknowledge setbacks not as defeats but as instructive experiences. I utilize these lessons to recalibrate my course and persist with heightened resolve.

My personal development transcends mere self-interest. As I evolve, I emerge as a source of encouragement and assistance for those around me, uplifting and empowering them on their own paths.

I cultivate gratitude daily, acknowledging that even amidst my pursuits, there is much to cherish in the present moment.

My mindset stands as a cornerstone of my achievements. I elect positivity, resilience, and adaptability, recognizing that these attributes empower me to surmount any hurdle.

I welcome life's uncertainties with open arms, for it is amidst challenges and change that I genuinely unveil my strength and potential.

I am the architect of my growth narrative, and each chapter serves as a testament to my resilience, determination, and unwavering confidence in my capacity to realize my fullest potential.

The GPS

GPS stands for the Global Positioning System. We are all familiar with what the GPS is for, but in case you are not, the GPS allows you to get from one point to another by providing you with step-by-step instructions. By utilizing the GPS, it is simpler for anyone to get from point A to point B. But in order for the GPS to work it requires information from the user.

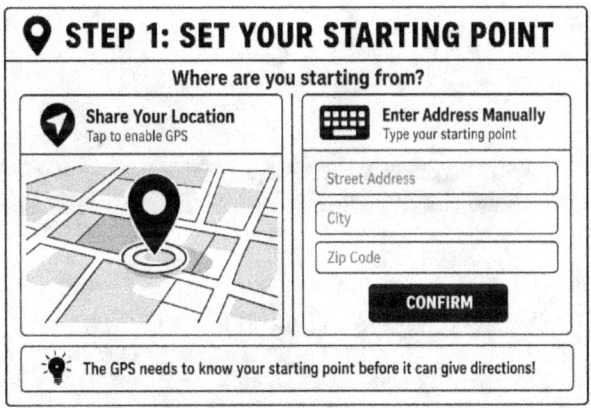

STEP 1: The first thing the GPS needs to know is where you are. What is your starting point? You can either share your location with the GPS or you can manually input your location. Without this information it is literally impossible for the GPS to give you the directions you need without knowing where you are.

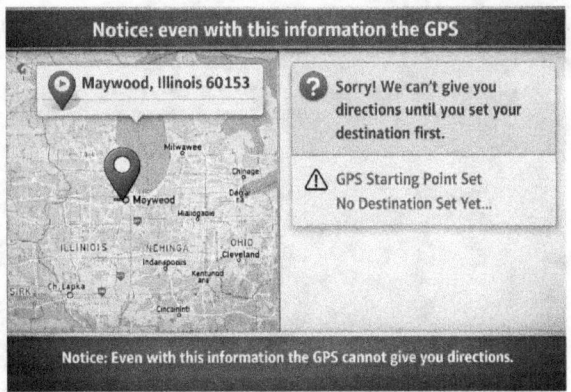

STEP 2: The second thing that is required by the GPS is where you desire to go. What is your destination? The GPS does not know where you want to go, and it requires that you tell it where you want to go. Without knowing where you need to go, the GPS cannot direct you anywhere.

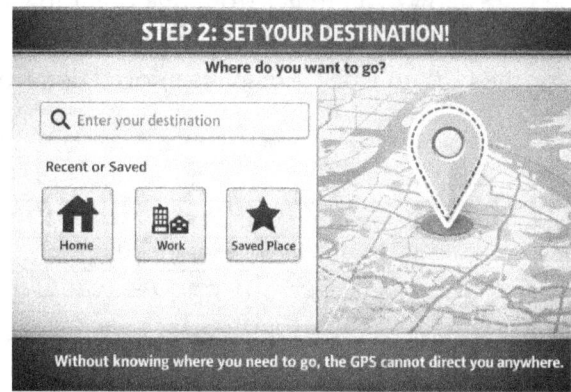

But once the GPS knows where you are going, watch what happens.

Once you have done the second step, the GPS does two things,

    1.   The GPS gives you choices.

        a. It gives you choices and the choices include these three things:
           i. The fastest route – if you want to get there quick.
          ii. The fuel saver route – if you want to use less fuel.
         iii. The scenic route – requires more time and more miles.

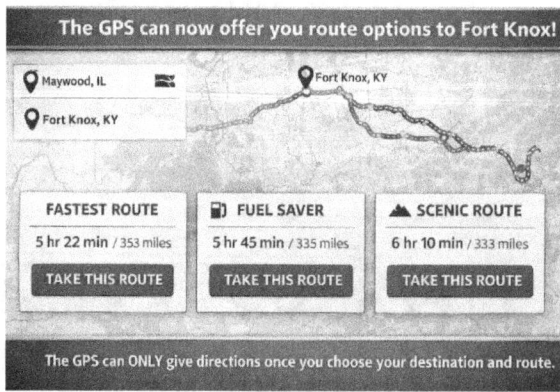

        b. It forewarns you of obstacles that you may encounter, such as:
           i. Traffic congestion
          ii. Accidents
         iii. Tolls

      iv. Road Construction

      v. Road Closures

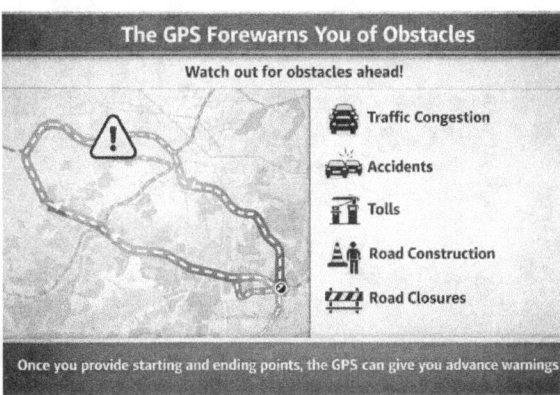

2.   The GPS gives you options:

  a. The first options are things to avoid.
      i. Highways
      ii. Tolls
      iii. Ferries

  b. The second is distance unit measurements.
      i. Automatic – Determined by the GPS
      ii. Miles
      iii. Km

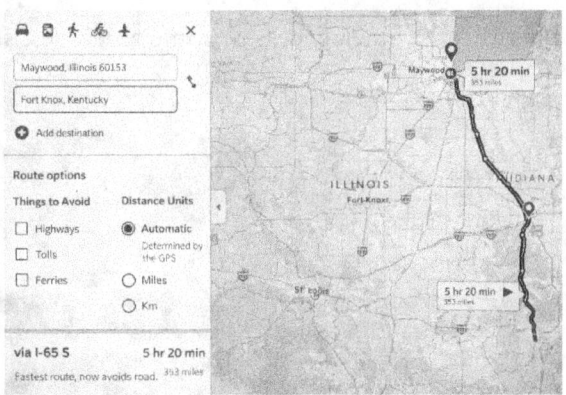

STEP 3: Once you have determined the best route for you by considering the obstacles that you may encounter and selected your options and determined how your trip is measured, the GPS is prepared to give you the directions you need based on how you have determined to get there.

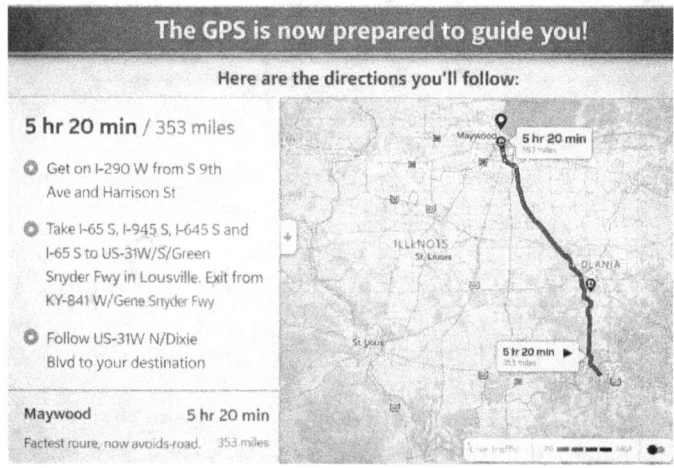

Now that you have your directions, reaching your destination is simple and easy. The only thing that you need now, depending on how far your destination is, is to gas up when you are running low on fuel, take a bathroom break or even stop and get rest.

STEP 4: Here is the sweet part about the GPS, once you have your directions it gives you amenities to choose on your route, these route options include:

The GPS includes hot buttons for quick access to some amenities, such as

1. Hotels
2. Gas
3. Rest stops
4. More

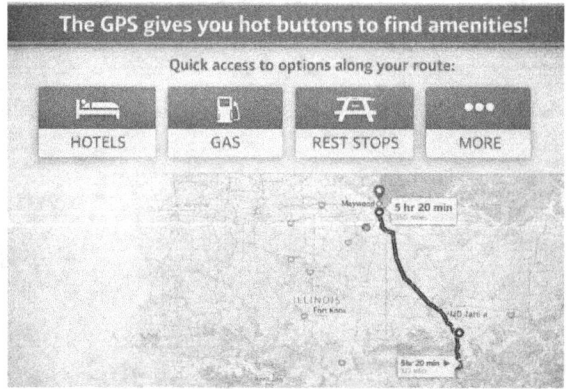

Under the more "hot button" you will find the following amenities, such as:

  a. Accommodation
      i. Hotels
      ii. Campgrounds

  b. Food & Drinks
      i. Restaurants
      ii. Coffee
      iii. Fast Food
      iv. Groceries

  c. Services
      i. Rest stops
      ii. Gas
      iii. EV charging
      iv. Banks – ATM

  d. Things to do.
      i. Attractions
      ii. Events
      iii. Parks
      iv. Museums

These amenities are very helpful to you along your route, especially for long trips, they allow you to get the things needed during your trip as well as an opportunity to see and experience things along the way.

Now that you fully understand the GPS and how it works, oh no wait a minute, I forgot one of the key factors of the GPS and that is what mode of travel will you use? Let's make this step 5.

STEP 5: Here you want to determine your travel method and depending on the GPS you will have 5 maybe 6 choices.

Travel Methods:

  1. Recommended Travel (may not be available on all GPS systems)
  2. Driving
  3. Transit
  4. Walking
  5. Cycling
  6. Airplane

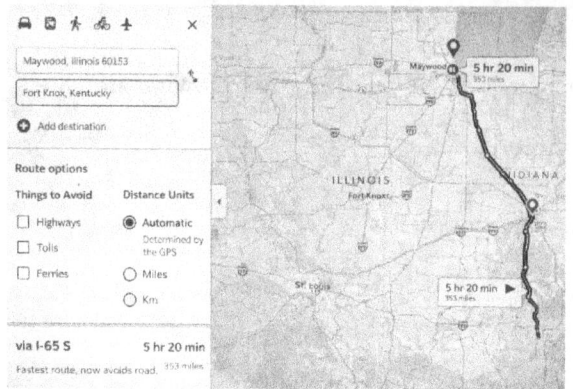

Choosing your method determines your time factor, walking is slower than cycling, cycling is slower than transit, transit is slower than driving (in most cases) and driving is slower than airplane. Also walking, cycling and transit would not be an option depending on the distance you have to travel.

Now with that being said, you should fully understand how the GPS is operated. So, here's what I need you to do, I want you to consider this same concept if you apply it to your life. Could you imagine if you had a GPS that would allow you to get where you wanted to go in life? How awesome would that be! Well, the truth of the matter is that we do, but most of us don't realize that it is available, or we don't use it in the proper manner. I call it the Life Progression System or the LPS for short.

The LPS

What if I introduced you to a system that could help you achieve the progress you desire in life? Imagine a system where you could input your goals, dreams, and aspirations, and then effortlessly live the life you've always envisioned. Surprisingly, this system has been around for years, yet many of us have never fully realized its potential or learned how to use it effectively.

Enter the Life Progression System (LPS). It comprises several familiar tools, but the challenge lies in using them correctly and synergistically to create a systematic approach to life. Let's explore these tools:

Tool #1: SELF-ASSESSMENT

Often overlooked, self-assessment is the critical first step in the LPS. Before we can progress, we must understand where we currently stand. By delving into our morals, obedience, values, and ethics, we establish a foundation for growth and set boundaries for our journey.

Tool #2: GOAL SETTING

Setting goals is essential, but many of us struggle to turn our aspirations into reality. We become dreamers, setting goals without taking action to achieve them. However, merely setting goals isn't enough—we must implement strategies to reach them.

Tool #3: ACTION STEPS

Breaking down our goals into manageable action steps is vital for progress. Without action, our goals remain mere fantasies. It's the execution of these steps that transforms dreams into tangible achievements.

Tool #4: RESOURCES

Identifying and leveraging our resources is crucial for success. Whether it's knowledge, finances, relationships, or time, understanding what we have and what we need propels us forward on our journey.

Tool #5: TIME MANAGEMENT

Effective time management extends beyond creating daily schedules. It involves maximizing every minute of our day, ensuring that each moment contributes to our progress.

Now, let's draw parallels between these tools and the GPS navigation system. Just as the GPS requires accurate location and destination information to chart a course, the LPS relies on self-assessment and goal setting to map our path forward. Action steps serve as the directions, guiding us towards our objectives. Resources are the fuel that propels us forward, while time management ensures we stay on track throughout our journey.

By understanding and utilizing these tools effectively, we can unlock the full potential of the Life Progression System, paving the way for personal growth and fulfillment.

Using the tools of the LPS like a GPS

Finding Your Starting Point

Much like a GPS needs a starting point, the LPS relies on understanding where you are in life and, more importantly, who you are. Self-assessment is key. It's about comprehending not just your physical location but your identity and values. After all, how can you map out a journey without knowing your current position? In the same way, the LPS requires a deep dive into self-awareness before embarking on your desired path. It's like setting a destination on your GPS without enabling location services—it just won't work. Similarly, without knowing who you are, your journey toward personal growth will be directionless.

Some might argue, "I don't need to change who I am; I just want to change my circumstances." But have you considered that your circumstances are often a reflection of who you are? For instance, if you're a shopaholic aspiring to become a millionaire, wouldn't you need to alter your spending habits? Similarly, if procrastination is your default mode, achieving your goals requires a shift in mindset. To change your outcomes, you must first change yourself, and that begins with understanding your current self through self-assessment.

Setting Your Destination

Just as the GPS requires a destination, the LPS relies on goals. But goal-setting isn't as straightforward as it seems. Most people only focus on the tangible aspects—possessions, career, physical health—without delving into the psychological transformation required for success. It's like inputting an address into your GPS without specifying the city or state; you'll end up lost. Likewise, solely focusing on external goals often leads to failure.

However, the LPS introduces a critical second phase: the psychological transformation. This phase, often overlooked, is where true success lies. It's about reshaping your beliefs, overcoming fears, and adopting a growth mindset. By aligning your internal identity with your external goals, you dramatically increase your chances of success. This phase, though less emphasized, is the linchpin of the entire system.

Mapping Your Route

While a GPS provides step-by-step directions and warns of obstacles, the LPS requires manual action steps. Each goal requires a detailed plan of action, akin to plotting a route on your GPS. These action steps not only guide you toward your objectives but also anticipate and prepare for obstacles along the way. By breaking down your goals into manageable steps, you empower yourself to navigate challenges effectively.

Consider Barbara, a single mother aiming to buy a house. She identifies obstacles—insufficient savings and a low credit score—and explores various strategies to overcome them. Through careful planning and resourcefulness, she uncovers alternative options, much like choosing different routes on a GPS to avoid traffic or road closures. Action steps, choices, and options are the tools that enable her to navigate toward her goal effectively.

Choosing Your Method

Just as a GPS offers different travel modes, time management plays a dual role in the LPS. It determines both your method of progress—whether you proceed slowly or swiftly—and the timing of your milestones. Your chosen pace affects your journey's duration and efficiency, much like selecting a travel mode on a GPS influences your estimated time of arrival. Procrastination, akin to ignoring GPS directions, can derail your progress and lead you astray.

Understanding Your Resources

Resources, crucial in the LPS, are akin to amenities on a GPS journey. They encompass knowledge, finances, relationships, and time—essential for a smooth journey to success. Like stopping for fuel or rest on a trip, utilizing your resources strategically ensures you reach your destination efficiently. The more abundant your resources, the faster your progress. Replenishing and adjusting your resources along the journey ensures flexibility and adaptability, much like procuring amenities during a trip to maintain comfort and efficiency.

In essence, by treating your journey to success like a guided GPS trip, you can navigate life's challenges with confidence and clarity. Self-awareness, goal alignment, strategic planning, efficient time management, and resource utilization are the keys to unlocking your full potential and reaching your desired destination.

PART I
The Pre-Trip Inspection

PRE-TRIP INSPECTION

Preparing for the Journey

Just as we ensure our vehicle is road-ready before a trip, it's vital to prep ourselves for the journey toward a better life. Picture this: you're about to embark on a road trip, but before you hit the highway, there's a checklist to go through. First, you check the fluids, ensuring they're clean and topped up. Next, you inspect the lights, making sure they're shining bright. Lastly, you examine the brakes and tires, ensuring they're up to the task. Only then do you load up the car and set off.

Similarly, before we begin our journey of personal growth, there's a mental pre-trip inspection to undertake. Our minds are like the engines powering us forward. We need them to be clean and open to change, fueled by belief and powered by will. If we're willing to make the necessary changes and take action, there's no limit to what we can achieve.

In this chapter, we'll focus on priming our minds for the journey ahead. Without a positive mindset, steadfast belief, and strong will, we won't even get started. Think of it like a car unable to start without an engine, fuel, or oil. Are you ready? Let's explore the three essential steps we need to take before we can begin our journey.

Before we set off, gather these items:

1. A pen

2. A pencil (for any adjustments)

3. The LPS Workbook

   - Alternatively, a large spiral notebook or a three-ring binder with plenty of paper will suffice.

   - You can also use a Word or Google Doc.

These tools are essential for the exercises and note-taking ahead. While you can manage with basic supplies, investing in the LPS Workbook not only saves time but also provides valuable additional information. It's available digitally for $9.95 or in print for $29.95. Visit www.basspublishing.com/workbook to place your order.

With the tools in hand, let's embark on our journey of personal growth.

BE OPEN-MINDED

Being open-minded is a powerful trait that can transform the way we perceive the world and interact with others. It's like having a wide-open road ahead, inviting us to explore new ideas, perspectives, and experiences with curiosity and a willingness to learn, grow, and change. Let's delve into the benefits of embracing open-mindedness, how to nurture it, and why it's crucial in today's world.

The Benefits of Open-Mindedness

Embracing an open-minded mindset brings numerous benefits, both personally and professionally. When we're open-minded, we're more inclined to explore new ideas and approaches, sparking greater creativity and innovation in both our work and personal lives. Considering diverse perspectives enriches our problem-solving abilities, leading to more effective and comprehensive solutions. Moreover, open-mindedness fosters empathy and understanding, strengthening our relationships and connections with others. By seeing things from different viewpoints, we expand our empathy and deepen our understanding of others' experiences, fostering personal growth and development.

Cultivating Open-Mindedness

While some may naturally possess open-mindedness, it's a trait that can be nurtured through practice. Actively listen to others without interrupting or passing judgment, seeking to understand their perspective and the reasons behind their opinions. Recognize and challenge your own biases and preconceptions, especially when faced with situations that challenge your assumptions. Expand your exposure to diverse opinions and viewpoints by engaging with literature, events, and groups representing different backgrounds and beliefs. Embrace the discomfort of uncertainty, remaining open to the possibility of evolving beliefs and opinions as you continue to learn and grow.

Why Open-Mindedness Matters Today

In our information-saturated world, cultivating an open-minded attitude is more crucial than ever. Open-mindedness serves as a bridge across cultural, social, and ideological divides, fostering greater understanding and cooperation. By embracing diverse perspectives, we nurture tolerance and acceptance, crucial elements for societal progress and harmony. Furthermore, open-mindedness fuels social and political change by challenging existing norms and envisioning new possibilities. It empowers us to adapt, learn, and grow, fostering creativity, empathy, and effective communication. In a rapidly evolving world, open-mindedness is not just advantageous but essential for personal fulfillment and collective advancement.

Embracing open-mindedness is like unlocking the door to endless possibilities. It fuels creativity, enhances problem-solving skills, strengthens relationships, and fosters personal growth. By remaining receptive to new ideas and experiences, we cultivate resilience, adaptability, and lifelong learning. In today's dynamic world, where change is constant and diversity is celebrated, open-mindedness is not just a trait but a guiding principle for success and fulfillment. So, let's embrace the journey of personal growth with open hearts and open minds, ready to explore, learn, and evolve every step of the way.

OUR BELIEFS

Understanding Beliefs

Beliefs are the lenses through which we perceive the world, shaping our thoughts, actions, and decisions. They're the ideas or convictions we hold about ourselves, others, and the world around us. These beliefs are crafted through our experiences, interactions, and upbringing, influencing everything from our attitudes to our behaviors.

Influences on Beliefs

Our beliefs are like seeds planted in the soil of our minds, nurtured by various influences. They're shaped by our upbringing, culture, religion, education, and personal encounters. For instance, our family background and cultural heritage mold our views on God, family, and success. Similarly, exposure to media, peer groups, and political ideologies can sway our beliefs about current affairs and societal issues.

The Impact of Beliefs

Our beliefs are the architects of our reality, constructing the framework within which we operate. They influence every facet of our lives, from our career choices to our relationships and health decisions. For instance, believing in our abilities and the power of hard work can propel us towards success, while negative beliefs can act as roadblocks on our journey.

Challenging and Changing Beliefs

Sometimes, our beliefs need a reality check. By questioning their validity and examining the evidence, we can discern whether they're constructive or limiting. If we find our beliefs holding us back, it's time for a makeover. By transforming negative beliefs into positive affirmations and setting actionable goals, we pave the way for growth and success.

So let's take a moment and write down our beliefs and determine whether they help or hinder us. Then we need to identify any beliefs that are holding us back from taking action on the positive beliefs that we have. Sound confusing, turn to page 1 of your workbook if you have it or get a sheet of paper and write your beliefs down, whether they help or hinder and what is holding you back. Here's an example:

Belief	Help	Hinder	What's holding me back
I believe I can become a real estate investor	Y	N	Bad Credit Not enough money

		Negative feedback from others

These items that are holding you back are negative beliefs, when we encounter these negativities, we need to acknowledge that they are in facts beliefs that we hold in our minds and now add them to our negative beliefs. See page 4 in your workbook or write these negative beliefs, change to positive beliefs and what goals need to be set.

Here's an example:

Negative Belief	Positive Belief	Goals to set
Bad credit is stopping me from being a real estate investor	I can change my credit from bad to good or excellent	1. Repair my credit. 2. Use a credit builder to increase my credit score. 3. Open secure credit cards
Not enough money is stopping me from being a real estate investor.	Money is not an issue, because I know how to create or raise what I need.	1. Look for no money down deals. 2. Use crowdfunding sites. 3. Use other people's money. 4. Find a capital partner. 5. Do wholesale deals to build capital
Negative feedback from others is stopping me from being a real estate investor	If they haven't done it their feedback is irrelevant. If it's been done by someone, I can do it too.	1. Find successful real estate investors to talk to. 2. Join a real estate investment club. 3. Go to real estate seminars

After challenging our negative beliefs, we need to replace them with positive ones and create goals to overcome the negative beliefs. This could involve reframing negative self-talk into positive affirmations or focusing on our strengths and accomplishments rather than our weaknesses. To make the new positive beliefs stick, we need to practice them consistently. This could involve repeating positive affirmations, visualizing ourselves succeeding, or taking small steps towards our goals. Changing our beliefs can be challenging, and it can be helpful to seek support from friends, family, or a therapist. Supportive communities can also help us stay motivated and accountable.

Remember, changing our beliefs takes time and effort, but it can have a transformative impact on our lives. By cultivating positive beliefs, we can increase our confidence, resilience, and ability to achieve our goals.

Following Our Beliefs

Our convictions are like guiding stars, illuminating our path in the darkest of nights. When our beliefs are strong and aligned with our values, we're empowered to navigate life's challenges with confidence. Yet, there are times when we must recalibrate our beliefs in light of new insights or experiences, adapting to the ever-changing landscape of life.

Beliefs are the silent architects of our destiny, shaping the course of our lives in profound ways. By cultivating positive beliefs and staying true to our values, we unlock the door to boundless possibilities. So, let's embrace the journey of self-discovery, guided by the wisdom of our beliefs, and embark on a path towards fulfillment and growth.

THE WILL

The will, a cornerstone of human nature, propels us towards our aspirations, guiding our actions and shaping our destiny. Whether facing monumental challenges or minor hurdles, the strength of our will influences our journey's trajectory.

Strength through Adversity

Our will's potency stems from a blend of genetics, upbringing, and life's tapestry. While some possess an inherent fortitude, others navigate a path to fortify their resolve. Regardless of our starting point, intentional efforts can bolster our willpower. Setting clear objectives, fostering self-discipline, and embracing challenges expand our capacity to harness this inner force.

Navigating Challenges

A defining trait of robust willpower is its ability to navigate obstacles with resilience and creativity. Rather than succumbing to defeat, individuals with unwavering resolve approach setbacks as opportunities for growth. Their adaptive mindset transforms barriers into stepping stones towards success.

Driven to Achieve

The tenacity of will drives individuals relentlessly towards their ambitions. Fueled by focus and perseverance, they chart a steady course towards their goals. This pursuit demands not only discipline but also the audacity to venture beyond comfort zones, embracing risks in pursuit of greatness.

Living with Purpose

Ultimately, the power of will extends beyond mere accomplishments; it steers us towards a life rich in fulfillment and purpose. Grounded in self-awareness, individuals with robust willpower make deliberate choices aligned with their core values. They navigate life's complexities with clarity and intention, striking a harmonious balance between immediate gratification and lasting fulfillment.

Embracing Openness

An open mind, complementing the will, broadens our horizons and enriches our journey. It fosters social adeptness, fosters resilience, and cultivates a growth-oriented mindset. By embracing diverse perspectives, we deepen our understanding of the world, forge stronger connections, and propel ourselves towards greater fulfillment.

Moving Forward

As you embark on this transformative journey, fueled by the fusion of open-mindedness and unwavering will, remember: your potential is boundless. Armed with newfound clarity and determination, you're poised to sculpt a future brimming with purpose and promise. So, with anticipation coursing through your veins, let's embark on this odyssey of self-discovery and growth.

FEAR

Fear, though intimidating, can be a powerful catalyst for growth and transformation. It is a natural human emotion that pushes us to confront the unknown and step outside our comfort zones. Embracing fear and channeling it into motivation can unlock untapped potential within us. It is a reminder that we are alive and capable of experiencing life's challenges. It fuels our determination to face adversity head-on and emerge stronger than before.

Beyond fear lies the realm of endless possibilities. It is the gateway to discovering our true potential and realizing the extraordinary feats we are capable of achieving. Embracing fear allows us to break free from self-imposed limitations and transcend our perceived boundaries. It is the key to unlocking the doors to a life beyond our wildest dreams. Just as a phoenix rises from the ashes, facing our fears empowers us to rise above setbacks, failures, and doubts, emerging with newfound resilience and courage. It acts as a compass, guiding us toward the path we are meant to traverse. It serves as a reminder that greatness lies beyond our comfort zones.

The journey of personal growth requires navigating through fear, for it is through these trials that we build the foundation of our character and strength. When fear knocks on the door of our minds, we can choose to let it cripple us or use it as a stepping stone to progress. It is within our power to harness fear for our benefit. Fear is a temporary visitor on the road to success; as we keep moving forward, it gradually loses its hold on us, paving the way for confidence and self-assurance. Like a wind propelling a sailboat, fear can become the driving force behind our ambitions, propelling us forward on the waters of triumph and achievement.

Embracing fear is an act of faith in ourselves and our capabilities. It is a declaration that we are ready to seize every opportunity that comes our way, regardless of the challenges it presents. In the face of fear, let us remember that we are resilient beings capable of overcoming obstacles and transcending limitations. Embrace fear not as a roadblock but as a stepping stone to a life of growth, fulfillment, and extraordinary achievement. With courage and determination, fear becomes a mere blip on our journey to greatness. Understand that bravery is acting despite the fear that exists. Embrace the unknown, for it is where our greatest potential lies, waiting to be unleashed by our unwavering belief in ourselves.

Fear as an Acronym

Fear can indeed be an acronym for:

Faith Extinguished After Rationalization

This concept reminds us of the power we hold within ourselves to overcome fear's grip and ignite the flame of courage. According to the Bible, God has not given us the spirit of fear; but of power, and of love, and of a sound mind.

In the journey of life, it is common to encounter moments when we extinguish our faith after rationalization, unwittingly allowing fear to take root within us. However, it is crucial to recognize this pattern and shift our perspective to embrace courage and unwavering belief. When we overthink and rationalize our dreams, we sometimes convince ourselves that they are too grand to achieve, dousing the flames of faith that once burned brightly within us. When fear takes hold, it can smother our faith in ourselves and our abilities. But it is essential to remember that fear is often rooted in irrational thoughts and limiting beliefs that can be challenged. Rationalization can lead us to focus on the obstacles rather than the possibilities, causing us to doubt our capabilities and extinguish the belief in our potential.

Fear is born when we rationalize ourselves into a state of stagnation, fearing failure more than we value the rewards of taking a leap of faith towards our dreams. Rationalization becomes a breeding ground for fear when we dwell on past failures or negative outcomes, overlooking the invaluable lessons and growth that they provide. By analyzing every potential pitfall, we inadvertently snuff out the hope that once fueled our ambition, creating space for fear to cast its shadow on our aspirations. Excessive rationalization can lead to paralysis by analysis, leaving us feeling trapped and unsure, suffocating the spirit of faith that propels us toward our goals. Instead of embracing the unknown with excitement, we find ourselves entangled in a web of doubt, rationalizing away the possibilities that await us, allowing fear to take hold. Rationalization breeds fear when we become overly concerned about the opinions of others, eroding the self-belief that is essential for pursuing our passions. The moment we succumb to fear, we dim the light of faith that guides us toward our dreams and aspirations.

However, by actively questioning our fears and examining them critically, we can reignite the flame of belief in our potential. Faith requires an open heart and the willingness to embrace uncertainty, while rationalization thrives on certainty, leading us to forego opportunities for growth and transformation. Let us be mindful of how rationalization can give birth to fear and instead choose to cultivate faith in our abilities and the potential of our dreams. By trusting in ourselves and nurturing our faith, we can conquer fear's grip, igniting the flames of courage to move forward with determination and resilience. As we understand the delicate interplay between rationalization and fear, we gain the power to break free from its grasp. Let us challenge the thoughts that dampen our faith and embrace a mindset of possibility and belief. With unwavering faith in ourselves, we can face fear head-on, stepping boldly into the unknown and unlocking a world of endless opportunities and personal growth. Remember, within every challenge lies the potential for greatness, and with faith as our guiding light, we can conquer fear and become the architects of our destiny.

But what if, instead of rationalizing our faith, we rationalize our fear? Rationalization can be both positive and negative. If we rationalize our faith, it is a negative connotation, but when we rationalize our fears, it is a positive connotation. When we rationalize the negative, it results in a positive outcome; when we rationalize the positive, it results in a negative outcome. Rationalization encourages us to question the validity of our fears, reminding us that they often arise from a place of uncertainty and doubt. With this understanding, we can choose to face our fears head-on and confront them with courage. As we rationalize our fears, we develop a more objective perspective, allowing us to see them for what they are — temporary barriers that can be overcome with unwavering faith in ourselves.

Fear can distort our perception of reality and make us lose sight of our inner strength. Yet, through positive rationalization, we can gain clarity and dispel the illusions that fear casts upon us. Faith, when aligned with positive rational thinking, can help us conquer fear and propel us toward action. By acknowledging our fears and evaluating them logically, we empower ourselves to navigate through challenging situations with confidence. Fear may try to extinguish the fire of our dreams, but we must never forget that rational thought can reignite our passion and determination to pursue what truly matters to us. By dissecting our fears with positive rational thinking, we discover that they hold no power over us unless we allow them to. Our faith in our abilities can dismantle fear's stronghold and lead us toward personal growth and success.

Rationalization strengthens our resolve to face fear with a balanced perspective. Instead of being paralyzed by doubt, we can find the courage to take calculated risks, knowing that every step forward is a testament to our resilience. Ultimately, understanding fear as "Faith Extinguished After Rationalization" empowers us to embrace the unknown with newfound confidence. By combining faith in our potential with questioning and denouncing the fear that exists, we can soar beyond fear's constraints and embrace a life filled with limitless possibilities. Knowing that we can do all things through Christ who strengthens us. Fear may cast its shadow on our journey, but it is within our power to dispel that darkness with the light of positive rational thought and unwavering faith in ourselves. Where there is light, darkness cannot exist. As we face our fears with courage and understanding, we open the door to a world of growth, achievement, and boundless potential. So let us embrace fear not as a barrier but as an opportunity for self-discovery and transformation. Together, faith and rationalization of our fears will guide us toward a future filled with triumph and resilience.

Why We Fear

Fear is a natural and universal emotion that resides within all of us. Despite its intimidating presence, fear serves a crucial purpose in our lives, urging us to evolve, learn, and grow. Fear arises from our instinct for self-preservation, protecting us from potential harm and danger. It is an innate mechanism that has helped humans survive and thrive throughout history. Fear can be a powerful motivator, propelling us to take action and face challenges that push us beyond our comfort zones. It inspires us to reach for our dreams and achieve greatness.

In times of uncertainty, fear can be a guiding compass, reminding us to proceed with caution and consider the consequences of our choices before taking action. Fear teaches us invaluable lessons about resilience and adaptability. It strengthens our character by showing us that we can overcome obstacles and emerge stronger than before. Fear is an integral part of human experience, demonstrating that we are not alone in our vulnerabilities. Acknowledging our fears fosters empathy and compassion for ourselves and others. By confronting our fears, we gain a deeper understanding of our true desires and aspirations. It prompts us to reflect on what truly matters to us and what we are willing to fight for.

Fear challenges us to rise above our limitations and doubts, showing us that we are capable of achieving far more than we initially believed. When we embrace fear as a catalyst for growth, we open ourselves to new experiences and opportunities, enriching our lives and expanding our horizons. Fear helps us appreciate moments of triumph and achievement even more profoundly, as we recognize the courage and perseverance it took to overcome challenges. Embracing fear empowers us to live life to the fullest, for it reminds us that every step taken in the face of fear is a declaration of our courage and determination to create a life of purpose and fulfillment.

Let us remember that fear, while formidable, can be a source of empowerment and inspiration. Embrace fear as a catalyst for personal growth, knowing that it is an integral part of the human experience. When we face fear with courage and resilience, we unlock the boundless potential within ourselves, transcending limitations and soaring towards our dreams. It is through our willingness to embrace fear that we discover the true depth of our strength and the extraordinary heights we can reach on our journey of self-discovery and personal development. So, let us rise to the challenge, embrace our fears, and step confidently into the unknown, for it is in those moments that we truly come alive and uncover the greatness that lies within us.

We all have some type of fear; it is only natural. But just because we have them does not mean we have to succumb to them. One thing that encourages me when I am fearful is Psalms 27, which states: "The Lord is my light and my salvation; whom shall I fear? the Lord is the strength of my life; of whom shall I be afraid? When the wicked, even mine enemies and my foes, came upon me to eat up my flesh, they stumbled and fell. Though an host should encamp against me, my heart shall not fear: though war should rise against me, in this will I be confident."

Understand that the confidence of knowing that the end result will allow us to grow stronger than we are should be more than enough to give us the courage to push beyond our fear and claim what is ours. As long as we hold fast to our beliefs and have a willingness to take action even in the midst of fear, we will always attain the victory we are seeking. Understand that you already have the victory; all you have to do is take the necessary actions to claim it. You are more than a conqueror; you are confident, courageous, and victorious because you have the belief, willingness, and persistence to use your fear as a stepping stone to growth.

Identifying Fear

Identifying our fears is a powerful and transformative journey that empowers us to embrace vulnerability and catalyzes personal growth. Embracing the process of identifying our fears is a courageous act in itself. As we confront these apprehensions head-on, we discover the hidden barriers that have been holding us back from our true potential. Self-discovery and growth: Identifying our fears opens doors to self-discovery and self-awareness. By delving deep into our emotions and experiences, we unravel the intricacies of our psyche, leading to profound personal growth. Recognizing our fears grants us the power to break free from their grip. By understanding the roots of our anxieties, we reclaim control over our thoughts and emotions, empowering ourselves to overcome obstacles. Fear often masks itself as limiting beliefs, preventing us from pursuing our aspirations. As we unearth these beliefs, we liberate ourselves from self-imposed restrictions, allowing us to dream without constraints. Identifying our fears necessitates vulnerability, a quality that fosters genuine connections with others. By embracing vulnerability, we cultivate empathy and compassion for ourselves and those around us. As we bring our fears into the light, they lose their power over us. We liberate ourselves from the shadows of uncertainty and emerge stronger, guided by a newfound sense of clarity and purpose.

Embracing and Overcoming Fear

Fear is a natural part of the human experience. Identifying and acknowledging these fears is the first step towards overcoming them and fostering personal growth. By facing our fears with courage and resilience, we can unleash our true potential and lead a life of purpose, authenticity, and fulfillment. This process, though challenging, holds immense potential for transformation. As we navigate through our inner world, we understand that fear is not an enemy but a companion on our journey of self-discovery. Embrace the path of uncovering your fears with an open heart and a curious mind, for it leads to a more authentic and empowered version of yourself. In doing so, you pave the way for a life that transcends limitations and embraces the full spectrum of human experience. Remember, the power to identify your fears lies within you; let it be the catalyst for an extraordinary and fearless existence.

Identifying Fear

Go through each of the fears identified, list the fears you currently have on page 7 of your workbook in the Identify Fear Worksheet, or create it in your notebook. For now, only write the fears that you have; don't worry about how to overcome them for now. Here is an example for you to use:

Identifying Fear	
Fear	**How to overcome**
Fear of Failure	
Fear of Success	
Fear of Change	
Fear of rejection	
Fear of Not Being Enough for Others	

By identifying our fears, we now have power over them because we know and acknowledge their existence. Next, we determine what we need to do and how we can overcome them.

Overcoming Your Fears

Overcoming fears is a crucial aspect of our personal growth journey, enabling us to unlock our true potential and live a fulfilling life. Conquering fears allows you to embrace your authentic self without the limitations imposed by anxiety and self-doubt. You become free to express your true identity and passions. By overcoming fears, you gain the confidence to pursue your dreams and aspirations, no longer allowing fear to hold you back from achieving your goals. It strengthens your resilience and adaptability in the face of challenges, helping you bounce back stronger from setbacks and obstacles. Confronting fears pushes the boundaries of your comfort zone, leading to personal growth and a sense of empowerment. Each fear you conquer adds to your reservoir of courage, developing the bravery to tackle future challenges.

Letting go of fears opens doors to new opportunities and experiences you might have otherwise missed out on, reducing stress and anxiety and contributing to improved emotional well-being and overall happiness. Facing your fears cultivates empathy and understanding, enabling deeper connections with others. It inspires those around you, showing them that obstacles can be surmounted with determination and courage. The act of conquering fears transforms you into a powerful agent of change in your own life, allowing you to shape your destiny.

Steps to Overcome Fear

The first step to overcoming fears is acknowledging and accepting their existence, which we have already done. Embrace your vulnerabilities and understand that fear is a natural part of growth. Dig deep to understand the root cause of your fears, uncovering past experiences or beliefs that might have contributed to their development. Challenge negative thought patterns associated with your fears, replacing self-doubt with self-empowering affirmations to build resilience. View fear as an opportunity for learning and growth rather than a setback. Visualize yourself successfully overcoming your fears, using positive imagery to rewire your brain and reduce anxiety. Step outside your comfort zone and embrace discomfort, understanding that growth and transformation often occur beyond the boundaries of familiarity. Stay present and mindful in moments of fear, observing your emotions without judgment and practicing breathing exercises to calm your mind.

Return to the previous exercise in your workbook or notebook. Think of ways that would cause you to push beyond your fears and allow you to gain strength and momentum in your personal growth journey.

Fear	How to overcome
Fear of Failure	Embrace failure as an opportunity for growth and learning.

	Challenge negative self-talk and replace it with positive affirmations.
	Focus on the process rather than solely on the end result.
Fear of Success	Examine any limiting beliefs you have about success and challenge their validity.
	Use visualization techniques to imagine yourself succeeding and living your best life.
	Recognize that success may bring new challenges and uncertainties.
Fear of Change	Shift your focus from the potential negative outcomes to the positive possibilities that change can bring.
	Gradually introduce change into your life.
	Embrace change as a new adventure in life.
Fear of rejection	View rejection as redirection or a necessary step towards finding the right path or opportunity.
	Focus on building your self-esteem and self-worth
Fear of Not Being Enough for Others	Embrace your uniqueness and accept yourself for who you are.
	Seek validation and approval from within rather than relying solely on external sources.

Share your fears with trusted friends, family, or a therapist. Having a support system can provide encouragement and a different perspective. Embrace failure as a steppingstone toward success. Celebrate every milestone achieved in conquering your fears. Acknowledge your efforts, no matter how small, and use them as motivation to keep moving forward. Overcoming fears is a journey of self-discovery and empowerment. By facing our fears with courage, resilience, and self-compassion, we open doors to a life filled with boundless possibilities. As we embrace the challenges that once held us back, we step into a new realm of growth and transformation, where fears no longer dictate our choices or define our destiny. Let your journey of fearlessness be a testament to your strength and determination to craft a life that knows no bounds—a life of authenticity, fulfillment, and endless growth.

PART II
Determining Your Starting Point

SELF-ASSESSING

Self-assessment is a critical tool for personal and professional growth. It involves taking a step back and reflecting on our actions, thoughts, and behaviors to gain a better understanding of ourselves. This process helps identify strengths and weaknesses, uncover areas for improvement, and develop a plan for achieving goals. Self-assessment fosters self-awareness, which is essential for success in all aspects of life. Through self-assessment, we can take control of our lives, build better relationships, and improve performance in any area that matters to us. In this fast-paced and ever-changing world, self-assessment is a vital skill that helps us stay relevant, adaptable, and fulfilled.

It involves a critical process of introspection that allows us to evaluate our skills, knowledge, abilities, and personal qualities. This close and honest look at ourselves helps us identify strengths and weaknesses, areas for improvement, and potential opportunities for growth. Regular self-assessment enables us to make informed decisions about our personal and professional lives, set realistic goals, and work towards achieving them. It serves as a powerful tool for self-improvement, enabling us to achieve greater success and fulfillment in all areas of our lives.

Self-assessment can take many forms, including reflective journaling, self-evaluation questionnaires, and feedback from others. By engaging in self-assessment, we become more self-aware and better equipped to navigate our personal and professional lives with greater confidence and effectiveness. Although challenging and sometimes uncomfortable, the benefits of self-assessment are numerous, leading to greater self-understanding, personal growth, and a more fulfilling life.

Why Self-Assessment is Important

Self-assessment is important because it allows us to gain a deeper understanding of ourselves, our strengths, weaknesses, and areas for improvement. It helps us take ownership of our personal and professional growth by providing a framework for identifying goals and evaluating progress toward those goals.

Through self-assessment, we can identify our unique strengths and leverage them to achieve success, while also identifying areas where we need to improve or develop new skills. By taking a proactive approach to self-improvement, we can increase our confidence, build resilience, and enhance our ability to adapt to changing circumstances.

Self-assessment provides a sense of control and agency over our lives, allowing us to take responsibility for our actions and decisions. It helps us better understand our values, motivations, and aspirations, aligning our actions with our personal and professional goals.

In the context of career development and lifelong learning, self-assessment is crucial. By regularly assessing our skills, knowledge, and abilities, we can identify areas where we need further development or new skills, ensuring we remain competitive in the job market and continue to grow professionally.

Overall, self-assessment is a powerful tool for personal and professional growth, enabling us to gain insight into our strengths and weaknesses, set meaningful goals, and take action to achieve success.

Benefits of Self-Assessing

Self-assessment offers several benefits. It enables us to evaluate our skills, knowledge, strengths, and weaknesses, leading to increased self-awareness. By understanding our strengths and weaknesses, we can improve our communication skills and interactions with others.

Self-assessment helps us identify areas needing improvement. By taking steps to develop new skills and enhance our knowledge, we experience personal growth. It also encourages us to set realistic and achievable goals based on our current skills and abilities, keeping us motivated and focused on our objectives.

Engaging in self-assessment promotes active learning, identifying gaps in knowledge or skills, and developing plans to overcome them. Seeing progress through self-assessment motivates us to continue improving and reaching our goals. It helps us make better decisions by reflecting on experiences and assessing what worked and what didn't.

Regular self-assessment leads to improved performance by identifying areas needing improvement and creating plans to address them. It helps us reflect on our strengths and weaknesses, improving our effectiveness in various areas of life, such as work, school, or personal relationships. By reflecting on our actions, we can make adjustments and learn from our mistakes, leading to better outcomes in the future.

Self-assessment is an important tool for career development, allowing us to identify skills and strengths that can be leveraged in our current job. Regularly assessing our skills and knowledge helps us stay up-to-date with the latest trends and techniques in our field, useful when pursuing career opportunities or seeking a promotion.

Self-assessment promotes accountability. By assessing ourselves, we take ownership of our strengths and weaknesses, holding ourselves accountable for our actions and decisions. It can improve performance and accountability in the workplace.

Overall, self-assessment is a valuable tool for personal growth, goal setting, and improved performance. It helps us gain a better understanding of ourselves and our capabilities, taking responsibility for our own development. It is a valuable tool for personal and professional development, as it allows us to gain self-awareness, set realistic goals, and take responsibility for our learning and growth. It also allows us to reflect on our strengths and weaknesses and make improvements to enhance performance and achieve success.

Common Barriers to Effective Self-Assessment

To overcome these barriers, it is important to develop self-awareness, seek feedback from others, stay open to different perspectives, set aside time for self-assessment, and focus on progress rather than perfection. Working with a coach or mentor can also provide guidance and support.

Several common barriers to effective self-assessment include lack of self-awareness, fear of criticism, biases, overconfidence, or underestimation of abilities, limited perspective, perfectionism, lack of feedback, lack of motivation, and time constraints.

Lack of self-awareness makes it difficult to assess ourselves accurately. Fear of criticism or negative feedback can prevent honesty in self-assessment. Biases, whether conscious or unconscious, affect self-assessment accuracy. Overconfidence can lead to overestimating abilities, while underestimation can lead to underestimating potential.

Self-assessment requires a broad perspective, but many of us have a limited perspective of ourselves, focusing too much on flaws or not seeing strengths. Perfectionism makes it difficult to accept and learn from mistakes. Self-assessment can be more effective when combined with feedback from others, but lack of feedback makes accurate self-assessment challenging. Motivation and commitment are required for effective self-assessment, but lack of motivation makes progress difficult. Self-assessment can be time-consuming, and many feel they do not have enough time to devote to it.

To overcome these barriers, develop self-awareness, seek feedback from others, and regularly assess yourself. Working with an accountability partner, coach, or mentor can provide guidance and support.

How Do We Assess Ourselves?

Assessing yourself involves taking a critical look at your own thoughts, feelings, behaviors, and experiences. It is a valuable tool for personal growth and development, useful for gaining self-awareness and understanding strengths, weaknesses, and tendencies. Ensuring your mind is equipped for the journey ahead requires reflection on experiences, both positive and negative, as they shape values and beliefs.

Reflect on past experiences, considering what you have learned and how they have impacted you. Identify and categorize negative experiences to better understand their effects. Create a new positive belief from each negative experience to develop new values and standards in your life.

Focus on converting negative experiences into positive beliefs. This process involves writing out negative experiences, categorizing them by their effects, and creating a new positive belief from each one.

By doing so, you develop a healthier and more fulfilling life, using your past as a stepping stone into your future. Understanding the things that hold us back and addressing them allows us to reach higher heights and fulfill our goals with ease.

Reflect on your experiences, taking time to think about past experiences, both positive and negative, and how they have impacted you. Categorize your negative experiences to better understand why you dwell on them. If you have the workbook this exercise is on page 11 or create it in your notebook.

Here is an example:

Identifying and Categorizing Negative Experiences				
#	Experience	Positive	Negative	What I learned from it:
1	Purchased my first property	Y	N	You can own property without a down payment
2	Joined gift giving opportunity	N	Y	Never put money into something that does not provide a service or product and involves your return being based on others putting money being put into it.
3				

Categorizing Negative Experiences

Write out your negative experiences and determine why you remember them by placing them in the following categories:

1. Emotional Impact: Memories and experiences with strong emotional impact.

2. Nostalgia: Sentimental longing for the past.

3. Regret: Negative emotion arising from mistakes or missed opportunities.

4. Learning from Mistakes: Learning from both positive and negative experiences.

5. Uncertainty About the Future: Anxiety about the future leading to focus on the past.

If you have the workbook this exercise is on page 14 if you don't use your notebook and write it out. We are only focusing on negative experiences in this exercise, write the number of all the negative experiences you have had in column one, then check the column(s) that are applicable. Here is an example of categorizing negative experiences:

Experience Effects					
#	Emotional Impact	Nostalgia	Regret	Learning from mistake	Uncertainty about the future
2	☐	☐	☒	☒	☐
	☐	☐	☐	☐	☐

Converting Negative Experiences to Positive Beliefs

Reflect on your negative experiences and determine what you learned from them to create new positive values in your life. Remember that our beliefs are the determining factor of whether we fail or succeed. Whatever we believe directly affects who we are and what we do, if we believe we cannot then we won't, if we believe something is too hard then it is, but if we believe that all things are possible then they are. I know you are probably tired of hearing me say this, but it has to be said before each exercise, so get used to it. If you have the workbook this exercise is on page 16 under the previous exercise is the Negative Experience Conversion Table if you don't use your notebook and write it out. Here is an example:

Negative Experience Conversion Table	
Negative Experience	**Positive Belief**
Joined gift giving opportunity	Multi-level Marketing is a good investment as long as the product or service is worth the money. Avoid money making schemes that are based on other people joining without a product or service attached.

By creating new positive beliefs, you develop new values and standards to prevent repeating negative experiences. Embrace negative experiences as growth moments to live a healthier and fulfilled life, using your past as a stepping stone into your future.

Understanding our experiences and addressing them helps us move forward and achieve our goals with ease. This process of self-assessment is crucial for personal and professional growth, enabling us to lead a life of purpose, authenticity, and fulfillment.

STRENGTHS AND WEAKNESSES

Strengths and weaknesses play a key role in our progress towards personal growth. Strengths are wonderful to have, but only if they are utilized correctly and we are aware that they exist. Unused strengths can be just as detrimental as weaknesses and can hinder our personal growth. Misused or overused strengths can be more dangerous than our greatest weakness. However, personal growth does not start with our strengths; it actually starts by acknowledging our weaknesses, which is what we will work on next.

Acknowledging Weaknesses

Acknowledging our weaknesses can be challenging, but it is an essential step towards personal growth and improvement. Since we have already discovered and acknowledged our negative experiences, we can easily identify some of our weaknesses through those experiences. Our negative experiences often expose our weaknesses. We can take what we have learned from these experiences to discover our weaknesses and develop a plan to strengthen those areas.

First, let's acknowledge the fact that everyone has weaknesses, and it's okay to have them. Be honest with yourself. Understand that failures, mistakes, and mishaps are part of life; they are meant to teach us valuable lessons as long as we view them as learning experiences. For example, when I joined the Family Gift Giving scheme, I was focused on getting more back than I put in, not realizing that the only way I would get my money was to convince others to join or put more money in. This negative experience taught me to recognize it for what it really was a Ponzi scheme.

Rather than seeing our weaknesses as fixed traits, we should approach them as opportunities for learning and growth. Fixed traits often fester, consume us, and become part of who we are. Instead of accepting them, we should work on improving them. Justifying our weaknesses stunts our personal growth. For example, I used to be late for everything and justified this by telling myself that I was always right on time. This annoyed my wife to the point that she adjusted times for occasions to ensure we arrived on time. Eventually, I realized that being fashionably late was still late. Embracing our weaknesses as opportunities to improve allows us to grow both personally and professionally.

List of weaknesses an individual may have

Here is a list of the top 25 weaknesses an individual may have:

1. Inadequate belief system
2. Resistance to change or difficulty in adapting to new situations.
3. Lack of self-confidence or self-esteem: Feeling unsure of oneself and doubting one's abilities.
4. Lack of self-motivation or self-discipline
5. Poor decision-making skills or inability to make timely decisions.
6. Procrastination or difficulty in starting or finishing tasks.
7. Poor time management skills

8. Difficulty with public speaking or presentations.
9. Inadequate technical or computer skills
10. Inability to prioritize tasks effectively.
11. Difficulty in working in a team or collaborating with others.
12. Poor communication skills, including written and verbal communication.
13. Inability to delegate tasks or micromanagement
14. Lack of assertiveness or difficulty in saying "no"
15. Inadequate leadership skills or difficulty in managing people.
16. Inability to manage stress or cope with pressure.
17. Lack of creativity or innovation
18. Difficulty in balancing personal and professional responsibilities
19. Tendency to be disorganized or messy.
20. Inability to handle criticism or feedback.
21. Poor customer service skills
22. Inflexibility or rigidity in thinking or approach.
23. Poor listening skills or lack of empathy
24. Lack of attention to detail
25. Inability to handle conflict or difficult situations effectively.

Overcoming Weaknesses

Now that we know what weaknesses look like, review the list below and see which weaknesses you have. Write them down and note what you can do to strengthen them. Here's an example of how to convert a weakness into a strength:

Weakness Conversion Sheet	
Weakness	**How to strengthen or correct**
Poor time management skills	Practice being 15-minutes early for occasions. Schedule all occurrences to allow for travel time and incidents. Get the advice of people who have mastered time management. Learn to schedule everything. Use 15-minute intervals for time management instead of 30 minutes or hourly
Procrastination	Learn to prioritize. Create a to do list. Give start time and deadlines for what must be done.

Sometimes, acknowledging your weaknesses can help you understand your strengths better. Think about what tasks or activities you struggle with and consider the opposite qualities that may be your strengths. By acknowledging our weaknesses and knowing what needs to be done to strengthen or correct them, we create goals and actionable steps to overcome them. Overcoming our weaknesses requires discipline and effort. We will discuss goals in chapter 27 and action steps in chapter 32, but for now, we will move forward to identifying our strengths.

Identifying Strengths

Identifying your strengths is an important part of understanding yourself and developing a successful career or personal life. This exercise can help you make better decisions and improve your overall performance and well-being. Sometimes, the best way to identify your strengths is through trial and error. Trying new things, taking on new challenges, and experimenting with different activities can help you discover what you excel at and enjoy.

Pay attention to activities or tasks that come naturally to you and that you enjoy doing. Look for patterns in your behavior or preferences that indicate your strengths. Reflect on past experiences and accomplishments. Think about what you enjoyed doing, what you were good at, and what gave you a sense of satisfaction or achievement. These can often be indicators of your strengths. For example, if you enjoy problem-solving and are good at it, this could be a strength.

List of Strengths

Here are some examples of strengths individuals can possess:

Accountability	Open-mindedness
Active listening	Organization
Adaptability	Patience
Analytical thinking	Perseverance
Assertiveness	Positive attitude
Attention to details.	Problem-solving
Communication	Public speaking
Compassion	Resilience
Conflict resolution	Resourcefulness
Creativity	Risk-taking
Critical thinking	Sense of humor
Customer service	Self-discipline
Decision making	Self-motivation
Diplomacy	Strategic thinking
Emotional intelligence	Teamwork
Empathy	Time management
Enthusiasm Leadership	Trustworthiness
Listening	Vision
Mentoring	Willingness to learn.
Networking	Work ethic
Negotiation	

Identifying Strengths

Now, let's identify our strengths. List your positive experiences, the strengths used in these experiences (1-3), and how they made you feel. Be honest about the strengths you have. If it is one you want to have, make it a goal. Here's an example:

Identify Strengths		
Experience	**Strengths used**	**How you felt**
Purchased my first property	*Negotiation* *Creativity* *Communication*	*Buying my first property was one of the most exciting moments in my life, it gave me a feeling of power.*
Becoming a father	Patience Independence Compassion	Becoming a father was both a happy, joyous, and yet scary feeling.

Since we now know what strengths we used in our positive experiences, we can determine how they can help us in our personal growth and in achieving our goals. Categorize your strengths to understand how they can be used effectively. Here's an example:

Categorizing Strengths

Strengths Categorization			
Strength	**Learned/Natural**	**Professional/Personal**	**How can I use this in my personal growth:**
Negotiation	Natural	Professional	Create a win/win outcome in any deal
Communication	Learned	Professional	Develop relationship by gaining clarity and understanding others point.
Creativity	Natural	Professional	Realize that there is always more than one way of doing things
Patience	Learned	Personal	*Take the time to care for other*
Independence	Learned	Personal	*Don't wait for others when I can do it myself*

Compassion	Natural	Personal	Always show kindness and gratitude.

Understanding how our strengths were used in the past will also help us use them in the future. Remember that everyone has unique strengths and talents, and it's important to identify and cultivate them to achieve your goals and live a fulfilling life. Identifying and categorizing your strengths is an ongoing process and may require self-reflection and experimentation. With time and practice, you can develop a clearer understanding of your unique talents and abilities.

Keep in mind the importance of using your strengths wisely. We don't want to waste our strengths by not utilizing them, nor do we want to misuse them, turning them into weaknesses. Be conscious of your strengths and utilize them in every situation possible. Doing so will allow you to excel in whatever you set out to do.

FEEDBACK

Feedback is a powerful tool that helps us improve ourselves and our work. Asking for feedback can be intimidating, but it is essential if we want to grow and reach our full potential. We will explore the benefits of asking for feedback and how to do it effectively. We will also discuss different types of feedback and how to use them to your advantage.

Feedback is essential for both personal and professional growth. Whether you are a student, employee, manager, or entrepreneur, it will help you improve your skills, knowledge, and performance. It will help us gain insights into our strengths and weaknesses, identify areas for improvement, and make positive changes. In our personal lives, it helps us build positive relationships, increase self-awareness, and set achievable goals. In our professional lives, it is critical for career development, performance management, and continuous improvement. Feedback provides us with guidance and support to improve our performance, develop new skills, and reach our full potential. It is a valuable tool that should be embraced as an opportunity for learning and development, leading to personal and professional growth and success.

Feedback helps us identify areas of improvement, refine our skills, and learn from our mistakes. It also enhances our self-awareness, helps us build better relationships, and promotes a culture of continuous improvement. Without feedback, we may be unaware of our blind spots, miss out on valuable insights, and fail to achieve our full potential.

However, asking for feedback can be a challenging task. Many people feel uncomfortable or anxious about receiving criticism and may not know how to ask for it effectively. We will explore the importance of feedback, the benefits of asking for feedback, who to ask for feedback, and strategies to ask for feedback in a constructive and meaningful way.

Types of Feedback

Constructive feedback is intended to help the recipient improve their performance or behavior. It is specific, actionable, and focused on the issue at hand. The purpose of constructive feedback is to provide information that can be used to make positive changes and achieve goals. It is not meant to be negative or critical; instead, it is delivered in a respectful and supportive way. The goal is to build trust, enhance relationships, and foster a culture of continuous improvement. When delivered effectively, it can help us grow, increase our self-awareness, and achieve personal and professional goals.

Critical feedback is intended to point out the recipient's weaknesses, mistakes, or areas needing improvement. It often focuses on negative aspects of performance or behavior. While difficult to hear and sometimes perceived as harsh, it can be valuable for growth and development when delivered effectively. It helps us identify areas needing improvement and make positive changes. The key to providing critical feedback is to be specific, objective, and focused on the issue, delivering it respectfully and supportively to help the recipient improve.

Positive feedback is intended to recognize and reinforce strengths, accomplishments, and positive behavior. It focuses on the positive aspects of performance. Positive feedback can be a powerful motivator, acknowledging efforts and accomplishments and reinforcing positive behavior. It builds trust, enhances relationships, and fosters a positive environment. Positive feedback should be specific, genuine, and timely. It increases self-confidence, improves morale, and promotes personal and professional growth.

Negative feedback identifies and addresses areas where performance or behavior needs improvement, focusing on the negative aspects of performance. Although difficult to hear and sometimes perceived as critical, it can be valuable for growth and development when delivered effectively. It helps us identify areas needing improvement and make positive changes. Negative feedback should be specific, objective, and focused on the issue, delivered respectfully and supportively to help us improve.

Formal feedback is a structured and planned process, often used in professional settings like performance evaluations or development programs. It involves setting specific goals, gathering information about performance, and providing feedback in a formal setting. Delivered by a supervisor, manager, or other authority figures, it is often documented for future reference and focused on specific performance metrics.

Informal feedback is given on an ongoing basis, in an informal setting, without a structured process. It can be given by anyone, regardless of position or authority, and can be either positive or negative. Often given in real-time in response to specific situations, informal feedback provides immediate insights that can be used to improve performance or behavior. It is used in day-to-day interactions and aims to provide timely, relevant feedback to enhance skills and achieve goals.

Understanding the type of feedback, we are receiving is important because it helps us interpret the feedback correctly and use it effectively to improve performance or behavior. Different types of feedback have different implications and require different responses. By understanding the type of feedback, we can determine how to respond to it in a way that aligns with our goals and supports our personal and professional growth. This helps us make better decisions, improve performance, and build stronger relationships with those providing feedback. It's important to approach all feedback with an open mind and use it as an opportunity to learn and grow.

Who to Ask for Feedback

Identifying potential sources of feedback is important for receiving feedback that can help improve performance or behavior. Consider sources like colleagues, supervisors, mentors, friends, family members, and even customers or clients. Identify people who can provide honest, objective feedback relevant to your goals. Consider those most familiar with your work or behavior and those with expertise in your area of work or experience with similar challenges. Using feedback tools, such as surveys or assessments, can gather feedback from a broader range of sources. For personal growth, focus on feedback from family, friends, mentors, and associates. For professional growth, consider work colleagues, supervisors, or managers.

Choosing the right people to ask for feedback ensures that we receive relevant and constructive feedback that can help improve performance or behavior. Select individuals familiar with your work, experienced in your field, and trusted to give honest feedback. Choose people who understand your strengths and weaknesses and can provide feedback relevant to your goals. Consider the person's communication style and approach to giving feedback. Choose individuals who can communicate effectively, provide specific examples and actionable feedback, and do so constructively and respectfully. Diversity in feedback providers offers a broader perspective and helps identify blind spots. Make a list of people to ask for feedback, including family members, friends, colleagues, associates, and mentors.

Feedback Request List

- **Name**: Patricia Bass
    - o **Relationship**: Wife
    - o **Topic**: Me as a husband
- **Name**: Pastor Anthony
    - o **Relationship**: Pastor/Mentor
    - o **Topic**: How can I be a better man of God
- **Name**: Renwick Walker
    - o **Relationship**: Friend
    - o **Topic**: What can I do better

Asking for Feedback

Asking for feedback has many benefits. It demonstrates that we are open to learning and willing to improve. It shows that we value other people's opinions and perspectives. By asking for feedback, we gain a deeper understanding of how others perceive us, our work, and our behavior. We also receive specific and actionable suggestions to improve performance, enhance communication skills, and develop leadership abilities. Asking for feedback builds trust, fosters collaboration, and promotes a culture of continuous learning and growth.

Overcoming Obstacles to Asking for Feedback

Many people feel anxious or uncomfortable about receiving feedback. They may fear criticism, rejection, or failure. However, these fears can hold us back from achieving our full potential. To overcome the fear of feedback, shift your mindset from a fixed mindset to a growth mindset. A fixed mindset believes that our abilities are fixed and cannot be changed, while a growth mindset believes that we can learn and develop our abilities over time. By adopting a growth mindset, we can embrace feedback as an opportunity to learn and improve, rather than a threat to our self-esteem.

Overcoming fear, anxiety, and resistance to feedback is important for personal and professional growth. Reframe feedback as an opportunity for growth and learning, rather than as a personal attack or criticism of abilities or character. Seek feedback in a safe and supportive environment, such as from a trusted mentor or colleague. Practice active listening and focus on understanding the feedback, rather than becoming defensive or dismissive. Recognize that receiving feedback is a normal and necessary part of growth, and it helps identify blind spots and areas for improvement. Seek additional resources or support, such as counseling or coaching, to overcome underlying fears or anxieties. By overcoming the fear of asking for feedback, you can receive valuable insights that help you achieve your goals and improve your performance. Implement these strategies to overcome fear, anxiety, and resistance to feedback, and use it as a powerful tool for development.

Approach to Asking for Feedback

Asking for feedback from a friend can provide valuable insights into your behavior and performance. When approaching a friend for feedback, be clear about what you are seeking and why it's important to you. Explain the specific area or behavior you want to improve and ask for honest feedback. Approach the conversation in a non-confrontational manner and avoid becoming defensive. Listen actively to what your friend says and ask clarifying questions to ensure you fully understand their perspective. Thank your friend for their feedback and let them know how you plan to use it to improve. By approaching the conversation with openness and a willingness to learn, you can gain valuable insights from a trusted friend and take meaningful steps toward personal and professional growth.

Asking for feedback from a family member can be challenging but rewarding. Be clear about what you are looking for and why it's important to you. Choose a time and place for an open and honest conversation. Express your desire to improve and grow and explain the specific area or behavior you are seeking feedback on. Ask for honest feedback and listen actively. Avoid becoming defensive or argumentative and ask clarifying questions to gain a better understanding of their perspective. Thank your family members for their feedback and let them know how you plan to use it to improve. By approaching the conversation with openness and a willingness to learn, you can gain valuable insights from a trusted family member and take meaningful steps toward personal and professional growth.

Asking for feedback from a mentor can provide valuable insights and guidance. Be clear about what you are looking for and why it's important to you. Ask for a specific time to speak with your mentor and come prepared with a list of questions or topics. Be open and honest about your strengths and weaknesses and ask for feedback on areas where you can improve. Listen actively and ask clarifying questions to fully understand their perspective. Take notes and use the feedback to create a plan for improvement. Thank your mentor for their time and feedback, and follow up as you make progress. By approaching the conversation with respect and a willingness to learn, you can gain valuable insights from your mentor and take meaningful steps toward personal and professional growth.

Approaching individuals for feedback can be challenging but is important for receiving constructive feedback that can help improve performance or behavior. Be clear about your goals and why you're seeking feedback. Explain that you value their opinion and expertise and are looking for specific feedback to help you grow and develop. Choose an appropriate time and place to ask for feedback, ensuring the person is comfortable and willing to provide it. Be prepared to receive feedback that may be critical or uncomfortable to hear, and be open-minded and receptive. Thank the person for their time and feedback, and follow up to discuss action plans or progress made. By approaching individuals for feedback in a respectful and professional manner, we can receive valuable insights that help achieve personal and professional goals.

When approaching others for feedback, be clear about what you are looking for and let them know you want them to be honest and forthright. Emphasize that you want to hear the truth to grow and improve. Give them full authority to speak openly and honestly, assuring them that it will not affect your relationship but will improve it. Whatever they say, especially the bad, is only to help you grow and become a better person.

Receiving Feedback

Active listening and responding to feedback are important for receiving feedback effectively. Be fully present and give the person providing feedback your undivided attention. Avoid distractions and the urge to interrupt or defend yourself. Focus on listening to the feedback and ask clarifying questions to ensure understanding. Reflect on the feedback and consider how it aligns with your personal and professional goals. Be open-minded and receptive, avoiding defensiveness. If you disagree with the feedback, ask for additional context or examples. Express gratitude for the feedback and discuss specific actions or changes based on the feedback. By actively listening and responding to feedback, you demonstrate a commitment to growth and improve relationships.

Handling negative feedback constructively is essential for growth. Remain calm and avoid becoming defensive or dismissive. Process the feedback and consider the person's perspective before responding. Focus on understanding the feedback and how it can help you improve. Ask questions to clarify the feedback and discuss specific examples or situations. Be open-minded and willing to accept feedback, even if difficult to hear. Develop a plan to address the feedback and take steps to incorporate it into your development plan. Handling negative feedback constructively turns a potentially negative situation into an opportunity for growth and improvement.

When asking for feedback, include questions about your strengths and weaknesses, what you do that is annoying or bothersome, how you can be a better family member or friend, and areas where you are good and need improvement.

Incorporating Feedback into Personal and Professional Development

Using feedback to improve performance is key to growth. Start by reviewing the feedback and identifying specific areas for improvement. Consider both positive and negative feedback and look for patterns or trends to guide your efforts. Develop a plan for addressing the feedback, including specific actions or changes. Seek additional resources or support, such as training or mentorship. Track your progress and continue to seek feedback as you work toward your goals. By using feedback to improve performance, we enhance our skills, achieve our goals, and build stronger relationships.

In this exercise, we will examine the feedback we received, categorizing it as either negative or positive. If negative, determine how to improve; if positive, determine how to use it to achieve goals. Write down the feedback you received, select whether it was positive or negative, and note how you can use or improve it.

Feedback Evaluation

- **Feedback**: Never on time
    - **Positive (P)/Negative (N)**: Negative
    - **How can we use it or improve it**: Schedule 30 minutes ahead of time. Embrace the mindset that fashionably late is still late.
- **Feedback**: Fails to meet deadlines or provide information in time stated
    - **Positive (P)/Negative (N)**: Negative
    - **How can we use it or improve it**: Provide information or documentation ahead of the promised time.
- **Feedback**: Creative thinker
    - **Positive (P)/Negative (N)**: Positive
    - **How can we use it or improve it**: Use creative thinking to help others solve problems and design new methods of doing things.
- **Feedback**: Helpful
    - **Positive (P)/Negative (N)**: Positive
    - **How can we use it or improve it**: Always be willing to help when there is a need.

Creating a plan for incorporating feedback into personal and professional development is important for improvement. Review the feedback and identify specific areas for improvement. Develop a clear and actionable plan with specific goals and a timeline. Seek additional resources or support to achieve your goals. Determine how to measure progress and adjust your plan as needed. Regularly review your plan and adjust it based on new feedback or changes in goals. By creating a plan for incorporating feedback, we ensure continuous improvement and goal achievement.

Measuring progress in feedback is important for improvement. Identify clear and specific goals based on feedback and establish a timeline. Determine how to measure progress and set regular checkpoints to review progress. Seek additional feedback at these checkpoints to ensure progress. Track progress and adjust your plan as needed. Celebrate successes to maintain motivation. By measuring progress in feedback, we ensure continuous improvement and goal achievement.

Celebrating success is important for reinforcing positive changes and maintaining motivation. When achieving a goal or making progress based on feedback, acknowledge and celebrate your success. This helps reinforce the value of feedback and its positive impact on growth. Celebrating success can take many forms, such as sharing your success with others, treating yourself, or reflecting on your progress. By celebrating success, you reinforce the value of feedback and its impact on growth.

We will cover creating a plan, measuring progress, and celebrating success in chapter 30, "Setting Goals," as these are part of the goal-setting process. For now, let's focus on feedback.

Encouragement to Regularly Get Feedback

Make feedback a regular part of your development process. Create a culture of feedback in your personal and professional life. Encourage those around you to share feedback openly and constructively and be willing to do the same. While it can be uncomfortable to receive feedback, remember it is an opportunity to learn and grow. Set clear goals and seek feedback regularly to monitor progress and adjust your approach. Embrace feedback and use it to achieve your goals and aspirations. The more feedback you receive, the more opportunities you have to improve and grow. By making feedback a regular part of your development process, you can unlock your full potential and achieve greater success in all aspects of your life.

Final Thoughts on the Importance of Feedback

In conclusion, feedback is an essential tool for personal and professional growth. By seeking out feedback from others, we gain valuable insights into our strengths and weaknesses and identify areas for improvement. We build better relationships, enhance our communication skills, and promote a culture of continuous improvement. Whether constructive, critical, positive, or negative, formal or informal, feedback provides the information needed to make meaningful changes and reach our full potential. Actively seek out feedback and create a culture of feedback in your personal and professional lives to continually improve performance and achieve greater success. Embrace feedback, use it to guide your development, and achieve greater heights in all aspects of your life.

PERSONALITY AND STRENGTHS ASSESSMENTS

Personality Assessment

A personality assessment is designed to evaluate and measure different aspects of our traits, characteristics, values, interests, and behavior patterns. It provides insights into our strengths, weaknesses, and tendencies, and helps identify areas for personal growth or development. These assessments are commonly used in clinical psychology, career counseling, and organizational management.

Personality assessments can be administered in various formats, including self-report questionnaires, tests, interviews, and behavioral observations. The most commonly used are self-report questionnaires, where individuals answer a series of questions about themselves, often using Likert scales, to rate the degree to which they agree or disagree with statements about their personality. These assessments can be based on different theoretical frameworks, such as the Big Five personality traits, Myers-Briggs Type Indicator (MBTI), DISC Assessment, or the Enneagram.

The results of a personality assessment provide information about our personality and its impact on our lives and interactions with others. Overall, these assessments aim to provide a deeper understanding of our personality and how it interacts with our environment. They can be used for career development, personal growth, and improving interpersonal relationships. However, personality assessments are not definitive measures and should be used alongside other sources of information.

Benefits of Personality Tests

Personality tests can be powerful tools for personal growth and self-improvement. By taking a personality test, we can gain insights into our strengths, weaknesses, and tendencies. This information can help develop strategies for personal growth, identify areas for improvement, and make better decisions in various aspects of life. For example, if a personality test reveals a tendency toward procrastination, we can develop strategies to overcome this habit and improve productivity. Similarly, if we score low in emotional intelligence, we can focus on developing these skills to improve relationships and communication.

Personality tests can also help us develop greater self-awareness, identify limiting behavior patterns, and recognize thoughts that may hinder personal growth. For instance, a high score in neuroticism might indicate a propensity for anxiety and stress. By recognizing these patterns, we can take steps to manage thoughts and emotions, develop coping mechanisms, and improve overall well-being. Understanding our personality traits and preferences can also help us identify our passions and interests, leading to a greater sense of purpose and direction in life, increased motivation, and happiness.

Finally, personality tests can provide a sense of direction and purpose by helping us identify career paths, hobbies, and activities suited to our strengths and interests. This self-awareness can lead to better decision-making, goal-setting, and overall well-being, enabling us to pursue activities that align with our natural inclinations and talents.

Online Personality Tests

Online personality tests are assessments administered via the internet, designed to measure our personality traits and characteristics. These tests typically involve a series of questions or statements asking us to indicate our level of agreement or disagreement.

The four most common types of online personality tests are:

- **Big Five Personality Test**: Measures openness, conscientiousness, extraversion, agreeableness, and neuroticism.

- **Myers-Briggs Type Indicator (MBTI)**: Categorizes individuals into one of 16 personality types based on four dichotomies.

- **Enneagram**: Categorizes individuals into one of nine personality types based on motivations, fears, and desires.

- **DISC Assessment**: Measures dominance, influence, steadiness, and conscientiousness, often used in workplace settings.

Each of these tests provides valuable insights for personal growth, self-awareness, career planning, and team building. However, it is important to use these tests as tools for reflection and self-discovery rather than making important decisions based solely on their results.

When taking any personality test, it is crucial to approach the questions with honesty, answering based on true characteristics and past behaviors rather than how we wish to perceive ourselves. Authenticity in responses ensures more accurate results.

How to Use Personality Test Results

Personality tests can provide valuable tools for self-awareness and understanding our thoughts, feelings, and behaviors. Here are some ways to use personality test results:

- **Personal Growth**: Identify areas for improvement and develop strategies for becoming a better version of yourself. For example, if you score low in emotional intelligence, work on developing empathy and social skills.

- **Self-Awareness**: Use insights from the test to understand your strengths and weaknesses, improving interpersonal relationships, communication skills, and work performance.

- **Relationship Building**: Understand your communication style and how you relate to others, adjusting behavior to better connect and build stronger relationships.

- **Leadership Development**: Use test results to develop leadership skills, such as taking risks, leading groups, or achieving goals.

- **Conflict Resolution**: Understand your personality traits to better navigate conflicts and find solutions that work for everyone involved.

By using personality test results as a starting point for self-reflection and personal growth, you can make informed decisions about your personal and professional lives, increasing your chances of success and happiness.

BIG FIVE PERSONALITY TEST

The Big Five personality test, also known as the Five-Factor Model (FFM), describes and categorizes human personality based on five core dimensions: Openness, Conscientiousness, Extraversion, Agreeableness, and Neuroticism (OCEAN). The test typically consists of a series of questions rated on a Likert scale, with scores ranging from strongly agree to strongly disagree.

Questions on the Big Five Personality Test

- Openness: "I have a vivid imagination."

- Conscientiousness: "I always make plans and stick to them."

- Extraversion: "I enjoy being the center of attention."

- Agreeableness: "I am sympathetic and compassionate toward others."

- Neuroticism: "I often worry about the future."

Benefits of the Big Five Personality Test

- **Self-Awareness**: Gain insights into your personality traits and tendencies, aiding in better decision-making.

- **Personal Growth**: Identify areas for improvement and work on developing traits that benefit various aspects of life.

- **Improved Relationships**: Understand your tendencies and preferences to better communicate and build relationships.

- **Career Development**: Identify career paths suited to your strengths and interests.

Free Big Five Tests Online

- Open Psychometrics - https://openpsychometrics.org/tests/IPIP-BFFM/

- Truity - https://www.truity.com/test/big-five-personality-test

- Personality Assessor - https://www.personalityassessor.com/big-five2/

- PsychologyToday - https://www.psychologytoday.com/us/tests/personality/big-five-personality-traits-test

- Personality Max - https://personalitymax.com/tests/big-five-personality-test/

Results of the Big Five Personality Test

The results provide scores for each of the five dimensions, typically represented on a scale from 1 to 100. These scores offer insights into your strengths, weaknesses, and areas for improvement. Use the results to enhance self-awareness and guide personal growth.

Exercise for The Big Five Personality Test Reflective Questions

1. Which of the Big Five traits do you resonate with the most, and why?

2. Are there any traits you were surprised to see in your results? How do they manifest in your life?

3. How do your dominant traits influence your interactions with others?

4. In what ways have your traits contributed to your successes and achievements?

5. Are there any traits you would like to develop further? How can you work on them?

Strengths and Weaknesses Analysis

Identify your top strengths and consider ways to leverage them in different areas of your personal growth. Similarly, identify your weaknesses and develop strategies to improve them.

Creating Goals Using the Big Five Personality Assessment

The Big Five personality assessment can help in creating goals by providing insights into your personality traits, strengths, and weaknesses. For example, if you score high in openness, consider setting goals that involve learning a new skill or pursuing a creative project. If you score high in conscientiousness, focus on improving productivity or developing new skills. Understanding your personality traits helps align goals with your strengths and areas for improvement, leading to greater fulfillment and satisfaction.

MYERS-BRIGGS TYPE INDICATOR

The Myers-Briggs Type Indicator (MBTI) measures and categorizes various personality traits based on the work of Carl Jung. It identifies preferences in how we perceive the world and make decisions, resulting in 16 possible personality types based on four dichotomies: Extraversion-Introversion, Sensing-Intuition, Thinking-Feeling, and Judging-Perceiving.

Questions on the Myers-Briggs Type Indicator Assessment

- "Do you prefer to spend time alone or with other people?"

- "Do you tend to focus on concrete details and practical information, or do you look for patterns and connections?"

- "Do you prioritize objective analysis and logic when making decisions, or do you consider personal values and emotions?"

- "Do you prefer a structured and organized approach, or do you like to keep things open-ended and spontaneous?"

Benefits of the Myers-Briggs Type Indicator Assessment

- **Self-Awareness**: Gain insights into personality preferences, helping you make informed decisions.

- **Improved Communication**: Understand different communication styles and preferences to connect better with others.

- **Career Planning**: Identify work environments and roles that align with your strengths and interests.

- **Team Building**: Foster better teamwork and collaboration by understanding diverse personality types.

- **Personal Growth**: Identify areas for development and stretch beyond natural preferences to enhance capabilities.

Free Myers-Briggs Type Indicator Assessment Online

- 16personalities.com

- truity.com

- personalityhacker.com

- humanmetrics.com

- personalityperfect.com

Results of the Myers-Briggs Type Indicator Assessment

The results provide a four-letter code representing your personality type, reflecting preferences across the four dimensions. These results offer insights into your strengths, weaknesses, and preferred ways of interacting with the world. Use the results for self-awareness and understanding diverse perspectives.

Exercise for The Myers-Briggs Type Indicator Assessment Reflective Questions

1. How can I use my MBTI insights to enhance self-awareness and cultivate a growth mindset?

2. How can I use my MBTI insights to build stronger relationships with colleagues, friends, or romantic partners?

3. In what ways can I embrace and develop my non-preferred MBTI preferences to become more adaptable?

4. Are there specific skills or knowledge areas I need to improve based on my MBTI results?

5. How can I use my MBTI type to enhance problem-solving abilities and think more strategically?

Strengths and Weaknesses Analysis

Identify your top strengths and consider ways to leverage them in different areas of personal growth. Similarly, identify your weaknesses and develop strategies to improve them.

Creating Goals Using the Myers-Briggs Type Indicator Assessment

Use the MBTI assessment to create goals aligned with your unique personality preferences. Understand your type, identify growth areas, and set goals that incorporate your strengths and address areas for improvement. For example, extraverts might focus on expanding their network, while introverts might prioritize personal reflection. Sensors might enhance attention to detail, while intuitives might explore new possibilities. Tailor your goals to align with your preferred methods and natural inclinations for greater success and satisfaction.

ENNEAGRAM

The Enneagram test is a personality assessment tool describing nine distinct personality types, providing insights into motivations, fears, desires, and core beliefs. Each of the nine types represents a pattern of thoughts, emotions, and behaviors shaping individuals' perspectives and interactions.

Questions on an Enneagram Test

- "When faced with a problem, do you seek logical solutions, consider the impact on others, or trust your instincts?"

- "In social situations, do you maintain a reserved demeanor, engage in lively conversations, or observe and listen?"

- "When under stress, do you become perfectionistic, feel overwhelmed by emotions, or withdraw to figure things out?"

- "In personal relationships, do you value loyalty and practical support, connection and emotional depth, or independence and growth?"

Benefits of an Enneagram Test

- **Self-Awareness**: Gain insights into thoughts, emotions, behaviors, and motivations.

- **Personal Growth**: Identify specific patterns and tendencies for self-improvement.

- **Improved Relationships**: Understand different personality types to develop empathy and better communication skills.

- **Conflict Resolution**: Navigate conflicts effectively by recognizing different motivations and perspectives.

- **Workplace Insights**: Recognize strengths, identify areas for improvement, and understand work styles for career satisfaction.

Free Online Enneagram Test

- www.truity.com/test/enneagram-personality-test

- www.crystalknows.com/enneagram-test

- www.idrlabs.com/enneagram/test.php

Results of the Enneagram Assessment

The results provide your primary Enneagram type, core motivations, fears, desires, strengths, weaknesses, and patterns of thinking, feeling, and behaving. Some tests may also identify your wing type, which influences and complements your primary type. Use these insights for self-awareness, personal growth, and understanding diverse perspectives.

Exercise for The Enneagram Assessment Reflective Questions

1. Does the Enneagram type identified by the test resonate with me?

2. Do the core motivations, fears, and desires described align with my experiences and behaviors?

3. Are there any aspects of my Enneagram type that surprised me or that I initially resisted? Why might that be?

4. How do I relate to the strengths and weaknesses associated with my Enneagram type?

5. Which strengths do I recognize in myself, and how have they positively influenced my life?

Strengths and Weaknesses Analysis

Identify your top strengths and consider ways to leverage them in different areas of personal growth. Similarly, identify your weaknesses and develop strategies to improve them.

Creating Goals Using the Enneagram Assessment

The Enneagram provides insights into core motivations, fears, and desires, helping us set meaningful and aligned goals. Identify your dominant type, recognize specific growth areas, and set goals addressing these areas. For example, if you are prone to perfectionism, set goals to cultivate self-compassion and flexibility. Align goals with your core values for greater fulfillment and satisfaction.

DISC ASSESSMENT

The DISC assessment evaluates personality types and behavioral styles based on four primary dimensions: Dominance (D), Influence (I), Steadiness (S), and Conscientiousness (C). It helps individuals and teams understand communication styles, build stronger relationships, and improve teamwork.

Questions on a DISC Assessment

- "When working on a project, do you prefer to take charge and make decisions quickly, or listen to others' opinions and work collaboratively?"

- "How would you describe your communication style? Are you outgoing and talkative, or more reserved and quieter?"

- "When faced with conflict, do you confront it head-on or avoid it and hope it goes away?"

- "Do you prefer tasks requiring detail and precision, or creative and open-ended tasks?"

- "Do you prefer a strict timeline and schedule, or to be flexible and adaptable?"

Benefits of Taking a DISC Assessment

- **Self-Awareness**: Understand behavior and communication styles to improve interactions and relationships.

- **Team Building**: Foster stronger teams by understanding diverse behavioral styles.

- **Personal Development**: Identify strengths and areas for improvement, and develop strategies for achieving goals.

- **Improved Communication**: Adapt communication styles for more effective interactions.

- **Leadership Insights**: Enhance leadership skills by understanding strengths and areas for development.

Free Online DISC Assessment

- www.mydiscprofile.com/en-us/free-personality-test.php

- www.123test.com/disc-personality-test/

- www.tonyrobbins.com/disc/

- www.openpsychometrics.org/tests/ODAT/

- www.crystalknows.com/disc-personality-test

- www.truity.com/test/disc-personality-test

Results of the DISC Assessment

The results provide insights into behavior across Dominance, Influence, Steadiness, and Conscientiousness dimensions. The report includes analysis of behavioral tendencies, strengths, communication style, and areas for development. Use the results to improve communication, teamwork, and overall performance.

Exercise for The DISC Assessment Reflective Questions

1. How accurately do the DISC assessment results align with your perception of your own behavioral tendencies?

2. What specific behaviors or traits highlighted in the assessment resonate strongly with your self-perception?

3. Are there any surprising or unexpected insights from the assessment results that challenge your self-perception?

4. In what situations or contexts do you find yourself exhibiting behaviors associated with your dominant DISC style?

5. How do your dominant DISC style and associated behaviors impact your interactions and relationships with others?

Strengths and Weaknesses Analysis

Identify your top strengths and consider ways to leverage them in different areas of personal growth. Similarly, identify your weaknesses and develop strategies to improve them.

Creating Goals Using the DISC Assessment

The DISC assessment helps create goals by providing insights into behavioral tendencies, strengths, and areas for development. Understand your natural tendencies, communication style, and teamwork preferences to set goals that capitalize on strengths and address areas for improvement. Align goals with values and priorities for greater success and satisfaction.

MOVE

MOVE is an acronym for Morals, Obedience, Values, and Ethics. I call it MOVE because our Morals, Obedience, Values, and Ethics should determine every action we take. However, many people today are not obedient to their morals, values, and ethics; some may not even understand their importance. That's why I want to explain how powerful MOVE is for personal growth and success in life.

Embracing strong morals fosters integrity and authenticity. By adhering to our sense of right and wrong, we build a solid foundation for ethical decisions and cultivate trust in ourselves and others. Morals guide us in choosing actions aligned with our principles, allowing us to navigate challenges with a clear conscience and develop a strong moral compass that strengthens our character.

In our pursuit of personal growth, obedience plays a vital role. By embracing obedience, we learn discipline, respect for authority, and the importance of adhering to societal and organizational norms. Obedience helps us develop responsibility and accountability, enabling us to work effectively in teams, navigate professional settings, and contribute positively to our communities.

Our values serve as guiding beacons that direct our choices and actions. By clarifying our core values, we establish a solid framework for personal growth. Embracing our values empowers us to make decisions in alignment with our true selves, leading to a life of authenticity, fulfillment, and purpose. Our values shape our relationships, career choices, and overall life direction.

Ethics form the foundation of our personal growth journey, shaping our behavior and interactions with others. By embracing ethical principles, we develop a heightened sense of integrity, fairness, and responsibility. Ethical conduct allows us to navigate challenges with moral clarity, fostering trust and respect in our relationships. It enables us to make choices that positively impact our communities and contribute to a more just and compassionate society.

When we embody MOVE—Morals, Obedience, Values, and Ethics—we can profoundly impact ourselves and those around us. Our commitment influences our actions, inspiring others and creating a ripple effect of positive change. By leading with integrity and adhering to ethical standards, we become catalysts for personal growth, fostering a culture of honesty, compassion, and accountability.

MOVE encourages the development of a growth mindset—an attitude that embraces challenges, values effort, and seeks opportunities for learning and improvement. By embodying MOVE principles, we cultivate resilience, adaptability, and a hunger for personal and professional growth. We see setbacks as opportunities for growth, persevere in the face of obstacles, and continually seek self-improvement.

Incorporating MOVE into our personal growth journey promotes self-reflection. By evaluating our actions through the lens of morals, obedience, values, and ethics, we deepen our self-awareness and gain valuable insights into our behaviors and decision-making. Self-reflection enhances our personal growth by helping us identify areas for improvement, align our actions with our values, and foster a greater understanding of ourselves and others.

MOVE fosters empathy—a vital attribute in personal growth. By embracing morals, obedience, values, and ethics, we develop the ability to understand and connect with others' perspectives, experiences, and emotions. Empathy enhances our relationships, communication skills, and leadership capabilities, allowing us to create inclusive and supportive environments that promote personal and collective growth.

By embodying MOVE principles, we cultivate consistency in our behaviors and actions. Consistency allows us to build trust, both in ourselves and in our relationships. It reinforces our commitment to our morals, values, and ethical standards, leading to increased credibility and respect from others. Consistency ensures that our personal growth journey is grounded in integrity and authenticity.

When we embrace MOVE in our personal growth journey, we leave a lasting legacy. By exemplifying strong morals, obedience, values, and ethics, we inspire others to do the same. Our actions and choices become a positive influence on those around us, shaping the next generation and contributing to a more compassionate, ethical, and harmonious society. Our legacy is built upon the values we embody and the impact we create through our commitment to MOVE.

Differentiating Morals, Values, and Ethics

Morals, values, and ethics are distinct but interconnected concepts that shape our character, guide our actions, and influence our decision-making. Morals refer to our personal beliefs and principles about what is right and wrong. They stem from our individual conscience and provide a sense of direction and an internal compass, guiding our behavior and helping us navigate ethical dilemmas.

Values encompass a set of beliefs and principles that we consider important and meaningful in our lives. They are influenced by our upbringing, culture, and personal experiences. Values shape our attitudes, priorities, and overall worldview, defining what we hold dear and guiding our choices and actions.

Ethics focus on the study and application of moral principles within specific contexts, such as professional or social settings. Ethics provide a framework for evaluating the moral implications of our actions and decisions. They encompass societal norms, standards, and codes of conduct that guide our behavior and interactions with others.

In short, morals are our individual sense of right and wrong, values are our broader beliefs and principles that guide our lives, and ethics provide a framework for evaluating and applying moral principles within specific contexts. Understanding these distinctions allows us to navigate ethical challenges with clarity, live in alignment with our principles, and contribute to a more just and compassionate world.

Obedience Connection

Obedience plays a vital role in upholding our morals, values, and ethics. It serves as a bridge between our inner principles and their manifestation in our actions and choices. By embracing obedience, we demonstrate our commitment to living in alignment with our deeply held beliefs and ethical standards, translating our moral compass into tangible behaviors that reflect our values. Obedience empowers us to put our principles into action, acting in accordance with our moral code even when faced with challenges or temptations. It reinforces our commitment to honesty, integrity, compassion, and other virtues that form the bedrock of our moral framework.

Moreover, obedience provides the necessary discipline to navigate complex ethical dilemmas. It encourages us to consider the broader impact of our actions and make choices that prioritize the greater good over personal gain. By obeying ethical guidelines and standards, we contribute to a just and harmonious society where fairness, respect, and integrity prevail.

Obedience also fosters trust and credibility in our relationships. When others witness our consistent adherence to our morals, values, and ethical principles, they develop confidence in our character and reliability. Obedience builds a foundation of trust, enhancing our connections with others and enabling us to collaborate effectively in various spheres of life.

Furthermore, obedience nurtures personal growth and self-mastery. It instills self-discipline and self-control, allowing us to overcome impulsive behaviors and align our actions with our higher ideals. By obeying our morals, values, and ethics, we cultivate a sense of purpose, authenticity, and fulfillment in our lives.

Ultimately, obedience in our morals, values, and ethics allows us to live with integrity and make choices that honor our deepest convictions. It is a conscious commitment to being the best version of ourselves, aligning our actions with our inner compass of righteousness. By embracing obedience, we become catalysts for positive change, shaping a world that reflects the values and ethics we hold dear.

Morals

Morals are the guiding principles that shape our character and behavior, reflecting our inner compass. They provide a moral framework to navigate life's complexities, enabling us to make ethical choices, act with integrity, and uphold our principles. Morals serve as a moral anchor, offering clarity and direction, and helping us navigate difficult situations and ethical dilemmas with conviction and honesty.

Strong morals foster trust and respect in our relationships. When we consistently act according to our moral principles, we build a reputation for reliability and integrity. Others recognize our steadfastness and are more likely to place their trust in us. Our moral compass becomes a beacon that guides us toward meaningful connections and positive interactions.

Morals give us a sense of purpose and meaning. By aligning our actions with our morals, we create a life in harmony with our values and beliefs, providing a sense of fulfillment and authenticity. They also contribute to a just and ethical society, influencing others to uphold fairness, honesty, and compassion, and laying the foundation for a harmonious and ethical community.

Having strong morals helps us overcome challenges and temptations. Our moral compass guides us toward choices that align with our values, even when it may be easier to compromise our integrity. Morals provide the strength and resilience to stay true to ourselves, even in adversity.

Morals provide a sense of accountability. With clearly defined morals, we hold ourselves to a higher standard of behavior, taking responsibility for our actions and their impact on others. Morals instill personal accountability, encouraging reflection and making amends when needed. They cultivate empathy and compassion, encouraging consideration of others' well-being and perspectives.

Ultimately, having strong morals gives our lives a sense of purpose, direction, and fulfillment. They shape our identity, guide our choices, and define our character, empowering us to make a positive difference in the world and leaving a legacy of integrity and ethical conduct.

Realizing Your Morals

This exercise helps individuals reflect on their morals and uncover their deeply held values and principles. Find a quiet and comfortable space for self-reflection without distractions. Grab a pen and notebook or turn to page 98 in your workbook. A list of 90 morals in Appendix A on page 318 will help you.

1. Reflect on your upbringing: Think about your childhood, family, and cultural background. Consider the values and morals emphasized or instilled in you during that time. Write down any morals that come to mind because of your reflection.

   o Memories/Cultural Background: "Don't bust hell wide open by lying" (Honesty), "Always apologize when you're wrong" (Forgiveness), "Respect your elders" (Respect)

2. Identify influential figures: Think about individuals who have significantly impacted your life, such as mentors, role models, or inspirational figures. Consider the qualities or morals you admire most in these individuals. Write down any morals that resonate with you. (See page 100 in your workbook.)

   o Individuals Name: Rev. Morgan James (Bluntness), Clara James (Compassion), Pastor Anthony (Generosity)

3. Contemplate significant life experiences: Reflect on meaningful experiences or moments in your life. Consider how these experiences may have shaped your values and morals. Write down any morals that arise from these reflections. (See page 101 in your workbook.)

   o Meaningful experience/Moment: Joining the Army to take care of my daughter (Responsibility)

4. Evaluate your guiding principles: Assess what you consider to be the most important principles in your life, such as honesty, kindness, justice, compassion, respect, or fairness. Write down the morals that align with your guiding principles. (See page 102 in your workbook.)

   o Important Principal: [Write your principal here]

5. Consider moral dilemmas: Imagine hypothetical scenarios or recall real-life situations where you faced a moral dilemma. Reflect on how you approached those situations and the morals that guided your decisions. Write down any morals that emerged from these reflections. (See page 103 in your workbook.)

   o Scenario/Real-life situation: [Write your scenario here]

6. Reflect on your behavior: Evaluate your actions and behaviors. Consider moments when you felt a deep sense of alignment with your values and morals. Write down the morals that you find most important based on this self-reflection. (See page 104 in your workbook.)

   o Action/Behavior: [Write your action here]

7. Reflect on your behavior: Evaluate your actions and behaviors. Consider instances where you may have acted in a way that conflicted with your morals. Write down the morals that you find most important based on this self-reflection. (See page 105 in your workbook.)

   o Action/Behavior: [Write your action here]

8. Analyze the common themes: Review the list of morals you have written down. Look for common themes or recurring values. Identify the top five morals that resonate most deeply with you. (See page 106 in your workbook.)

   o Morals: Honesty, Respect, Responsibility, Forgiveness, Gratitude

9. Personalize your morals: Reflect on how these morals manifest in your life. Consider specific actions or behaviors that demonstrate these morals. Write down practical ways you can integrate these morals into your daily life. (See page 106 in your workbook.)

- Morals: How to use them daily

  - Honesty: Speak the truth in all things

  - Respect: Give respect to others at all times

  - Responsibility: Take responsibility for my actions and inactions, regardless of the ramifications

  - Forgiveness: If you have a problem with someone, do not let the sun go down until you have forgiven them

  - Gratitude: Be grateful for my family, each day that God blesses me with, and all that I have

Revisit and revise: Over time, your morals may evolve and change as you gain new experiences and perspectives. Periodically revisit this exercise to assess whether your morals remain consistent or if any modifications are necessary. By engaging in this exercise, you can gain a clearer understanding of your morals and values, providing a foundation for personal growth and a guide for living a more authentic and purposeful life.

Obedience

Obedience is a powerful attribute that plays a significant role in personal growth. It involves respecting and adhering to rules, laws, and guidelines that govern our lives. By embracing obedience, we develop discipline, self-control, and a sense of responsibility that propels us forward on our personal growth journey. Obedience provides structure and order in our lives, allowing us to establish routines, follow schedules, and stay organized. By honoring commitments and obligations, we create a sense of stability that fosters personal growth and success.

Obedience helps us navigate challenges and overcome obstacles. It teaches us to persevere and work diligently towards our goals, even when faced with setbacks. By committing to obedience, we develop resilience and the ability to overcome adversity, enabling personal growth and transformation. Embracing obedience nurtures self-discipline, essential for personal growth. It involves making conscious choices and taking actions that align with our long-term aspirations. Self-discipline allows us to prioritize our goals, stay focused, and maintain consistency in our efforts.

Obedience promotes accountability. When we are obedient, we take ownership of our actions and accept the consequences of our choices. This accountability fuels personal growth by encouraging self-reflection, learning from mistakes, and striving for continuous improvement.

Obedience encourages us to listen, learn, and accept guidance from others. Humility opens doors to new perspectives and growth opportunities, as it allows us to recognize that personal growth involves a lifelong journey of learning from others and ourselves. Obedience fosters trust and reliability. When others perceive us as obedient individuals, they develop confidence in our abilities and character. Trust is vital in personal growth, as it opens doors to new opportunities, collaborations, and meaningful relationships.

Obedience facilitates learning and growth from mentors and role models. When we exhibit obedience towards those who possess wisdom and experience, we create opportunities to absorb their knowledge and benefit from their guidance. By being receptive and obedient, we accelerate our personal growth journey. Obedience cultivates humility, self-control, and emotional intelligence. It teaches us to manage our impulses, emotions, and reactions, enabling us to make thoughtful decisions and respond effectively to various situations. Self-control and emotional intelligence are crucial components of personal growth and contribute to our overall well-being.

Ultimately, obedience propels us towards self-mastery and personal excellence. It helps us cultivate the necessary habits, attitudes, and behaviors that foster growth, achievement, and fulfillment. By embracing obedience, we unlock our full potential, step into our greatness, and become the best versions of ourselves.

Obedience and Self-discipline

Obedience and self-discipline are the dynamic duo that propel us towards our goals and aspirations. By cultivating these qualities, we gain control over our actions, thoughts, and habits, allowing us to direct our lives with intention and purpose. Together, they are the keys to unlocking our full potential. They enable us to overcome procrastination, resist distractions, and stay focused on what truly matters. With these qualities, we can harness our inner drive and commitment to achieve remarkable feats.

Obedience and self-discipline foster a strong work ethic. They instill within us the mindset of consistent effort and perseverance, even in the face of challenges or setbacks. Through diligent practice and unwavering dedication, we can achieve excellence in our pursuits. They fuel personal growth, pushing us beyond our comfort zones and into the realm of continuous improvement. By embracing obedience and self-discipline, we create an environment where growth becomes the norm, and mediocrity is left behind.

Obedience and self-discipline empower us to make wise choices and resist instant gratification. They enable us to delay short-term desires for long-term fulfillment and success. With these qualities, we become the architects of our own destiny, shaping our lives according to our deepest aspirations. They build resilience and inner strength, teaching us to persevere through difficulties, setbacks, and failures. By developing these qualities, we develop the capacity to bounce back from challenges and use them as stepping stones to greater achievements.

Obedience and self-discipline enhance our self-esteem and self-confidence. When we consistently honor our commitments and follow through on our goals, we develop a sense of trust in ourselves. This self-trust becomes the foundation for self-belief and the fuel that propels us forward in our personal and professional endeavors.

Obedience and self-discipline cultivate a growth mindset. They encourage us to embrace challenges and view failures as opportunities for learning and growth. With these qualities, we develop a resilient mindset that sees setbacks as temporary roadblocks on the path to success. They allow us to maximize our time and energy. By prioritizing our tasks, eliminating distractions, and staying focused, we optimize our productivity and accomplish more in less time. These qualities help us make the most of each day and create a life of purposeful action.

Ultimately, obedience and self-discipline lead to a life of fulfillment and personal satisfaction. When we honor our commitments, show up consistently, and put in the effort required for our goals, we experience a deep sense of fulfillment. We realize that our disciplined actions have the power to shape our destiny and create a life of purpose and meaning.

Embrace obedience and self-discipline as powerful allies on your journey of personal growth. Cultivate these qualities with intention and perseverance, knowing that they are the keys to unlocking your true potential and achieving extraordinary success. With obedience and self-discipline as your guiding principles, you have the power to create a life of purpose, fulfillment, and lasting impact.

Values

Values are the guiding principles that define who we are at our core. They represent our fundamental beliefs and priorities, serving as the foundation upon which we build our lives. Having clear values provides a sense of identity and purpose, helping us navigate the complexities of life with clarity and integrity. Values act as a compass, directing our decisions and actions. They help us make choices aligned with our authentic selves, enabling us to live a life that is true to our deepest aspirations and ideals. Values provide a sense of direction, ensuring that we are on a path that resonates with our innermost desires.

Values bring meaning and fulfillment to our lives. When we align our actions with our values, we experience a sense of congruence and purpose. Our values provide a sense of significance, as they reflect what we hold dear and consider important. Living in accordance with our values allows us to lead a life that feels meaningful and fulfilling.

Values guide our relationships and interactions with others. They shape the way we treat others, our approach to teamwork, and our ability to establish deep connections. By honoring our values, we foster trust, respect, and authenticity in our relationships, creating a supportive and nurturing environment.

Values act as a source of strength and resilience during challenging times. When we face obstacles or adversity, our values provide a solid foundation for making decisions and navigating difficulties with courage and perseverance. They remind us of our priorities and help us stay grounded, even in the face of uncertainty.

Values serve as a moral compass, guiding us towards ethical behavior and responsible choices. They act as a guidepost, helping us distinguish between right and wrong, and encouraging us to act in accordance with our principles. Values provide a sense of integrity and encourage us to uphold honesty, fairness, and compassion in our interactions with others.

Values promote self-awareness and personal growth. By clarifying our values, we gain insight into what truly matters to us. This self-awareness allows us to assess our actions and make intentional choices that align with our values. Values provide a framework for personal development, inspiring us to continually strive for growth and improvement.

Values foster a sense of authenticity and individuality. Each person's set of values is unique and reflective of their own experiences and beliefs. Embracing our values allows us to express our true selves and honor our individuality. It encourages us to celebrate our uniqueness and make choices that align with our authentic nature.

Values provide a sense of stability and consistency in a rapidly changing world. In the face of external influences and societal pressures, our values act as an anchor, allowing us to stay true to ourselves. Even in the midst of uncertainty, values provide a sense of continuity and resilience.

Ultimately, values are the building blocks of a purpose-driven life. They shape our character, define our priorities, and influence our actions. By embracing and living in alignment with our values, we create a life that is meaningful, fulfilling, and reflective of our true selves. Values give us a sense of direction and provide the framework for personal growth, authentic relationships, and a positive impact on the world around us.

Syncing Morals and Values

Our morals and values are intricately intertwined, creating a powerful synergy that shapes our character and influences our actions. When our morals align with our values, we experience a profound sense of integrity, authenticity, and fulfillment. When our values align with our morals, we create a strong foundation for living a life of purpose and meaning. Our values become the driving force behind our moral compass, guiding us to make choices that align with our deepest beliefs and principles. When they are aligned, we experience a deep sense of congruence and authenticity. Our actions become a reflection of our innermost convictions, and we find ourselves living in alignment with our true selves. This alignment creates a sense of inner harmony and peace, as we are honoring the core essence of who we are and what we stand for.

Moreover, when our morals align with our values, we experience a greater sense of integrity and coherence. Our values provide the framework for ethical behavior and responsible decision-making, while our morals serve as the internal compass that directs us towards what we perceive as right and wrong. This alignment allows us to navigate life's challenges and complexities with clarity and conviction.

Living in alignment with our morals and values empowers us to create a positive impact on the world around us. When our actions are guided by our deeply held principles, we contribute to the well-being of others and the betterment of society. We become catalysts for positive change, inspiring others to embrace their values and live with integrity. Eventually, the alignment of our morals with our values is the foundation for personal growth, fulfillment, and a life well-lived. It enables us to pursue our goals and aspirations in a way that is authentic and meaningful. When our morals and values are in harmony, we cultivate a life of purpose, integrity, and joy, creating a legacy of compassion, fairness, and positive impact.

Aligning Values with Morals

Aligning your values with your morals is a powerful catalyst for personal growth and fulfillment. When you consciously choose to live in alignment with your deeply held beliefs and principles, you create a solid foundation for making decisions and taking actions that are in harmony with your authentic self. This alignment provides a sense of integrity and purpose, fueling your motivation to strive for excellence in all aspects of your life. When your values and morals are in sync, you experience a profound sense of clarity and direction. You know what truly matters to you and what you stand for, which allows you to navigate life's challenges with unwavering determination. By aligning your values with your morals, you cultivate a strong internal compass that guides your choices, ensuring that you consistently act in ways that align with your deepest convictions.

The alignment of values and morals fosters a sense of authenticity and genuineness. When your actions and decisions reflect your true self, you radiate a genuine and magnetic presence that inspires others. People are naturally drawn to those who embody their values, and by aligning your values with your morals, you become a beacon of inspiration, motivating others to also embrace their beliefs and strive for a life of integrity.

Aligning values with morals empowers you to live a life of purpose and meaning. By identifying the principles and ideals that are most important to you and ensuring that your actions align with them, you infuse your life with a profound sense of significance. You no longer wander aimlessly through life; instead, you embark on a journey driven by a higher purpose, where each step you take is in harmony with your deeply held beliefs.

When your values and morals are aligned, you experience a deep sense of inner peace and fulfillment. There is a sense of congruence and harmony between your thoughts, words, and actions. This internal coherence brings about a profound sense of well-being, allowing you to approach life's challenges with resilience and grace. By aligning your values with your morals, you cultivate a state of inner alignment that fuels your motivation and propels you forward.

The alignment of values and morals is the key to creating a life of integrity and making a positive impact on the world around you. When your values guide your decisions and actions, you become a force for good, contributing to the betterment of society. By living in alignment with your morals, you set an example for others, inspiring them to also align their actions with their deeply held beliefs. Together, we can create a world where integrity, compassion, and ethical behavior are the norm, making a lasting difference in the lives of others and leaving a positive legacy for future generations.

Value Exercise

Using your top 5 morals, which you previously selected, convert them into values. Turn to page 108 in your workbook or create it in your notebook. Here are some examples of aligning values to morals:

- **Honesty**: I will live with integrity in both my personal and professional environment

- **Respect**: I will treat those who I encounter with dignity and honor

- **Responsibility**: I will hold myself accountable for my actions and assignments

- **Forgiveness**: I will give grace to others just as God has given it to me

- **Gratitude**: I will always show and give appreciation for what I have and for what others do for me

These examples illustrate how specific morals can be transformed into corresponding values. Values are broader concepts that encompass the essence of the underlying moral and provide a guiding framework for living in alignment with one's principles. Embracing these values allows individuals to manifest their morals in everyday actions, fostering personal growth and contributing to a more ethical and compassionate world.

Now, these were your top 5 morals, which you have now formed into values; these values are known as your core beliefs. It is through these core beliefs that we make our decisions and live our lives. This is who you are right now! But what about who you want to become? How do we determine that? It's easier than you think. Look at the list of morals that are in Appendix B; from this list, consider which of these morals you would like to have. You can choose as many as you like, and you can even add some that may not be on the list; it's entirely up to you.

Now that you have selected the morals you want to possess, I want you to turn them into values you desire to have. (See page 109 in your workbook or create it in your notebook.)

- Desired Moral: **Patience**

  o Desired Value: I will be resilient in all situations maintaining a calm manner

- Desired Moral: **Perseverance**

  o Desired Value: I will persist until I have achieved success

- Desired Moral: **Balance**

  o Desired Value: I will recognize the significance of nurturing all aspects of my life, including physical, emotional, mental, and spiritual dimensions.

- Desired Moral: **Wisdom**

  o Desired Value: I will continue to educate myself on things I do not understand

- Desired Moral: **Teamwork**

  o Desired Value: I will rely on others that are better at the things I need done

Once you have completed this assignment, you will have the values that you want to have in your life. Later, we will use these new morals and values to create goals that will enhance our personal growth journey. As we use the morals and values that we have, others will see that we are men and women of ethics adhering to the morals and values that guide our every decision and the way we live our lives.

Ethics

Ethics, the guiding light of our moral compass, empowers us to make choices that align with our deepest values and principles. It reminds us that our actions have consequences and that we possess the power to shape a world that reflects our highest ideals. Embracing ethics enables us to rise above self-interest and consider the greater good, fostering a culture of integrity, fairness, and compassion. When we prioritize ethics, we become catalysts for positive change, inspiring others to embrace the path of moral responsibility. Our commitment to ethical living not only uplifts our own lives but also creates a ripple effect that reaches far beyond ourselves. So let us embrace ethics as a guiding force, igniting our potential to make a profound impact, and together, let us build a brighter, more ethical world for generations to come.

Put simply, ethics are the laws by which we govern ourselves. It is mainly about abiding by the morals and values that we have set for ourselves. When we do not adhere to our ethics, several negative consequences can arise, both on a personal and societal level. Going against our ethics creates inner conflict and a sense of warfare within ourselves. We experience feelings of guilt, regret, and dissatisfaction, knowing that our actions contradict our moral compass. This internal turmoil can lead to diminished self-esteem and a lack of inner peace.

Failing to uphold our ethics erodes our personal integrity and credibility. Others may view us as inconsistent or untrustworthy, damaging our reputation and the trust others place in us. This erosion of integrity can strain relationships and hinder opportunities for growth and collaboration. Our actions may hurt or betray the trust of those close to us, leading to feelings of resentment, betrayal, and even the breakdown of relationships. Lack of ethical behavior can create distance and hinder meaningful connections with others.

On a broader scale, when individuals or institutions do not adhere to ethics, it can lead to negative consequences for society. Unethical practices can result in exploitation, injustice, and social inequalities. It undermines the trust and well-being of communities, erodes social cohesion, and perpetuates harmful systems and behaviors.

Acting against ethics may also result in legal ramifications. Unethical behavior can violate laws, regulations, or professional codes of conduct, leading to legal consequences, fines, or even criminal charges. Such legal repercussions can have long-lasting effects on one's personal and professional life.

When we deviate from our ethics, we may experience a loss of self-identity and purpose. Our actions no longer align with our values and beliefs, leading to a sense of disconnect from our authentic selves. This can lead to feelings of emptiness, confusion, and a loss of direction in life.

It is crucial to understand the impact of not adhering to our ethics and strive to live in alignment with our values. By making conscious choices that align with our moral compass, we uphold our integrity, maintain positive relationships, contribute to a more ethical society, and foster personal growth and fulfillment.

Ethics Categories

Ethics can be categorized in many ways, but to be truly ethical means conducting ourselves in a manner that is always empowering and uplifting others, even when we must be brutally honest about their behavior. Here are some examples of ethical categories:

- **Professional Ethics**: Ethical standards and principles that guide conduct within specific professions or industries, such as medical ethics, legal ethics, or engineering ethics.

- **Business Ethics**: Principles and values that govern ethical behavior in the business world, including honesty, fairness, transparency, and responsibility towards stakeholders.

- **Environmental Ethics**: Moral considerations and values related to the responsible stewardship of the environment, including sustainability, conservation, and minimizing harm to ecosystems.

- **Research Ethics**: Ethical guidelines and principles that govern the conduct of research, including the protection of human subjects, integrity in data collection and analysis, and the responsible use of resources.

- **Bioethics**: Ethical considerations surrounding medical and biological research, healthcare practices, and moral dilemmas related to topics such as genetic engineering, organ transplantation, or end-of-life care.

- **Digital Ethics**: Principles and guidelines regarding ethical behavior in the digital realm, including issues such as data privacy, cybersecurity, online harassment, and responsible use of technology.

- **Social Ethics**: Ethical principles and values that govern interpersonal relationships, societal norms, and issues related to social justice, equality, and human rights.

- **Legal Ethics**: Ethical standards and rules that guide the behavior of legal professionals, including attorneys and judges, ensuring fairness, confidentiality, and loyalty to clients.

- **Media Ethics**: Principles and values that guide responsible and ethical practices within the media industry, such as truthfulness, accuracy, unbiased reporting, and respect for privacy.

- **Personal Ethics**: Individual moral principles and values that guide one's behavior and decision-making, reflecting personal beliefs, character, and integrity.

These examples represent various domains in which ethics play a crucial role in guiding behavior, decision-making, and promoting responsible and morally sound actions. Ethics provide frameworks for addressing moral dilemmas, shaping professional conduct, and fostering a just and ethical society. For this writing, we will mainly be focusing on personal ethics and social ethics.

Ethics Exercise

While ethics are based on real-life circumstances, we can simulate dilemmas to test our ethical principles. If you have the workbook, we have given you a few simulated dilemmas on page 111. Here are two for you to gain an understanding of testing your ethics.

1. You receive a shut-off notice from the electric company stating that $75 must be paid by the following business day, but you don't get paid until the next week and only have $10. You need to buy detergent to wash your clothes to go to work the following week. You go to the store to buy the detergent, and the cashier rings you up, and your total is $8.79. You give her the $10, and she gives you $91.21 back in change. Do you:

   o Count it as a blessing that you have enough to pay the electric bill.

   o Tell the cashier she made a mistake and return the $90.

   o Keep the change, pay the light bill, and return the money when you get paid.

2. A friend calls and asks you to confirm to their spouse that the two of you went out to dinner last night should they call and ask because your friend went out to dinner with their ex and doesn't want the spouse to get angry and leave them. Even though you were at home with your spouse last night, do you:

   o Agree to cover for your friend and hope their spouse does not ask.

   o Agree to cover for your friend and tell the spouse you were together.

   o Tell your friend you won't do it and leave it at that.

   o Tell your friend she needs to tell her spouse what happened and deal with the consequences because you won't cover for them.

The answers to these questions depend on your values, and there is no wrong answer. It is a question of where your values lie. Personally, I would answer "b" for the first question and "d" for the second. I would not want the cashier to have to pay the $90 out of their pocket or lose their job, even though it was their mistake. For the second, I would tell my friend to come clean with their spouse because knowing what they did would bother me until it was resolved between them. If it caused discord in their marriage, as a friend, I would talk to the spouse and ask them to give my friend another chance. For me, these are the ethical things to do, but as individuals, we are all different.

Hopefully, you have learned the importance of living a life with Morals, Obedience, Values, and Ethics. You should also understand why I use the term MOVE for these four attributes—they dictate how we need to move in life to have peace and tranquility. From these four, we learn to set boundaries in our lives and live a harmonious life.

Boundaries

Boundaries are the loving limits we set to protect our well-being, honor our values, and create space for personal growth. They define what is acceptable and what is not in our lives. Boundaries remind us and others of our worthiness, deservingness, and self-respect, allowing us to navigate life with clarity, authenticity, and integrity. Boundaries empower us to say "yes" to what aligns with our values and priorities and confidently say "no" to what drains our energy or compromises our boundaries. They create healthy relationships, foster self-care, and nurture our emotional, mental, and physical health. Embrace the power of boundaries, honor your needs, and watch as your life transforms into one of balance, fulfillment, and empowered authenticity.

Setting Boundaries

Setting boundaries is an empowering act that honors our self-worth. It declares to the world that we value ourselves and our needs. Boundaries create a protective shield around our emotional, mental, and physical well-being, allowing us to navigate life with a sense of confidence and self-respect. Embrace the power of boundaries and watch as we cultivate healthier relationships, build stronger self-esteem, and unlock a life of authenticity and fulfillment.

When we set boundaries, we prioritize our well-being and make self-love a top priority. Boundaries enable us to establish limits that align with our values and needs. By saying "no" when necessary and asserting our boundaries, we create space for self-care, personal growth, and genuine connections. Remember, it is not selfish to protect our well-being—it is an act of self-love that allows us to show up as our best self for others.

Boundary setting helps us manage our time, emotions, and resources in a way that aligns with our priorities and values. By setting boundaries around demanding commitments, toxic relationships, or draining activities, we reclaim our energy and create a life that nourishes and energizes us. Embrace the power of boundaries to live a life filled with passion, purpose, and sustainable joy.

Boundaries establish mutual respect, create clear expectations, and promote authentic connections. By communicating our boundaries openly and respectfully, we invite others to honor our needs and values. Boundaries nurture relationships built on trust, understanding, and genuine acceptance. Embrace boundaries to foster healthy connections that bring joy, support, and growth to our life.

Boundaries are a path to personal freedom. Setting boundaries is an act of liberation that allows us to embrace our authenticity. It frees us from others' expectations and demands, empowering us to live according to our values and desires. Boundaries provide the space for us to explore our passions, pursue our dreams, and express our true selves. Embracing and maintaining healthy boundaries is a transformative practice that enables us to protect our well-being, nurture meaningful relationships, and embark on a journey of self-discovery and personal growth. By setting and respecting boundaries, we embrace our power, honor our needs and values, and create a life aligned with our true selves.

Boundaries MOVE

Morals set the foundation of boundaries, serving as the bedrock for establishing boundaries in our lives. They provide us with a clear understanding of our values and principles, helping us discern what is acceptable and what crosses our personal limits. By honoring our morals, we establish the foundation for healthy relationships, self-respect, and personal integrity.

Obedience respects boundaries and limits playing a crucial role in setting boundaries. When we respect the boundaries set by others, we demonstrate consideration, empathy, and a willingness to honor their autonomy. By obeying reasonable rules and agreements, we foster trust, harmonious interactions, and cultivate an environment of mutual respect.

Values guide boundaries with authenticity, acting as guiding lights, shaping the boundaries we set for ourselves. By aligning our actions with our core values, we establish boundaries that reflect our authentic selves. Our values enable us to prioritize what truly matters to us, empowering us to say "no" when needed and creating a space where we can thrive in alignment with our deepest convictions.

Ethics provide a framework for setting boundaries that promote fairness, justice, and the greater good. By embracing ethical principles, we establish boundaries that ensure equal treatment, respect for others' rights, and accountability. Ethical boundaries cultivate an environment of trust, inclusivity, and positive impact, fostering healthy relationships and social harmony.

When we set our boundaries based on our morals, obedience, values, and ethics, it safeguards our personal well-being. By clearly defining what is acceptable and what is not, we protect ourselves from emotional, mental, or physical harm. Boundaries help us to create a space where we feel safe, respected, and can nurture our overall health and happiness. When boundaries are rooted in our morals, obedience, values, and ethics, they empower us to express ourselves authentically. Boundaries enable us to communicate our needs, preferences, and limitations, fostering healthy assertiveness and self-advocacy. Creating an environment where our voice is heard, valued, and respected allows us to carve out time for rest, relaxation, and introspection. By setting boundaries, we prioritize self-care practices, recharge our energy, and create opportunities for personal growth and self-discovery.

Boundaries nurtured by morals, obedience, values, and ethics contribute to personal growth and empowerment. They enable us to make intentional choices, take ownership of our lives, and create boundaries that align with our evolving sense of self. By setting and honoring boundaries, we grow in self-awareness, develop resilience, and embrace the power to shape our narratives.

Boundaries Alignment Exercise

This exercise is designed to help you set boundaries that align with your existing morals, obedience, values, and ethics. It encourages self-reflection, introspection, and the intentional creation of boundaries that honor your authentic self. Find a quiet and comfortable space where you can reflect without distractions. Turn to page 114 in your workbook or write it in your notebook.

In this exercise, I want you to remember what your morals and values are; setting your boundaries is dependent on them. Have them readily available, if necessary, to complete this exercise. I will walk you through this exercise as we go through it.

1. Choose the moral and value you will be using to set your boundary.

   o Moral: Honesty

   o Value: I will live with integrity in both my personal and professional environment

2. Identify Areas Requiring Boundaries: Reflect on different aspects of your life—relationships, work, personal time, commitments, etc. Identify areas where you feel your existing boundaries may be blurred or need strengthening. Be specific about the situations or interactions that call for clearer boundaries.

   o Area: Marriage/Relationship

3. Set Clear Boundaries: Based on your morals, values, and ethics, establish clear boundaries for the identified areas. Determine what behaviors, actions, or situations are within your boundaries and what falls outside of them. Be firm in defining what you will and will not tolerate in these areas.

   o Will tolerate: Open communication, full transparency, hurtful truth, undivided attention to listening

   o Will not tolerate: Lying, half-truths, brutal verbal attacks, being interrupted while speaking

4. Communicate Boundaries: Consider how you will communicate your boundaries to others. Reflect on assertive and respectful ways to express your limits and expectations. Practice assertive communication techniques that enable you to effectively communicate your boundaries to others.

   o Method of Communication: Verbal with examples of boundaries

5. Practice Self-Observation: Begin implementing your boundaries in real-life situations. Observe your reactions, emotions, and thoughts as you navigate these situations. Reflect on any challenges or resistance you encounter and remind yourself of the importance of honoring your boundaries.

   o By implementing these boundaries, communication in our relationship has improved. I am happier and no longer wonder if there are secrets in our relationship.

   o The greatest challenge for me was being judged by what I say or having it taken the wrong way. My resistance came in speaking without being interrupted or my spouse immediately going on the defensive, causing anger or resentment towards one another.

6. Adjust and Reinforce Boundaries: Regularly assess your boundaries and make adjustments as needed. Reflect on their effectiveness and whether they align with your morals, values,

and ethics. Reinforce your boundaries by consistently practicing self-compassion and self-advocacy.

- o Adjustment: Speak in love, remind spouse when boundaries are crossed in a kind manner.

If you face challenges in setting or maintaining boundaries, seek support from trusted friends, family, or professionals. Share your experiences, seek guidance, and learn from others who have navigated similar situations. Regularly reflect on your progress in living with aligned boundaries. Celebrate each step forward, acknowledging the positive impact that honoring your boundaries has on your well-being and relationships.

This exercise may take some time to complete as you need to have boundaries for each moral and value that you have in your life. By engaging in this exercise, you cultivate a deep sense of self-awareness and empower yourself to establish boundaries that are aligned with your morals, obedience, values, and ethics. Remember, setting boundaries is an ongoing process, and it requires practice and self-compassion. Embrace this journey of self-discovery and growth and honor the authentic expression of who you are through the boundaries you set.

Got them all done? Outstanding! You now know exactly where your starting point is on this personal growth journey. Before you move on, I want you to reflect on everything that you have learned about your starting point and who you are right now. Knowing where you are is the most important part of any journey. If you don't know where you are, how will you know in which direction you need to go? Let me answer that—you can't know; you merely start guessing which way to go, which only gets you more lost and confused. But because you have identified where you are, 60% of your trip planning is already complete. Before we can determine which direction to go in, we need to know where we are going, and we can only determine that by envisioning where we want to be. This is what Part III will teach us to do!

Part III
Determining your Destination

YOUR DESTINATION

The GPS requires two important factors before it can direct you where to go: knowing your starting point (where you are) and knowing your destination (where you want to go). These two factors are crucial for the GPS to provide adequate directions to reach your destination. Similarly, the Life Progression System (LPS) works the same way—it needs a starting point (who you are) and a destination (who you want to become). In the previous section, we discussed your starting point, and now you should know where you are or who you are. In this section, we will determine where you want to go and who you want to become.

Determining your destination is easier than most people imagine. In fact, we try to do it every day by dreaming of living a life better than the one we have. These are not just dreams; they are possible destinations we want to travel to, representing untapped potential we can achieve. However, we often fail to figure out how to get there. In this section, we will determine our destination by envisioning the life we want to live—not just dreaming, but deciding to change our destination in life and the direction we go. The LPS needs to know where you want to go to give you directions on how to get there. Your destination is just as important as your starting point.

Determining your destination in life is a transformative journey of self-discovery and personal growth. It requires introspection, reflection, and a deep understanding of your passions, values, and aspirations. When you define your destination, you gain clarity on the path you want to pursue, empowering you to live a purpose-driven life aligned with your authentic self. The power of determining your destination lies in living a life of intention and focus. By knowing where you want to go, you can make deliberate choices and take purposeful actions that steer you in the right direction. Rather than drifting aimlessly through life, you become the captain of your own ship, charting a course towards a destination that excites and fulfills you.

Determining your destination sparks a sense of excitement and motivation. When you have a clear vision of where you want to be, you awaken a powerful drive within yourself. This drive fuels your enthusiasm and determination, propelling you forward, even in the face of challenges or setbacks. Your destination becomes a beacon of inspiration, igniting a fire within you to persevere and achieve great things.

Setting a destination in life allows you to align your actions with your values and passions. When you know what truly matters to you, you can make decisions that align with your authentic self. By pursuing a path that resonates with your core beliefs and desires, you create a life of authenticity and integrity, experiencing a deep sense of fulfillment and purpose. It empowers you to overcome obstacles and navigate uncertainties. When challenges arise or roadblocks appear, having a clear destination provides you with the resilience and determination needed to overcome adversity. Your destination acts as a guiding light, helping you persevere, learn from setbacks, and adapt to changing circumstances while staying focused on the bigger picture.

The power of determining your destination lies in its ability to unlock your potential and push you beyond your comfort zone. By setting a destination that stretches your capabilities and encourages growth, you tap into your hidden talents and unleash your full potential. As you strive towards your chosen destination, you discover strengths you never knew you had and achieve remarkable feats. Creating a sense of purpose and meaning, it gives you a reason to wake up each morning with enthusiasm and excitement. When you have a destination to work towards, every action you take becomes infused with purpose, contributing to the bigger picture of your life's journey. Your sense of purpose fuels your drive, propelling you forward with passion and determination.

Having a clear destination allows you to make the most of your time and resources. You can prioritize your efforts, focus on what truly matters, and avoid distractions that derail you from your path. Time becomes a precious resource that you allocate intentionally, ensuring that each moment contributes to your journey towards your desired destination. It fosters self-confidence and belief in your abilities. When you set a destination, you declare to yourself and the world that you can achieve great things. Your belief in your potential strengthens as you progress towards your destination, overcoming challenges and experiencing small victories along the way. With each milestone reached, your self-confidence grows, fueling your determination to keep pushing forward.

The power of determining your destination lies in its ability to create a life of fulfillment and happiness. When you have a clear vision of where you want to be, you can design a life that aligns with your passions, values, and purpose. By pursuing your chosen destination, you create a life that brings you joy, fulfillment, and a profound sense of accomplishment. You become the architect of your own destiny, forging a path that is uniquely yours and living a life that truly matters.

Determining your destination starts with your vision—knowing where you want to go, what you want in life, and most importantly, who you want to become. Then, set goals that align with your passion and values. Understand that goal setting and achievement is the difference between success and a dream.

ENVISIONING YOUR IDEAL FUTURE

Envisioning your ideal future is a powerful exercise that allows you to tap into your imagination, explore your deepest desires, and create a roadmap for your life. By painting a vivid picture of your ideal future, you unlock your potential and set the stage for a life of purpose, fulfillment, and limitless possibilities. In this chapter, we will delve into the transformative power of envisioning your ideal future and discover practical strategies to bring your vision to life.

Your ideal future begins with giving yourself permission to dream big. Allow your imagination to soar and visualize the life you truly desire. Imagine every aspect: your career, relationships, health, personal growth, and contributions to the world. Visualizing your ideal future provides clarity and direction, serving as a compass that guides your choices and decisions. As you paint a detailed picture of your desired future, you gain clarity on your values, aspirations, and priorities. This clarity empowers you to make choices that align with your vision and move you closer to the life you want to create.

Envisioning your ideal future fuels motivation and drive. When you have a clear vision of what you want to achieve, you tap into a wellspring of intrinsic motivation. Your vision becomes a source of inspiration, propelling you forward even in the face of challenges. It ignites a burning desire within you and fuels your determination to take action and make your vision a reality. Your ideal future lies in its ability to overcome limiting beliefs. When you vividly imagine the life you desire, you challenge the beliefs that hold you back. You expand your sense of what's possible and shatter the boundaries of self-imposed limitations. By envisioning a future beyond your current circumstances, you create space for growth, transformation, and breakthroughs. Let go of limitations and believe in the possibility of creating a future that excites and inspires you.

Envisioning your ideal future cultivates a positive mindset. It allows you to focus on possibilities rather than limitations, on solutions rather than problems. When you envision a future filled with success, abundance, and joy, you program your mind to seek out opportunities and attract positive outcomes. Your mindset becomes a magnet for the experiences and circumstances that align with your vision. Knowing what your ideal future looks like helps you set meaningful goals. When you have a clear vision, you can break it down into actionable steps and set goals that align with your desired outcomes. Your vision becomes the driving force behind your goals, providing the motivation and direction to pursue them with passion and commitment. Each goal you achieve becomes a steppingstone towards your ideal future.

The process of envisioning your ideal future fosters self-discovery and personal growth. As you explore your desires, values, and passions, you gain a deeper understanding of who you are and what truly matters to you. This self-awareness empowers you to make choices that align with your authentic self and lead to a life of fulfillment and authenticity. It encourages you to take proactive steps towards creating the life you desire. It propels you out of a passive mindset and into a proactive mindset, where you actively seek opportunities and take deliberate action to bring your vision to life. Your vision becomes a source of inspiration and a catalyst for positive change. When you encounter challenges along the way, your vision acts as a beacon of hope and resilience. It reminds you of the bigger picture and motivates you to persevere, adapt, and learn from setbacks. Your vision becomes the anchor that keeps you grounded amidst the storms of life.

The process of envisioning your ideal future is an ongoing journey of self-discovery and growth. As you move forward, remember that your vision may evolve and change over time, and that is okay. Embrace the process with curiosity and an open mind, and allow your vision to guide you towards a future that reflects your truest desires. Envision the life you want to create, take courageous steps towards it, and watch as your ideal future unfolds before your eyes.

Right now, relax and clear your mind of all the stress and worries in your life. Do not think of life as it is right now, but how you would like it to be. Before we start, if you have the workbook, turn to page 118; if not, grab your notebook or a paper and pen. We are about to embark on a journey in our minds, and it is important to keep a record of everywhere we are going. We will begin our journey with the most important destination: ourselves. Let us look at who we want to become. This new you should align with your morals, values, and ethics, and not take you beyond your personal boundaries. When I first took this journey, it was an awakening moment that allowed me to see all the things that I was missing in who I was as a man.

This journey contains many stops along the way. There are several places we must go to attain our future life, and as much as we want to envision a life with material things, like a new home, new exotic and luxury cars, new designer wear, and even our bank accounts filled with millions of dollars. These are not the first steps we need to take; they are actually part of the end of our journey. It's like I have told thousands of people who come to me telling me about their dreams of being rich and successful. I tell them it doesn't matter how rich or successful you are; if you don't have the right mindset, you will ultimately end up right back where you are today. There are millions of people right now praying to God for a new home, a new car, or a lump sum of money to make their lives better. But the problem they have is that they never prepare themselves for what they are asking for. Praying for something or setting goals for things that you want but are not ready for or capable of managing is like a five-year-old asking his father for a book of matches or a lighter. What responsible father would give his son a book of matches or a lighter? None that I know of! It would be foolish and irresponsible for any man to do that. Well, asking God or dreaming of having a billion dollars to just fall in your lap is the most foolish thing that you can do. I say this because many of us are not even responsible enough to manage the finances that we currently have, so why would you think you could manage more? This is why our first stop is all about preparing ourselves for the new life we envision for ourselves.

This may sound selfish, but it actually is not, because when we start by fixing ourselves, we are not just doing it for ourselves but for all those we love and those we will encounter later in life. What appears to be an act of selfishness is actually a selfless act. I say this because what we are doing is sacrificing ourselves for the greater good of humanity. When we are new and improved, we have the ability to empower others; when we are better, we make the world better. When we are whole and complete, we equip ourselves to inspire others. Understanding these key facts is what should drive us to achieve our personal growth, which is why our journey must begin with ourselves.

How We View Ourselves

How we view ourselves is the foundation of our self-esteem, confidence, and personal growth. It shapes our beliefs, attitudes, and actions. By cultivating a positive and empowering self-perception, we can unlock our full potential and create a life filled with joy, purpose, and fulfillment. Our self-view sets the boundaries of what we believe is possible. When we view ourselves as capable, resilient, and deserving of success, we open doors to new opportunities and embrace challenges as steppingstones to growth. By nurturing a mindset of self-belief, we break free from self-imposed limitations and unlock our true potential.

Self-awareness is crucial to how we view ourselves. When we cultivate a deep understanding of our values, strengths, and areas for improvement, we can align our actions with our true selves. By embracing self-reflection and seeking personal growth, we become more authentic, leading to greater fulfillment and a stronger sense of identity. Self-compassion is key to how we view ourselves. When we extend kindness and understanding to ourselves, we create a nurturing and supportive inner dialogue. By embracing our flaws, celebrating our strengths, and treating ourselves with love and compassion, we build a foundation of self-acceptance and foster a positive self-image.

How we view ourselves influences our relationships. When we hold a positive self-image, we attract healthier connections and establish boundaries that reflect our self-worth. By valuing ourselves and surrounding ourselves with uplifting and supportive individuals, we create a positive social circle that fosters growth and mutual respect. Our self-view affects our ability to overcome obstacles. When we view ourselves as resilient and capable of overcoming challenges, we develop a mindset of perseverance and resilience. By reframing setbacks as opportunities for growth, we learn from our experiences and bounce back stronger, ready to face new challenges with confidence.

The way we view ourselves influences our level of self-confidence. When we believe in our abilities and trust ourselves, we radiate confidence and attract opportunities. By acknowledging our achievements, focusing on our strengths, and embracing growth, we build a strong foundation of self-assurance that propels us towards success. Our self-view impacts our mental and emotional well-being. When we view ourselves with love, acceptance, and kindness, we cultivate a positive sense of self-worth and inner peace. By prioritizing self-care, practicing self-compassion, and embracing our unique qualities, we nurture a healthy self-esteem that supports our overall well-being.

How we view ourselves is a choice. We have the power to shape our self-perception through self-reflection, self-love, and intentional mindset shifts. By embracing a positive self-view, we step into our true potential, embody our worth, and create a life filled with confidence, purpose, and limitless possibilities. The lens through which we view ourselves shapes our self-talk. By cultivating positive self-talk, we reframe negative thoughts into empowering affirmations. By replacing self-doubt with self-belief and criticism with self-compassion, we create a positive internal dialogue that uplifts and motivates us towards achieving our goals.

Overall, how we see ourselves involves looking at the four major aspects of who we are:

1. Our psychological self

2. Our physical self

3. Our personal self

4. Our professional self

These four foundational parts allow us to see who we truly are and envision who we want to become. There is also a fifth element that some of us see ourselves through and often use to measure our riches and success: our Possessional self. While this self neither truly defines our riches nor success, it can build self-confidence and self-esteem through the items and things we possess. In the upcoming sections, we will envision each of these selves to fully attain our personal growth destination. Are you ready? Well, ready or not, it is time to take a cold, hard look at yourself.

ENVISIONING MY PSYCHOLOGICAL SELF

Creating a Better Me

Becoming a better person is a lifelong journey of self-improvement and personal growth. It starts with a commitment to continuous self-reflection, learning, and growth. By striving to be the best version of yourself, you can positively impact every aspect of your life and the lives of those around you. The first thing I want you to do is commit to becoming the best you the world will ever experience. Write a letter committing to becoming a better person to yourself.

What does a better you look like? How does a better you feel? How does a better you act? These are some of the questions we need to ask ourselves to become who we desire to be. While I cannot walk with you on this journey of creating a better you, I can guide you along the way. No one knows you better than you except God Himself! No one knows what you want in life better than yourself. I know who I want to be, do you? Taking the time to know who you want to become is one of the most aggravating, painful, and cumbersome experiences we can have in life, but it is also the most exhilarating, peaceful, and graceful experience. How is this possible? Well, the best way for me to describe it is to say it is the pleasure of pain. If you have ever worked out or been part of a sports team at any point in your life, you know exactly what I am talking about. To perform at our peak, we must rigorously practice, pushing ourselves beyond the limit of comfort to a place of pain. But the results of the pain are more beneficial to us than the pain itself. For us to create a better self, we must go through the pain of the reality that we have faults, need work, are lacking, are awful, and, in other words, need to improve. Some of you may think you are already where you need to be, and if you are happy with it, so am I. But remember, this you that you are happy with is the same you that has brought you where you are now. For those of you who know you can grow and become better than who you are now, let us begin the journey.

In this first step of envisioning our future inner self, answer the questions in your workbook on page 118 or ask yourself the following questions to help you gain clarity and direction:

1. How do I want to feel on a daily basis? What emotions and states of mind do I want to cultivate within myself?

2. What are my core values, and how do I want to embody them in my actions and interactions with others?

3. How do I envision my level of self-confidence and self-assurance? What steps can I take to cultivate a powerful sense of self-belief?

4. What habits and thought patterns do I want to let go of to create a more positive and empowering mindset?

As you answer these questions, remember that envisioning your future inner self is a dynamic and evolving process. Be open to exploring new insights and be compassionate with yourself as you navigate the journey of self-discovery and personal growth. Don't stop with these questions; ask yourself whatever you can think of that will help you become the you that you want to be. Use your responses as a guide to set meaningful intentions and take purposeful steps towards becoming the person you aspire to be.

Now you should have a blurred image of the future emotional and mental you, or as I call it, the Psychological you. Notice I said a blurred image, so what we need to do is bring it into focus. We will do this by focusing our internal lens to have a vivid image of our psychological selves. We will utilize what I call the self-assessment form. You can find this form on page 118 of your workbook, or you can create it in your notebook using the example that I will show you in a moment. First, understand what the psychological you consist of, which includes the inner you:

1. Your fears

2. Your strengths and weaknesses from self-assessments

3. Your feedback from others.

4. Your strengths and weaknesses from The Big Five Personality Test

5. Your strengths and weaknesses from Myers-Briggs Type Indicator

6. Your strengths and weaknesses from Enneagram Test

7. Your strengths and weaknesses from The DISC Assessment

8. Along with your MOVE

In this exercise, we will compile them all to create a psychological profile of the new you. This will mainly consist of transferring existing data from several areas to one central location. This may seem redundant, but there is a method to what you see as madness. As a minister and coach, I have learned that people subconsciously learn by repeatedly writing things down. The more you write it, the more it takes root in your subconscious. This will help you when you begin to travel on this journey of personal growth. Also, doing this exercise will make setting your goals much easier and more productive. You may need to take a break before we finish your psychological self, and that is understandable. Feel free to take a break at any time during this exercise.

Let us get started. The first thing I want you to do is turn to page 7 of your workbook or the notes from page 32 of the book in your notebook. You will find the data we need to transfer. In this exercise, we took our fears and created ways to overcome them in the second column entitled "how to overcome them." What you have listed in the second column are the items we want to transfer to our psychological assessment form. Got it? Okay, let's write them on our psychological assessment form on page 121 of our workbook or in our notebook. Here is an example of the psychological assessment:

Psychological Assessment Form

Traits	Already have	Need to work on
1. Embrace failure as an opportunity for growth and learning.		X
2. Challenge negative self-talk and replace it with positive affirmations.		X
3. Focus on the process rather than solely on the end result.		X

Now repeat this process for each of your fears until you have completed them all. Finished? Good, make sure you have completed them all before you move on; otherwise, you will waste a lot of time in the latter chapters.

As we continue on our journey, we will be working on our strengths and weaknesses. This will take considerable time because our strengths and weaknesses are found in several places. They are in the self-assessment, The Big Five assessment, the Myers-Briggs Type Indicator (MBTI), the Enneagram Test, and the DISC Assessment. We will start with our weaknesses identified on page 23 of your workbook or use your notes from pages 42 of the book. We will extract the information from column two entitled "how to strengthen or correct." Using the same psychological assessment form, list each "how to strengthen or correct" item that you identified under the last fear. Weaknesses, like fears, will have the "need to work on" box checked. See the example below:

Traits	Already have	Need to work on
3. Focus on the process rather than solely on the end result.		X
4. Practice being 15-minutes early for occasions.		X
5. Schedule all occurrences to allow for travel time and incidents.		X
6. Get the advice of people who have mastered time management.		X
7. Learn to schedule everything.		X
8. Use 15-minute intervals for time management instead of 30 minutes or hourly.		X
9. Learn to prioritize.		X
10. Create a to-do list.		X
11. Give start time and deadlines for what must be done.		X

Hopefully, you have completed all of your weaknesses from the exercise. Next, we will go to the strengths which we categorized on page 37 of your workbook or from your notes on page 44 of the book in your notebook. In column four entitled "how can I use this in my personal growth," you will find the data that you need. Unlike weaknesses and fears, our strengths will require you to check the "already have" box. Using the same psychological assessment form, list each strength that you categorized under the last weakness. See the example below:

Traits	Already have	Need to work on
11. Give start time and deadlines for what must be done.	X	
12. Create win/win outcome in any deal.	X	
13. Develop relationship by gaining clarity and understanding others' point.	X	
14. Realize that there is always more than one way of doing things.	X	

Traits	Already have	Need to work on
15. Take the time to care for others.	X	
16. Don't wait for others when I can do it myself.	X	
17. Always show kindness and gratitude.	X	

Now that we have completed all of our strengths, we finished in the self-assessment section of the book. Our next stop will be in Incorporating Feedback into Personal and Professional Development exercise, where we listed the feedback that we received from others. You will find this in your workbook on page 46 or from your notes on page 50 in your notebook. Are you there yet? Okay, we will be using column two entitled "how can we use it or improve it" and extract the information from there. Negative feedback consists of things we need to work on, and positive feedback are things we already have, remember to check the appropriate box. Using the same psychological assessment form, list each feedback item that you categorized under the last strength. See the example below:

Traits	Already have	Need to work on
17. Always show kindness and gratitude.	X	
18. Embrace the mindset that fashionably late is still late.		X
19. Provide information or documentation ahead of the time promised.		X
20. Use creative thinking to design new methods of doing things.	X	
21. Always be willing to help when there is a need.	X	

Finished? Great, our next stop will be The Big Five Personality Test under Strengths and Weaknesses Analysis. You will find this in your workbook on page 57 or from your notes on page 61 in your notebook. Got it? Okay, we will begin with the strengths, using column two entitled "how can I use this in my personal growth" and extract the information from there. Remember, strengths are things we already have. Start on the psychological assessment form where you left off. See the example below:

Traits	Already have	Need to work on
21. Always be willing to help when there is a need.	X	

Traits	Already have	Need to work on
22. Seek opportunities to think outside the box and generate innovative ideas.	X	
23. Mentor or coach individuals who can benefit from my expertise and guidance.	X	
24. Develop strong listening skills to understand and connect with others on a deeper level.	X	
25. Use setbacks and failures as opportunities for growth and learning.	X	
26. Embrace change and uncertainty by seeking new experiences and stepping out of your comfort zone.	X	

Now that you are done with the strengths, it's time to move on to the weaknesses. You will find this in your workbook on page 61 or your notebook right after the strengths. Use column two entitled "how can I improve this in my personal growth" and extract the information from there. Remember, weaknesses are things we need to work on. Start on the psychological assessment form where you left off. See the example below:

Traits	Already have	Need to work on
26. Embrace change and uncertainty by seeking new experiences and stepping out of your comfort zone.	X	
27. Learn to look at things from at least three different points of view.		X
28. Learn to make decisions faster and delegate things to others.		X
29. Get in the habit of listening twice as much as you speak; don't interrupt those who are speaking.		X
30. When you fail at something, don't quit; figure out another way.		X
31. Always be open to change and new adventures.		X

All done? Awesome! What we just did with the Big Five Personality Test, we will repeat for the Myers-Briggs Type Indicator, The Enneagram Test, and The DISC Assessment. We will use the Strengths and Weaknesses Analysis of each, beginning with the strengths and extracting the information from column two entitled "how can I use this in my personal growth." Then move on to the weaknesses, extracting the information from column two entitled "how can I improve this in my personal growth." Remember, strengths are things we already have, and weaknesses are things we need to work on. For those of you with workbooks, if you are running out of room, feel free to make copies of the Assessment form on page 497 of your workbook at any time. Also, be cautious of duplicate strengths and weaknesses since these tests give similar results.

Our next stop will be Myers-Briggs Type Indicator. You will find this in your workbook on pages 69 and 73 or in your notes on page 68 in your notebook. Remember, the weaknesses will be directly following the strengths in your workbook or notebook. Found it? Let's Go!

Traits	Already have	Need to work on
31. Always be open to change and new adventures.		X
32. Seek opportunities to lead projects or teams, and focus on developing your skills in delegation, motivation, and strategic thinking.	X	
33. Embrace your confidence and decisiveness to take action and make decisions.	X	
34. Tap into your resilience and determination to overcome obstacles and persevere in the face of challenges.	X	
35. View setbacks as opportunities for growth and remain focused on your long-term goals.	X	
36. Harness your charisma and leadership presence to inspire and motivate others around you.	X	
37. Utilize your strong communication skills to articulate your ideas clearly and persuasively.	X	
38. Practice mindfulness techniques, such as deep breathing or stepping back to assess the situation objectively before responding or making decisions.		X
39. Be open to different perspectives and actively seek out diverse viewpoints.		X
40. Learn to deliver feedback and engage in discussions with diplomacy and tact.		X
41. Make a conscious effort to understand and validate others' emotions and perspectives.		X
42. Recognize the value of collaboration and shared decision-making.		X

Our next stop will be The Enneagram Test. You will find this in your workbook on pages 81 and 84 or in your notes on page 74 in your notebook. Remember, the weaknesses will be directly following the strengths in your workbook or notebook. Found it? Let's do this!

Traits	Already have	Need to work on
42. Recognize the value of collaboration and shared decision-making.		X
43. Recognize that setbacks and failures are opportunities for growth and learning.	X	
44. Embrace your true self and share your genuine experiences with others.	X	
45. Embrace healthy competition by setting personal benchmarks and challenging yourself to surpass your own achievements.	X	
46. Shift your focus from seeking external validation to cultivating intrinsic motivation.	X	
47. Practice being present with your own emotions and those of others.	X	
48. Recognize that it's okay to show vulnerability and share your struggles with others.		X
49. Challenge the tendency to set unrealistically high expectations for yourself.		X
50. Recognize that taking care of yourself physically, emotionally, and mentally is essential for overall well-being.		X
51. Focus on building genuine and authentic relationships with others rather than transactional or image-based connections.		X
52. Embrace the idea that mistakes and failures are part of the learning process and a natural part of being human.		X

Our next stop will be The DISC Assessment. You will find this in your workbook on pages 92 and 96 or from your notes on page 80 in your notebook. Remember, the weaknesses will be directly following the strengths in your workbook or notebook. Made it? Let's hit it!

Traits	Already have	Need to work on
52. Embrace the idea that mistakes and failures are part of the learning process and a natural part of being human.		X
53. Recognize that setbacks and failures are opportunities for growth and learning.	X	

Traits	Already have	Need to work on
54. Embrace your true self and share your genuine experiences with others.	X	
55. Embrace healthy competition by setting personal benchmarks and challenging yourself to surpass your own achievements.	X	
56. Shift your focus from seeking external validation to cultivating intrinsic motivation.	X	
57. Practice being present with your own emotions and those of others.	X	
58. Focus on building collaborative relationships rather than exerting control.		X
59. Cultivate self-awareness and consider the impact of your communication on others.		X
60. Slow down and take time to evaluate options and potential consequences before making decisions.		X
61. Develop a balanced approach by assessing risks more thoroughly and considering potential drawbacks.		X
62. Surround yourself with individuals who excel in attention to detail and collaborate with them to ensure accuracy.		X

WOW! We made it through all of our strengths and weaknesses. Now it is time to move on to our MOVE. We will start by realizing your morals on page 106 of your workbook or your notes from page 86 of the book. We will be working on the chart from question #9. We will extract information from column two entitled "how to use them daily." Put the information in your psychological assessment form following the last weakness from your DISC Assessment. Your morals can go either way; they can be something you already have or something you feel you need to work on. Okay, have at it!

Traits	Already have	Need to work on
62. Surround yourself with individuals who excel in attention to detail and collaborate with them to ensure accuracy.		X
63. Speak the truth in all things.	X	
64. Give respect to others at all times.	X	
65. Take responsibility for my actions and inactions, regardless of the ramifications.	X	

Traits	Already have	Need to work on
66. If you have a problem with someone, do not let the sun go down until you have forgiven them.		X
67. Be grateful for my family, each day that God blesses me with, and all that I have.	X	

All done? Great, let's move on to our values, which are found on page 108 of your workbook or in your notes from page 90 of the book. We will extract information from column two entitled "values" onto our psychological assessment form following the last moral. Values, like morals, can either be something we already have or something we need to work on. In the case of values, we have already separated the two. This set of values are values that we already have.

Traits	Already have	Need to work on
67. Be grateful for my family, each day that God blesses me with, and all that I have.	X	
68. I will live with integrity in both my personal and professional environment.	X	
69. I will treat those who I encounter with dignity and honor.	X	
70. I will hold myself accountable for my actions and assignments.	X	
71. I will give grace to others just as God has given it to me.		X
72. I will always show and give appreciation for what I have and for what others do for me.	X	

Once you have completed these values, our final stop will be values that we desire to have, which can be found on page 109 of your workbook or your notes from page 91 of the book. We will extract information from column two entitled "desired value." Put the information in your psychological assessment form following the last value. These desired values are always something we need to work on.

Traits	Already have	Need to work on
72. I will always show and give appreciation for what I have and for what others do for me.	X	
73. I will be resilient in all situations, maintaining a calm manner.		X
74. I will persist until I have achieved success.		X
75. I will recognize the significance of nurturing all aspects of my life, including physical, emotional, mental, and spiritual dimensions.		X
76. I will continue to educate myself on things I do not understand.		X
77. I will rely on others that are better at the things I need done.		X

By completing this section, you know almost all there is to know about your psychological self and what it needs to allow your mind to operate at maximum performance. Allowing your mind to operate this way also causes your spirit to be accelerated, enhancing your total being to perform at its peak. Soon we will refer back to the information that you have generated to set goals and action steps. Some of the information generated will also be used to assist in managing our time. Before we close our psychological self, there is one more area of your psychological being that needs to be addressed.

The Spiritual You

The importance of the spiritual aspect of a person cannot be overstated when it comes to personal growth and development. Nurturing your spiritual self can provide a profound sense of purpose, inner peace, and resilience in the face of life's challenges. It is essential for achieving a sense of purpose and overall well-being. Spirituality involves connecting with something larger than oneself, whether it be a higher power, the universe, or one's inner self. A strong spiritual foundation brings inner peace. Psalm 46:10 reminds us, "Be still, and know that I am God." It encourages self-reflection and understanding. Proverbs 20:27 teaches, "The spirit of a man is the lamp of the Lord, searching all his innermost parts." Connecting with a higher power provides comfort and assurance during turbulent times. Embracing spirituality allows us to seek guidance and wisdom beyond our understanding. Seeking spiritual guidance provides direction in decision-making. Proverbs 3:5-6 advises, "Trust in the Lord with all your heart, and do not lean on your own understanding. In all your ways acknowledge Him, and He will make straight your paths." Trusting God in your personal growth journey will cause you not to be led astray.

Spiritual beliefs provide a deeper sense of meaning and purpose in life. Jeremiah 29:11 states, "For I know the plans I have for you, declares the Lord, plans for welfare and not for evil, to give you a future and a hope." Embracing your spirituality helps you discover your life's purpose. By being spiritually connected to God, the plan that He has for us begins to manifest and align with our personal growth. The spiritual self is grounded in values and morals that guide ethical decision-making. Colossians 3:17 emphasizes, "And whatever you do, in word or deed, do everything in the name of the Lord Jesus, giving thanks to God the Father through him."

Spirituality fosters resilience, helping us cope with challenges and adversity. Isaiah 41:10 reassures, "Fear not, for I am with you; be not dismayed, for I am your God; I will strengthen you, I will help you, I will uphold you with my righteous right hand." In challenging times, our spiritual strength provides resilience. Psalm 55:22 reminds us to "cast your burden on the Lord, and he will sustain you." Spiritual growth helps overcome fear with faith. Psalm 27:1 affirms, "The Lord is my light and my salvation; whom shall I fear?" The spiritual journey fosters self-awareness and personal growth, leading to positive transformations. Romans 12:2 encourages, "Do not be conformed to this world, but be transformed by the renewal of your mind." Engaging in spiritual practices promotes emotional well-being and reduces stress. Philippians 4:6-7 reminds us, "Do not be anxious about anything, but in everything by prayer and supplication with thanksgiving let your requests be made known to God. And the peace of God, which surpasses all understanding, will guard your hearts and your minds in Christ Jesus."

Spirituality fosters a sense of interconnectedness and compassion towards others. Galatians 6:2 encourages, "Bear one another's burdens, and so fulfill the law of Christ." Nurturing your spiritual self will foster compassion and empathy towards others, leading to stronger relationships and acts of kindness. Colossians 3:12-14 not only tells us what to equip ourselves with and what actions to take but also how to reach perfection. It states: "Therefore, as the elect of God, holy and beloved, put on tender mercies, kindness, humility, meekness, longsuffering; bearing with one another, and forgiving one another, if anyone has a complaint against another; even as Christ forgave, so you also must do. But above all these things, put on love, which is the bond of perfection."

Practicing gratitude as part of spirituality leads to increased contentment and appreciation for life's blessings. 1 Thessalonians 5:18 urges, "Give thanks in all circumstances; for this is the will of God in Christ Jesus for you." Embracing your spiritual self helps cultivate gratitude and contentment, as stated in 1 Thessalonians 5:18, "Give thanks in all circumstances." Spirituality encourages forgiveness, both towards oneself and others, promoting emotional healing. Ephesians 4:32 advises, "Be kind to one another, tenderhearted, forgiving one another, as God in Christ forgave you." Spirituality encourages forgiveness and letting go of grudges, as exemplified by Jesus' teaching in Matthew 6:14-15.

Finally, embracing the spiritual self provides a profound connection with the Divine, leading to a sense of peace and unity with the universe. Integrating spirituality into your life fosters holistic growth, encompassing emotional, mental, and physical well-being. In 3 John 1:2, we are reminded, "Beloved, I pray that all may go well with you and that you may be in good health, as it goes well with your soul."

In conclusion, nurturing the spiritual you is an essential aspect of personal growth. Embracing your spirituality leads to a deeper understanding of self, purpose, and interconnectedness with others. It provides strength, resilience, and guidance, contributing to a more balanced and fulfilling life journey. Incorporating spirituality into personal growth allows individuals to lead more fulfilling lives, anchored in their values, guided by faith, and embracing the journey towards self-discovery and enlightenment.

Spiritual Reflection Questions

Asking yourself meaningful questions about your spiritual self and personal growth can lead to greater self-awareness and a deeper understanding of your beliefs, values, and purpose. These questions and others are on page 126 of your workbook. Here are some questions to consider:

1. What does spirituality mean to me?

2. Do I feel a connection to something greater than myself?

3. How do I nurture my spiritual well-being on a daily basis?

4. Do I feel a sense of purpose in life, and if so, what is it?

5. What role does gratitude play in my life, and how do I express it?

6. How do I handle challenges and setbacks from a spiritual perspective?

7. Am I able to forgive myself and others, and how does forgiveness impact my personal growth?

8. What spiritual practices or rituals do I engage in, and how do they contribute to my well-being?

9. Do I find meaning and fulfillment in my daily activities and interactions?

10. What brings me a sense of inner peace and contentment?

These questions are meant to encourage introspection and self-discovery. Take time to reflect on them and be open to exploring your spiritual self in a way that resonates with your beliefs and values. Embrace the journey of personal growth and remember that spiritual development is an ongoing and enriching process.

Spiritual Growth

I would be ever so concerned if I did not discuss ways to grow your spiritual self during your personal growth. Understand that personal growth involves the entire you, meaning mind, body, and soul. To leave out how to grow spiritually would be a catastrophe, because without being spiritually aligned with our personal growth, we will continue to wander in the wilderness just like the children of Israel. Enhancing your spiritual self is a powerful and transformative journey that can deeply enrich your personal growth. Let me briefly explain some things that we can do to grow spiritually.

Start by embracing moments of solitude and reflection to explore the depths of your being. Connecting with our inner self through practices like meditation, prayer, or mindfulness is pivotal in our spiritual growth. Understand that this is the means by which we communicate with our spirits and with God. Prayer is us talking, and meditation is us listening. Many of us tend to talk to God (pray), but we never stay long enough to hear what He has to say (meditation). How rude is that? You want Him to listen to you, but you don't want to hear what He has to say? As we delve into the core of our being, we'll uncover profound insights that lead to a stronger spiritual foundation.

Feed your spiritual growth by immersing yourself in spiritual literature, sacred texts, and teachings. Embrace the wisdom of spiritual leaders and scholars to gain new perspectives and deepen your understanding of life's mysteries. Practice gratitude daily, acknowledging the abundance in your life to show God that you are thankful. Nurture compassion and kindness towards yourself and others to extend the grace of God to yourself and others. By fostering a loving heart, you'll experience a heightened sense of interconnectedness and harmony with the world around you.

Spend time in nature, marveling at its beauty and complexity to gain a better understanding of creation. Cultivate mindfulness, being fully present in each moment. Nature and mindfulness offer gateways to a more profound spiritual awareness and appreciation for the wonders of existence. Engage with like-minded individuals seeking spiritual growth. Join spiritual groups, attend retreats, or participate in communal activities centered around love, unity, and support. Sharing experiences with others can amplify your spiritual journey.

Regularly examine your thoughts, actions, and intentions. Engage in journaling to record your insights and progress. Self-reflection promotes self-awareness, allowing you to align your behaviors with your spiritual values. Release grudges and past grievances to free your heart from negative burdens. Forgiveness liberates the soul, creating space for healing and growth. Embracing forgiveness empowers you to live authentically and fully.

Embrace holistic well-being by nurturing your mind, body, and spirit. Engage in physical activities that promote balance, nourish your body with wholesome foods, and devote time to spiritual practices that uplift your soul. Infuse mindfulness into your daily routines, whether eating, working, or interacting with others. Being mindful heightens your awareness, enabling you to make intentional choices that align with your spiritual journey. Embrace the flow of life and trust in divine timing. Accept that challenges and lessons are essential parts of your spiritual growth. Surrender to the journey, knowing that each step leads you closer to your higher self.

If you desire to grow spiritually, I want you to add your spiritual growth goals to your Psychological Assessment where you left off. It is my prayer that all of my readers have a spiritual relationship, but again that is entirely up to you. But I can tell you that it makes for a smoother personal growth journey. Are you finished with your spiritual goals? Now there is one more aspect that I need to speak on in our spiritual growth and that is tithing.

Tithing According to the Bible, we are to pay a tithe of 10% to the Lord. This tithe consists of three things: your time, your talent, and your treasure. There is a reason why God instructed us to tithe, and it has very little, if anything, to do with money, but it has everything to do with our obedience. When we tithe, God blesses us. He not only protects and stretches the 90%, but He increases it through new insights, concepts, and ideas. While we give thanks and exalt our employer for the paycheck we receive each week, we need to realize that it is God who allowed us to have a paycheck, not your education, not your experience, and not anyone you know. God gave you the job, He allowed your employer to choose you over someone else, He allowed the job to be created, He gave the owner of the company the idea to start the company. Yes, I give all the credit to God, and you should too. Our tithes are equivalent to a farmer planting a seed, from that one seed another hundred will grow; from the hundred, there will be thousands. Are you tithing or tipping? If you are not giving 10% of what you make each week, you are tipping, and it will have no effect on your increase. If you are spending less than 2 hours and 24 minutes a day, that's 16 hours and 48 minutes per week you are tipping. When it comes to your talent, it is sometimes used in your time. For example, if you play the piano or serve in church service, that is both time and talent. It is hard to measure our talent when it comes to tithing, but our time and treasure can easily be measured. How much are you tithing?

On page 128 of your workbook, you will find the Tithing Calculations worksheet or write it in your notebook from the example below, it will tell you if you are tipping or tithing:

Tithing Calculations						
Treasure			**Time**			
Monthly Income	$5,000.00		Task	Hrs.	Min.		Volunteering	Hrs.	Min.
Multiply by .10	X.10		Praying	1	45		Church Set-up	1	30
Amount to Tithe	$500		Praise & Worship	2			Food Pantry		30
			Reading the Bible	7					
			Sunday School	0					
			Bible Class	1					
			Church Service	3					
			Total Time	**16**	**45**		**Total Time**	**2**	**0**

When we cheerfully tithe out of obedience, not out of anticipation of getting more, God blesses us with more. But as I told you, I am not here to sway anyone, but you need to know the truth. When we tithe our time, talent, and treasure, we receive more in abundance. If you want to see the results of not tithing, take the time to read Deuteronomy 27:14-26, but if you want to see the true benefits of tithing, read Deuteronomy 28:7-14. If you are or want to start tithing, make it a goal, add your tithing to your Psychological Assessment Form.

Congratulations! You have completed the psychological assessment forms; it is through this assessment that you will soon know exactly where you want to go psychologically and how to get there. The picture is no longer blurred but is now vivid and crystal clear. In order for us to know who we want to become psychologically and have it ingrained within us, so that we maintain a drive to reach our destination, we need to incorporate another tool into our life progression system. It is what is known as an affirmation. Let me explain what an affirmation is and why we want to have them.

AFFIRMATIONS

Affirmations are powerful tools that can transform our mindset and shape the trajectory of our lives. Just as a GPS provides direction on a road trip, affirmations guide us toward positivity and self-belief, nurturing a resilient and confident outlook. Writing and consistently repeating affirmations plants seeds of self-empowerment in our subconscious mind. By affirming our worth, potential, and abilities, we lay the foundation for a strong and unshakeable self-image.

The importance of writing affirmations lies in their ability to rewire our thought patterns. By consistently affirming positive beliefs, we override negative self-talk and cultivate a mindset of optimism and possibility. Affirmations act as a compass, guiding us toward our goals. As we write affirmations aligned with our dreams, we become more focused and driven, steering our actions in the direction of success. Writing affirmations is an act of self-compassion, reminding us to nurture our inner growth with love and acceptance.

Affirmations are like motivational mantras that keep us uplifted during challenges. When we encounter obstacles, our affirmations act as a source of encouragement, reminding us of our strength and resilience. The importance of writing affirmations lies in their ability to boost our confidence and self-esteem. As we affirm our positive qualities, we begin to embody them, radiating self-assurance in every aspect of our lives. They have a ripple effect on our behavior and choices. When we write and embrace positive statements, we naturally align our actions with the belief that we can achieve greatness.

Writing affirmations helps us cultivate a growth mindset. We shift our focus from limitations to possibilities, allowing us to embrace challenges as opportunities for learning and growth. They are a form of manifestation. By consistently writing and visualizing our desired outcomes, we set the stage for the universe to respond to our positive intentions. Affirmations can create a harmonious connection between our mind, body, and spirit. As we immerse ourselves in positive thoughts and emotions, we tap into the infinite potential within us and open doors to a fulfilling and abundant life.

Incorporate the power of affirmations into your daily routine. Write them, repeat them, and internalize them with unwavering belief. Embrace the transformative force of positive affirmations, for they have the remarkable ability to create a life that reflects the limitless potential that resides within you.

Writing Your Affirmation

Writing your affirmations is not as hard as you may think. You have used the tools correctly, and now it is just a matter of transferring the data from one place to another and reformatting it. The affirmation is nothing more than an "I am" statement that transforms your mindset and attitude to create positive change. In this exercise, we will simply be transferring the information from the psychological assessment form(s) and creating an affirmation. Also, include how you want to feel emotionally and your confidence level if they are not part of your psychological form.

My Psychological Affirmation

I embrace failure as an opportunity for growth and learning. I challenge negative self-talk and replace it with positive affirmations. I focus on the process rather than solely on the end result. I practice being 15 minutes early for occasions, schedule all occurrences to allow for travel time and incidents, take the advice of people who have mastered time management, and learn to schedule everything. I use 15-minute intervals for time management instead of 30 minutes or hourly, prioritize, create a to-do list, and give start times and deadlines for what must be done.

I create win/win outcomes in any deal. I develop relationships by gaining clarity and understanding others' points. I realize that there is always more than one way of doing things. I take the time to care for others and don't wait for others when I can do it myself. I always show kindness and gratitude and embrace the mindset that fashionably late is still late. I provide information or documentation ahead of the time promised, use creative thinking to design new methods of doing things, and am always willing to help when there is a need. I seek opportunities to think outside the box and generate innovative ideas. I mentor or coach individuals who can benefit from my expertise and guidance, develop strong listening skills to understand and connect with others on a deeper level, use setbacks and failures as opportunities for growth and learning, and embrace change and uncertainty by seeking new experiences and stepping out of my comfort zone. I learn to look at things from at least three different points of view, make decisions faster, and delegate tasks to others. I get in the habit of listening twice as much as I speak and don't interrupt those who are speaking. When I fail at something, I don't quit until I figure out another way.

I am always open to change and new adventures. I seek opportunities to lead projects or teams and focus on developing my skills in delegation, motivation, and strategic thinking. I embrace my confidence and decisiveness to take action and make decisions. I tap into my resilience and determination to overcome obstacles and persevere in the face of challenges. I view setbacks as opportunities for growth and remain focused on long-term goals. I harness my charisma and leadership presence to inspire and motivate others around me. I utilize my strong communication skills to articulate my ideas clearly and persuasively. I practice mindfulness techniques, such as deep breathing or stepping back to assess the situation objectively before responding or making decisions. I am open to different perspectives and actively seek out diverse viewpoints. I learn to deliver feedback and engage in discussions with diplomacy and tact. I make a conscious effort to understand and validate others' emotions and perspectives. I recognize the value of collaboration and shared decision-making. I recognize that setbacks and failures are opportunities for growth and learning. I embrace my true self and share my genuine experiences with others. I embrace healthy competition by setting personal benchmarks and challenging myself to surpass my achievements. I shift my focus from seeking external validation to cultivating intrinsic motivation. I practice being present with my emotions and those of others.

I recognize that it's okay to show vulnerability and share struggles with others. I challenge the tendency to set unrealistically high expectations for myself. I recognize that taking care of myself physically, emotionally, and mentally is essential for overall well-being. I focus on building genuine and authentic relationships with others rather than transactional or image-based connections. I embrace the idea that mistakes and failures are part of the learning process and a natural part of being human. I recognize that setbacks and failures are opportunities for growth and learning. I embrace my true self and share my genuine experiences with others. I embrace healthy competition by setting personal benchmarks and challenging myself to surpass my achievements. I shift my focus from seeking external validation to cultivating intrinsic motivation. I am present with my emotions and those of others. I focus on building collaborative relationships rather than exerting control. I cultivate self-awareness and consider the impact of my communication on others. I slow down and take time to evaluate options and potential consequences before making decisions. I develop a balanced approach by assessing risks more thoroughly and considering potential drawbacks. I surround myself with individuals who excel in attention to detail and collaborate with them to ensure accuracy. I speak the truth in all things, give respect to others at all times, and take responsibility for my actions and inactions, regardless of the ramifications. If I have a problem with someone, I do not let the sun go down until I have forgiven them. I am grateful for my family, each day that God blesses me with, and all that I have.

I will live with integrity in both my personal and professional environments. I will treat those I encounter with dignity and honor. I will hold myself accountable for my actions and assignments. I will give grace to others just as God has given it to me. I will always show and give appreciation for what I have and for what others do for me. I will be resilient in all situations, maintaining a calm manner. I will persist until I have achieved success. I will recognize the significance of nurturing all aspects of my life, including physical, emotional, mental, and spiritual dimensions. I will continue to educate myself on things I do not understand. I will rely on others who are better at the things I need to be done.

Your affirmation may not sound perfect at first, especially when you go line by line. You will need to revise it several times until you feel confident and empowered by reading it. That's the purpose of having and reading it. Here's a revised example to make it more confident and empowering:

My Psychological Affirmation (*Revised*)

I recognize that taking care of myself physically, emotionally, and mentally is essential for my overall well-being. I embrace my true self and share my genuine experiences with others. I recognize the significance of nurturing all aspects of my life, including physical, emotional, mental, and spiritual dimensions. I am energetic, full of love and laughter. I am confident in knowing who I am, and I love myself. I will live with integrity in both my personal and professional environments, speaking the truth about all things. I give respect to others at all times and treat those I encounter with dignity and honor. I am always willing to help when there is a need. I mentor or coach individuals who can benefit from my expertise and guidance. I take the time to care for others. I don't wait for others when I can do it myself. If I have a problem with someone, I do not let the sun go down until I have forgiven them. I give grace to others just as God has given it to me. I always show kindness and gratitude, being grateful for my family each day that God blesses me with them, and all that I have. I always show and give appreciation for what I have and for what others do for me. I develop relationships by gaining clarity and understanding others' points. I have developed strong listening skills to understand and connect with others on a deeper level. I get in the habit of listening twice as much as I speak. I don't interrupt those who are speaking. I practice mindfulness techniques, such as deep breathing or stepping back to assess the situation objectively before responding or making decisions. I make a conscious effort to understand and validate others' emotions and perspectives. I embrace my true self and share my genuine experiences with others. I practice being present with my emotions and those of others. I focus on building genuine and authentic relationships with others rather than transactional or image-based connections. I cultivate self-awareness and consider the impact of my communication on others. I challenge negative self-talk and replace it with positive affirmations.

I realize that there is always more than one way of doing things. I use creative thinking to design new methods of doing things, focusing on the process rather than solely on the end result. I seek opportunities to think outside the box and generate innovative ideas. I look at things from at least three different points of view. I create win/win outcomes in any situation. I schedule everything. I use 15-minute intervals for time management instead of 30 minutes or hourly. I schedule all occurrences to allow for travel time and incidents. I embrace the mindset that fashionably late is still late. I practice being 15 minutes early for occasions. I prioritize, create a to-do list, and get the advice of people who have mastered time management. I give start times and deadlines for what I must commit to doing. I provide information or documentation ahead of the time promised.

I seek opportunities to lead projects or teams and focus on developing my skills in delegation, motivation, and strategic thinking. I harness my charisma and leadership presence to inspire and motivate others around me. I focus on building collaborative relationships rather than exerting control. I recognize the value of collaboration and shared decision-making. I surround myself with individuals who excel in attention to detail and collaborate with them to ensure accuracy. I utilize my effective communication skills to articulate my ideas clearly and persuasively. I am open to different perspectives and actively seek out diverse viewpoints.

I deliver feedback and engage in discussions with diplomacy and tact. I embrace my confidence and decisiveness to take action and make decisions. I slow down and take time to evaluate options and potential consequences before making decisions, allowing me to make better decisions faster and delegate things to others. I have a balanced approach by assessing risks more thoroughly and considering potential drawbacks.

I recognize that it's okay to show vulnerability and share my struggles with others. I rely on others who are better at the things I need to be done. I continue to educate myself on things I do not understand. I will hold myself accountable for my actions and assignments. I will take responsibility for my actions and inactions, regardless of the ramifications.

When I fail at something, I do not quit; I figure out another way. I embrace and use failure as an opportunity for growth and learning. I live by the idea that mistakes and failures are part of the learning process and a natural part of being human. I also recognize that setbacks and failures are opportunities for growth and view them as opportunities for growth and remain focused on my long-term goals. I am always open to change and new adventures. I embrace change and uncertainty by seeking new experiences and stepping out of my comfort zone. I shift my focus from seeking external validation to cultivating intrinsic motivation. I tap into my resilience and determination to overcome obstacles and persevere in the face of challenges. I welcome healthy competition by setting personal benchmarks and challenging myself to surpass my achievements. I challenge the tendency to set unrealistically high expectations for myself. I am resilient in all situations, maintaining a calm manner. I persist until I have achieved success.

NOTE: This version is more polished and empowering. Remember that your affirmation is a personal document that should be written to help you and no one else. It should give you the ability to see the future you desire to be, empower you, motivate you, and build your confidence. Writing affirmations is a key part of personal growth. They provide the courage to persist and be resilient in achieving your goals.

Write your affirmation in your workbook on page 129 or in your notebook. You may want to use a pencil for this, or you could use a scratch sheet of paper and write your revision in your workbook or notebook.

Reading Your Affirmations

Reading your affirmations is like taking a nourishing sip from the well of self-empowerment. As you immerse yourself in the positive words you have written, you invite a surge of confidence, motivation, and belief in your abilities. The act of reading your affirmations is a powerful reminder of the incredible potential that lies within you. Each affirmation serves as a gentle nudge, urging you to step into your greatness and embrace the limitless possibilities that await. When you read your affirmations, you are reprogramming your subconscious mind. By consistently exposing yourself to positive and empowering statements, you replace self-doubt and limiting beliefs with a mindset of self-belief and resilience.

Reading affirmations is an act of self-care. It is a moment of stillness and reflection, a chance to reconnect with your inner strength and rekindle the fire within your soul. It is a time to prioritize your well-being and affirm your worthiness. The importance of reading affirmations lies in their ability to anchor you in the present moment. As you immerse yourself in the positive words, you cultivate mindfulness and shift your focus to the present, allowing worry and anxiety to melt away. It is an act of self-empowerment and self-fulfillment. It is a declaration to the universe and to yourself that you are deserving of all the blessings, success, and happiness that life has to offer. It is a powerful step toward creating a life aligned with your truest desires and aspirations. Make it a daily ritual to read your affirmations with intention and presence. Allow the words to penetrate your being, igniting a sense of purpose and clarity. Embrace the transformative power of affirmations and watch as they guide you towards a life filled with joy, fulfillment, and endless possibilities.

Now that we have completed the psychological, it is time to move into the next arena, which is the physical.

ENVISIONING YOUR PHYSICAL SELF

The physical aspect of your being is crucial to your personal growth journey. It's like the foundation of a house, enabling you to build a thriving life. Prioritizing your physical health creates a solid platform for personal growth, empowering you to face life's challenges with vitality and resilience. Think of it as establishing a strong mind-body connection. Physical health directly impacts mental well-being, enabling you to approach personal growth with clarity and focus.

Prioritizing your physical health is an act of self-love and self-care. By showing kindness to your body, you send a powerful message of self-worth and empowerment. This foundation of physical health propels you forward in your journey. When you focus on your physical well-being, you unlock boundless energy and productivity. A healthy body fuels a focused mind, enabling you to accomplish tasks, pursue goals, and embrace new opportunities with vigor.

As you prioritize your well-being, you experience higher energy levels and greater vitality. A healthy and vibrant body provides the strength needed to pursue your dreams and aspirations. This boost in energy propels you forward, enabling you to tackle challenges with enthusiasm. Nurturing your physical self also enhances your confidence and self-esteem. When you feel good about your body, you radiate a positive aura that attracts success and fosters the belief that you are capable of achieving your personal growth goals.

Embracing physical health instills confidence and bolsters self-esteem. Feeling good in your own skin fosters a positive self-image that spills over into all areas of your life. By honoring and respecting your physical self, you communicate self-worth and self-respect to the world. This authentic self-love sends a powerful message that others mirror back, reinforcing your personal growth journey.

When others witness your dedication to physical health, they are inspired to follow suit. Your commitment to personal growth through physical well-being becomes a guiding light for those seeking positive transformation. Prioritizing your physical self will set a positive ripple effect in motion. As you improve your physical health and lead by example, others are motivated to embrace their journeys of self-improvement.

A physically healthy and strong individual is better equipped to face obstacles and overcome setbacks. Physical resilience translates into mental resilience, making you more tenacious and determined in your personal growth pursuits. A strong and resilient body equips you to navigate life's challenges with grace and determination. As you push your physical limits, you cultivate mental fortitude that extends to other aspects of your journey.

A well-maintained physical body leads to increased productivity. By ensuring adequate rest, nutrition, and exercise, you optimize your ability to stay focused and achieve personal growth milestones. When your physical health is at its best, you become more productive in all aspects of life. Improved focus, efficiency, and mental clarity empower you to achieve your goals effectively.

Taking care of your physical health positively impacts emotional regulation. Engaging in regular physical activity releases endorphins, reducing stress and anxiety, and promoting emotional resilience. This newfound emotional balance allows you to navigate challenges with a clear and composed mindset, facilitating personal growth.

By nurturing your physical self, you demonstrate ownership and empowerment over your well-being. Engaging in regular exercise, nourishing foods, and adequate rest fosters a positive mind-body connection. This sense of control extends to other areas of your life, fostering a proactive approach to personal growth.

Nurturing your physical self-demands discipline and commitment. Embracing healthy habits instills a sense of discipline that extends to other areas of your life, inspiring you to stay focused on your goals and aspirations. By staying dedicated to healthy habits, you cultivate these qualities, which are transferable to other areas of your personal growth journey.

Fostering healthy habits in the physical realm extends beyond immediate benefits. These habits become integral to your lifestyle, translating into positive habits that enhance personal growth in all dimensions. Taking care of your physical self encourages body awareness and mindfulness. It reminds you to honor the present moment and appreciate each step you take toward becoming the best version of yourself.

While nurturing your physical health, you also encourage other positive lifestyle choices. From nutrition to sleep and stress management, each decision fosters a holistic approach to personal growth. Personal growth is a multidimensional journey, and embracing physical wellness ensures a holistic approach to your development. Your physical body is the temple that houses your soul. Treating it with respect and care is essential for nurturing a harmonious connection between your mind, body, and spirit.

By nurturing your body alongside your emotional, mental, and spiritual aspects, you embrace a balanced approach to personal growth that harmonizes all dimensions of your being. Your physical body is a canvas for transformation. As you grow and evolve on your personal growth journey, you'll witness positive changes in your physical self, reflecting the inner transformation you're experiencing.

Investing in your physical health enhances your longevity and quality of life. A strong, healthy body allows you to savor life's experiences fully, contributing to a more meaningful and fulfilling personal growth journey. Optimal physical health opens doors to new experiences and opportunities. Whether it's embarking on an adventurous journey or pursuing your passions, a healthy body equips you for exciting endeavors.

Remember, the physical you is an essential aspect of your holistic growth. Personal growth is a multidimensional journey, and nurturing your physical well-being is an integral part of the process. Do it with love, gratitude, and care, for it is the vessel through which you'll thrive and bring your dreams to fruition. Nurturing your body, mind, and spirit creates a powerful synergy that fuels your personal growth journey. Embrace healthy habits, exercise regularly, nourish your body with nutritious food, and prioritize self-care. As you build a strong and healthy physical foundation, you'll discover a renewed sense of vitality, confidence, and inner strength that propels you forward in your personal growth journey. By investing in your physical well-being, you embark on a path of holistic growth that enriches every aspect of your life. Take this journey with enthusiasm, knowing that your commitment to the physical you will lay the groundwork for a fulfilling and empowered life. Every step you take towards nurturing the physical you will propel you forward on your journey to becoming the best version of yourself.

Reflecting on Your Physical Self

Before we start envisioning a healthier and better-groomed self, let's ask some questions to guide you in visualizing a healthier and well-groomed self. In your workbook on page 130 or in your notebook, consider these questions:

What does "healthier" mean to me? Define what health and well-being look like in terms of your physical aspects. What specific aspects of my health do I want to improve? Identify areas such as fitness, nutrition, sleep, stress management, or overall lifestyle habits. How do I want to feel in my body daily? Consider the energy level, vitality, and overall sense of well-being you want to experience. What kind of physical activities do I enjoy or want to incorporate into my routine? Explore activities that resonate with you to make fitness enjoyable and sustainable. What adjustments can I make to my diet to support my health goals? Consider incorporating more fruits, vegetables, whole grains, lean proteins, and reducing processed foods and sugary snacks.

Visualizing a new healthier and well-groomed you is key to success. Review your answers to ensure they are clear and leave no room for speculation or additional questions. Later, in our goal-setting exercise, we will create small, consistent steps to ensure that our vision becomes a reality. These questions are just to break the ice. Being well-groomed is a matter of choice, and we should already know what we desire in terms of grooming. In the next few sections, we will do a deep dive into visualizing a healthier, well-groomed you.

A Well-Groomed You

Envisioning a well-groomed you creates a captivating and confident presence that radiates from within. Close your eyes and see yourself as your best, well-groomed version, exuding self-assurance and elegance, embracing a poised and polished demeanor. Envision self-care as a daily ritual where grooming becomes an act of self-love and self-expression. Nourish your body, mind, and soul with care and attention.

A well-groomed appearance sends a powerful message of self-confidence to the world. Envision walking into any room with your head held high, knowing you are deserving of admiration and respect. Develop a personal style that reflects your individuality and showcases your best features. Dressing in a way that aligns with your personality boosts your self-esteem and leaves a lasting impression.

Imagine glowing skin and a radiant smile resulting from consistent skincare and oral hygiene. A well-groomed you exudes vibrancy and good health. Envision the care you put into every aspect of your appearance, from well-maintained nails to polished shoes. Your attention to detail sets you apart and showcases your commitment to excellence.

Visualize the positive impact of grooming habits on your overall well-being. A well-groomed you feels ready to conquer challenges and embrace new opportunities. Grooming goes beyond the surface. Nurturing your inner beauty, self-esteem, and emotional well-being shines through in your outward appearance. Envision the positivity you exude when you feel well-groomed and put-together. A radiant smile, good posture, and an aura of confidence draw others to your magnetic energy.

Grooming is an art of self-expression. Embrace your uniqueness and celebrate your journey to becoming a well-groomed you. Your authenticity and self-care inspire others to do the same. Recognize that grooming is not about conforming to societal standards but about embracing your authentic self with love and care. It's a transformative journey where your inner beauty aligns with your external presentation. Embrace this empowering vision, step into your spotlight, and let the world witness the radiance of a well-groomed you.

Reflection and Questions for a Well-Groomed You

Before we go further, note that being well-groomed doesn't mean becoming vain. Vanity can lead to arrogance. Being well-groomed is about how you feel about yourself, not just how you look. It's about the love you have for yourself and the empowerment it gives to your overall well-being. Becoming a well-groomed version of yourself involves thoughtful self-reflection and a commitment to self-care. On page 133 in your workbook or in your notebook, ask yourself these questions:

How do I currently perceive my grooming habits and appearance? Take an honest look at your grooming routine and assess areas that may need improvement. What specific grooming goals do I want to achieve? Define clear and achievable grooming objectives that align with your desired image. What aspects of my appearance do I feel most confident about? Acknowledge your strengths and build upon them to enhance your overall grooming. What steps can I take to improve my skincare and personal hygiene practices? Explore skincare products and hygiene habits that promote a healthier and more radiant appearance. How can I enhance my personal style to reflect my unique personality and preferences? Embrace clothing, accessories, and hairstyles that make you feel comfortable and confident.

Remember, the journey to becoming a well-groomed you is personal. Approach it with kindness and patience. Embrace your uniqueness and let your grooming routine become an expression of self-love and care. By consistently investing in yourself and your appearance, you will project confidence and radiate the beauty that comes from embracing your true self.

The Grooming Maintenance Chart

A grooming maintenance chart helps you stay organized and maintain regular self-care practices. It typically includes a list of grooming tasks and a schedule for when each task should be completed. It can be in the form of a weekly or monthly planner, checklist, or calendar. The chart can cover a wide range of self-care activities, such as:

Daily tasks: Brushing teeth, washing face, applying skincare products, and combing hair. Weekly tasks: Shaving, haircuts, and nail care. Monthly tasks: Deep conditioning hair, exfoliating skin, or cleaning makeup brushes. Occasional tasks: Getting a massage, facial, changing a toothbrush, or participating in other self-care rituals.

Creating a grooming maintenance chart helps establish a consistent and well-rounded grooming routine. It prevents grooming tasks from being overlooked or forgotten. By staying on top of personal grooming, you can enhance your overall well-being, confidence, and self-esteem.

The chart can be customized to fit personal preferences and specific grooming needs. Some people prefer using digital tools like smartphone apps or online planners, while others might prefer a physical, printed chart posted in their bathroom or bedroom for easy reference.

By maintaining a grooming maintenance chart, you can prioritize self-care, establish healthy habits, and ensure that you look and feel your best every day. It serves as a useful reminder to take care of yourself and make grooming a seamless part of your daily routine.

Turn to page 136 in your workbook and complete the chart or create a chart in your notebook. Put in the grooming task, check whether it is a daily, weekly, monthly, or occasional task. Here is an example:

Grooming Chart

Grooming Chart				
Grooming Task	Daily	Weekly	Monthly	Occasional
Brush Teeth	X			
Mouthwash	X			
Wash-up/Shower	X			
Take a Bath		X		
Hair – Comb/Brush	X			
Haircut/Hairdo			X	
Manicure			X	
Pedicure			X	
Message				X
Change under garments	X			
Get Dressed	X			
Iron/Press Clothes		X		
Wash & Dry Clothes			X	

Review the chart and make sure you haven't missed any grooming tasks. Next, we'll create three charts from the one above.

Daily Grooming Chart

List each item checked off as daily and then check the appropriate box or boxes for the daily grooming task whether it is morning, afternoon, or evening, or a multiple of the three. Here is an example:

Daily Grooming Chart			
Daily Grooming Task	**Mornings**	**Afternoons**	**Evenings**
Brush Teeth	X		X
Mouthwash	X		X
Wash-up/Shower	X		
Hair – Comb/Brush	X		
Change under garments	X		
Get Dressed	X		X

All six grooming tasks are done each morning, and three are done both morning and evening. This will be helpful later when creating routines. Next, we'll create a weekly grooming chart.

Weekly Grooming Chart

List all your tasks that have been checked weekly and choose the day of the week for each task. Here is an example:

Weekly Grooming Chart							
Grooming Task	**Mon**	**Tue**	**Wed**	**Thurs**	**Fri**	**Sat**	**Sun**
Take a Bath	X		X		X		X
Iron/Press Clothes			X			X	

It's up to you how often you do each task throughout the week. This will become useful when creating routines later on. Lastly, we'll create a monthly grooming chart.

Monthly Grooming Chart

List your grooming tasks selected as monthly in your grooming chart. Determine which weeks of the month these tasks will be performed. Here is an example:

Monthly Grooming Chart					
Grooming Task	1st Week	2nd Week	3rd Week	4th Week	5th Week
Haircut/Hairdo		X		X	
Manicure	X		X		
Pedicure			X		
Wash & Dry Clothes		X			X

Finished? Later, we will break all the grooming charts down to create a grooming routine for managing our time. This completes the well-groomed section; now let us move on to the healthier you part of this journey.

A Healthier You

A healthier self is the foundation of a fulfilled and purposeful life. When you prioritize your well-being, you unlock limitless potential within yourself, paving the way for personal growth and self-discovery. Embrace the importance of a healthier self as a commitment to self-love and self-respect. By nurturing your physical well-being, you acknowledge your worth and create a solid base for a positive and rewarding life. A healthier self will empower you to take charge of your life, gaining the energy and vitality needed to pursue your dreams and aspirations with unwavering determination.

The significance of a healthier self lies in its profound impact on your overall happiness and contentment. As you practice self-care and cultivate a balanced lifestyle, you foster a sense of inner peace and fulfillment. A healthier self leads to greater resilience and adaptability in the face of challenges. By taking care of your body, you build the strength to overcome obstacles and thrive in times of adversity.

The importance of a healthier self extends to your relationships with others. When you are in tune with your well-being, you become a more compassionate and empathetic individual, fostering deeper connections with those around you. Prioritizing a healthier self allows you to tap into your creative potential and unleash your talents. A clear and focused mind enables you to explore your passions and pursue endeavors that bring you joy and fulfillment.

A healthier self inspires and motivates others. Your dedication to self-improvement serves as a beacon of inspiration, encouraging those around you to prioritize their well-being and embark on their own journeys of personal growth. The significance of a healthier self lies in its ability to break free from limiting beliefs and self-imposed barriers. When you prioritize self-care, you embrace your full potential and step into a life of possibility and abundance.

A healthier self is the key to balance and harmony in all aspects of your life. As you cultivate a sense of well-being, you experience greater alignment and flow in your personal and professional endeavors. But most importantly, a healthier self, bestows upon you the gift of a life lived to the fullest. Embrace the journey of self-discovery and self-improvement, for within a healthier self lies the promise of a purpose-driven and extraordinary existence.

A healthier self begins with small, intentional steps. Embrace self-compassion and patience as you embark on this journey of growth and transformation. Embrace the significance of a healthier self, for it is the foundation upon which you can build a life of joy, fulfillment, and boundless possibilities.

SHEEP: The 5 Key Areas for Physical Health

There are five areas to focus on for physical health, referred to as SHEEP to keep it memorable and simple. By focusing on these areas, you can embark on a path toward a healthier physical self. Remember, it is a continuous journey, so be patient, stay committed, and enjoy the process of becoming a healthier and happier version of yourself.

Sleep

Sleep is a powerful pillar of health that often gets overlooked in our busy lives. Prioritizing sleep is a declaration of self-love and care. When you grant your body the rest it deserves, you nourish yourself at the core, allowing your mind, body, and spirit to recharge and rejuvenate. Sleep is the secret ingredient to unlocking your full potential. As you rest, your brain consolidates memories, processes information, and reboots your creativity, giving you the mental clarity and sharpness needed to thrive in every aspect of your life. During deep sleep, your body repairs tissues, balances hormones, and supports your immune system, helping you ward off illnesses and perform at your peak.

Embracing sufficient sleep can be the key to achieving your health and fitness goals. As you sleep, your body balances hunger hormones, which can help you resist unhealthy cravings and maintain a balanced diet. Adequate sleep enhances your mood, boosts your emotional intelligence, and fosters an optimistic outlook on life. Prioritize this fundamental aspect of self-care and witness the remarkable transformation as you become a healthier, more energized, and invigorated version of yourself.

How much sleep does the average person need to maintain a healthy self? The recommended amount of sleep for the average adult to maintain a healthy self is generally between 7 to 9 hours per night. However, individual sleep needs can vary based on factors such as age, lifestyle, genetics, and overall health.

Hydrate

Hydration is the elixir of life, and embracing the importance of staying adequately hydrated can be the key to becoming a healthier and more vibrant version of yourself. Hydration fuels your body's engine. When you keep yourself well-hydrated, you provide the essential support your organs need to function optimally. From digestion to circulation, hydration is the secret behind your body's seamless operation. Water is nature's detoxifier. As you hydrate, you flush out toxins and waste products, cleansing your system and promoting clearer, healthier skin.

Hydration is vital for maintaining cognitive function, focus, and mental clarity. By staying hydrated, you enhance your memory and boost your ability to concentrate on tasks. Drinking water supports emotional well-being. When you're properly hydrated, you feel more balanced and energized, helping you tackle stress and challenges with greater ease and resilience. The significance of hydration extends beyond physical health; it nourishes your soul too. Sipping water mindfully can become a sacred ritual, a moment of self-care and reflection that keeps you in tune with your body's needs.

The general recommendation for daily water intake to maintain a healthier self, varies depending on factors such as age, gender, physical activity level, and climate. The Institute of Medicine (IOM) provides general guidelines for total daily water intake, which includes water from all beverages and foods. These recommendations are as follows:

- Adult men: About 3.7 liters (or about 13 cups) of total water intake per day.

- Adult women: About 2.7 liters (or about 9 cups) of total water intake per day.

Reflecting on Hydration

- How much water do you drink per day (in ounces)?

- What kind of fluids other than water do you drink?

- How much of each of the other fluids do you drink per day (in ounces)?

- Based on the weight factor, how much water should you be drinking (in ounces)?

- What is the difference between the amount of water you drink and how much water you should drink?

- Are you drinking more, less, or the correct amount of water?

Eat

Embracing a healthy and mindful approach to eating is the cornerstone of becoming a healthier and happier you. Your relationship with food can profoundly impact your overall well-being, and its time to nourish your body, mind, and soul with the goodness that comes from a balanced and positive eating experience. Food is your fuel for life. When you choose to fill your plate with nourishing and wholesome foods, you are providing your body with the energy and nutrients it needs to thrive. Every bite is an opportunity to nourish your cells, support your immune system, and promote your vitality. Embracing mindful eating is an act of self-compassion. By savoring each bite and eating with intention, you create a deeper connection with your body and its signals of hunger and satiety. This mindful approach allows you to appreciate the flavors and textures of your food, fostering a healthier relationship with eating. Food is a celebration of life. It's not just about sustenance; it's about pleasure and enjoyment. By choosing a variety of colorful and nutritious foods, you can indulge in the joy of eating while still nurturing your well-being.

A balanced diet is the key to unlocking your potential. When you fuel your body with the right nutrients, you enhance your cognitive function, boost your mood, and elevate your energy levels, empowering you to tackle life's challenges with clarity and resilience. Mindful eating helps you break free from emotional eating patterns. By tuning in to your hunger cues, you can distinguish between physical and emotional hunger, empowering you to address your emotions in healthier and more constructive ways. The importance of a healthy relationship with food extends beyond your physical health; it impacts your mental and emotional well-being too. As you cultivate a positive attitude towards eating, you nurture self-esteem and build a foundation of self-love that radiates through all aspects of your life.

Reflecting on Eating Habits

- Do my meals incorporate a variety of food groups? Ensure that your plate includes a mix of fruits, vegetables, whole grains, lean proteins, and healthy fats.

- Am I getting enough vegetables and fruits? Aim to fill half of your plate with a colorful array of vegetables and fruits to ensure you get a wide range of vitamins, minerals, and antioxidants.

- Is my protein intake sufficient? Check if your meals contain enough lean protein sources such as fish, poultry, tofu, beans, or lentils to support muscle maintenance and growth.

- Are my grains whole grains? Choose whole grains like brown rice, quinoa, oats, and whole wheat to increase fiber intake and promote better digestion.

- Is my meal high in added sugars or unhealthy fats? Examine your food choices to avoid excessive added sugars and unhealthy fats often found in processed and sugary snacks.

By asking these questions regularly, you can evaluate and adjust your eating habits to ensure you are on track to consuming balanced, nutrient-rich meals that contribute to your overall well-being. Remember, healthy eating is a journey, and small, mindful changes can make a big difference in your health and happiness.

I don't want you to get the impression that I don't eat healthy meals at all. I prefer baked foods over fried any day, I love eating 1-2 veggies with every meal. I am not a big bread eater, except when I have spaghetti or fried fish, bread is a must. I eat plenty of fruits, nuts, cheese, and yogurts, I also love soups and salads. I prefer fresh foods over processed and frozen foods, I prefer a home cooked meal over restaurant foods. Not to say I don't eat restaurant foods, because it does happen on rare occasions. I will not eat any food that was prepared in a microwave, I barely like having my food heated in one, but it makes it easier for my wife when I eat leftovers. I may not be a health food nut, but I consider myself to be somewhat of a healthy eater.

Exercise

Exercise is not just a means to a fit body; it is the pathway to becoming a healthier and more empowered version of yourself. Embrace the importance of exercise, and you will unlock a myriad of physical, mental, and emotional benefits that will enrich your life beyond measure. Exercise is a celebration of your body's potential. When you move, you discover the incredible strength and resilience that resides within you. Each step, each rep, and each stretch are a testament to your body's capability to conquer challenges and push beyond limits.

The power of exercise extends far beyond physical appearance. Regular physical activity boosts your cardiovascular health, strengthens your muscles, and improves flexibility, promoting overall well-being and reducing the risk of chronic illnesses. It is an elixir for mental clarity and focus. As you engage in physical activity, your brain releases endorphins, the "feel-good" chemicals that enhance your mood and reduce stress, anxiety, and depression.

Embracing exercise empowers you to set and achieve goals. Whether it is running a mile or lifting heavier weights, each achievement fuels your confidence and reinforces your belief in your own abilities. It is the art of self-discipline and dedication. When you commit to a fitness routine, you cultivate consistency and resilience, teaching yourself that you can overcome obstacles and stay committed to your health journey.

The joy of exercise lies in its versatility. With countless forms of physical activity to explore, from dancing to hiking to yoga, you can find a mode of movement that brings you pure delight and encourages you to stay active. It is your daily act of self-love and self-care. By prioritizing your fitness, you honor your body's needs and nurture the temple that houses your beautiful soul. Physical strength begets mental strength. The mental fortitude developed through exercise spills into other areas of your life, empowering you to face challenges with resilience, determination, and grace.

Exercise is the journey to discovering your inner athlete. You will surprise yourself with newfound abilities and feats you never thought possible, proving that the limitations you once perceived were merely illusions. The ripple effect of exercise reaches far beyond yourself. As you become healthier and happier, you inspire those around you to do the same. Your commitment to fitness becomes a beacon of light, motivating others to embark on their healthy journeys.

So, step into the realm of exercise with courage and enthusiasm. Embrace the journey, not just for the physical rewards, but for the transformation it brings to your mind, body, and spirit. As you exercise, you will unlock the door to a healthier, happier, and more fulfilled version of yourself, ready to embrace all of life's wonders with open arms.

The amount of time spent on exercising to become a healthier you can vary depending on your fitness level, goals, and overall lifestyle. The American Heart Association (AHA) and other reputable health organizations recommend at least 150 minutes of moderate-intensity aerobic activity or 75 minutes of vigorous-intensity aerobic activity per week for adults.

If you plan to do moderate-intensity exercises, aim for about 30 minutes of moderate-intensity aerobic activity most days of the week. This can include activities like brisk walking, cycling, swimming, or dancing. If you prefer more intense workouts, aim for about 25 minutes of vigorous-intensity aerobic activity three days a week. Examples include running, high-intensity interval training (HIIT), or participating in intense sports. Additionally, include strength training exercises at least two days a week. Focus on all major muscle groups, such as lifting weights, bodyweight exercises, or using resistance bands.

Keep in mind that you do not have to do all the exercise at once; you can break it down into shorter sessions throughout the day. For instance, you can do three 10-minute walks or two 15-minute sessions of exercise per day. It is essential to listen to your body and choose activities that you enjoy. Gradually increase the duration and intensity of your workouts over time as your fitness level improves. If you are new to exercise or have health concerns, consider consulting with a healthcare provider or a certified fitness professional to create a personalized exercise plan that suits your needs and abilities. The most important thing is to stay consistent with your exercise routine and find activities that bring you joy and satisfaction. By incorporating regular physical activity into your life, you'll be on your way to becoming a healthier and happier version of yourself.

Reflecting on Exercise Habits

- What types of physical activities do I enjoy or have enjoyed in the past? Identifying enjoyable activities increases the likelihood of adhering to your exercise routine.

- How much time can I realistically dedicate to exercise each week? Determining your availability helps in planning the frequency and duration of workouts.

- What are my current fitness levels and any physical limitations I should consider? Assessing your starting point allows for a safe and gradual progression.

- What aspects of fitness do I want to focus on (e.g., cardiovascular endurance, strength, flexibility, balance)? Identifying your priorities helps tailor your exercise routine accordingly.

- How can I make exercise a part of my daily routine or lifestyle? Exploring ways to incorporate physical activity into your daily life promotes consistency.

By asking yourself these questions, you can envision a customized and sustainable exercise plan that fits your future lifestyle, preferences, and goals. Remember that consistency is key, and finding activities that you genuinely enjoy will make your fitness journey more enjoyable and successful. If you have any health concerns or medical conditions, it is always a good idea to consult with a healthcare provider or fitness professional before starting a new exercise program. For now, let's start planning a new exercise program for our future self.

Exercise Chart

Go to page 145 in your workbook and complete the Exercise Planning Chart or create a chart in your notebook. Yes, in case you were wondering, I love charts—they make life and learning so much simpler. Here are the instructions: put in the exercise (if you have the workbook your exercises have been listed for you, feel free to add at the end what was not listed), check whether it is a daily, weekly, or monthly exercise. Here is the example:

Exercise Chart

Exercise	Daily	Weekly	Monthly	Occasional
Push-Ups	☒			
Sit-Ups	☒			
Squats (Standard, Sumo, Narrow)	☒			
Lunges (Forward, Reverse, Lateral)	☒			
Jogging		☒		
Kickboxing			☒	
Planks	☒			
Crunches	☒			
Swimming			☒	
Cycling			☒	
Karate		☒		
Basketball practice		☒		
Hiking				☒
Skating				☒
Bowling				☒
Racquetball				☒

To help remind you, I have made a list of exercises in Appendix C. Go through it, and make sure you did not miss anything, then review and adjust your tasks accordingly. Next, we are going to create three charts from the one above, the first will be our daily exercise chart.

Daily Exercise Chart

You can find this chart on page 146 of your workbook, or you can create it in your notebook. In our daily exercise chart, we will write each item that has been checked off as daily and then check the appropriate box or boxes for the daily exercises whether it is morning, afternoon, or evening or a multiple of the three. Here is an example, using the information from the exercise task chart:

Daily Exercise Chart

Exercise	Mornings	Afternoon	Evenings
Push-Ups	☒		☒
Sit-Ups	☒		☒
Squats (Standard, Sumo, Narrow)	☒		
Lunges (Forward, Reverse, Lateral)	☒		
Planks	☒		
Crunches	☒		

Based on the information above, all 6 exercises are done each morning and 2 are done both morning and evening. This information will be helpful later as we get into creating our exercise program. Next, we will create a weekly exercise chart.

Weekly Exercise Chart

You can find this chart on page 147 of your workbook, or you can create it in your notebook. The weekly exercise chart is slightly different from the one above because in it, you will list all your exercises that you have checked as weekly, but instead of choosing a time of day, you will choose the day of the week. Here is an example, using the information from the exercise chart:

Weekly Exercise Chart

Exercise	Mon	Tue	Wed	Thurs	Fri	Sat	Sun
Jogging				☒	☒	☒	
Karate		☒		☒			
Basketball practice	☒		☒			☒	

Simple, right? It will be up to you how often you do any particular exercise throughout the week. Again, this will become useful when we get into creating our exercise program later on. On to our final chart and I am sure you have figured out it will be our monthly exercise chart.

Monthly Exercise Chart

You can find this chart on page 148 of your workbook, or you can create it in your notebook. In this chart, we will list the exercises that you have checked as monthly in your exercise chart. We will also determine what weeks of the month we will be performing these exercises. Okay, let's do this!

Monthly Exercise Chart

Exercise	1st Week	2nd Week	3rd Week	4th Week	5th Week
Kickboxing	☒		☒		
Swimming	☒		☒		☒
Cycling		☒			

Done? Splendid! Later in the exercise programming, we will break all the exercise charts down to create an exercise routine that can be used in managing our time. Remember, as I told you before starting an exercise program, it is important to consult a physician. Well, it's that time. Let's go see the doctor!

Physician

Having a physician as a partner in your journey towards becoming a healthier you is invaluable. Their expertise, guidance, and support play a crucial role in your overall well-being. Physicians have years of education and training, making them the most qualified professionals to provide accurate and evidence-based health advice. Trusting their expertise can lead to informed decisions and better health outcomes. They take the time to understand your unique health needs, creating a tailored plan that addresses your specific goals and challenges. Focusing not only on treating existing health conditions but also on preventing future illnesses through early detection and lifestyle interventions, they empower you to take a proactive stance on your health. A good physician considers the physical, mental, and emotional aspects of your health, recognizing that they are interconnected. This comprehensive approach ensures that all aspects of your well-being are addressed. Having a physician by your side means having a dedicated supporter who encourages you to stay on track, celebrates your progress, and provides guidance during setbacks. Regular check-ins with your physician help you stay accountable to your health goals, ensuring that you remain committed to making positive changes.

Physicians educate you about your health conditions, treatment options, and ways to improve your lifestyle. Armed with this knowledge, you become an empowered advocate for your own well-being. If you have any health concerns or questions, a physician is there to provide clarity and alleviate any fears or uncertainties. Developing a strong patient-physician relationship fosters trust and open communication, leading to better health management and shared decision-making. They often serve as role models, showcasing the benefits of a healthy lifestyle through their actions and commitment to their own well-being. Know that your physician is not just a healthcare provider but a partner in your health journey. Embrace the opportunity to work together and make the most of their knowledge, support, and dedication to guide you towards a healthier, happier, and more fulfilling life. With a physician by your side, you have a trusted ally who will help you navigate the path to becoming a healthier you with confidence and determination.

I was not a big fan of doctors. For me to see a doctor, it had to be an emergency, and I found out later that this mindset is common among many men. But all that changed when I got married. My wife insisted that I go to the doctor at least twice a year. I know you're probably thinking that either my wife has me whipped or I am a hen-pecked man, and she wears the pants. No, it's neither, I just like peace and don't want to hear constant complaints and reminders. Happy wife, happy life!

But back to the story, as we began to search for a doctor for me, it was the most aggravating experience I ever had to go through. I went through about eight doctors in the span of a year, then I met Doctor Lu. She had wonderful bedside manners, was knowledgeable and believed in more than writing a prescription. Dr. Lu was the perfect doctor for me. In time, we became friends and talked about family and life during each visit. When Dr. Lu discovered I had arthritis, she sat me down and referred me to an endocrinologist, her friend Dr. Schoenberger. She could see my hesitation about going to see another doctor and assured me that I would like her. So, I trusted her words and I did.

Soon, Dr. Lu decided to leave my network because they were only allowing seven minutes with each patient. On my next visit, the doctor came in and literally in seven minutes was gone. I hadn't gotten a chance to talk to him about the stiffness in my arm. When I told the nurse, she said my seven minutes was up and I had to schedule another appointment. I told her, "Don't worry about it, I am out," and I meant out of that practice. Dr. Lu kept in touch with me and asked Dr. Schoenberger to take care of my health, and for several months, she did. Then, on one of my visits, she told me that she was not a primary physician and I needed to get one because my insurance would no longer pay for the number of visits I was accruing with her. She referred me to her colleague Dr. Gantner. Trusting her word, I scheduled a visit and, to my surprise, she was the perfect doctor for me. To make this a little shorter, Dr. Schoenberger later referred me to Dr. B, or at least that is what I call her, who was a rheumatologist. These three doctors have been my health team for more than ten years now; they know me and my body well. Over the years, they have made me healthier than I have ever been before, and they continue to improve me more and more.

The moral of this is to find a physician that you are comfortable with or, in my case, a health team, but get a physician even if you are healthy. It is better to have it verified. Trust me, I have seen many guys wait until they had no choice but to go to the hospital and then find out that they were so bad off that there was nothing the doctors could do except make them comfortable. Don't be that guy!

As you consider the importance of having a physician in your journey to becoming a healthier you, here are some questions to reflect upon (see page 149 in your workbook):

- Have I established a good relationship with my physician? Assess whether you feel comfortable discussing your health concerns openly and honestly with them.

- Do I trust my physician's expertise and medical advice? Reflect on whether you value and trust their recommendations regarding your health.

- How often do I schedule regular check-ups with my physician? Consider the frequency of your visits to ensure you stay proactive about your health.

- Do I ask my physician questions about my health and treatment options? Evaluate if you actively seek information and engage in discussions about your well-being.

- Am I open to following my physician's recommendations for lifestyle changes or treatments? Reflect on your willingness to embrace their advice and make necessary changes.

As you ponder these questions, keep in mind that having a physician in your corner is an essential component of becoming a healthier you. A strong patient-physician relationship built on trust, communication, and shared decision-making can empower you to take charge of your health and make informed choices for a more fulfilling and vibrant life. If any concerns arise from your reflections, do not hesitate to discuss them with your physician. Open communication is key to building a successful and proactive approach to your well-being.

When I talk about physicians, I am not just referring to general practitioners. Physicians include general practitioners, specialists, surgeons, otolaryngologists (ear, nose, and throat doctors), dentists, and even though they are not medical doctors, optometrists. Of these, there are four that should be a must:

- General Practitioner

- Dentist

- Otolaryngologist

- Optometrist

If you do not have all four of these as a part of your medical team, then it's time to start looking for the one(s) you are missing. They all play a vital role in your healthcare needs. In this next exercise, we will be doing a health assessment on ourselves. In the following exercise, we will list our medical team. You can find this form on page 150 of your workbook, or you can create it in your notebook.

Physician Contact Form

Physician Name	Type of Physician	Physician Phone
Dr. Gantner-Overmyer	General Practitioner	(123) 555-1234
Dr. Patel	Optometrist	(123) 555-9574
Dr. Wyatt	Otolaryngologist	(123) 555-1563
Dr. Daniels	Dentist	(123) 555-8439
Dr. Schoenberger	Endocrinologist	(123) 555-7532

Physician Name	Type of Physician	Physician Phone
Dr. Bukiej	Rheumatologist	(123) 555-2546
Dr. Brown	Gastrologist	(123) 555-6297

Health Assessment Questions

Asking the right questions can provide valuable insights into your well-being. I have omitted some questions on sleep, hydration, and nutrition as they would be redundant to what we have already covered. Here are some questions to consider:

General Health:

1. How would you describe your overall health and energy levels?

2. Do you have any ongoing health concerns or medical conditions? (Yes or No)

Stress and Mental Well-Being:

1. How do you manage stress and cope with daily challenges?

2. Do you experience anxiety or mood fluctuations regularly?

Medical History:

1. Have you undergone any medical treatments, surgeries, or hospitalizations in the past?

2. Do you have any family history of specific health conditions?

Lifestyle Habits:

1. Do you smoke, and if so, how frequently?

2. Do you consume alcohol, and if so, how frequently?

3. Are you exposed to environmental factors that may impact your health?

Body Measurements:

1. What is your current weight and height?

2. Do you have any specific weight or body composition goals?

Vital Signs:

1. Do you regularly check your blood pressure, heart rate, and other vital signs?

2. If yes, are they normal, high, or low?

Pain and Discomfort:

1. Are you experiencing any chronic pain or discomfort in specific areas of your body?

Personal Well-Being:

1. How do you feel about your current lifestyle and overall happiness?

Social Connections:

1. Do you have a strong social support system and maintain healthy relationships?

Medical History Report

This is an important document to have in case of any unforeseen emergency. Even though it is easily accessible to your hospital or doctor, what if something happens and you need immediate medical treatment on the scene and you are unable to communicate? Wouldn't it be nice for someone to be able to provide this document so that you could receive the proper care? This document can be shared with your spouse, family, and employer in case of an unforeseen emergency, allowing you to receive the proper medical treatment you may need. You will find this document on page 151 of your workbook, or you can create it in your notebook. Complete the document as best you can. If needed, feel free to contact your physician for additional information. This is a vitally important document. But remember to keep it safe as it contains much of your personal information as well as your medical history.

Medical History Report

Personal Information

Full Name:	Prefix	First	Middle	Last	Suffix

Date of Birth:		Gender:	Male Female		

Contact info:	Street Address	Apt. or Unit #	City	State	Zip Code

Home Phone:		Mobile Phone:		Email:	

Medical Conditions

Current or Past Condition	Date Diagnosed	Last Treated on	Remission Date

Medication History

List of current and past medications	Prescription Date	Dosage	Frequency (daily, twice daily, etc.)	Completion Date

Surgical History

Previous Surgeries	Date	Outcome	Anesthesia
			Y / N
			Y / N
			Y / N
			Y / N
			Y / N

Hospitalizations History

Reasons for Admission	Admission Date	Release Date	Outcome

Medical Procedures History

Treatments	Admission Date	Release Date	Outcome

Family Medical History

Medical Condition	Relationship	Date Diagnosed or # of Years	Attributed to Death
			Y / N
			Y / N
			Y / N

			Y / N
			Y / N
			Y / N
			Y / N

Immunization History

Vaccination Type	Given By	Date Received	Batch #

Screenings and Tests

Health Screenings (e.g., mammograms, colonoscopies, pap smears, etc.)	Date Received	Results
Diagnostic Tests	Date Received	Results

(blood tests, X-rays, MRIs, etc.)		

Allergies and Sensitivities

Medication Allergies (Penicillin, Amoxicillin, Hydrocodone, etc.)	Date Diagnosed	Date of Last Occurrence	Medication Used to Resolve

Food Allergies (Shellfish, Dairy, Eggs, Berries, etc.)	Date Diagnosed	Date of Last Occurrence	Medication Used to Resolve

Environmental Allergies (Seasonal, Dust, Cat, Dog, etc.)	Date Diagnosed	Date of Last Occurrence	Medication Used to Resolve

Environmental Exposures

Hazardous Substances (Hydrochloric acid, Lead, Arsenic, Radon Gas, etc.)	Date of Exposure	Date Treated	Results

Hazardous Environments (Mines, Nuclear Power Plant, Chemical Plant, etc.)		Date Visited	Duration of Stay	Symptoms

Emergency Contacts

Contact Name	Relationship	Mobile Phone #	Other Phone #	Email

Additional Information

Do you have a signed DNR in place?	Y / N	Are you an organ donor?	Y / N
Do you give permission to treat you if incapacitated?	Y / N	Do you give permission to be transported to the nearest medical facility if you are incapacitated?	Y / N

Additional Notes

Example of a Medical History Report

Caution: Due to the sensitive and confidential information contained on this page, we suggest that it not be shared with employers or other individuals that you do not feel need to know the contents of this page.

Psychosocial History				
Mental Health Disorder *(Depression, Bipolar, Schizophrenia, etc.)*	**Date Diagnosed**	**Date of Last Treatment**	**Treated by**	**Date of Release from Treatment**

Reproductive Health *(Women Only)*				
Pregnancy History *(Childbirth, Miscarriage, Stillborn, etc.)*	**Date of Pregnancy**	**Duration of Pregnancy**	**Procedure Type** *(Natural, C-Section, Surgical, etc.)*	**Date of Incident**

Lifestyle and Behavioral Factors				
Tobacco Usage				
Product Type *(If user state cigarette, cigar, snuff, etc.)*	**Date Started or # of Years**	**How often** *(Daily, Weekly, etc.)*	**Number of Products Used**	**Considered Quitting**
Alcohol Usage				
Product Type *(If user state beer, wine, whiskey, etc.)*	**Date Started or # of Years**	**How often** *(Daily, Weekly, etc.)*	**Number of Products Used**	**Considered Quitting**
Recreational Drug Usage				
Drug Type *(If user state Marijuana, Cocaine, etc.)*	**Date Started or # of Years**	**How often** *(Daily, Weekly, etc.)*	**Number of Products Used**	**Considered Quitting**

Sexually Transmitted Disease				
Type *(HIV, AIDS, Herpes, Gonorrhea, etc.)*	**Date Transmitted**	**Date of Treatment**	**Date of Remission**	**Result**

Remember to share the first three pages of your Medical History Report with your employer, spouse, and other close family members. It is important to be assured that if something should happen, your information may be readily available for first responders and the hospital you may be taken to.

This covers all five areas of becoming a healthier you. By now, you should know your SHEEP (Sleep, Hydrate, Eat, Exercise, Physician) and what you need to grow your SHEEP. By completing this section, you know almost all there is to know about your physical self and what it needs to allow your body to operate at maximum performance. Allowing your body to operate this way also causes your mind and spirit to be accelerated, enhancing your total being to perform at its peak. Soon, we will be referring back to the information that you have generated to create routines, an exercise program, goals, and action steps. Some of the information generated will also be used to assist in managing our time.

This concludes our physical self. Now, we need to create our physical assessment form just as we did in our psychological assessment form. We will gather the data from grooming and SHEEP to see our new physical self.

Physical Assessment Form

On page 155 of your workbook, you will find your physical assessment form or create it in your notebook from the example below. First, we will transfer the information from the daily, weekly, and monthly grooming charts. Then we will input how many hours we sleep per day, how much water and other fluids we drink each day, how often we eat per day, what we eat, how many times we snack, what our snacks consist of, and next, we will transfer the data from our daily, weekly, and monthly exercise charts. Finally, we will use the data from our medical report and our physicians team to input our health information.

Physical Assessment Form			
	Traits	Already have	Need to work on
1	I brush my teeth each morning and evening	☒	☐
2	I rinse my mouth with mouthwash each morning and evening	☒	☐
3	I wash-up or take a shower each morning	☒	☐
4	I take a bath three times a week in the evenings	☒	☐
5	I iron my clothes twice a week	☐	☒
6	I get a haircut 2-3 times per month	☐	☒
7	I get a manicure twice a month	☐	☒
8	I get a pedicure twice a month	☐	☒
9	I wash & dry my clothes twice a month	☒	☐
10	I sleep 6 hours per night	☒	☐

11	I drink 16 ounces of water per month	☒	☐
12	I drink 80-100 ounces of other fluids per day	☒	☐
13	I eat one meal per day	☒	☐
14	I eat a meat, a starch and 1-2 vegetables per day	☒	☐
15	I snack on fruits and nuts each day	☒	☒
16	I stay away from processed and microwaved foods	☒	☐
17	I rarely eat at restaurants	☒	☐
18	I do 25 push-ups each morning and evening	☐	☒
19	I do 25 sit-ups each morning and evening	☐	☒
20	I do 25 squats each morning	☐	☒
21	I do 10 planks each morning	☐	☒
22	I do 25 crunches each morning	☐	☒
23	I jog 3 miles three times per week	☐	☒
24	I go to karate twice a week	☐	☒
25	I go to basketball practice three times per week	☐	☒
26	I see Dr. Gantner twice a year for my check-ups	☒	☐
27	I see Dr. Schoenberger every three months for my hyperthyroid	☒	☐
28	I see Dr. Bukiej every four months for my rheumatoid arthritis	☒	☐
29	I see Dr. Brown once a year to check my esophagus	☐	☒
30	I see Dr. Patel once a year for an eye exam	☒	☐
31	I see Dr. Daniels twice a year for semi-annual cleaning	☒	☐

I did not use all the information; this was just meant to be an example. But it is important that you use all your information as it will be needed later. Once you are done completing the Physical Assessment Form, write an affirmation for your physical self.

Are you done with your Physical Self? Excellent! By completing this task, you have now seen the new you from a psychological perspective and a physical perspective. This means you are ready for the next step in your journey. We will now look at you from a personal perspective. The personal perspective is mainly about how you personally interact with others, your mood, your attitude, and your responses.

ENVISIONING YOUR PERSONAL SELF

We have covered your psychological and physical self. Now, it's time to explore your personal self, which focuses on improving your relationships for the benefit of others. This aspect deals with how you relate to various people in your life. Here is a list of relationships:

- Parental (Child to Parent, Parent to Child)

- Sibling

- Family (excluding parents, children, and siblings)

- Spouse/Love

- Friendly

- Acquaintance

- Professional

Becoming a Better Spouse

Becoming a better spouse is a journey of growth, love, and commitment. It starts with a genuine desire to nurture and strengthen the bond with your partner. This means actively listening to your partner's needs, showing empathy, and being present in your relationship. Being a better spouse involves continuous self-improvement, taking responsibility for your actions, and demonstrating a willingness to learn and evolve. It means understanding and appreciating your partner's individuality, prioritizing quality time, and nurturing your emotional connection.

Embrace generosity and selflessness, showing consideration for your partner's needs and happiness. Invest in daily acts of love and kindness, and maintain open and honest communication. By doing so, you create an environment where both partners feel heard, understood, and valued.

Exercise to Become a Better Spouse

1. How do I show love and affection to my partner daily?

2. How well do I listen to my partner's needs, desires, and concerns?

3. Do I support my partner's dreams and aspirations?

4. How do I handle conflicts and disagreements in our relationship?

5. How do I contribute to the emotional well-being of my partner?

Becoming a Better Child

Becoming a better child involves showing gratitude and love for the sacrifices your parents have made. Take the time to listen to and understand your parents' perspectives, appreciate the lessons and values they have instilled in you, and show gratitude for their love and support. Embrace forgiveness, let go of past grievances, and focus on building a harmonious relationship based on understanding, acceptance, and unconditional love.

Exercise to Become a Better Child

1. How do I communicate with my parents?

2. How do I express gratitude for all that my parents have done for me?

3. How do I handle disagreements and conflicts with my parents?

4. How do I prioritize spending quality time with my parents?

5. How do I support my parents during challenging times?

Becoming a Better Parent

Being a better parent involves nurturing your children while also focusing on your personal development. It means fostering a loving and supportive environment, being empathetic to your children's needs, and communicating effectively with them. Setting boundaries, teaching values, and being willing to admit mistakes are key components of good parenting. Celebrate your children's successes and support them through their struggles.

Exercise to Become a Better Parent

1. How do I prioritize spending quality time with my child?

2. How do I communicate with my child?

3. What are my child's unique strengths and interests?

4. How do I handle discipline and setting boundaries?

5. How do I manage my own stress and emotions when dealing with parenting challenges?

Becoming a Better Family Member

Being a better family member means offering unconditional love, support, and belonging to your loved ones. Strive to be a pillar of strength and positivity, take the time to understand each family member, and celebrate their individuality. Prioritize family gatherings, embrace forgiveness, and practice active listening and empathy.

Exercise to Become a Better Family Member

1. How do I prioritize spending quality time with my family?

2. How do I contribute to the overall harmony within the family?

3. How do I show appreciation for my family members' efforts and contributions?

4. How do I demonstrate empathy and understanding towards my family members?

5. How do I actively listen to my family members' thoughts and concerns?

Becoming a Better Friend

Friendship is a treasure that enriches our lives. Being a better friend involves building trust, understanding, and support. It means being there for your friends during challenging times, celebrating their successes, and offering empathy and encouragement. Friendships positively impact mental and emotional well-being, providing a support network that enriches our lives.

Exercise to Become a Better Friend

1. How do I actively listen to my friends?

2. How do I demonstrate empathy and understanding towards my friends' needs and emotions?

3. How do I show appreciation for my friends' presence in my life?

4. How do I prioritize spending quality time with my friends?

5. How do I support my friends' dreams and aspirations?

Becoming a Better Acquaintance

Building relationships with acquaintances can blossom into meaningful friendships. Embrace every interaction as an opportunity to create a bond. Engage in small talk and casual conversations, be present, and show genuine interest. Building relationships with acquaintances fosters a sense of camaraderie and belonging within your community.

Exercise to Become a Better Acquaintance

1. Am I approachable and friendly when meeting new acquaintances?

2. Do I actively listen and show genuine interest when acquaintances share their thoughts?

3. How do I demonstrate empathy and understanding towards acquaintances' challenges?

4. Do I remember important details shared by acquaintances?

5. Am I respectful and considerate of acquaintances' boundaries?

Becoming a Better Professional

Building professional relationships is essential for career growth and success. These connections provide access to knowledge, resources, and support. Cultivating positive and supportive connections creates a more inclusive and productive environment. Professional relationships enhance reputation, provide a safety net during challenging times, and contribute to personal growth.

Exercise to Become a Better Professional

1. How do I actively listen to my colleagues and superiors?

2. How do I demonstrate empathy and understanding towards my colleagues' needs and challenges?

3. How do I communicate with clarity and professionalism?

4. How do I contribute to a positive and collaborative work environment?

5. How do I handle conflicts or disagreements with my colleagues?

By reflecting on these questions and working towards improvement, you can enhance your relationships and become a better person in all aspects of your life.

Becoming a Better Community Member

Being a part of a community means contributing to its growth, well-being, and harmony. Becoming a better community member involves being actively engaged, showing respect and empathy towards others, and working collaboratively to create a positive environment. It means understanding the needs of your community and finding ways to make meaningful contributions.

Exercise to Become a Better Community Member

1. How do I contribute to my community?

2. Am I involved in community activities or initiatives?

3. How do I show respect and understanding towards my community members?

4. How can I help address the needs and challenges within my community?

5. Am I fostering a sense of unity and collaboration among community members?

Putting It All Together

You have now explored various aspects of your personal self, focusing on improving your relationships with others. By working on becoming a better spouse, child, parent, family member, friend, acquaintance, and professional, you create a positive ripple effect that enhances your life and the lives of those around you. Each relationship is an opportunity for growth, learning, and deeper connection.

Creating Your Personal Self-Assessment Form

Now that you have reflected on your relationships and identified areas for improvement, it is time to create your Personal Self-Assessment Form. This form will help you track your progress and stay committed to becoming the best version of yourself in all your relationships. You can find this form on page 185 of your workbook, or you can create it in your notebook. Here is an example of what the form might look like:

Personal Self-Assessment Form

Traits	Already Have	Need to Work On
I actively listen to my partner's needs and concerns.	☒	☐
I show appreciation and gratitude towards my parents.	☐	☒
I spend quality time with my children.	☒	☐
I contribute to a positive family atmosphere.	☐	☒
I prioritize spending time with my friends.	☐	☒
I am approachable and friendly with acquaintances.	☒	☐
I communicate effectively with my colleagues.	☐	☒
I am involved in community activities.	☐	☒

Writing an Affirmation for Your Personal Self

Once you have completed the Personal Self-Assessment Form, write an affirmation that encapsulates your commitment to becoming a better person in all your relationships. Here is an example:

"I am committed to nurturing and strengthening my relationships with my spouse, family, friends, acquaintances, and community. I actively listen, show empathy, and offer support. I prioritize spending quality time with my loved ones and contribute positively to my community. I am dedicated to personal growth and continuous improvement, creating a harmonious and loving environment for all."

Conclusion

By envisioning and working on your personal self, you take significant steps towards becoming a better person in all aspects of your life. Remember that this journey is ongoing and requires continuous effort, reflection, and growth. Embrace the opportunity to improve your relationships, foster deeper connections, and create a positive impact on the lives of those around you.

Your commitment to personal development will not only enrich your life but also inspire and uplift others, contributing to a more compassionate, understanding, and connected world.

Seeing the New You

We've created a blueprint for our personal self; now it's time to envision and build the new version of you. Picture yourself in each of the relationships we've discussed, and based on your answers to the questions provided, create a list of attributes you need to have in order to be an asset in those relationships. Indicate whether you already possess these attributes or need to work on them. Use the self-assessment chart in your workbook on page 186 or create your own in your notebook.

Example of Relationship Assessment Chart:

Relationship: Husband

Attributes	Already have	Need to work on
I tell my wife I love her every day	☒	☐
I greet her each morning with three kisses and a smile	☒	☐
I give my wife my undivided attention when she expresses her needs, desires, and concerns	☒	☐
I get clarity from my wife after she has expressed her needs, desires, and concerns	☐	☒
I give feedback on my wife's needs, desires, and concerns	☒	☐
I ask how I can help her concerning her needs, desires, and concerns	☒	☐
I support my wife in her dreams and aspirations	☒	☐

Attributes	Already have	Need to work on
I encourage my wife and support her to achieve her dreams and aspirations	☒	☐
I am actively involved in helping my wife achieve her goals towards fulfilling her dreams and aspirations	☐	☒
I am patient and empathetic to my wife when we have disagreements and strive to find a resolution	☐	☒
I never respond in anger during a disagreement with my wife but with love and understanding	☐	☒
I seek to see her point of view before giving a response in a disagreement	☐	☒
I provide comfort, understanding, and a safe space for my wife to express her emotions	☒	☐
I share the responsibility of household chores with my wife	☒	☐
When I see that my wife needs help in her household chores, I take the initiative to do it for her	☐	☒
I set aside quality time to spend with my wife each day	☒	☐
I pray with my wife each day	☐	☒
I have a devotional each morning with my wife	☐	☒
I date my wife 1-2 times per month so that we can have meaningful connections and shared experiences	☐	☒
I show my wife appreciation by telling her how grateful I am to have her on a regular basis	☒	☐
I acknowledge the sacrifices and contributions my wife has made each week	☐	☒
I respect my wife's right to privacy and give her personal space	☒	☐
I give my wife "love is" clippings on a regular basis to show the importance of my love for her	☒	☐

Now, apply this method to each of the relationships we discussed and list all the attributes you've identified from your answers. Indicate whether you possess them or need to work on them. Pause and complete this exercise.

Creating Affirmations for Each Relationship

After completing the self-assessment charts for each relationship, create affirmations for each type of relationship. You can find the forms on pages 198-204 in your workbook.

Example of a Husband Affirmation:

"I am a great husband to my wife. I tell my wife I love her every day, greet her each morning with three kisses and a smile. I give my wife my undivided attention when she expresses her needs, desires, and concerns. I get clarity from my wife after she has expressed her needs, desires, and concerns. I give feedback on my wife's needs, desires, and concerns. I ask how I can help her concerning her needs, desires, and concerns. I support my wife in her dreams and aspirations by encouraging her and being supportive to inspire her to achieve her dreams and aspirations. I am actively involved in helping my wife achieve her goals towards fulfilling her dreams and aspirations. I am patient and empathetic to my wife when we have disagreements and strive to find a resolution. I never respond in anger during a disagreement with my wife but with love and understanding. I seek to see her point of view before giving a response in a disagreement. I provide comfort, understanding, and a safe space for my wife to express her emotions. I share the responsibility of household chores with my wife. When I see that my wife needs help in her household chores, I take the initiative to do it for her. I set aside quality time to spend with my wife each day. I pray with my wife each day and have a devotional each morning with her. I date my wife 1-2 times per month so that we can have meaningful connections and shared experiences. I show my wife appreciation by telling her how grateful I am to have her on a regular basis. I acknowledge the sacrifices and contributions my wife has made each week. I respect my wife's right to privacy and give her personal space. I give my wife 'love is' clippings on a regular basis to show the importance of my love for her. I respect the relationship my wife has with her family and try to duplicate that love to them. I express my feelings and thoughts to my wife regularly. I trust my wife to do things that are in the best interest of our family. Each day I strive to be the best husband that my wife could ever dream of."

Creating Your Personal Assessment Form

Transfer all the data from each relationship into your Personal Assessment Form. This will give you a comprehensive view of your personal self. Use page 205 of your workbook, or create it in your notebook. Here's an example using the spousal relationship chart:

Example of Personal Assessment Form:

Attributes	Already have	Need to work on
I tell my wife I love her every day	☒	☐
I greet her each morning with three kisses and a smile	☒	☐

Attributes	Already have	Need to work on
I give my wife my undivided attention when she expresses her needs, desires, and concerns	☒	☐
I get clarity from my wife after she has expressed her needs, desires, and concerns	☐	☒
I give feedback on my wife's needs, desires, and concerns	☒	☐
I ask how I can help her concerning her needs, desires, and concerns	☒	☐
I support my wife in her dreams and aspirations	☒	☐
I encourage my wife and support her to achieve her dreams and aspirations	☒	☐
I am actively involved in helping my wife achieve her goals towards fulfilling her dreams and aspirations	☐	☒
I am patient and empathetic to my wife when we have disagreements and strive to find a resolution	☐	☒
I never respond in anger during a disagreement with my wife but with love and understanding	☐	☒
I seek to see her point of view before giving a response in a disagreement	☐	☒
I provide comfort, understanding, and a safe space for my wife to express her emotions	☒	☐
I share the responsibility of household chores with my wife	☒	☐
When I see that my wife needs help in her household chores, I take the initiative to do it for her	☐	☒
I set aside quality time to spend with my wife each day	☒	☐
I pray with my wife each day	☐	☒
I have a devotional each morning with my wife	☐	☒
I date my wife 1-2 times per month so that we can have meaningful connections and shared experiences	☐	☒
I show my wife appreciation by telling her how grateful I am to have her on a regular basis	☒	☐
I acknowledge the sacrifices and contributions my wife has made each week	☐	☒

Attributes	Already have	Need to work on
I respect my wife's right to privacy and give her personal space	☒	☐
I give my wife "love is" clippings on a regular basis to show the importance of my love for her	☒	☐
I respect the relationship my wife has with her family and try to duplicate that love to them	☒	☐
I express my feelings and thoughts to my wife regularly	☐	☒

Visioning Your Future Self

Now that you've completed the Personal Assessment Form, it's time to see your future self. Stand in front of a mirror and read all your affirmations. This exercise will empower you to envision the new you with clarity and conviction. Close your eyes and picture yourself using all your strengths, viewing your weaknesses as strengths, receiving feedback for growth, living within your values, and being the vibrant, healthy person you aspire to be.

Continuing the Journey

You have made significant progress, but the journey is far from over. We've covered your psychological, physical, and personal self, but there are still two more areas to address: your professional self and your possessional self. Before we dive into those areas, take a moment to celebrate your growth. Reflect on how far you've come and imagine how much more you will grow as we continue this journey.

Next, we'll move on to exploring and enhancing your professional self.

Envisioning Your Professional Self

Envisioning a new professional life is like crafting a masterpiece where you are the artist, the canvas, and the storyteller. Imagine yourself achieving your professional aspirations, breaking barriers, and reaching heights you once thought impossible. Embrace the feeling of accomplishment and let it fuel your determination.

Envision a career that aligns with your passions and values. When you are fueled by purpose and enthusiasm, each day becomes an opportunity to thrive and make a meaningful impact. Visualize challenges not as roadblocks but as stepping stones towards your goals. Each obstacle presents a chance to learn, adapt, and become stronger.

Give yourself permission to dream big and set audacious goals. Your vision should stretch your limits and inspire you to take bold actions. Picture yourself in an environment that fosters creativity, collaboration, and respect. A positive workplace can enhance your motivation and sense of fulfillment. See a professional life where you continuously seek growth and improvement. Embrace a mindset of lifelong learning and embrace new opportunities for skill development.

Surround yourself with like-minded individuals who inspire and uplift you. A strong support network can provide guidance and encouragement during your journey. Envision celebrating your successes, no matter how small. Recognize and appreciate your progress, as each step brings you closer to your vision. The power of visualization lies in believing that your dreams are attainable. Embrace self-belief and trust in your abilities to navigate the path towards your new professional life. As you envision a new professional chapter, remember that you have the power to shape your destiny. Take ownership of your dreams, and let your vision guide you towards creating a fulfilling and rewarding professional life that reflects the best version of yourself. Embrace the journey with courage, resilience, and a steadfast belief in the limitless potential within you.

Remember when you were little and dreaming of what you would do when you grew up? For most of us boys, we dreamed of being a firefighter, police officer, doctor, or lawyer. We wanted action or lots of money. But we never asked ourselves what would make us happy or what we love doing. Many people enter fields they studied for years only to find it's not what they want to do for the rest of their lives. I know someone who dreamed of being a lawyer, went through all the schooling, and found it too stressful and against his morals. He shifted to being a political advisor and now loves his work while maintaining his ethics.

Understand you can be anything you choose, but it should be something you love and see yourself doing for the rest of your life. It's never too late to change your profession. Envisioning yourself doing what makes you happy is better than wondering what if.

I am 57 years old. Twenty years ago, no one could have told me I would become a life and financial coach or an author. But I love people, helping, empowering, and enriching their lives. Looking back, I've been doing this all my life; now, I do it full time. I've been in finance most of my adult life. I love numbers and helping others overcome financial distress. I've worked in various finance roles, including financial auditor for Citibank, medical collector, credit analyst, insurance sales, and real estate investor. Each job involved finance and people, even my ministry. But most jobs were more about helping corporations than people.

Three years ago, I shifted to becoming a financial coach to help people. When envisioning a new career path, it's crucial to know why you want to make the change. You can be whoever you want and do whatever you want.

Reflective Questions for Envisioning Your New Profession

Before you envision your new profession, it's essential to ask yourself reflective questions that explore your passions, interests, values, and goals. Here are some questions to guide your introspection:

- What am I passionate about?

- What are my core values?

- What skills and strengths do I possess?

- What type of work environment do I thrive in?

- What kind of impact do I want to make?

- What are my long-term career goals?

Professional Exercise

See yourself in the position and ask these questions. Envisioning a new profession is an opportunity for self-discovery and growth. Be open to exploring different possibilities and trust your instincts as you embark on this transformative journey towards a career that resonates with your true self. On page 208 of your workbook, you will find a professional questionnaire or write in your notebook the following questions with your answers.

1. What career or profession have I chosen?

2. Why am I choosing this career path?

   o   To make more money

   o   Fulfill your passion

   o   Help others

3. How much will I earn in this profession?

4. Am I willing to invest time and effort into acquiring any necessary qualifications or certifications?

5. What are the potential challenges or obstacles I may face in pursuing this new profession?

Professional Assessment Form

Now that you have answered these questions, turn to page 210 of your workbook to the Professional Assessment Form or create your self-assessment chart in your notebook. It's okay to have more than one profession. Here is an example:

Example of a Professional Assessment Form

Traits	Already have	Need to work on
I am an Assistant Pastor	☒	☐
As an Assistant Pastor I earn $2,400 per year	☒	☐
As an Assistant Pastor I help others grow spiritually	☒	☐
As an Assistant Pastor I listen to the issues and concerns of others and help them find a resolution	☒	☐
As an Assistant Pastor I preach 1-2 times per month	☒	☐
As an Assistant Pastor I am licensed in the ministry	☒	☐
As an Assistant Pastor I have no set schedule as I am on call 24/7	☒	☐
As an Assistant Pastor I must take care in the advice that I give to members	☒	☐
As an Assistant Pastor I need to be mindful of work and family balance	☒	☐
As an Assistant Pastor I am fulfilling the need to help others	☒	☐
As an Assistant Pastor I am continuously spreading the Gospel	☒	☐
As an Assistant Pastor my ministry aligns with my morals, values, and ethics	☒	☐
I am a Life Coach	☒	☐
As a Life Coach I earn $100,000 per year	☐	☒
As a Life Coach I assist others in their personal growth	☒	☐
As a Life Coach I am certified	☒	☐
As a Life Coach I have many obstacles and challenges to overcome	☐	☒
As a Life Coach I see obstacles and challenges as a learning lesson	☒	☐
As a Life Coach I understand that each individual is different and I treat them according to their needs and level of understanding	☒	☐

Traits	Already have	Need to work on
As a Life Coach I assess each client to determine their needs	☒	☐
As a Life Coach I work 8-10 hours per week	☐	☒
As a Life Coach I always schedule clients around my family life, always prioritizing one from the other	☒	☐
As a Life Coach I fulfill my purpose of helping others	☒	☐
As a Life Coach I fulfill my purpose of being a provider to my family	☒	☐
As a Life Coach my conduct and actions align with my morals, values, and ethics	☒	☐
I am a Financial Coach	☒	☐
As a Financial Coach I earn $150,000 per year	☐	☒
As a Financial Coach I assist individuals in their personal financial growth	☒	☐
As a Financial Coach I educate individuals on finance, teaching financial literacy in elementary, middle, and high schools and in the evenings to adults	☒	☐
As a Financial Coach there are few obstacles and challenges that I have not already overcome	☒	☐
As a Financial Coach I assess each client's finances and understand that each client and their financial goals are different	☒	☐
As a Financial Coach I create a budget	☒	☐
As a Financial Coach I create new revenue streams for clients	☒	☐
As a Financial Coach I develop customized systems for clients to pay off debts faster	☒	☐
As a Financial Coach I create a savings plan that includes a rainy-day fund and an emergency fund	☒	☐
As a Financial Coach I help clients to start/increase their retirement funds	☒	☐
As a Financial Coach I fulfill my purpose of helping others	☒	☐

Traits	Already have	Need to work on
As a Financial Coach I fulfill my purpose of financially educating those I come in contact with	☒	☐
As a Financial Coach I work 10-12 hours per week	☐	☒
As a Financial Coach I fulfill my purpose of being a provider for my family	☒	☐
As a Financial Coach my conduct and actions align with my morals, values, and ethics	☒	☐
I am a Real Estate Investor	☒	☐
As a Real Estate Investor, I earn $250,000 per year	☐	☒
As a Real Estate Investor, I make money	☒	☐
As a Real Estate Investor, I wholesale 5-7 deals per month	☐	☒
As a Real Estate Investor, I Fix and flip 2 properties per month	☐	☒
As a Real Estate Investor, I buy and hold 4 properties per year	☐	☒
As a Real Estate Investor, I create win/win deals for both buyer and seller	☒	☐
As a Real Estate Investor, I increase the value of properties I rehab	☒	☐
As a Real Estate Investor, I know that capital is always an obstacle to overcome	☒	☐
As a Real Estate Investor, I know that maintaining the rehab schedule can be challenging	☐	☒
As a Real Estate Investor, I help others by creating new homeownership	☒	☐
As a Real Estate Investor, I help others by providing great rental units to rent	☐	☒
As a Real Estate Investor, I work 4-6 per week over a period of 9 months	☐	☒
As a Real Estate Investor, I fulfill my purpose of creating a better life for my family	☒	☐
As a Real Estate Investor, my conduct and actions align with my morals, values, and ethics	☒	☐

Traits	Already have	Need to work on
I am an Author	☐	☒
As an Author, I write self-help books to encourage, empower and enlighten others	☐	☒
As an Author, I wrote the Life Progression System	☐	☒
As an Author, I wrote the Financial Progression System	☐	☒
As an Author, I help readers in personal and financial growth	☐	☒
As an Author I encounter many obstacles and challenges such as obtaining the right information, writer's block, getting books published, marketed, and sold, and family interruptions	☐	☒
As an Author, I will sell 1 million copies of the Life Progression System	☐	☒
As an Author, I will sell 300,000 copies of the LPS Workbook	☐	☒
As an Author, I will sell 1.5 million copies of the Financial Progression System	☐	☒
As an Author, I will sell 500,000 copies of the FPS Workbook	☐	☒
As an Author, I work 8-12 hours per day over a 2-month period per book	☐	☒
As an Author I earn $15 million in one year	☐	☒
As an Author, I fulfill my purpose of creating a better life for my family	☐	☒
As an Author, I fulfill my purpose of living an abundant life	☐	☒
As an Author, I fulfill my purpose of living a debt-free lifestyle	☐	☒
As an Author my conduct and actions align with my morals, values, and ethics	☐	☒
I am a Course Creator	☐	☒
As a Course Creator I help other people	☐	☒
As a Course Creator I make money	☐	☒

Traits	Already have	Need to work on
As a Course Creator I created the Debt Eliminator Course	☐	☒
As a Course Creator I created the Debt Annihilator Course	☐	☒
As a Course Creator I created the Debt Conqueror Course	☐	☒
As a Course Creator I help millions of Americans to live a debt-free life in as little as 9 months	☐	☒
As a Course Creator I have over 2 million monthly subscribers	☐	☒
As a Course Creator I generate $100 million per month in revenue	☐	☒
As a Course Creator I helped hundreds of thousands of clients become debt-free	☐	☒
As a Course Creator I fulfill my purpose of building a $1 billion corporation	☐	☒
As a Course Creator I fulfill my purpose of living an abundant life	☐	☒
As a Course Creator my conduct and actions align with my morals, values, and ethics	☐	☒

Creating Your Professional Affirmation

Now that you have completed your Professional Assessment, write your professional affirmation. State what you do for a living and personalize it to what you will be in your new profession. Be as detailed as possible. Go get it done! Stop reading.

Reflect and Empower Yourself

Go to a mirror and read your professional affirmation to yourself. Reflect on how it made you feel. Are you empowered, on fire, ready to start your new profession? Good, that is how you should feel. This inspiration will drive you to take action towards becoming this new professional.

Transition to the Possessional Self

We are now going into the part of envisioning that everyone loves—your possessional self. The possessional self is all about the material things you possess. This is often the first stop many people make, but without preparing the other selves, it can lead to feeling lost. Let's dive into this exciting phase, envisioning the material possessions that reflect your new, empowered self.

Embrace the excitement and possibilities as we move forward!

ENVISIONING YOUR POSSESSIONAL SELF

Envisioning the material possessions and financial wealth you want in life opens the door to boundless opportunities and financial freedom. Allow yourself to dream big and visualize the material possessions you desire. Let your imagination soar beyond any limitations, knowing that anything is possible with determination and hard work. Envision a life of abundance, where you have the financial means to not only meet your needs but also indulge in the luxuries that bring joy and fulfillment. Paint a vivid picture of the material possessions you want, from your dream home to luxurious travel experiences. This will fuel your motivation and direct your actions. Setting ambitious financial goals empowers you to take decisive steps toward building wealth. Envision yourself achieving these milestones, one step closer to financial independence. Envisioning financial abundance helps cultivate a wealth mindset. Embrace the belief that you are worthy of success and prosperity, attracting opportunities to grow your wealth. Envision yourself using your financial wealth to make a positive impact on the lives of others and contribute to causes that are dear to your heart.

As you envision material possessions and financial wealth, challenge any limiting beliefs about money that may be holding you back. Believe in your ability to create wealth and abundance. Envision yourself continuously learning about finances and investing, becoming financially savvy and making informed decisions to grow your wealth. Alongside envisioning your desires, cultivate gratitude for what you already have. Gratitude attracts more abundance and allows you to appreciate your current blessings. Envisioning is powerful, but it must be followed by action. Take inspired steps towards your financial goals, make strategic investments, and persevere with determination. Understand, envisioning material possessions and financial wealth is not about materialism but about creating a life of freedom, security, and opportunity. Embrace the journey of growing your wealth with integrity and purpose, and never forget the potential impact you can have on your life and the lives of others through your financial success. As you align your thoughts, feelings, and actions with your visions, watch as the universe conspires to turn your dreams into a tangible reality of prosperity and fulfillment.

Envisioning your material possessions and financial wealth usually involves a multitude of things, but in this book, I will only be focusing on what I call the majors. You know exactly what I am talking about: the new home, the new car, and an abundance of money. These are the top three possessions that most people focus on when envisioning their possessional self. If I were to include everything we desire in this book, you would not even consider reading it. Why? Because it would be well over five hundred pages. This is why I will be writing a second book entitled "The FPS" or the Financial Progression System, in fact, depending on when you are reading this book, I am probably busy writing it. You need to understand that our possessional wants and desires will always exceed our current earnings and incomes, which is why I am writing the second book, it will teach you financial stewardship, how to increase your monthly income, how to generate passive income streams, and goal setting to reach all of your possessional expectations. But for now, we are going to focus on the top three. I already know you are ready so let's get started.

Envisioning Your New Home

Envisioning your new home is an exhilarating journey of design, comfort, and possibility. Visualize your dream home as the cornerstone of your dream life. Every detail reflects your personality, tastes, and aspirations. Compile images, colors, and decor that resonate with your dream home. A vision board serves as a powerful reminder of your desired space. Envision not only the physical elements but also the emotions your new home evokes - a sanctuary of tranquility, joy, and belonging. See each room with purpose and functionality. Imagine a kitchen that inspires culinary adventures and a bedroom that offers serene rest. Picture a home with a seamless flow and positive energy, where each area complements and enhances the next. Look at your new home as a canvas for creating cherished memories with family and friends, filled with laughter and love. Realize the ability to customize your home to suit your needs, creating a haven that perfectly aligns with your lifestyle. Picture large windows inviting natural light and greenery into your home, connecting you to the beauty of the outdoors. Determine whether it is spacious or cozy, envision a home that allows you to feel abundant, unburdened by clutter and stress.

Embrace the feeling of walking through the door of your new home, knowing that you've manifested your dreams and are living the life you've envisioned. As you visualize your new home, remember that this process is not just about the physical structure but the embodiment of your aspirations and values. Immerse yourself in the joy and excitement of creating your dream space, and trust everything will align to bring you the home that you've envisioned. Your new home is a canvas for self-expression and personal growth, where each corner reflects your unique story and journey. With determination and a clear vision, your dream home is within reach, and soon, you'll be walking through the doors of the place you've always envisioned as home.

New Home Exercise

Before you envision your home, ask yourself some key questions about where you want to live, what your house will look like, its style, its structure, and the materials it consists of. You will find this questionnaire on page 214 of your workbook. Here are some questions you should consider asking yourself before visualizing your new home:

- What type of location suits my lifestyle best? Evaluate the ideal setting for your new home, do you want to live in the city, in the suburbs, or in the country?

- What architectural style or design elements do I love? Explore different architectural styles and interior designs to identify what resonates with your taste and preferences.

- What are my must-have features in a new home? Consider the structure and style of the home. What will the exterior of the home be made of? How many floors do I want? Consider the essential elements that your dream home should include, such as how many bedrooms and bathrooms do I want? What style of a Kitchen do I want? How big should the living room be? Do I want a dining room? Do I want a home office? Do I want a basement?

- Consider what amenities you want in your new home. Do I want a garage? If so, how many cars? Do I want a pool? Do I want it to be fenced in? Do I want a security system? Do I want a deck?

- How do I want my home to feel? Reflect on the emotions and atmosphere you want your new home to evoke, such as cozy, vibrant, serene, or welcoming.

- What lifestyle aspects are important to me? Consider how your new home will support your daily routines, hobbies, and interests.

- How much space do I need for my family's future growth or for potential guests? Anticipate your future needs and ensure your new home can accommodate them.

- How will my new home contribute to my overall well-being? Consider factors such as natural light, outdoor space, and proximity to amenities that can enhance your quality of life.

- Do I want a move-in ready home or a fixer-upper? Decide whether you prefer a ready-to-live-in home or if you're willing to invest time and effort in renovating and personalizing a fixer-upper.

- What are my long-term plans for this home? Envision how this new home fits into your future and if it aligns with your long-term goals and aspirations.

- How important is the neighborhood and community to me? Evaluate the importance of community amenities, proximity to schools, parks, and social activities.

Taking the time to answer these questions will help you clarify your vision and set the foundation for envisioning your ideal new home. It allows you to create a detailed and purposeful image that reflects your unique lifestyle, aspirations, and values, making your dream home a true reflection of you and your family. Now, close your eyes and envision the home that you desire, I want you to do a virtual walkthrough of your home in your mind. Write down what it looks like on the outside, write the details down as you walk through your new home, include the floor coverings, paint color, trim, and moldings. Write down everything you envision on the New Home Chart on page 217 of your workbook or create the chart in your notebook. Here is an example:

New Home Chart

	Description
1	I live in the suburbs of South Barrington
2	I live in a 15,000+ sqft home
3	I live in a traditional style home
4	My home is made of brick and cement
5	My home has three levels and an attic
6	My home has 6 Bedrooms
7	My home has 6.5 baths

	Description
8	My home has an eat-in kitchen
9	My home has an office
10	My home has a library
11	My home has a dining room
12	My home has a living room
13	My home has a recreation room
14	My home has an exercise room
15	My home has a home theater
16	My home has a game room
17	My home has a sunroom
18	My home sits on 10+ acres
19	My home has a 5-car garage
20	My home has an outdoor in-ground swimming pool
21	My home has a pool house
22	My home has a guest house
23	My home has zoned central heating and air
24	My home has a deck outside of the master bedroom
25	My home has his and her closets in the master bedroom
26	My home is located in an excellent school district
27	My home is in a low crime area
28	My home has a state-of-the-art home security system
29	My home has a multi-room intercom and stereo system
30	My new home costs me $850,000.00

Here is a bit of wisdom that I have learned in life: if you are not grateful for the house, condo, or apartment you are in and being a good caretaker of it, it will be extremely hard for you to achieve a new home. So be grateful for where you are, take care of it as if it were your dream home and watch how easier it will be for your new home to manifest.

Envisioning Your New Car

Envisioning your new car is an exhilarating journey into the world of possibilities, style, and adventure. Allow your imagination to run wild and envision the car of your dreams. Picture yourself behind the wheel, experiencing the thrill of owning your ideal vehicle. Consider your lifestyle, family size, and driving preferences to envision a car that perfectly suits your daily needs and desires. Envision a car that reflects your personality and complements your individuality. Let your new car become an extension of your identity. Imagine the sense of pride and joy you'll experience as you take possession of your dream car, a symbol of your achievements and hard work. Picture the adventures and road trips that await you with your new car, creating lifelong memories with loved ones along the way. Envision a car that offers the utmost comfort and luxury, turning every drive into a delightful experience. Your dream car isn't just about aesthetics; envision a vehicle that prioritizes safety and reliability for your peace of mind.

As you envision your new car, consider the places you will visit and the destinations you'll explore, fueled by the freedom of your wheels. Believe in the abundance of possibilities and that the car you envision is within reach. Trust that God will bless you to make your vision a reality. Envisioning your new car is the first step; take inspired action towards making it happen. Research, save, and plan to manifest your dream on wheels. As you immerse yourself in the vision of your new car, remember that this is a journey of excitement, determination, and reward. Embrace the feeling of driving your dream car and trust in your ability to make it a reality. Visualize yourself cruising through life with confidence and joy, knowing that the car you desire is awaiting you just around the corner. With dedication and a clear vision, your dream car will soon become a tangible symbol of success and a source of endless joy and pride. You will find this questionnaire on page 218 of your workbook.

New Car Exercise

Before envisioning your new car, take time to consider these important questions to ensure your dream vehicle aligns with your needs and preferences:

- Am I open to exploring both new and used car options? Decide if you're open to considering both new and used vehicles to widen your choices.

- What are my primary reasons for getting a new car? Identify the specific needs your new car should fulfill, such as daily commuting, family transport, or weekend adventures.

- What are my preferred brands and models? Explore different car brands and models that appeal to your tastes and preferences.

- How many passengers and cargo space do I require? Assess the number of people you need to accommodate regularly and consider your storage needs.

- What features are essential for my lifestyle? Determine which features are must-haves, such as fuel efficiency, safety technology, entertainment systems, or advanced driver assistance features.

By thoughtfully answering these questions, you can develop a clear and informed vision of your ideal new car. This helps you make the best decision that not only brings joy but also serves as a practical and reliable companion on your journey ahead. Remember to trust your instincts and take the time to research and test-drive various options to find the perfect match for you.

I know that some of you may be like me, I want more than one car. I want a pick-up truck, a luxury car, a van for road trips, and a sports car. I know it seems to be a bit much, but remember I dream big, I love cars, I am a versatile guy. Understand the pick-up is for daily use and for cargo space. The luxury car is for church and special events that I attend. The van is for taking the family on vacation and other events. The sports car is for me to have lots of fun. So, if you want more than one car then complete the questions for each car you want.

New Car Chart

On page 220 of your workbook, you will find the new car chart or write it in your notebook from the example below. Before you start, take a look at my example below, then read the next paragraph after you have read my New Car Chart.

New Car Chart	
Vehicle Make and Model	2023 SIERRA 3500 HD DENALI Pick-up
#	Description
1	Ebony Twilight Metallic exterior paint
2	20" LT275/65R20 all-terrain, black wall tires with 20" multi-dimensional Chrome aluminum wheels
3	Jet Black, Forge Perforated Leather seating surfaces
4	Technology Package
5	Snowplow Prep / Camper Package
6	Cargo Convenience Package
7	Denali Illumination Package
8	Denali Ultimate Package
9	6.6L V8 Gas engine
10	8" diagonal Premium GMC Infotainment System with Navigation
11	6-speed, heavy-duty, electronically controlled automatic transmission
12	Power sunroof
13	GMC Illuminated door sills and puddle lamp emblem
14	GMC MultiPro tailgate Step Lights

New Car Chart	
15	It will cost $98,044.00 for my 2023 GMC Sierra Denali

I am only doing one of my vehicles at this time as it would become several pages long. Notice the detail for the vehicle, the better the detail, the more vivid the picture is when you envision it. I must share a little secret that will help you complete this assignment: I used the build-my-vehicle feature at GMC.com to gather the details on my vehicle. You can go to whichever car brand website you want and build your vehicle. They will even allow you to print out a summary report of the vehicle after you have built it with all the packages and options included. This will make envisioning your new car even easier than just using your mind. Isn't technology wonderful! Now that you have my cheat information, go ahead and complete your New Car Chart.

Remember the wisdom I shared with you on the house applies to your new car; if you are not grateful for the car you drive and being a good caretaker of it, it will be extremely hard for you to achieve a new car. So be grateful for what you drive, take care of it as if it were your dream car and watch how easier it will be for your new car to manifest. Now let's talk about money.

Envisioning Your Finances

Envisioning your finances is an empowering journey of financial self-discovery and abundance. Allow yourself to dream big when envisioning your finances. Picture a life where financial freedom is your reality, and your goals are within reach. Visualize yourself making smart financial decisions, investing wisely, and enjoying the fruits of your hard work as you achieve your financial goals. Envision a future where you have a robust emergency fund, insurance coverage, and a solid financial safety net to handle any unexpected challenges. Picture a life without the burden of debt, where financial freedom gives you the freedom to pursue your passions and dreams. Embrace the belief that there is an abundance of opportunities to grow your wealth and achieve financial success. Envision yourself making a positive impact on the world through generous giving and supporting causes close to your heart. See yourself making informed investment decisions that grow your wealth and secure your financial future.

Envision a life where financial worries are a thing of the past, and you have the freedom to pursue your passions without constraints. Define specific financial goals and visualize yourself taking purposeful steps towards achieving each one. As you envision your finances, trust in your ability to overcome challenges and stay committed to your financial plan. Envisioning your finances is not just about material wealth but about aligning your financial decisions with your values and aspirations. It is about embracing a mindset of abundance and recognizing the potential within yourself to achieve financial success. Take inspired action towards your goals and maintain unwavering faith in your ability to create the financial future you desire. With determination, discipline, and an unobstructed vision, you have the power to manifest a life of financial freedom, security, and abundance.

Finance is the number one thing that most people dream of, and I say dream because most people are looking for financial blessings that don't require anything from them, that is not how it works.

We have the ability to acquire any amount of money that we set our mind to having, but it requires us to take action in order to get it. Many of us are often looking for something for nothing and this is why we end up with nothing more than a dream. To be honest, we can never achieve financial freedom if we don't learn to be good stewards in the first place. I am sure that many of you have heard of the story of the three servants and the talents. It goes like this: there was a rich ruler who was going on a journey, and he gave one servant five talents, another two talents, and the last servant he gave one talent, and he told them to take care of his talents until he returned. The ruler then left and after a long period of time he returned home and called the three servants to him that they may give a report of the talents. Well, the first servant came and said to the ruler, "I have taken the ten talents which you gave me and turned them into ten talents, the ruler was pleased and said to him good and faithful servant well done. You have been faithful over a little; I will set you over much. Enter into the joy of your master." Then the second servant to whom he had given two talents reported that he had turned the two talents into four; the ruler was pleased and said to him "good and faithful servant well done. You have been faithful over a little; I will set you over much. Enter into the joy of your master." Finally, the third servant to whom he had given one talent, came in and said to his master, "Master, I knew you to be a hard man, reaping where you did not sow, and gathering where you scattered no seed, so I was afraid, and I went and hid your talent in the ground." Here is the talent you gave me. But his master answered him, "You wicked and slothful servant! You knew that I reap where I have not sown and gather where I scattered no seed? Then you ought to have invested my money with the bankers, and on my coming, I should have received what was my own with interest. So, take the talent from him and give it to him who has the ten talents."

You are wondering why I am telling you this story; well, it is for two reasons: The first is the master gave the talents according to each servant's ability. If we don't have the ability to handle five hundred dollars, what makes us think we can handle fifty thousand dollars. To receive more, we must be able to handle what we already have. When you envision your finances, I need you to first envision yourself being able to handle what you already have before you envision having more. Now the second reason, and this is my belief, God has given each of us talents, but it is up to us to enhance them or bury them and do nothing with them. If you embrace your talents, your passions, and purpose, you will find that it is much easier to have a means of achieving the financial security you are envisioning. For us to expect that we will become financially secure without having a means to do it is mere foolishness. When we envision financial success, we need to have a means by which to earn that financial success. For example, when I envision my financial success, I envision having one million dollars in the bank and a passive income of $5,000 per month. This may sound crazy to some of you, but for me it is achievable. I envision myself writing a book, this book and the accompanying workbook, making $7 from the sale of each book and selling at least 150,000 copies of the book. Now let's do the math: 150,000 copies times $7 profit per copy, which would equal $1,050,000.00. Now as for the $5,000 per month, I envision two ways of achieving that. The first would be to buy rental real estate so that I could earn $200 per month off each unit, which means I would need a minimum of 25 units to meet my goal. The second way would be through financial coaching seminars, creating a seminar that would allow people to attend for $197 and learn how to stop living paycheck to paycheck. By doing one seminar each month and booking 50 attendees that would allow me to profit $5,000 each month. I know what you are thinking that's more than $5,000 a month, it's actually $9,850, but you have to realize there are costs involved. My actual profit from the $197 will be about $100.

Finance Exercise

When you envision your financial success, I want you to envision a revenue stream that will allow it to happen! With that being said, let's move on to envisioning our finances. But before envisioning your finances and setting financial goals, it's crucial to ask yourself these essential questions to gain clarity and plan for a secure financial future:

- What is my current financial situation? Assess your income, expenses, debts, savings, and investments to get a clear picture of your current financial standing.

- What are my short-term and long-term financial goals? Define specific financial objectives for the near future and those that align with your long-term aspirations.

- What are my priorities in life that require financial planning? Consider the things that matter most to you, such as education, retirement, travel, or buying a home, to prioritize your financial goals.

- What level of financial security do I want to achieve? Define what financial security means to you and the level of savings or assets you want to have for peace of mind.

- How can I improve my financial literacy? Explore resources and educational materials to enhance your knowledge of personal finance and money management.

- What strategies can I use to increase my income or improve my earning potential? Consider ways to boost your income through career advancement, side hustles, or investing.

- How much debt do I have, and what steps can I take to manage and reduce it? Develop a plan to address your debts and create a timeline for repayment.

- Am I saving and investing for my future? Review your savings and investment strategies to ensure they align with your financial goals.

- Do I have an emergency fund to handle unexpected expenses? Determine the amount you need to set aside in an emergency fund to safeguard against unforeseen financial challenges.

- How can I develop good financial habits and avoid common financial pitfalls? Reflect on your spending habits and identify areas for improvement to enhance your financial well-being.

Asking yourself these questions lays the groundwork for envisioning a secure financial future. By having a clear understanding of your current financial situation and setting thoughtful financial goals, you can build a robust financial plan that leads to long-term prosperity and peace of mind. Remember that envisioning your finances is not just about monetary gain but also about aligning your financial decisions with your values and life aspirations.

Now that you have answered those questions, I need you to answer a few more questions. Turn to page 223 of your workbook or write the answers in your notebook. To envision your financial needs, you need to know how much you really need; these questions will help you:

- How much do I need to pay off all of my debts? Consider all your creditors, even the mortgage company and people who you have borrowed money from.

- How much do I need for my rainy-day fund? Consider the amount you would want in a savings account for any unforeseen mishap, such as auto repair, appliance repair, unexpected trip, etc.

- How much do I need for my emergency fund? Consider an amount you would need in case of job loss, death of an income producer in the house, etc. This should be 3-6 months of the loss income.

- How much do I want to increase my monthly income by? Consider how much additional money you would like to see coming in each month above your current income.

- What method can I use to acquire my additional monthly income? Think of ways that you can earn the additional monthly income you desire to have.

- How much, if any, of a lump sum amount of money do I want to have? Consider how much money you want to acquire at one time that you would like to see in your bank account.

- How much am I going to spend on my new home? You should already have this amount in your new home chart.

- How much am I going to pay for my new car(s)? You should already have this amount in your new car chart. List each car separately.

Once you have completed answering these questions, you will know the financial position you need to envision. You will also have a general idea of your financial goals. Now close your eyes and envision yourself paying off all your debts, saving for a rainy day and your emergency funds, creating a new monthly passive income, generating a lump sum, and buying your new home and car(s) in cash. Don't forget to set aside 35% of the total for taxation, not that you will pay this much but it is better to have more to pay in taxes than not enough. Include taxation at the end. Can you see it? Okay, it is time to complete your Financial Assessment Form on page 224 of your workbook or create the chart in your notebook from the example.

Financial Assessment Form

Source	Amount
Debt Repayment	$163,000.00
Rainy Day Fund	$2,500.00
Emergency Fund (3-6 months of current top household income)	$48,000.00
New monthly income (1 year)	$60,000.00
Lump Sum	$1,000,000.00

Source	Amount
New home	$850,000.00
2023 GMC Sierra Denali	$98,044.00
Retirement Fund	$20,000,000.00
Taxation	$7,796,090.40
Total	$30,070,634.40

Finance Chart

Now, turn to page 225 in your workbook to the Finance Chart or create the chart in your notebook. Your entry should include how it was allocated (paid, saved, spent, etc.), the dollar amount, what your money was used for, and where it came from. Here is the example:

Finance Chart	
#	Description
1	Pay off $163,000 in debt by allocating 65% of my income from coaching
2	I saved $2,500 for a rainy day by saving half of the money I earned from my first wholesale deal
3	I saved $48,000 for an emergency fund by saving 25% of the money I earned from my first four fix and flips
4	I increased my income by $60,000 per year by adding 1 additional wholesale deal per month
5	I will generate a lump sum if $1,000,000 through the sale of my first 143,000 copies of The Life Progression System book
6	I paid $850,000 for my new home by selling 170,000 copies of The Life Progression System book
7	I paid $98,044 for my 2023 GMC Sierra Denali by selling an additional 14,007 copies of the Life Progression System book
8	I paid $53,000 for my 2023 Kia Carnival MPV by selling an additional 7,572 copies of the Life Progression System book
9	I built a $20 million retirement fund by allowing my company that does course creations to pay 2% of monthly revenue into a SEP account each month as the CEO until SEP account balance reaches $20 million

Possessional Assessment Form

Now to close out your possessional self, we need to complete a Possessional Assessment Form. You will find the form on page 226 of your workbook, or you can create it in your notebook. All we are doing here is taking the information from our new home, new car(s), and finance charts and transferring them onto the Possessional Assessment Form. Also, everything in your Possessional Assessment Form will be checked as need to work on. In the example, I will only be using the first five from each chart, but you will list them all. Ready? Ok, let's get done. Here is the example:

Possessional Assessment Form	
Description	Already have
1	I live in the suburbs of South Barrington
2	I live in a 15,000+ sqft home
3	I live in a traditional style home
4	My home is made of brick and cement
5	My home has three levels and an attic
6	I drive a 2023 SIERRA 3500 HD DENALI SINGLE REAR WHEEL DENALI 4WDMC Sierra Denali Pick-up
7	My 2023 GMC Sierra Denali has Ebony Twilight Metallic exterior paint
8	My 2023 GMC Sierra Denali has 20" LT275/65R20 all-terrain, black wall tires with 20" multi-dimensional Chrome aluminum wheels
9	My 2023 GMC Sierra Denali has Jet Black, Forge Perforated Leather seating surfaces
10	My 2023 GMC Sierra Denali has a Technology Package
11	Pay off $163,000 in debt by allocating 65% of my income from coaching
12	I saved $2,500 for a rainy day by saving half of the money I earned from my first wholesale deal
13	I saved $48,000 for an emergency fund by saving 25% of the money I earned from my first four fix and flips
14	I increased my income by $60,000 per year by adding 1 additional wholesale deal per month
15	I will generate a lump sum if $1,000,000 through the sale of my first 143,000 copies of The Life Progression System book

When you are done, I want you to create an affirmation of your Possessional Self, starting with your dream house beginning with the sentence: "I live in a __ bedroom, ___ bathroom home in whatever location you choose." Include everything you want inside, outside, and around where your home is located. Next, when you are done with your new home, I want you to talk about the new car(s) that you will be driving and just like I did earlier tell why you drive it and its purpose. In your affirmation, start with the sentence: "I drive a (year) (make) (model) with (paint color) exterior." Include everything you want inside and outside your new car. Finally, when you are done with your car(s), I want you to talk about your finances. You will start with a positive message to yourself, something like "my finances are in order" or "my finances are well managed and under control." Everything in your affirmation should be written in the past tense because you are speaking as if it has already happened. By now you should be an experienced affirmation writer. I know it won't take you long! Go ahead and write your affirmation.

See, I knew it wouldn't take you long. This completes our journey of envisioning, now it is time for us to set goals for the vision of our new selves. In the upcoming chapter "Setting Goals" we will talk about the power of setting goals, how to make our goals SMART, and aligning our goals with our MOVE and boundaries

THE POWER OF GOAL SETTING

THE POWER OF GOAL SETTING

Goal setting has the transformative power to turn your dreams into reality. It gives you a target to aim for, a vision to pursue, and a purpose to live by. When you set clear and compelling goals, you unlock your inner potential and tap into the limitless possibilities that await you. Goals act as a catalyst for growth and personal development, challenging you to stretch beyond your comfort zone, break through self-imposed limitations, and discover new levels of capability. With each goal you set and pursue, you become stronger, more resilient, and more empowered to tackle even greater challenges. Goals fuel motivation and drive you forward, even in the face of adversity. When you have a goal that excites and inspires you, you develop an unwavering determination to overcome obstacles, push through setbacks, and persist until you achieve what you set out to accomplish.

The power of goal setting lies in its ability to provide focus and clarity. Goals help you filter out distractions and prioritize your time and energy on what truly matters. They give you a roadmap to follow, ensuring that every action you take aligns with your ultimate vision and moves you closer to your desired destination. Goals expand your comfort zone and enable you to unleash your full potential. When you set audacious goals, you tap into your inner reservoir of strength and creativity, propelling yourself beyond the boundaries of what you thought was possible. With each goal you achieve, you raise the bar for your future accomplishments, cultivating resilience and perseverance. Goals teach you to embrace failure as a steppingstone to success, to learn from setbacks, and to bounce back stronger than before. By embracing challenges and setbacks as part of the journey, you develop the tenacity and determination necessary to overcome any obstacle.

Goals also have the ability to instill a sense of purpose and direction in your life. When you have a clear vision and well-defined goals, you wake up each day with a sense of purpose and excitement, knowing that you are working towards something meaningful and fulfilling. Goals empower you to take control of your destiny, giving you the power to design the life you desire, and to shape your future according to your own aspirations and values. With each goal you set and achieve, you gain confidence and belief in your ability to create the life you envision. Goals create momentum and a positive feedback loop. As you make progress towards your goals, you experience a sense of accomplishment and fulfillment, fueling your motivation to continue to take action. This positive momentum propels you towards even greater achievements and amplifies your personal and professional growth.

In the grand tapestry of life, goal setting allows you to make a lasting impact and leave a meaningful legacy. By setting goals that are aligned with your values and contribute to the greater good, you have the power to create positive change in your own life and in the lives of others. Embrace the power of goal setting, and let it propel you towards a future that is filled with purpose, fulfillment, and endless possibilities.

Your goals are the destination you want to reach, not the directions. But in order to know what goals you need to set you must first visualize your destination; you must know where you are trying to go. I know that may sound confusing, but think of it like this: your goal is the exact address you are trying to reach, and your vision is the city and state where the address resides. In other words, putting an address in the GPS without a city or state can take us to the wrong place, because it will give us the nearest address of our current location. For example, if I want to go to Moving and Storage at 123 Main St. in Los Angeles, CA, and I am in Chicago, IL, and all I do is put in 123 Main Street, the GPS will give me directions to Downtown Food Mart in Downers Grove, IL. Not that I would follow the directions, but if I were to follow these directions, I would be totally confused and lost. The same holds true with the LPS setting goals without a vision will only leave us totally confused and lost. So let's start by creating a vision of where we want to go and then set goals.

Making Goals SMART

SMART goals are a framework used to define clear and actionable objectives. The acronym "SMART" stands for Specific, Measurable, Achievable, Relevant, and Time-bound. Here's a breakdown of each component:

Specific: A goal should be well-defined and clearly articulated. It answers the questions: What exactly do you want to accomplish? Why is it important? Who is involved? Where will it take place?

Measurable: Goals should include criteria that allow you to track progress and determine when you have achieved them. They answer questions such as: How much? How many? How will I know when the goal is accomplished?

Achievable: Goals should be realistic and attainable. While they may stretch your abilities, they should still be within your reach. It's important to consider available resources and constraints when setting goals.

Relevant: Goals should align with your overall objectives and be relevant to your broader aspirations. They should have a meaningful impact and contribute to your personal or professional growth.

Time-bound: Goals should have a defined time frame or deadline for completion. This helps create a sense of urgency and provides a clear target to work towards. It answers the question: When will this be accomplished?

By following the SMART framework, you can create goals that are specific, measurable, achievable, relevant, and time-bound, which increases the likelihood of success and provides a clear roadmap for achieving your desired outcomes.

I am going to break each one of these down so that you will have a better understanding of what SMART goals look like from each of the five guidelines. Understand as I breakdown each of these guidelines, I just want you to get a full understanding of each one of them so that when we start setting goals, it will be easier for you to follow the method and understand it.

Making Goals Specific

Setting specific goals is crucial for achieving success and making meaningful progress in any area of life. Specific goals provide clarity, direction, and focus, allowing you to allocate your time, energy, and resources effectively.

The Power of Specificity: When goals are specific, they are more actionable and easier to understand. Specific goals provide a clear target to aim for, helping you to focus your efforts and avoid distractions. They eliminate ambiguity and allow you to define precisely what you want to achieve. They enhance motivation and commitment by creating a vivid picture of the desired outcome. When you can clearly envision what you're working towards, it becomes easier to stay motivated and dedicated to your goals. Specific goals are easier to measure, which means you can track your progress and determine when you have achieved them. This measurability enhances accountability, as you can objectively assess your performance and make adjustments if needed. When goals are specific, you can identify the resources, skills, and actions required to achieve them. This allows you to allocate your resources effectively, making the most efficient use of your time, money, and effort.

Strategies for Making Goals Specific: To make your goals specific, you need to clearly articulate what you want to accomplish. Be precise and avoid vague statements. For example, instead of saying, "I want to get in shape," specify, "I want to lose 10 pounds and increase my fitness level to run a 5K within three months." Establish measurable criteria that will determine when you have achieved your goal. Use quantifiable indicators such as numbers, percentages, or deadlines. For instance, if your goal is to increase sales, specify, "I want to increase monthly sales by 20% by the end of the quarter." Take into account any constraints or resources that may impact your goal. This could include factors such as time, finances, skills, or available support. By considering these factors, you can make your goals more realistic and achievable. Regularly review your goals to ensure they remain specific and aligned with your overall objectives. As circumstances change, you may need to refine your goals or adjust the specificity to stay on track.

Specific goals are the foundation for success and progress. By making your goals specific, you provide clarity, direction, and focus. Remember to define what, set measurable criteria, identify action steps, consider constraints and resources, and regularly review and refine your goals. Embrace the power of specificity and unlock your potential for achieving remarkable results.

Making Goals Measurable

Measuring goals is a vital aspect of the goal-setting process as it allows you to track progress, assess performance, and stay on course towards achieving your desired outcomes. Measuring goals serves several purposes that contribute to your success. It enables you to track your progress over time, providing a clear picture of how far you have come and helping you identify if you are moving closer to your desired outcome. It allows you to assess your performance objectively. By comparing actual results with the targets you set, you can determine whether you are meeting expectations or if adjustments are necessary. The act of measuring goals creates a sense of accountability. When you have specific metrics to evaluate, it motivates you to take consistent action and strive for improvement. It provides valuable data that can inform your decision-making process. By analyzing the results, you can identify patterns, strengths, weaknesses, and areas for improvement, which can guide your future actions.

Different goals require different methods of measurement. Here are some common approaches to measuring goals:

- Quantitative Measurement: involves using numerical data to assess progress and outcomes. This method relies on metrics such as sales figures, revenue growth, customer satisfaction ratings, or the number of completed tasks. It provides objective and tangible indicators of success.

- Qualitative Measurement: focuses on subjective assessments and observations. It involves gathering feedback, conducting surveys, or using qualitative criteria such as customer testimonials, peer evaluations, or personal reflections. This method provides insights into the quality, perception, and impact of your efforts.

- Key Performance Indicators (KPIs): are specific metrics that directly relate to the success of your goals. They are quantifiable and measurable indicators that reflect performance in critical areas. Examples of KPIs include conversion rates, website traffic, customer retention rates, or employee productivity. Choosing the right KPIs ensures you are tracking the most important aspects of your goals.

To effectively measure your goals, establish specific metrics that align with your goals. Define what success looks like and determine how you will measure it. Ensure your metrics are relevant, reliable, and reflect the progress or outcome you seek. Consistently monitor and record data related to your goals. This allows you to track trends, identify patterns, and make timely adjustments if necessary. Use tools like spreadsheets, project management software, or performance dashboards to streamline the tracking process. Regularly review your measurement data and analyze the results. Compare actual progress against your targets and assess the factors influencing performance. Look for insights, successes, challenges, and areas that require improvement. Based on your analysis, make informed decisions, and adjust your strategies as needed. If you are falling short of your goals, consider modifying your action plans, reallocating resources, seeking additional support, or refining your approach. Continuous iteration allows for continuous improvement. Recognize and celebrate your achievements along the way. Acknowledge milestones and progress, as this fosters motivation and a positive mindset. Celebrations can be personal or shared with others who contributed to your success.

Measuring goals is a crucial aspect of goal setting that enables you to track progress, evaluate performance, and make informed decisions. By employing appropriate measurement methods, setting clear metrics, consistently tracking progress, reviewing results, and adjusting strategies, you can effectively measure your goals and stay on the path to success. Embrace the power of measurement and use it as a guiding tool to drive your progress and achieve meaningful outcomes.

Making Goals Achievable

Setting achievable goals is essential for maintaining motivation, building confidence, and experiencing success. When goals are attainable, you are more likely to stay committed, take consistent action, and overcome challenges along the way. Achievability refers to setting goals that are realistic and feasible. When goals are achievable, you are more motivated to pursue them because you believe they are within your capabilities. Achieving realistic milestones builds confidence and reinforces the belief in your abilities. Realistic goals encourage persistence and resilience. You are more likely to persevere through setbacks and challenges when you believe that success is attainable. This helps you maintain momentum and overcome obstacles along the way. They enable you to allocate your resources effectively. When you set goals that are within reach, you can plan and utilize your time, energy, skills, and resources in a way that aligns with the goal's attainability.

To make your goals achievable, you should divide larger goals into smaller, manageable steps. This allows you to focus on one step at a time, making the overall goal feel less daunting. Each smaller step achieved provides a sense of progress and keeps you motivated. Consider the time required to achieve your goals and set realistic deadlines. Avoid setting overly aggressive timelines that may lead to frustration or burnout. Assess the resources available and the complexity of the goal to establish a timeframe that is both challenging and achievable. Evaluate the resources, skills, and support systems you have at your disposal. Identify any gaps and determine how to acquire or develop the necessary resources. This could involve seeking training, building relationships, or acquiring additional knowledge or tools. Determine which goals are most important and prioritize them accordingly. Focusing on a few key goals at a time allows you to direct your energy and efforts more effectively. By avoiding spreading, yourself too thin, you can devote ample resources to each goal, increasing the likelihood of success. Consider any limitations or constraints that may impact goal achievement. Evaluate factors such as time, finances, commitments, and potential obstacles. Adapt your goals and action plans to work within these constraints, finding alternative approaches or seeking support where needed. Share your goals with others who can provide guidance, feedback, and support. Seek mentors, coaches, or accountability partners who can help keep you on track, provide valuable insights, and offer encouragement during challenging times. Acknowledge and celebrate your progress by setting and celebrating milestones along the way. Recognizing and rewarding yourself for achieving smaller objectives within a larger goal reinforces your motivation and boosts confidence.

Making goals achievable is crucial for long-term success. By breaking goals into smaller steps, setting realistic timeframes, assessing available resources, prioritizing, and focusing, evaluating constraints, seeking feedback and support, and celebrating milestones, you can create a roadmap to success. Remember, achievable goals provide the motivation, persistence, and confidence needed to overcome challenges and experience meaningful progress.

Making Goals Relevant

Setting relevant goals is key to ensuring that your efforts are aligned with your values, aspirations, and broader objectives. Relevant goals are meaningful, impactful, and contribute to your personal or professional growth. Relevant goals serve as a driving force behind your actions and decisions. They hold personal significance and meaning for you. When goals align with your values, passions, and interests, they become a source of intrinsic motivation. Meaningful goals inspire and energize you, making it easier to stay committed and persevere through challenges. Contributing to your overall objectives and aspirations. They serve as steppingstones towards a larger vision or purpose. When your goals are aligned with your broader direction, you create a cohesive and purposeful path for personal or professional growth. They help you prioritize your efforts and resources. They guide your decision-making process and enable you to concentrate on activities that truly matter. By setting relevant goals, you avoid wasting time and energy on pursuits that do not align with your desired outcomes.

To make your goals relevant, reflect on your personal or organizational values and identify how your goals align with them. Determine how achieving your goals would reflect or support these values. This connection provides a sense of purpose and reinforces the relevance of your goals. Evaluate your long-term vision or desired outcome. Examine how your goals contribute to that vision and move you closer to achieving it. Ensure that your goals are steppingstones that propel you in the right direction and support your broader aspirations. Assess the potential impact of your goals on your life, others, or your organization. Ask yourself how achieving these goals would create positive change or make a difference. Focus on goals that have meaningful and lasting impact, beyond just immediate results. Consider the investment of time, energy, and resources required to achieve your goals. Assess whether the investment is worthwhile and aligned with your priorities. Avoid setting goals that may divert significant resources away from more relevant pursuits. Evaluate the relevance of your goals in the context of your current circumstances. Consider factors such as your skills, available resources, and external conditions. Ensure that your goals are realistic and achievable given the current environment. Regularly review and assess the relevance of your goals. As circumstances evolve, your goals may need adjustments to remain relevant. Periodically evaluate whether your goals still align with your values, aspirations, and the broader context. Share your goals with trusted individuals who can provide input and feedback. Seek perspectives from mentors, coaches, or colleagues who can help you assess the relevance and significance of your goals. Their insights can help you refine and strengthen your goal-setting process.

Setting relevant goals is crucial for meaningful progress and personal or professional fulfillment. By connecting goals to your values, aligning them with your long-term vision, considering impact and meaning, evaluating resource investment, assessing relevance to current circumstances, continuously aligning, and reviewing, and seeking input and feedback, you can ensure that your goals remain relevant and purposeful. Embrace the power of relevance and unlock the potential for achieving goals that truly matter to you.

Making Goals Time-Sensitive

Setting time-sensitive goals is essential for effective planning, prioritization, and execution. When goals have specific timelines, they become more actionable, accountable, and achievable. Time sensitivity in goal setting serves several crucial purposes. They help you prioritize your efforts by establishing clear deadlines. They enable you to allocate your time, energy, and resources effectively, focusing on tasks that align with your timeline and desired outcomes. Setting specific timeframes holds you accountable for your progress. It creates a sense of urgency and provides a measurable metric for tracking your performance. Time sensitivity helps you monitor progress, identify delays, and make necessary adjustments. Providing a sense of urgency and motivation. The presence of a deadline can stimulate action, prevent procrastination, and maintain momentum. A time-bound framework encourages consistent effort and helps you stay on track. They facilitate effective planning and resource allocation. With a specific timeframe in mind, you can better estimate the resources, tasks, and milestones required to achieve your goals. This enables you to create a realistic and actionable plan.

To make your goals time-sensitive, you need to establish specific deadlines for your goals. Consider the complexity and scope of the goal, along with your other commitments. Be realistic in your time allocations, ensuring they provide a sense of challenge without becoming unattainable. Divide larger goals into smaller milestones with individual deadlines. This allows for more focused planning and progress tracking. Breaking goals down into manageable chunks helps prevent overwhelm and ensures consistent progress. Utilize the SMART framework (Specific, Measurable, Achievable, Relevant, Time-bound) when setting goals. The "T" in SMART emphasizes the importance of setting time-sensitive goals. Ensure that each goal has a clear timeframe that aligns with your overall plan. Start with your desired outcome and work backward to determine the necessary steps and associated timelines. Consider the sequence of tasks, dependencies, and the time required for each phase. This approach helps create a realistic timeline for goal attainment. Once you have established deadlines, prioritize the tasks required to achieve your goals. Identify critical tasks that have the greatest impact on goal attainment and allocate time accordingly. By focusing on high-priority tasks, you can make efficient use of your time. Implement effective time management techniques to optimize your productivity and efficiency. Techniques such as time blocking, Pomodoro Technique, or Eisenhower Matrix can help you allocate time effectively and make progress toward your goals. (We will go into further details about these techniques in the time management section.) Continuously review your progress against the established deadlines. Assess if you are on track or if adjustments are needed. Be flexible in adapting your timeline as unforeseen circumstances or new information arises. Recognize and address tendencies toward procrastination. Break tasks into smaller, manageable steps and set deadlines for each. Utilize strategies like setting rewards or seeking accountability to combat procrastination and stay focused on your time-sensitive goals.

Making goals time-sensitive is crucial for effective goal setting and achievement. By setting clear deadlines, breaking goals into milestones, utilizing the SMART framework, reverse engineering, prioritizing tasks, employing time management techniques, reviewing, and adjusting timelines, and addressing procrastination tendencies, you can incorporate time sensitivity into your goals.

Hopefully, you fully understand the importance of having SMART goals by now. Having SMART goals will allow you to transition a lot smoother from being the person you are now into the person you want to become. By providing you with a clear understanding of SMART goals before actually setting our goals, eliminates having to revisit your goals in order to make them easier to achieve. Now when we write our goals, we already know that they should be specific, measurable, achievable, relevant and time-sensitive. Eliminating this step allows us to save time. There is one more thing that needs to be discussed before we actually begin writing our goals out, I have mentioned it before, but I need to make sure that you understand its importance. I cannot stress this enough: we need to ensure that our goals are in alignment with our MOVE and do not cause us to cross any of the boundaries we have set.

ALIGNING GOALS WITH MOVE

Aligning your goals with your morals, values, ethics, and obedience (MOVE) is a transformative journey that fosters profound personal growth. When your goals align with your morals and values, you embrace authenticity, staying true to who you are at your core. By aligning our goals with our ethics, we bring a sense of inner harmony, making decisions in line with our principles. Having goals in sync with our values gives our actions purposeful direction, igniting a passion that propels us forward. Goals rooted in morals and obedience build lasting character, shaping you into a person of integrity and resilience.

When your goals are aligned with your values, you attract opportunities that resonate with your authentic self, creating a fulfilling journey. Facing challenges with our values as a guiding compass strengthens our resilience, empowering us to overcome obstacles with grace. Our alignment with our morals and values inspires others to do the same, creating a ripple effect of positive change.

Personal growth becomes truly fulfilling when we strive for goals that align with our ethics, fostering a sense of purpose and contentment. Goals in harmony with our morals provide clarity in decision-making, enabling us to choose wisely and confidently. Aligning our goals with our values allows us to leave a meaningful legacy, impacting others and making the world a better place. In the pursuit of personal growth, it is vital to remember that the journey is just as important as the destination. Embrace the power of aligning your goals with your morals, values, ethics, and obedience as a compass guiding you towards a purpose-driven life. Let your principles shine through in every decision you make and watch as personal growth becomes a fulfilling and transformative experience. Aligning your goals with your authentic self-empowers you to create a life of significance and impact, leaving a profound mark on your journey and the lives of those around you. By aligning goals with your MOVE, you are assured that they are relevant.

How to Align Goals and MOVE

Aligning our goals with our morals, obedience, values, and ethics is a powerful process that ensures our actions are a true reflection of our authentic selves. Take time to introspect and identify your core values, the principles that guide your life. Use these values as a compass to shape your goals. When setting goals, be mindful of how they align with your values and ethics. Ensure that each goal is in harmony with your authentic self. Consider how each goal may impact your life and the lives of others. Choose goals that contribute positively to your well-being and the greater good. Check if your goals resonate with your inner desires and aspirations. True alignment brings a sense of excitement and purpose to your journey. Trust your intuition when evaluating your goals. Your inner voice can guide you toward choices that align with your highest principles. Stay true to your beliefs and avoid setting goals solely based on external pressures or societal expectations. Allow yourself to adjust and refine your goals if needed. Life may present new insights that lead to even more aligned aspirations. Share your goals with trusted individuals who can help hold you accountable to stay aligned with your morals and values. Celebrate your progress and achievements when you achieve goals that align with your ethics. This reinforces your commitment to staying true to yourself. If you realize your goals are not in harmony with your morals, treat it as a learning opportunity. Use the experience to grow and make more aligned choices in the future. By prioritizing alignment between our goals and our morals, obedience, values, and ethics, we embark on a transformative journey of self-discovery and growth. Aligning our goals with our authentic selves creates a life of fulfillment, joy, and impact. Remember that true success is not solely about achieving external milestones but also about being in harmony with our inner principles. When we align our goals with our deepest values, our journey becomes a meaningful and purposeful adventure that inspires and uplifts both ourselves and those around us.

Question Your Goals

To ensure that our goals are in alignment with our MOVE, we need to question our goals as we are creating them. Here are a few questions to ask yourself during your goal-setting process:

- Do my goals align with my core values and beliefs?

- Will achieving these goals require compromising my ethics or principles?

- Are my goals in line with the person I aspire to be and the legacy I want to leave?

- How will pursuing these goals impact my relationships with others and my community?

- Do my goals contribute positively to the well-being of others and the world at large?

- Will achieving these goals bring me a sense of fulfillment and joy without compromising my values?

- Have I considered the potential consequences of achieving these goals on my mental, emotional, and physical well-being?

- Are these goals driven by my authentic desires, or am I setting them based on external influences or expectations?

- Am I willing to dedicate the necessary time, effort, and resources to achieve these goals in a manner aligned with my values?

- Are there alternative approaches or adjustments to my goals that would be more in harmony with my values and ethics?

Asking ourselves these questions helps ensure that our goals are meaningful and fulfilling and aligned with our deepest values and ethical standards. By regularly reflecting on our aspirations and their impact, we can stay true to our authentic selves and create a life of purpose, integrity, and personal growth. Understand by asking the right questions concerning our goals to ensure that they are in alignment with who we are striving to become. These questions are a part of your Goal Sheet, which we will discuss momentarily.

Anticipating Obstacles and Challenges

Before we start to create our goals, there is one more crucial thing that we need to know: there will be obstacles and challenges. Don't see obstacles and challenges as a bad thing because, while they may look bad, they are actually strengthening exercises in our journey to a better self.

Knowing that they may happen allows us to prepare for them either as we are setting our goals or in the midst of achieving them. But it is better to see them ahead of time and prepare for them in the process of setting our goals. It's kind of like computer programming. One of the most important lines in programming is the if and then statements.

For example, have you ever gone online to sign into your account and entered the wrong password or user ID? You get an error message that may say something like this: "Invalid user ID or password, please try again." That is the if and then statement at work. Behind the scenes, there are codes written for every action that we are required to take. When we enter our user ID, the system has a line of code that says, "if user ID equals user then authenticate password" and on the next line of code it says, "if password equals user password then go to www.whatever.com/home". Now there is also another line of code that says, "if user ID not equal to user, then error message "Invalid user ID or password, please try again" and the next line states, "if password not equal to user password, then error message "Invalid user ID or password, please try again".

Our goals should contain an if and then statement for the moment we think of things that can and may go wrong. This approach allows us to navigate obstacles effectively, maintaining alignment with our values and ensuring steady progress toward our objectives.

OBSTACLES AND CHALLENGES

Obstacles and challenges are an inevitable part of our journey towards personal growth, and embracing them with a positive mindset empowers us to reach new heights. Obstacles are opportunities in disguise, testing our resilience and determination to overcome any hurdles that come our way. Challenges provide valuable learning experiences, teaching us important lessons that contribute to our personal development. Embracing obstacles builds strength of character, allowing us to discover untapped potential and inner resources. Overcoming challenges often reveals aspects of ourselves that we may not have known existed, unveiling our inner strength and tenacity. Challenges test our perseverance and dedication to our goals, fueling our motivation to keep pushing forward. Each obstacle presents an opportunity to develop our problem-solving skills, allowing us to tackle future challenges more effectively. Personal growth takes time, and challenges teach us the art of patience and the value of persistence. Conquering obstacles in our personal growth journey inspires those around us, serving as a beacon of hope and possibility. Every obstacle overcome becomes a milestone on our path to personal growth, reminding us of our progress and accomplishments. By embracing challenges, we accelerate our growth, transforming us into more resilient, self-aware, and compassionate individuals. In our pursuit of personal growth, it's essential to view obstacles and challenges not as roadblocks but as steppingstones on our path to becoming the best version of ourselves. Each challenge we overcome contributes to our growth, shaping us into individuals who can face any adversity with courage, grace, and determination. Embrace obstacles as catalysts for transformation, for they have the power to lead us to a future filled with possibilities and personal fulfillment. Remember that personal growth is a continuous journey, and every challenge you conquer brings you one step closer to the person you aspire to be.

Foreseeing Obstacles and Challenges

Foreseeing obstacles and challenges during the goal-setting stage of personal development empowers us to plan ahead and navigate our journey with wisdom and resilience. Look back on previous personal development endeavors to identify patterns of challenges you have encountered. This reflection will help us anticipate potential hurdles. Consult with mentors, coaches, or individuals who have achieved similar goals. Their insights can shed light on possible obstacles we may face. By talking about goals with those who have already achieved them, we gain access to the obstacles and challenges they faced and learn how they overcame them. Research the path you are embarking on, gathering information on potential obstacles and how others have overcome them. Develop backup plans for anticipated obstacles, allowing you to adapt and pivot when challenges arise. This is where that if and then statement comes in, that I talked about earlier. If we know what the obstacle and challenge may be, we can formulate a plan to overcome it simply by saying if this obstacle or challenge comes then I need to do this. Strengthen your emotional intelligence to handle obstacles with grace, maintaining a positive outlook despite setbacks. Cultivate mindfulness to stay present in your journey, noticing any signs of upcoming challenges and addressing them proactively. Divide your goals into smaller, manageable steps, making it easier to foresee challenges in each phase of your personal development journey. These are the action steps that we will discuss in the next part of the book. Analyze your strengths, weaknesses, opportunities, and threats related to your goals. Understanding potential threats will enable you to prepare accordingly. Adopt a growth mindset that views challenges as opportunities for learning and growth, transforming obstacles into steppingstones. Envision yourself overcoming obstacles with determination, visualizing how you will emerge stronger and more resilient on the other side. Foreseeing obstacles and challenges during the goal-setting stage is not about dwelling on potential difficulties but rather about equipping yourself with the tools and mindset to overcome them. Embrace the journey with open arms, knowing that each obstacle you encounter is an opportunity for personal growth and development. By planning ahead and maintaining a positive outlook, you'll navigate your path with confidence, forging a fulfilling and transformative personal development journey. Trust in your ability to face challenges head-on and remember that resilience and determination are your allies on the road to personal growth.

Identifying Obstacles and Challenges

During the goal-setting process, asking ourselves specific questions can help identify potential obstacles and challenges that may arise. Here are some questions to consider:

- What are the potential roadblocks that may hinder my progress towards achieving this goal?

- Have I encountered similar challenges in the past when pursuing similar goals or aspirations?

- Are there any external factors or circumstances that could pose challenges along the way?

- How might my current habits or behaviors impact my ability to achieve this goal?

- Are there any limiting beliefs or fears that could impede my progress? How can I address them?

By asking ourselves these questions, we can anticipate and address potential obstacles and challenges before they occur. This proactive approach allows us to develop strategies, build resilience, and stay focused on our goals, ultimately increasing our chances of success in our personal development journey. Remember that challenges are a natural part of growth, and by acknowledging and preparing for them, we become better equipped to turn obstacles into opportunities for learning and self-improvement.

Potential Obstacles and Challenges

In our personal growth journey, we may encounter various obstacles and challenges that can test our resolve and commitment to self-improvement. Some of these potential obstacles include:

- Self-Doubt and Fear: Negative self-talk and fear of failure can hinder our progress and prevent us from taking necessary risks.

- Procrastination: Putting off taking action towards our goals can delay our personal growth and hinder our success.

- Lack of Discipline: Inconsistent habits and routines may lead to a lack of progress and hinder our personal development.

- Time Management: Balancing personal growth efforts with other responsibilities can be challenging and requires effective time management.

- Negative Influences: Surrounding ourselves with negative or unsupportive individuals can hinder our motivation and growth.

- Past Traumas or Limiting Beliefs: Unresolved past traumas or limiting beliefs may hold us back from realizing our full potential.

- Comfort Zone: Fear of stepping outside our comfort zone can limit our personal growth and prevent us from embracing new opportunities.

- Unrealistic Expectations: Setting overly ambitious goals without realistic plans can lead to disappointment and discouragement.

- Lack of Focus: Failing to prioritize and focus on our most significant personal growth goals may lead to scattered efforts.

- Overwhelm: Attempting to tackle too many goals simultaneously can lead to overwhelm and burnout.

- External Challenges: Life events, financial constraints, or unexpected circumstances can disrupt our personal growth journey.

- Resistance to Change: Resisting necessary changes or unwillingness to adapt can hinder personal growth.

- Perfectionism: Striving for perfection may prevent us from taking action or accepting imperfect progress.

- Lack of Support: Not having a supportive network or mentorship can make the personal growth journey more challenging.

- Impatience: Expecting immediate results may lead to frustration and discourage continued effort.

Recognizing and understanding these potential obstacles empowers us to develop strategies and cultivate the resilience needed to overcome them. Embracing challenges as opportunities for growth and learning allows us to navigate our personal growth journey with determination, perseverance, and a positive mindset. Remember that personal growth is a continuous process, and every obstacle we face is an opportunity to become a stronger, wiser, and more fulfilled individual. Reviewing this list, you will find that most obstacles and challenges come from within. Many times, during our personal growth journey, our biggest obstacles and challenges come from our fears, phobias, lack of belief, stubbornness, or failure to take action. Overcoming these traits and flaws is essential to achieving our goals.

Overcoming Inner Obstacles and Challenges

Overcoming our inner obstacles and challenges in our goal-setting and personal growth journey is the key to unlocking our true potential and living a life of fulfillment and success. Confronting our inner obstacles leads to self-discovery and empowers us to break free from limitations, revealing the extraordinary capabilities within us. Each obstacle we conquer strengthens our resilience, equipping us to bounce back stronger and more determined to achieve our goals. Overcoming inner challenges fosters personal growth, inspiring us to embrace change and evolve into the best version of ourselves. Confronting obstacles sparks creativity as we search for innovative solutions to overcome hurdles on our path to success. Conquering inner obstacles bolsters our self-belief, allowing us to face new challenges with unwavering confidence. By facing our inner fears and doubts, we unlock hidden potential that propels us towards realizing our dreams. It pushes us beyond our comfort zones, encouraging us to explore new opportunities and grow. Teaching us to embrace change as a catalyst for personal transformation and progress. As we overcome inner hurdles, our determination intensifies, propelling us forward even when the journey gets tough. It aligns us with our purpose, infusing every step of our personal growth journey with meaning and fulfillment. Overcoming inner obstacles is not just about reaching our goals; it's about embracing the journey of personal growth and transformation. By facing our fears, doubts, and self-imposed limitations, we tap into our infinite potential and embark on a path of empowerment and self-realization. Remember that challenges are steppingstones towards greatness, and each obstacle conquered strengthens our resolve to create a life filled with purpose, joy, and a sense of accomplishment. Embrace the process, believe in yourself, and let the lessons from overcoming inner challenges propel you towards a future of limitless possibilities and extraordinary achievements.

Before I go any further, I want to address what I believe are the obstacles and challenges that affect and stunt most of our personal growth journeys: procrastination, fear, and disbelief. Towards the beginning of this book, I talked about belief and fear, and this is why. If you see fear as an obstacle or challenge you are facing, then go back and reread the fear section beginning on page 23. If you find that disbelief is an obstacle or challenge, then go back and reread the belief section beginning on page 17. This leaves procrastination.

Procrastination

Procrastination is a foe that can hinder our progress, but with determination and the right mindset, we can conquer it. Procrastination robs us of valuable time. Embrace the present moment and take action to seize opportunities and achieve your goals. Procrastination stifles our potential. Overcome it to unleash the greatness within you and achieve things you never thought possible. Train your mind to resist the temptation of procrastination. Cultivate self-discipline and focus on the task at hand. It often stems from fear of failure. Use it as a steppingstone to grow and learn, rather than letting it paralyze your progress; opt for progress over perfection. Taking small steps towards your goals consistently can lead to remarkable achievements. Breaking goals down into actionable steps often eliminates procrastination. Overcoming procrastination breaks the cycle of inaction. Each victory fuels your confidence and empowers you to face challenges head-on. Let your actions align with your purpose. Use your goals and passions as driving forces to overcome procrastination.

Share your goals with others and seek support and accountability to stay on track and conquer procrastination. Celebrate your victories, no matter how small. Acknowledging progress boosts motivation and helps overcome procrastination. Procrastination may persist, but so does your resilience. Rise above setbacks, dust yourself off, and forge ahead on your journey to success. Remember that procrastination is a common human tendency, but it's also conquerable. Shift your mindset, replace inaction with purposeful action, and watch as your life transforms. Embrace the power of determination, and you'll unlock a world of endless possibilities, growth, and accomplishment. Procrastination may have had a hold on you in the past, but now it's time to take charge and write your future with intention and action. The journey ahead is yours to create, and with the courage to face procrastination head-on, you will become the master of your destiny. Seize this moment and embark on a path of achievement, fulfillment, and unbridled success!

Let me tell a story about a friend of mine. I won't use her real name, but she was a young woman I will call Lily. She had big dreams and lofty goals, but she struggled with a persistent habit of procrastination. Lily's days were filled with grand visions and exciting plans, but when it came to taking action, she found herself putting things off for later. Lily aspired to start her own business, a cozy café that would bring joy to her community through delicious treats and warm ambiance. She envisioned a quaint space where people could gather, converse, and savor their favorite beverages. However, as days turned into weeks and weeks into months, the dream remained just that – a dream. Each morning, Lily would wake up determined to take steps towards her dream café. She would research the best locations, design ideas, and menu options. However, when it was time to make calls or visit potential suppliers, she would tell herself, "I'll do it tomorrow. Today, I need to relax."

As the weeks went by, Lily's passion for her café business started to wane. Doubts crept in, and she began to question whether she was capable of bringing her dream to life. Her friends and family, who had initially been excited about her venture, noticed her lack of progress and grew concerned. One day, I sat down with Lily for a heart-to-heart conversation. I saw the potential in Lily's dream and believed in her wholeheartedly. I gently reminded Lily that time was slipping away and that her dreams deserved more than just idle thoughts. I encouraged Lily to break her goals down into smaller, achievable tasks and tackle them one by one. Together, we devised a plan, setting deadlines for each step of the café's creation. Lily's excitement reignited, and she began taking action. As the days passed, Lily felt a newfound sense of purpose and determination. She reached out to landlords, negotiated with suppliers, and put her heart into crafting the perfect menu. Soon enough, the dream of her cozy café was no longer just a vision; it was becoming a reality.

With every hurdle she overcame, Lily gained confidence in her abilities. The café finally opened its doors to the world, and it was everything she had dreamed of and more. People flocked to her café, savoring every moment, and praising her for the warm and inviting atmosphere she had created. Lily's story serves as a powerful reminder that procrastination can hinder even the most passionate dreams. However, with the right support, determination, and a willingness to take action, we can overcome this obstacle and transform our dreams into realities. The journey may be challenging, but the rewards of finally bringing our visions to life make every step worth it.

Identifying Procrastination

Identifying procrastination is the first step toward breaking free from its grip and unleashing your full potential. Acknowledge that procrastination exists and be willing to confront it head-on. Awareness is the key to change. Pay attention to the excuses and justifications your mind generates to delay tasks. Challenge these thoughts and replace them with positive affirmations. Monitor how you spend your time each day. Recognize patterns of procrastination and take steps to redirect your focus. Identify the situations, emotions, or tasks that trigger procrastination. Knowing your triggers empowers you to develop strategies to overcome them. Establish specific and achievable goals. Clarity in your objectives minimizes the allure of procrastination and keeps you on track.

Organize your tasks in order of importance and create a plan to tackle them. Prioritization reduces overwhelm and makes progress feel more attainable. Large tasks can be daunting, leading to procrastination. Divide them into smaller, manageable steps, making them easier to approach and complete. Celebrate your achievements, no matter how small. Recognizing progress boosts motivation and helps combat procrastination. Share your goals with friends, family, or a mentor who can offer encouragement and hold you accountable to stay on track. Envision the satisfaction and fulfillment that come from completing your tasks on time. Use this positive imagery to stay motivated and focused. By identifying procrastination, you take back control of your time, energy, and productivity. Embrace the challenge of conquering procrastination as an opportunity for growth and personal development. Believe in your ability to overcome obstacles and let the desire for success fuel your determination. Remember that every step forward, no matter how small, brings you closer to your dreams. Embrace the power of self-awareness and commitment to create a life of purpose, productivity, and achievement. The journey to overcoming procrastination may have its challenges, but the rewards of increased focus, productivity, and a sense of accomplishment are well worth the effort. Step into the realm of action and watch your dreams transform into reality as you embrace a life of purpose, passion, and unyielding progress.

Questions to Prevent Procrastination

To prevent procrastination and stay on track with achieving our goals and personal growth development, we need to ask ourselves some pertinent questions. Asking yourself the following questions can be helpful:

- Why is this goal important to me? Reminding ourselves of the significance and purpose behind our goals can boost motivation and reduce procrastination.

- What potential obstacles or challenges might I face? Identifying potential roadblocks allows us to plan ahead and develop strategies to overcome them.

- How will I hold myself accountable? Establishing accountability measures, such as setting deadlines or seeking support from others, can help prevent procrastination.

- What are the consequences of procrastinating on this goal? Reflecting on the negative outcomes of delaying action can serve as a powerful deterrent against procrastination.

- How will I reward myself for the progress made? Creating a system of rewards for completing tasks can provide positive reinforcement and combat procrastination.

- How can I maintain focus and minimize distractions? Identifying distractions and implementing strategies to stay focused can help prevent procrastination.

- Am I being realistic with my time and resource management? Setting achievable timelines and allocating resources effectively can prevent overwhelm and procrastination.

- Have I learned from past instances of procrastination? Reflecting on past experiences of procrastination can offer insights and lessons to apply moving forward.

By asking these questions and honestly reflecting on our answers, we can gain clarity, focus, and a proactive mindset that helps us overcome procrastination and stay committed to achieving our goals and personal growth aspirations. Remember that progress, no matter how small, is significant, and each step forward brings you closer to becoming the person you aspire to be. Stay dedicated, embrace the journey, and watch as your efforts blossom into transformational results.

By using these simple questions, I have been able to help many clients overcome procrastination. One example is a client I will call Sarah. She was a talented artist with big dreams of holding her own art exhibition one day. Sarah told me of her inspiring vision for her artwork and knew that she had the potential to make a significant impact in the art world. However, despite her passion and talent, Sarah had a significant flaw – she was a chronic procrastinator. Sarah had a studio filled with half-finished canvases, paintbrushes scattered everywhere, and notebooks filled with brilliant ideas. She would spend hours imagining the grandeur of her future art exhibition, but when it came to taking action, she always found an excuse to delay. "I'll start tomorrow," she would tell herself, not realizing that this phrase would become her mantra. Days turned into weeks, and weeks into months, and months became years. Sarah watched as her artist friends showcased their work and gained recognition, while she remained stuck in a cycle of procrastination. Fear of failure and a nagging voice telling her that her work wasn't good enough held her back from taking the necessary steps to achieve her dream. She had even been approached by an art curator from a prestigious gallery, expressing interest in seeing her work. This was the opportunity she had been waiting for, but instead of seizing the chance, she hesitated once again. Doubts and insecurities paralyzed her, causing her to miss the deadline to submit her portfolio.

As time passed, Sarah's procrastination began to take a toll on her confidence and self-esteem. She saw her dreams slipping away, yet she couldn't break free from the chains of inaction. Each day, she felt the weight of her unrealized dream becoming heavier. One evening, as Sarah sat in her studio surrounded by unfinished masterpieces, she finally had an epiphany. She realized that her procrastination was not protecting her from failure; it was preventing her from living the life she had always envisioned. It was time to confront her fears and embrace her dreams wholeheartedly. With newfound determination, Sarah decided to seek help. This is what led her to me. I listened to her story and coached her in overcoming her procrastination. Because she understood her problem was procrastination, there was no reason for me to explain it to her; she had already realized her problem and was seeking my help. I asked her the same questions that I have asked you. I taught her how to take small steps towards her goals, to set daily goals for herself and commit to working on her art for at least an hour each day. Slowly but steadily, she started completing her paintings and refining her portfolio. I had helped her recognize that her work was indeed remarkable. With this encouragement, she mustered the courage to submit her portfolio to the gallery that had shown interest in her work before. This time, she met the deadline and waited anxiously for a response.

To her surprise and delight, the gallery curator loved Sarah's art and offered her the opportunity to hold her very own art exhibition. The moment she had dreamed of for so long was finally coming true. The day of the exhibition arrived, and Sarah stood proudly beside her paintings, which now adorned the gallery walls. As guests admired her work, she felt a sense of accomplishment and fulfillment she had never known before. She had overcome her procrastination, faced her fears, and achieved her dream. Sarah's journey should teach us that procrastination can hold us back from living our fullest potential. However, with self-awareness, determination, and a willingness to confront our fears, we can break free from procrastination's grasp and turn our dreams into reality. Just like Sarah, let us embrace the present moment and take inspired action towards the life we envision. For within each of us lies the power to create our own destiny and manifest the dreams that fill our hearts. But can you imagine Sarah's life without overcoming her procrastination? She would still be dreaming of becoming an inspiring artist. We need to know how dangerous procrastination really is!

Dangers of Procrastination

Procrastination is a thief of time, and its effects on achieving goals and personal growth can be profound. Procrastination robs us of valuable opportunities that could have accelerated our progress and led to remarkable achievements. By postponing tasks, we delay our journey towards success, making it harder to attain the level of personal growth we desire. Procrastination keeps us stuck in the same place, preventing us from evolving into the best versions of ourselves. The longer we procrastinate, the weaker our motivation becomes, making it challenging to muster the enthusiasm needed to achieve our goals. The weight of unfinished tasks and unfulfilled goals can lead to increased stress and anxiety, impacting both our mental and physical well-being. It breeds regret and self-doubt, causing us to question our abilities and worthiness of success. The habit of procrastination distracts us from our priorities, diverting our attention from what truly matters for our personal growth. It squanders our potential and unique talents, preventing us from making a meaningful impact on our lives and the lives of others. It can strain relationships, as unfulfilled promises and unmet commitments erode trust and reliability. Continuously putting off tasks can erode our self-esteem, leading us to doubt our capabilities and worthiness of achieving our goals. Overcoming procrastination is essential to unlocking our full potential and experiencing the profound effects of personal growth and goal attainment. Embrace the power of discipline, determination, and an initiative-taking mindset to break free from procrastination's grip. Take inspired action, even if it is small steps, and watch how each moment of progress accumulates to remarkable achievements. By focusing on the present and staying committed to our goals, we can build momentum, boost our confidence, and propel ourselves towards unparalleled success and personal growth. The journey may have its challenges but remember the transformational impact of overcoming procrastination.

I have a friend; I will call him Mark. He was a talented writer with a dream of publishing his first novel. However, Mark had a habit of procrastinating, and his dream seemed to slip further away with each passing day. Mark spent his days surrounded by stacks of unfinished manuscripts and a desk cluttered with notebooks and pens. He would often tell himself that he would start writing "tomorrow" or "when the time was right." But deep down, he knew that he was avoiding the hard work and vulnerability that came with pursuing his dream. One day I paid him a visit. I had always been supportive of Mark's writing aspirations and believed in his talent. Seeing Mark's struggle with procrastination, I offered my help. "I know how much you want to write that novel," I said, "and I believe in you. Let's work on it together. I can be your accountability partner." At first, Mark hesitated. He was embarrassed to admit that he couldn't find the motivation to write, even though it was his greatest passion. He declined my offer, convincing himself that he could overcome procrastination on his own.

Weeks turned into months, and Mark's unfinished manuscript remained untouched. He found himself sinking deeper into the pit of procrastination, unable to break free from its grip. Each day, he felt the weight of his unrealized dream becoming heavier. Meanwhile, I noticed Mark's withdrawal and frustration. I couldn't bear to see my friend struggle, knowing that he had the talent and potential to achieve greatness. Determined to help, I decided to try a different approach. One afternoon, I surprised Mark by showing up at his doorstep with my laptop in hand. "Let's write together," I said with a warm smile. "We can brainstorm ideas, outline your novel, and take the first steps towards making your dream a reality." This time, Mark couldn't refuse my unwavering support. As we sat side by side, I encouraged Mark to start writing, even if it was just a few sentences. With each word Mark typed, he felt a sense of relief and accomplishment. Over the next few weeks, Mark and I continued our writing sessions. With my gentle guidance and constant encouragement, Mark found the motivation and inspiration he had been lacking. The characters in his novel began to come alive, and the story took shape.

With the progress we were making, Mark started to believe in himself once again. He realized that he did not have to face procrastination alone and that seeking help was not a sign of weakness but a display of strength. Months passed, and Mark finally completed his novel. With my help, he revised, edited, and polished it until it shone brightly. When the day of publication arrived, Mark held his first novel in his hands, and tears of joy streamed down his face. Mark's journey taught him the value of accepting help and the power of having a supportive friend by his side. He learned that it is okay to ask for assistance when struggling with procrastination or any other challenges in life. And most importantly, he discovered that dreams are within reach when we allow ourselves to be vulnerable and accept the help that comes from the genuine love and care of a friend.

The lesson here is twofold. If you are a procrastinator, don't be afraid to allow others to help and support you. And if you know someone who procrastinates, as a friend, you should be persistent and resilient in helping and supporting them to overcome it.

By now, you should be well informed concerning goals. You have learned the power of goals, the importance of creating SMART goals, how to align your goals with MOVE, how to plan for potential obstacles and challenges, and how to take down the greatest foe, procrastination. It is now time to start setting our goals.

Setting Goals

Since we have done most of the heavy lifting already, setting goals will be an easy task. I hope you have completed all the exercises I have given you because it is from those results that you will find most of your goals have already been set. Throughout this entire journey, we have been making baby steps towards this very moment. Think back and remember the journey. Recall how we created the five assessment forms. Those forms actually contain most of your goals; all we have to do is use the Psychological, Physical, Personal, Professional, and Possessional Assessment Forms to set our goals. By restating the information in these assessment forms, we will set our goals. Notice I did say most of your goals; there is one that is not included, and we will find those in our belief exercise on page 4 of your workbook or note from page 18 of the book in your notebook.

Belief Goals

In this exercise, we took our negative beliefs, created a positive belief, and made a list of goals to set in the third column. What you have listed in the third column are the items we want to transfer to our goals forms. Got it? Okay, we are taking the goals to set column and writing them on either the goals form in our workbook on page 231 or in our notebook. Note: In your goals sheet, there is a Tracking and Monitoring section at the end. We will not be completing this section until we reach the chapter on Tracking and Monitoring. You will only see this section in this first example, but it is on every goal sheet in your workbook. Remember, we need to not only transfer the data from the column, but we need to make sure that they are specific, measurable, achievable, relevant, time-sensitive, and aligned with our MOVE.

Here is an example of what your goal form should look like:

Beliefs Goals Sheet

Goal: Repair my credit.

What is the expected outcome of this goal? I will repair my credit to attain a FICO score of 720.

How will I define success in this goal? By reaching a 720 or higher FICO score.

Where am I now in reference to this goal? My credit score is 584.

How will I measure progress and success? By the number of points my score has risen.

What metrics or criteria will I use to track my achievements? I will use the percentage my score has risen in respect to the number of points I need to gain, which is 136. So, 25% would be 34 points and 50% would be 68 points.

Are my goals realistic and attainable given my current resources and abilities? ☒Yes ☐No

If no, what resources do you need to acquire? N/A

What are some obstacles or challenges that can occur?

1. Having the erroneous or outdated items removed in a timely manner.

2. Contacting the creditors.

3. Losing a dispute.

4. Not having items removed even though I prove them to be outdated, erroneous, or illegal.

What steps can I take to overcome potential obstacles and challenges?

1. Be persistent to ensure that items are investigated within the timeline set by the Fair Credit Act.

2. Use several methods of contacting creditors such as certified mail, email, live chat, or calling daily.

3. Determine a way to work with creditors to have items removed through an agreement.

4. Send a letter to credit bureaus stating that the items were outdated, erroneous, and illegal and refusal to remove them will result in complaints and a lawsuit.

Does this goal align with my long-term aspirations and values?

☒Yes ☐No

If no, what changes can be made to align it? N/A

How will achieving this goal contribute to my personal growth and fulfillment?

1. It will increase my credibility with future lenders and creditors, allowing for better terms on future credit, such as interest rates, down payments, and credit limits.

2. It will give me a better sense of security.

Is it meaningful and worthwhile for me to pursue this goal? ☒Yes ☐No

If no, what will make it more meaningful and worthwhile? N/A

How much time do I need to complete this goal? 6 months

What date do you want to start working on this goal? August 15, 2023

What is the deadline for achieving this goal? February 15, 2024

Does this goal align with my core values and ethical principles? ☒Yes ☐No

If no, how can I align it? N/A

Will pursuing this goal uphold my personal integrity and not compromise my beliefs?
☒Yes ☐No

If no, what integrity or beliefs does it compromise? N/A

If no, in what way can I set this goal and allow it to uphold my personal integrity and not compromise my beliefs? N/A

Will this goal violate any of the boundaries I have set for myself? ☐Yes ☒No

If yes, what boundary(ies) does it violate? N/A

If yes, in what way can I attain the outcome of this goal without violating my boundaries? N/A

Using the information above, rewrite your goal to create a SMART goal.

SMART Goal: Repair my credit by raising my FICO score by 136 points to attain a score of 720 in 6 months.

Is this a short-term goal (less than 12 months)? ☒Yes ☐No

Is this a mid-term goal (1-3 years)? ☐Yes ☒No

Is this a long-term goal (4-10 years)? ☐Yes ☒No

Tracking and Monitoring

Method: ☐ Qualifying ☐ Quantifying Metrics:

Milestone 1:_____

    Reward 1:_____

Milestone 2:_____

    Reward 2:_____

Milestone 3:_____

    Reward 3:_____

Milestone 4:_____

    Reward 4:_____

Milestone 5:_____

    Reward 5:_____

Milestone 6:_____

    Reward 6:_____

Milestone 7:_____

    Reward 7:_____

Milestone 8:_____

Reward 8:—————————————————————————

Milestone 9:—————————————————————————

Reward 9:—————————————————————————

Milestone 10:—————————————————————————

Reward 10: —————————————————————————

Progress:

Repeat this process for each goal that you have in the third column until you have completed every goal. We will also be using this form in each of the areas that we will be procuring goals from. If you do not have enough forms in your workbook, feel free to copy the blank form in your appendix as much as you need to for your own personal use. Once you have completed all your belief goals, we can move on to our next set of goals, which is our psychological goals. Note: The Tracking and Monitoring section has been left blank; we will get to that section later in Chapter 33. For those of you who are creating the goals form in your notebook, I have shown it here so that you will know that it is at the end of every goal form, but I will not show it in future examples, so remember to add it at the end of each type of goal form that you see.

Psychological Goals

Our psychological goals can be found on our psychological assessment form on page 251 of your workbook or in your notes from page 106 of the book in your notebook. Your psychological assessment form contains the information from your fears, weaknesses, feedback, the Big Five Personality Test, the Myers-Briggs Type Indicator test, the Enneagram test, the DISC assessment, and MOVE. We will be taking each line in our psychological assessment form and creating our psychological goals. Turn to your next goals form in your workbook or create another goals form in your notebook and begin with the first line in your psychological assessment form. I will give you the first line example from the psychological assessment form example on page 106. Ready? Okay, here's the example:

Psychological Goals Sheet

Goal: Embrace failure as an opportunity for growth and learning.

What is the expected outcome of this goal? To take action even if I fail.

How will I define success in this goal? By taking action whether I fail or succeed.

Where am I now in reference to this goal? Paralyzed by the fear of failure.

How will I measure progress and success? By acting despite the presence of fear.

What metrics or criteria will I use to track my achievements? Based on my continued effort to take action even when I fear I will fail. By learning from actions that do fail and continuing to pursue the project in a different manner until I have gained the desired outcome or results.

Are my goals realistic and attainable given my current resources and abilities? ☐Yes ☒No

If no, what resources do you need to acquire? Accountability partner, motivational book on overcoming failure, mentor or life coach.

What are some obstacles or challenges that can occur?

1. Not acting.

2. Allowing fear to control me.

3. Procrastinating.

What steps can I take to overcome potential obstacles and challenges?

1. Do the action steps until completed!

2. Remind myself that fear has no power over me.

3. Talk to accountability partner, mentor, or life coach about what I am afraid of and get their advice or guidance.

Does this goal align with my long-term aspirations and values? ☒Yes ☐No

If no, what changes can be made to align it? N/A

How will achieving this goal contribute to my personal growth and fulfillment?

1. It will empower me to take action even if I do fail.

2. I may find that I have succeeded.

3. It will increase my confidence and self-esteem.

Is it meaningful and worthwhile for me to pursue this goal? ☒Yes ☐No

If no, what will make it more meaningful and worthwhile? N/A

How much time do I need to complete this goal? 60 days

What date do you want to start working on this goal? August 1, 2023

What is the deadline for achieving this goal? October 31, 2023

Does this goal align with my core values and ethical principles? ☒Yes ☐No

If no, how can I align it? N/A

Will pursuing this goal uphold my personal integrity and not compromise my beliefs? ☒Yes ☐No

If no, what integrity or beliefs does it compromise? N/A

If no, in what way can I set this goal and allow it to uphold my personal integrity and not compromise my beliefs? N/A

Will this goal violate any of the boundaries I have set for myself? ☐Yes ☒No

If yes, what boundary(ies) does it violate? N/A

If yes, in what way can I attain the outcome of this goal without violating my boundaries? N/A

Using the information above, rewrite your goal to create a SMART goal.

SMART Goal: To overcome my fear of failure by embracing failure as an opportunity to improve and grow through experiences within the next 60 days starting August 1, 2023.

Is this goal achievable? ☐Yes ☒No

If no, how can it be restructured to attain the outcome? Extend the amount of time to complete to 90 days and change the start date to September 15th.

Once you have answered this question, rewrite the goal. If you are not able to, then you must erase the goal.

Is this a short-term goal (less than 12 months)? ☒Yes ☐No

Is this a mid-term goal (1-3 years)? ☐Yes ☒No

Is this a long-term goal (4-10 years)? ☐Yes ☒No

Notice in this example, I checked the no box for is this goal achievable. I did this on purpose because this may happen. We may start writing a goal and realize that it is not achievable for some reason or another. In this case, I noticed that the timeframe was too short, and it conflicted with another goal I had. It is good to acknowledge that a goal is not achievable. This allows us the opportunity to make revisions. In this case, all I need to do is change my timeframe from 60 days to 90 days, change my start date from August 1, 2023, to September 15, 2023, and change my end date to December 14, 2023. Next, I will change my SMART Goal to state: "To overcome my fear of failure by embracing failure as an opportunity to improve and grow through experiences within the next 90 days starting September 15, 2023."

Now that you understand how to revise your goals, let's keep moving down the list of our psychological assessment form until we have completed each line. This will take some time, but I don't want you to become overwhelmed or stagnate in this exercise. Remember, this is a crucial part of your personal growth journey. We all want to grow, but understand in order for us to grow, we must take the necessary steps. You don't have to be in a rush to finish it, but you need to finish. Consider this an endurance race and know that the scripture tells us at the end of Hebrew 12:1, "and let us run with patience the race that is set before us." So, take as much time as you need to complete this exercise, and once you are done, you can continue to the next. Repeat this process for each line that you have until you have completed all your psychological goals.

Outstanding! I know it was a long process, but trust me, it is well worth it. Now that you have completed all your psychological goals, it's time to work on your physical goals. Notebook users, remember to add the Tracking and Monitoring portion of the goal form.

Physical Goals

Since we have done most of the heavy lifting already, setting goals will be an easy task. I hope you have completed all the exercises I have given you because it is from those results that you will find most of your goals have already been set. Throughout this entire journey, we have been making baby steps towards this very moment. Think back and remember the journey. Recall how we created the five assessment forms. Those forms actually contain most of your goals; all we have to do is use the Psychological, Physical, Personal, Professional, and Possessional Assessment Forms to set our goals. By restating the information in these assessment forms, we will set our goals. Notice I did say most of your goals; there is one that is not included, and we will find those in our belief exercise on page 4 of your workbook or note from page 18 of the book in your notebook.

Physical Goals

Our physical goals can be found on our physical assessment form on page 271 of your workbook or in your notes from page 144 of the book in your notebook. Your physical assessment form contains the information from grooming, SHEEP, and spiritual you. We will be taking each line in our physical assessment form and creating our physical goals. Turn to your next goals form in your workbook or create another goals form in your notebook and begin with the first line in your physical assessment form. I will give you the first line example from the physical assessment form example on page 144. Ready? Okay, here's the example:

Physical Goals Sheet

Goal: I iron my clothes twice a week.

What is the expected outcome of this goal? No wrinkles in clothes and a sharper dress appearance.

How will I define success in this goal? When I look in the mirror and don't see my clothes wrinkled.

Where am I now in reference to this goal? I barely iron and will wear wrinkled clothes.

How will I measure progress and success? By the number of non-wrinkled items I wear per week compared to the total number of items I wear.

What metrics or criteria will I use to track my achievements? I will count the total number of items I wear each week and determine what percentage of items were not wrinkled.

Are my goals realistic and attainable given my current resources and abilities? ☒Yes ☐No

If no, what resources do you need to acquire? N/A

What are some obstacles or challenges that can occur?

1. Changing my attitude about not caring how I dress

2. Allotting time to iron my clothes

3. Deciding to wear something that needs ironing at the last minute

What steps can I take to overcome potential obstacles and challenges?

1. By having the mindset of "your first impression is your best impression," and that requires my clothes to be wrinkle-free.

2. Schedule a time twice a week to iron clothes.

3. Prepare clothes I will wear at least 3-7 days in advance, this will allow them to be ironed on one of the scheduled days.

Does this goal align with my long-term aspirations and values? ☒Yes ☐No

If no, what changes can be made to align it? N/A

How will achieving this goal contribute to my personal growth and fulfillment?

1. It will allow me to meet my grooming needs.

2. Give me better self-esteem and character.

3. It will give me greater confidence.

4. It will show discipline.

5. It will support my endeavor to manage my time better.

Is it meaningful and worthwhile for me to pursue this goal? ☒Yes ☐No

If no, what will make it more meaningful and worthwhile? N/A

How much time do I need to complete this goal? 30-45 minutes twice per week.

What date do you want to start working on this goal? August 7, 2023.

What is the deadline for achieving this goal? August 6, 2024.

Does this goal align with my core values and ethical principles? ☒Yes ☐No

If no, how can I align it? N/A

Will pursuing this goal uphold my personal integrity and not compromise my beliefs? ☒Yes ☐No

If no, what integrity or beliefs does it compromise? N/A

If no, in what way can I set this goal and allow it to uphold my personal integrity and not compromise my beliefs? N/A

Will this goal violate any of the boundaries I have set for myself? ☐Yes ☒No

If yes, what boundary(ies) does it violate? N/A

In what way can I attain the outcome of this goal without violating my boundaries? N/A

Using the information above, rewrite your goal to create a SMART goal.

SMART Goal: I will iron every Wednesday and Saturday for 30-45 minutes per day starting August 7, 2023, to ensure all clothes for the next 3-7 days are wrinkle-free.

Is this goal achievable? ☒Yes ☐No

If no, how can it be restructured to attain the outcome? N/A

Is this a short-term goal (less than 12 months)? ☒Yes ☐No **Is this a mid-term goal (1-3 years)?** ☐Yes ☒No **Is this a long-term goal (4-10 years)?** ☐Yes ☒No

Just like the psychological goal form, this will take some time, but again, I don't want you to become overwhelmed or stagnate in this exercise. Remember, this too is a crucial part of your personal growth journey. So, take as much time as you need to complete this exercise, and once you are done, you can continue to the next. Repeat this process for each line that you have until you have completed all your physical goals. If you decide you want to continue reading and complete this exercise later, that is your choice, but do me a favor and at least do five so that you have a clear understanding of what you need to do.

If you completed the exercise, you are phenomenal, but if you decided to do five and keep reading, know that you will need to complete all of them before we get to part IV, as they will be needed to complete your action steps. Now, whether you have completed all your physical goals or decided to read on, it's time to work on your personal goals.

Personal Goals

Our personal goals can be found on our personal assessment form on page 291 of your workbook or in your notes from page 158 of the book in your notebook. Your personal assessment form contains information from being a better child, parent, sibling, family member, spouse/love, friend, acquaintance, and professional. We will be taking each line in our personal assessment form and creating our personal goals, just as we did with psychological and physical. I will give you the first line example from the personal assessment form example on page 158. Ready? Okay, here's the example:

Personal Goals Sheet

Goal: I get clarity from my wife after she has expressed her needs, desires, and concerns.

What is the expected outcome of this goal? To understand the needs, desires, and concerns of my wife clearly.

How will I define success in this goal? By being able to fulfill my wife's needs, desires, and concerns.

Where am I now in reference to this goal? I am learning to ask for clarification from her by restating what she says to make sure I have a clear understanding.

How will I measure progress and success? By the number of times I am able to fulfill her needs, desires, and concerns compared to the total requests being made.

What metrics or criteria will I use to track my achievements? Total number of requests divided by the total number of requests fulfilled.

Are my goals realistic and attainable given my current resources and abilities? ☒Yes ☐No

If no, what resources do you need to acquire? N/A

What are some obstacles or challenges that can occur?

1. Being distracted while she is talking

2. Having the time to fulfill her request

3. Seeing the request as valid

What steps can I take to overcome potential obstacles and challenges?

1. Give her my undivided attention when she is speaking or ask her to wait until I can.

2. Schedule a time to fulfill the request and give her an update as to when.

3. If it's important to her, then it should be important to me.

Does this goal align with my long-term aspirations and values? ☒Yes ☐No

If no, what changes can be made to align it? N/A

How will achieving this goal contribute to my personal growth and fulfillment?

1. It will make me a better listener.

2. It will make me more empathetic to my wife's needs.

3. It will make me a better husband.

4. It will create a stronger marital bond.

5. It will create more peace at home.

Is it meaningful and worthwhile for me to pursue this goal? ☒Yes ☐No

If no, what will make it more meaningful and worthwhile? N/A

How much time do I need to complete this goal? 9 months

What date do you want to start working on this goal? August 1, 2023

What is the deadline for achieving this goal? April 1, 2024

Does this goal align with my core values and ethical principles? ☒Yes ☐No

If no, how can I align it? N/A

Will pursuing this goal uphold my personal integrity and not compromise my beliefs? ☒Yes ☐No

If no, what integrity or beliefs does it compromise? N/A

In what way can I set this goal and allow it to uphold my personal integrity and not compromise my beliefs? N/A

Will this goal violate any of the boundaries I have set for myself? ☐Yes ☒No

If yes, what boundary(ies) does it violate? N/A

In what way can I attain the outcome of this goal without violating my boundaries? N/A

Using the information above, rewrite your goal to create a SMART goal.

SMART Goal: Listen to my wife's needs, desires, and concerns empathetically starting August 1st and fulfill as many as possible over a 9-month period.

Is this goal achievable? ☒Yes ☐No

If no, how can it be restructured to attain the outcome? N/A

Is this a short-term goal (less than 12 months)? ☒Yes ☐No **Is this a mid-term goal (1-3 years)?** ☐Yes ☒No **Is this a long-term goal (4-10 years)?** ☐Yes ☒No

Just like the physical and psychological goal sheets, this will take some time, but again, I don't want you to become overwhelmed or stagnate in this exercise. Remember, this is also a critical part of your personal growth journey. So, take as much time as you need to complete this exercise, and once you are done, you can continue to the next. Repeat this process for each line that you have until you have completed all your personal goals. If you decide you want to continue reading and complete this exercise later, that is your choice, but again, please do at least five so that you have a clear understanding of what you need to do.

If you completed the exercise, you are awesome, but if you decided to do five and keep reading, know that you will need to complete all of them before we get to part IV, as they will be needed to complete your action steps. Now, whether you have completed all your personal goals or decided to read on, it's time to work on your professional goals.

Professional Goals

Our professional goals can be found on our professional assessment form on page 311 of your workbook or in your notes from page # of the book in your notebook. Your professional assessment form contains information about your new profession. We will be taking each line in our professional assessment form that has been checked as "need to work on" and creating our professional goals. I will give you an example from the professional assessment form on page #. Ready? Okay, here's the example:

Professional Goals Sheet

Goal: To earn $100,000 per year as a Life Coach

What is the expected outcome of this goal? Increasing my annual income as a Life Coach to $100,000.

How will I define success in this goal? Profiting $100,000 per year.

Where am I now in reference to this goal? I am currently earning $28,500 per year as a Life Coach.

How will I measure progress and success? Progress will be measured based on the increase in dollars I earn as a Life Coach.

What metrics or criteria will I use to track my achievements? I will use the percentage method to measure my achievement on this goal. For example, earning $50,000 represents 50% progress in achieving my goal.

Are my goals realistic and attainable given my current resources and abilities? ☒Yes ☐No

If no, what resources do you need to acquire? N/A

What are some obstacles or challenges that can occur?

1. Finding new clients

2. Maintaining a suitable schedule that will not interfere with family time

3. Finding the right marketplace to advertise in

What steps can I take to overcome potential obstacles and challenges?

1. Create an advertising campaign that will attract more clients.

2. Schedule Life Coach clients around family time.

3. Do market research to find the best place to market in.

Does this goal align with my long-term aspirations and values? ☒Yes ☐No

If no, what changes can be made to align it? N/A

How will achieving this goal contribute to my personal growth and fulfillment?

1. It will help me realize debt freedom.

2. It will allow me to help more people in their personal growth.

3. It will allow me to meet more people.

4. It will give me an opportunity to learn more about marketing.

Is it meaningful and worthwhile for me to pursue this goal? ☒Yes ☐No

If no, what will make it more meaningful and worthwhile? N/A

How much time do I need to complete this goal? 3 months

What date do you want to start working on this goal? October 1, 2023

What is the deadline for achieving this goal? December 31, 2023

Does this goal align with my core values and ethical principles? ☒Yes ☐No

If no, how can I align it? N/A

Will pursuing this goal uphold my personal integrity and not compromise my beliefs? ☒Yes ☐No

If no, what integrity or beliefs does it compromise? N/A

In what way can I set this goal and allow it to uphold my personal integrity and not compromise my beliefs? N/A

Will this goal violate any of the boundaries I have set for myself? ☐Yes ☒No

If yes, what boundary(ies) does it violate? N/A

In what way can I attain the outcome of this goal without violating my boundaries? N/A

Using the information above, rewrite your goal to create a SMART goal.

SMART Goal: To earn $100,000 per year as a Life Coach by marketing to new clients over a 3-month period beginning October 1st.

Is this goal achievable? ☒Yes ☐No

If no, how can it be restructured to attain the outcome? N/A

Is this a short-term goal (less than 12 months)? ☒Yes ☐No

Is this a mid-term goal (1-3 years)? ☐Yes ☒No

Is this a long-term goal (4-10 years)? ☐Yes ☒No

Unlike the personal, physical, and psychological goal sheets, this will take you no time, but I don't want you to get lazy on me now. I know some of you have gotten in the habit of reading past the exercise and finishing it later. They say old habits are hard to break, but since this is a new one, let's break it now. It is important to know that this is a critical part of your personal growth journey. Many people lose focus on their dreams and visions because of the stress and worries brought on by their jobs, careers, or professions. Their need to achieve and succeed becomes just a dream that they die with. Don't let this be you! It's important to do what you love doing, even if it requires you to struggle to get there. I am not saying quit your job; what I am saying is prepare for that new career while working your current job. The struggle comes by sacrificing your current relaxation and sleep habits, giving up TV, not socializing as much, and cutting an hour, maybe two, on your sleep habits to get the necessary knowledge and credentials for the new career. It is better to work hard now and play hard later than to balance play and work; the outcome of such will cause you to continue to work all your life. Trust me, the sacrifices you make in your life while you are young well outweigh the struggle of working when you are older.

Repeat this process for each line that you have until you have completed all your professional goals. So, take as much time as you need to complete this exercise, and once you are done, you can continue to the next. Continuing to read is not an option on this one as it is almost the last one.

Now that you have completed all your professional goals, it's time to work on our last set of goals, which are our possessional goals.

Possessional Goals

Transforming our possessional assessment form into goals will require a slightly different version of our goal sheet, as the possessional goals require a different mindset and a different approach. Our possessional goals can be found on our possessional assessment form on page 162 of your workbook or in your notes from page 331 of the book in your notebook. Your possessional assessment form contains the information about your new possessions. We will be taking each material item in our possessional assessment form. I will give you an example from the possessional assessment form on page 162, line 14. Ready? Okay, here's the example:

Possessional Goals Sheet

Goal: I live in a 15,000+ sqft traditional style brick and cement home with three levels and an attic in the suburbs of South Barrington on 10 acres or more.

What is the underlying reason for wanting this specific material possession? To have more room, allow for guests when they come to town, and allow the space for family events.

How will obtaining this item contribute to my overall well-being and happiness? It will allow me and my family to sponsor more social and holiday events. It will also provide a more serene and peaceful atmosphere for the family.

How will this material possession add value to my daily life or experiences? It will provide safety and security, will be a long-term investment that will allow for equity and wealth creation, and become a family legacy throughout the ages.

Does it align with my personal interests, hobbies, or passions? ☒Yes ☐No

Have I considered whether I truly need this item or if it's more of an impulsive want? ☒Yes ☐No

Does acquiring this possession contribute positively to my overall financial health and stability? ☒Yes ☐No

Do I have a clear plan for saving or budgeting for it? ☒Yes ☐No

Does the cost of this material possession fit comfortably within my budget? ☒Yes ☐No

Have I considered the ongoing costs, maintenance, and upkeep associated with this possession? ☒Yes ☐No

Will acquiring it cause financial stress or impact my ability to meet other essential needs? ☐Yes ☒No

Does this material possession align with the person I aspire to become? ☒Yes ☐No

Will it enhance my personal development and contribute positively to my identity? ☒Yes ☐No

Will acquiring it cause financial stress or impact my ability to meet other essential needs? ☐Yes ☒No

How will this material possession impact my other financial or personal goals? It will enhance my financial position and fulfill my personal goal of making my family safe, secure, and happy.

Will owning this item add any additional responsibilities or tasks to my life? Yes, it will require regular cleaning, continued maintenance, and periodic repairs.

Will it bring a sense of fulfillment, happiness, or satisfaction beyond its functional purpose? ☒Yes ☐No

How will owning this material possession affect my emotions and mindset? It will give me joy, peace, and a sense of accomplishment. It will also increase my self-esteem and confidence.

Will its value and relevance to my life endure over time? ☒Yes ☐No

How long do I anticipate deriving satisfaction from owning this item? A lifetime.

Are there any other goals or experiences that will need to be postponed or sacrificed? ☐Yes ☒No

If yes, what goals or experiences will need to be postponed or sacrificed? N/A

Where am I now in reference to this goal? I am currently in the envisioning stages.

How will I measure progress and success? By tracking milestones such as acquiring the necessary funds, finding the right property, and completing the purchase.

What metrics or criteria will I use to track my achievements? Percentage completion of each milestone and overall progress towards acquiring the home.

Are my goals realistic and attainable given my current resources and abilities? ☐Yes ☒No

If no, what resources do you need to acquire? I will need money from the Debt Conqueror System. I will need 1 million subscribers to the DCS. I will need to increase my knowledge in marketing.

What are some obstacles or challenges that can occur?

1. Finding the right house with all the attributes and amenities that I desire in my new home.

2. Generating enough money to pay for it.

3. Procrastinating.

What steps can I take to overcome potential obstacles and challenges?

1. Be open-minded to a house that the attribute or the amenity can be added to the property.

2. Create an additional revenue stream or increase existing revenue streams to assist in generating the needed funding.

3. Do all the necessary action steps when they are required to be done no matter what.

How does acquiring this material possession align with my long-term goals and aspirations? ☒Yes ☐No

If no, what changes can be made to align it? N/A

Will this item enhance my quality of life or support a specific life milestone? ☒Yes ☐No

How will achieving this goal contribute to my personal growth and fulfillment?

1. It will give me a sense of confidence knowing that I am providing a safe, secure, and serene place for my family to call home.

2. It will comfort me to know that this new home will become a part of my family legacy.

3. It will give me leverage to increase my wealth.

4. It will allow me to have a peaceful space in which to think and be more creative, leading to new ideas, concepts, and creations.

5. It will allow me to socialize more and build a closer relationship with family and friends, as well as meet new people with the same mindset.

Is it meaningful and worthwhile for me to pursue this goal? ☒Yes ☐No

If no, what will make it more meaningful and worthwhile? N/A

How much time do I need to complete this goal? 4 years

What date do you want to start working on this goal? January 1, 2024

What is the deadline for achieving this goal? December 31, 2027

Will pursuing this goal uphold my personal integrity and not compromise my beliefs? ☒Yes ☐No

If no, what integrity or beliefs does it compromise? N/A

In what way can I set this goal and allow it to uphold my personal integrity and not compromise my beliefs? N/A

Will this goal violate any of the boundaries I have set for myself? ☐Yes ☒No

If yes, what boundary(ies) does it violate? N/A

In what way can I attain the outcome of this goal without violating my boundaries? N/A

Using the information above, rewrite your goal to create a SMART goal.

SMART Goal: I live in a 15,000+ sqft traditional style brick and cement home with three levels and an attic in the suburbs of South Barrington on 10 acres or more that costs me $6 million and took four years from when I started on January 1, 2024.

Is this goal achievable? ☒Yes ☐No

If no, how can it be restructured to attain the outcome? N/A

Is this a short-term goal (less than 12 months)? ☐Yes ☒No

Is this a mid-term goal (1-3 years)? ☐Yes ☒No

Is this a long-term goal (4-10 years)? ☒Yes ☐No

All finished? I know that was the easiest one of all. Now that you have completed your possessional goals, we are all done with our goal setting. That is, if you have completed all of your goals—belief, psychological, physical, personal, professional, and possessional goals—then you are golden. You are ready to move forward in the next part of the book. But if you decided not to complete any of the goal exercises, now is the time to go back and finish them all, otherwise you will be missing out on a lot of your personal growth journey. I urge you to complete all the goal exercises before you continue on; it will only make the journey easier for you. Go get it done, and then we can move forward to the next part.

Now that we have all of our goals set, we have a panoramic picture of where we want to go. Our destination has not only been determined, but we should now have a clear and vivid picture of it. We now know where we are and where we want to go. The next step is to get directions on how to get there. While the GPS automatically gives us various routes to take, the LPS does not work quite that way, even though I wish it did! In the next part of this book, we will be discovering how to develop our own routes, which will require some strategic planning.

Part IV

Developing your Route

Importance of Strategic Planning

Just as a ship needs a well-defined route to reach its destination, strategic planning serves as the compass for your personal development journey. It guides you through the uncertain waters of life, helping you navigate challenges and opportunities with purpose and clarity. Strategic planning transforms vague aspirations into actionable goals. It breaks down your larger vision of personal growth into manageable steps, making your dreams more achievable and motivating you to take consistent action. Without a roadmap, you might find yourself taking detours or wandering aimlessly. Strategic planning optimizes your efforts by prioritizing tasks, allocating resources wisely, and ensuring every action contributes to your overall progress.

Personal development isn't without its hurdles, but strategic planning equips you with the tools to overcome them. By anticipating potential challenges and devising contingency plans, you're better prepared to face setbacks head-on and persevere. Tangible progress fuels motivation. A well-structured strategic plan provides measurable milestones, allowing you to track your advancements and celebrate your achievements along the way. These small wins propel you forward, reinforcing your commitment to personal development.

Life is unpredictable, and unexpected shifts can disrupt your journey. Strategic planning encourages flexibility, helping you adapt to change while staying focused on your ultimate objectives. This resilience ensures you stay on track, even when faced with the unexpected. In the process of strategic planning, you delve deep into your strengths, weaknesses, and values. This self-awareness empowers you to make informed decisions aligned with your true self, fostering personal growth that is authentic and fulfilling.

Consistency is key to personal development. Strategic planning cultivates discipline by creating routines and setting specific deadlines. As you consistently work towards your goals, you strengthen your ability to stay dedicated and resilient in the face of challenges. Strategic planning pushes you beyond your comfort zone and encourages you to explore new avenues. By setting ambitious yet achievable targets, you challenge yourself to tap into your full potential and discover capabilities you might have never realized otherwise. Your personal development journey isn't just about you; it impacts the world around you. A well-executed strategic plan helps you create a positive and lasting legacy by inspiring others with your growth story and contributing meaningfully to your community.

Embarking on a journey of personal growth is akin to setting sail into uncharted waters. In this voyage, strategic planning becomes your guiding star, illuminating the path ahead and shaping your course. Just as a sailor charts a map to navigate the tides, you too must meticulously plan your route to self-discovery and transformation. Strategic planning empowers you to set clear intentions, define your objectives, and outline the steppingstones that will lead you towards your aspirations. However, a map alone does not guarantee progress; action steps are the sails that harness the winds of change. With each step you take, you propel yourself closer to the horizon of your potential, leaving behind the comfort of the shore. The harmony between strategic planning and action steps is the symphony of personal growth, orchestrating the transformation of dreams into reality. So, let your aspirations be your North Star, strategic planning your compass, and action steps your sails. As you navigate the currents of growth, remember that the journey is not solely in the destination, but in the wisdom gained and the strength cultivated through every strategic step you take.

ACTION STEPS

Action steps are specific, tangible tasks or activities you undertake to achieve a larger goal. They are the practical actions that turn your aspirations and plans into reality. Action steps provide a clear roadmap for accomplishing your goals by breaking down the overall process into manageable and actionable components.

In the realm of personal growth, action steps are the sparks that ignite the flames of transformation. They breathe life into your dreams, turning intentions into tangible achievements. With each step you take, you inch closer to becoming the person you envision, reshaping your identity through purposeful action. They empower you to transcend limitations and push boundaries. Through deliberate actions, you embrace discomfort, challenge your comfort zone, and unveil the limitless potential within you. Like a snowball gathering momentum as it rolls downhill, action steps generate their own force. The more you commit to these steps, the more unstoppable you become. With each accomplishment, your confidence grows, propelling you toward even loftier goals.

Dreams without action steps remain elusive fantasies. It's the strategic execution of these steps that bridges the gap between your aspirations and your reality. As you convert your dreams into actionable plans, you rewrite your story, demonstrating to yourself and the world that anything is attainable. The classroom of life is where you truly learn and grow, and action steps are your lessons. By actively engaging in your personal growth journey, you acquire wisdom, resilience, and insight that no amount of passive contemplation can provide. Embrace action as your teacher and guide.

Action steps foster a sense of self-reliance and autonomy. As you take charge of your growth journey, you develop the ability to shape your destiny, adapt to challenges, and overcome obstacles. Each step you conquer reinforces your belief in your capacity for greatness. The act of committing to action steps instills a powerful sense of determination. It sends a message to your subconscious that you're serious about your growth. This determination fuels your efforts, reminding you that you're in control of your trajectory. The path of personal growth is not always smooth, but action steps are bridges over adversity. They teach you to bounce back from setbacks, turning failures into opportunities for growth. The resilience you cultivate through action serves you not only in your journey but also in all aspects of life.

Action steps align your thoughts, emotions, and behaviors with your goals. The universe responds to your deliberate efforts, attracting opportunities and resources that support your growth. As you take action, you become a magnet for the very success you seek. In the symphony of personal growth, action steps are the notes that compose a harmonious melody of change. They form the rhythm of your progress, leaving an indelible mark on your character, accomplishments, and the legacy you leave behind. Action steps empower you to step into your potential, embrace challenges, and realize your aspirations. Through the consistent execution of action steps, you elevate yourself and inspire others to embark on their own transformative paths. Remember, it's in the act of doing that you truly become the architect of your destiny.

Without action steps, your goals are almost pointless. Setting goals without action steps is like planning a trip and never getting into the car. When we set goals but don't take action, we will never fulfill our dreams and aspirations. We will never grow and continue to be stagnated in the life we are in. James 2:17 puts it best: "Even so faith, if it hath not works, is dead, being alone." Our goals are based on faith and our action steps are the work. Goals without action are just pipe dreams that will never come to fruition. Galatians 6:9 also clearly states, "And let us not be weary in well doing: for in due season we shall reap, if we faint not." If you want to achieve success in this journey, you must take action. However, most people don't have a strategic plan that includes actual action steps. This causes them to lose momentum, become flustered, and give up on their dreams and aspirations. I don't want any of you to be one of those people. You have come too far not to finish the journey. So, let's turn our goals into actions by creating action steps.

Turning Goals into Action Steps

Your goals are the seeds of your dreams, but action steps are the nourishment that makes them grow. Each action step you take is a decisive move towards turning your aspirations into reality. Just as a sculptor shapes a masterpiece through careful strokes, your action steps mold your journey of success. Turning goals into action steps is like adding colors to a canvas. Your goals remain dainty until you take the brush of action and start painting. Action steps provide structure to your dreams, outlining the contours of your ambitions and bringing them into vivid existence.

Motivation alone is a spark; action steps are the fuel that keeps the fire burning. They transform fleeting enthusiasm into lasting dedication. As you embark on each action step, you stoke the flames of your passion, propelling you towards your desired destination. Goals can seem daunting when viewed as a whole, but action steps break them into manageable pieces. Like a puzzle, they allow you to tackle one piece at a time, gradually assembling the complete picture of your achievement. Action steps remind you that progress is more valuable than perfection. By taking consistent steps forward, you learn, adapt, and grow. Embrace imperfection as a sign of your active engagement and commitment to improvement.

The process of turning goals into action steps cultivates discipline—a vital trait on the path to success. Consistently executing each step hones your ability to focus, make deliberate choices, and stay committed even when challenges arise. They are the bridge that spans the gap between where you are now and where you want to be. They provide the practical means to cross over from the realm of intention to the realm of accomplishment. With each step, you traverse closer to the fulfillment of your dreams.

Just as a rolling stone gathers no moss, action steps create momentum that propels you forward. Each completed step energizes you, making the next one feel less daunting. Momentum becomes your ally, accelerating your progress and making achievement inevitable. Turning goals into action steps gives you ownership over your aspirations. It's a declaration that you are in control of your destiny and are committed to shaping your future. Each action step is a testament to your autonomy and the authorship of your story. Your goals represent your legacy in the making, and action steps are the chapters that compose it. By consistently turning your goals into actionable plans, you craft a narrative of determination, resilience, and achievement. Your legacy is a testament to your commitment to turning dreams into reality.

Turning goals into action steps is the art of making your ambitions come alive. It's the process of bridging intention and achievement, embracing progress, and leaving an indelible mark on the canvas of your life. Through deliberate action, you claim your place as the architect of your destiny, inspiring others to follow in your footsteps.

One of the greatest quotes I have ever heard about this matter came from Denzel Washington: "Dreams without goals are just dreams." In order for us to change a dream to reality, we must take a chance. Nothing in life is certain except death, and in order to take the chance, it requires action. I know most of you know the story of David and Goliath; it is an epic and memorable story, but most people only see the two main characters and miss one of the greatest lessons in life. What many people overlook is the army of Israel. They had gone out to battle with a goal to win, but because of Goliath, they were now living in fear. The goal of winning this battle had gone from being a goal to being a pipe dream. They had already made up their minds that they could not win. The fear of Goliath's size had paralyzed them, taking away all their courage and beliefs, but most importantly, it took away their ability to take the necessary action to fulfill their goal. David, on the other hand, a small, scrawny, teenage boy, believed he could win based on his belief. The difference between this small, scrawny teenager and the entire Israelite army of big, strong, well-built men trained to be soldiers was that David saw his obstacle and was willing, despite all the evidence compiled against him, to move forward.

The first thing that David did before facing Goliath was create a plan. He equipped himself with five stones and a slingshot. The plan was to kill Goliath with a slingshot and a stone. The second thing that David did was create an affirmation that empowered him. The final thing that David did was act, and not only did he take action, but he tackled it without haste. The story says that David ran. Then it says he took a stone from his bag, put it in the slingshot, and slung it right into the forehead of Goliath, causing Goliath to immediately fall dead to the ground. David then claimed his victory by cutting off the head of Goliath with a sword. Without David's action, the Israelites would have become the servants of the Philistines that very day. David saw his goal, affirmed it, and took the needed action to make it a reality.

Are you ready to take the necessary actions to make your goals a reality? I hope you answered yes. Otherwise, reading this book and all that you have done thus far has been not only in vain but a sheer waste of time. But I know if you have come this far, you are going all the way. You are fully invested in reaching your destination. You are not just ready and willing to turn your goals and aspirations into reality; you are able. It's time for us to take action by creating action steps to turn our goals into reality. Let's go!

STEP 1: Listing Your Action Steps

Turning goals into actionable steps involves breaking down your larger objectives into smaller, manageable tasks you can work on consistently. Turn to page 355 of your workbook to the Action Steps Sheet or create the sheet from the example I will give you below in your notebook.

Turning goals into action steps first requires us to have clear and concise goals already set, which we have already done. From our goal sheets, we will create our action steps.

I don't want to overwhelm you by giving you all the steps at one time, but instead, I want to walk you through this one step at a time. Right now, focus solely on one thing: brainstorming your action steps.

Here is what I need from you: use the Action Step Sheet and in the second column write all the tasks, actions, and activities that are required to achieve your goal. But before you start to write, think about what needs to be done from start to finish. The reason for this is to make sure your steps are in the right order, but because we may find some that were not done in order when we prioritize them, it is best to use a pencil for this assignment. That way, they can be easily corrected. Here is an example of my SMART Goal to repair my credit from my goal sheet:

Action Steps Sheet

SMART Goal: Repair my credit by raising my FICO score by 136 points to attain a score of 720 in 6 months.

#	Action Steps	Daily	Weekly	Monthly	Annually	Once
1	Request free credit reports from Equifax	☐	☐	☐	☐	☐
2	Request free credit reports from Experian	☐	☐	☐	☐	☐
3	Request free credit reports from TransUnion	☐	☐	☐	☐	☐
4	Review Experian credit reports for errors, inaccuracies, or outdated info	☐	☐	☐	☐	☐
5	Review Equifax credit reports for errors, inaccuracies, or outdated info	☐	☐	☐	☐	☐
6	Review TransUnion credit reports for errors, inaccuracies, or outdated info	☐	☐	☐	☐	☐
7	Dispute any errors or inaccuracies on your credit reports	☐	☐	☐	☐	☐
8	Write detailed letters to credit bureaus explaining discrepancies	☐	☐	☐	☐	☐
9	Monitor progress of each credit bureau	☐	☐	☐	☐	☐
10	Record credit score	☐	☐	☐	☐	☐
11	Call Capital One to change due date to the 11th of each month	☐	☐	☐	☐	☐
12	Call Chase to change due date to the 11th of each month	☐	☐	☐	☐	☐
13	Call AMEX to change due date to the 11th of each month	☐	☐	☐	☐	☐

#	Action Steps	Daily	Weekly	Monthly	Annually	Once
14	Call Walmart to change due date to the 25th of each month	☐	☐	☐	☐	☐
15	Call Kohl's to change due date to the 25th of each month	☐	☐	☐	☐	☐
16	Call Shell to change due date to the 25th of each month	☐	☐	☐	☐	☐
17	Call Amazon to change due date to the 25th of each month	☐	☐	☐	☐	☐
18	Pay all active bills, loans, credit card and mortgage payments early	☐	☐	☐	☐	☐
19	Negotiate better terms, such as lower interest or higher credit limit	☐	☐	☐	☐	☐
20	Make an additional $100 per month to Capital One or highest interest debt	☐	☐	☐	☐	☐
21	Open Credit Builder or Self account to save and rebuild credit	☐	☐	☐	☐	☐
22	Secure a secured credit card from Citibank	☐	☐	☐	☐	☐
23	Secure a secured credit card from Open Sky	☐	☐	☐	☐	☐
24	Become an authorized user on Joe's Discover Card	☐	☐	☐	☐	☐
25	Become an authorized user on Joe's B of A credit card	☐	☐	☐	☐	☐
26	Apply for new credit cards only after FICO score is over 610	☐	☐	☐	☐	☐
27	Celebrate reaching 618 FICO score	☐	☐	☐	☐	☐
28	Apply for new loans only after FICO is above 650	☐	☐	☐	☐	☐
29	Celebrate reaching 652 FICO score	☐	☐	☐	☐	☐
30	Celebrate reaching 686 FICO score	☐	☐	☐	☐	☐
31	Celebrate reaching 720 FICO score	☐	☐	☐	☐	☐
32	Refinance mortgage (if not paid off)	☐	☐	☐	☐	☐

STEP 2: Prioritizing Action Steps

Now that we have listed our action steps for repairing my credit, it is time to prioritize them. It is important that our action steps are in the correct order. This is why I asked you to use a pencil and not a pen. In this exercise, all we will be doing is assigning a number to each of the action steps and ensuring that they are in sequential order. If we did our steps right, they will be. If not, just move the step into the order it should be in. In column one, assign numbers to each action step based on the order in which it should be done, starting with the number one and continuing in sequential order. We will be using the same Action Steps Sheet we did before. Here is the example:

Action Steps Sheet

SMART Goal: Repair my credit by raising my FICO score by 136 points to attain a score of 720 in 6 months.

#	Action Steps	Daily	Weekly	Monthly	Annually	Once
1	Request free credit reports from Equifax	☐	☐	☐	☐	☐
2	Request free credit reports from Experian	☐	☐	☐	☐	☐
3	Request free credit reports from TransUnion	☐	☐	☐	☐	☐
4	Review Experian credit reports for errors, inaccuracies, or outdated info	☐	☐	☐	☐	☐
5	Review Equifax credit reports for errors, inaccuracies, or outdated info	☐	☐	☐	☐	☐
6	Review TransUnion credit reports for errors, inaccuracies, or outdated info	☐	☐	☐	☐	☐
7	Dispute any errors or inaccuracies on your credit reports	☐	☐	☐	☐	☐
8	Write detailed letters to credit bureaus explaining discrepancies	☐	☐	☐	☐	☐
9	Monitor progress of each credit bureau	☐	☐	☐	☐	☐
10	Record credit score	☐	☐	☐	☐	☐
11	Call Capital One to change due date to the 11th of each month	☐	☐	☐	☐	☐
12	Call Chase to change due date to the 11th of each month	☐	☐	☐	☐	☐
13	Call AMEX to change due date to the 11th of each month	☐	☐	☐	☐	☐

#	Action Steps	Daily	Weekly	Monthly	Annually	Once
14	Call Walmart to change due date to the 25th of each month	☐	☐	☐	☐	☐
15	Call Kohl's to change due date to the 25th of each month	☐	☐	☐	☐	☐
16	Call Shell to change due date to the 25th of each month	☐	☐	☐	☐	☐
17	Call Amazon to change due date to the 25th of each month	☐	☐	☐	☐	☐
18	Pay all active bills, loans, credit card and mortgage payments early	☐	☐	☐	☐	☐
19	Negotiate better terms, such as lower interest or higher credit limit	☐	☐	☐	☐	☐
20	Make an additional $100 per month to Capital One or highest interest debt	☐	☐	☐	☐	☐
21	Open Credit Builder or Self account to save and rebuild credit	☐	☐	☐	☐	☐
22	Secure a secured credit card from Citibank	☐	☐	☐	☐	☐
23	Secure a secured credit card from Open Sky	☐	☐	☐	☐	☐
24	Become an authorized user on Joe's Discover Card	☐	☐	☐	☐	☐
25	Become an authorized user on Joe's B of A credit card	☐	☐	☐	☐	☐
26	Apply for new credit cards only after FICO score is over 610	☐	☐	☐	☐	☐
27	Celebrate reaching 618 FICO score	☐	☐	☐	☐	☐
28	Apply for new loans only after FICO is above 650	☐	☐	☐	☐	☐
29	Celebrate reaching 652 FICO score	☐	☐	☐	☐	☐
30	Celebrate reaching 686 FICO score	☐	☐	☐	☐	☐
31	Celebrate reaching 720 FICO score	☐	☐	☐	☐	☐

Luckily, all of my steps were in sequential order and did not need to be changed, but trust me, this is not always the case. Sometimes we will need to make changes to the order of our action steps. This is not uncommon. Once you have completed your action steps and have them in sequential order, we move to the next part of the exercise, which is to assign frequency to our action steps.

STEP 3: Setting Frequency to Your Action Steps

Embracing the rhythm of consistent action is the heartbeat of progress on our journey of personal growth. Just as a musician creates a symphony through well-timed notes, we orchestrate our own masterpiece by assigning frequency to our action steps. Like the sun that rises and sets each day, our commitment to taking regular steps propels us forward with unwavering determination. Let us not be daunted by the scope of our dreams, but rather find solace in the cadence of our efforts. It's in the steady pulse of consistent action, whether daily, weekly, or monthly, that we cultivate the melody of transformation. So, as we assign the tempo of our progress, let us remember that even the smallest action resonates with the potential to create profound change. In the rhythm of our actions, we find the power to shape our destiny and compose a life that harmonizes with our highest aspirations.

In this exercise, we will continue using our Action Steps Sheet to determine how frequently we need to take each action. Some actions may become a part of our daily routine, while others may only be a one-shot wonder. Determining the frequency of our action steps will be based on the action step and the goal you are in the process of achieving. On our Action Steps Sheet, you will find in columns 3-7 the frequency by which you need for each action step. The columns are labeled "Daily, Weekly, Monthly, Annually, and Once." In this assignment, you will check the corresponding box that fits the frequency of the action step. This sounds simple, but there is a slight catch to it. For example, an action step that is needed on Monday, Wednesday, and Friday would not be marked daily. It would be marked as weekly because it occurs three times per week. Neither would an action step that is done in January, April, July, and October be marked as monthly, but as annually. Okay, you got it? Good, now let's start checking off the necessary box for each action step on our Action Steps Sheet.

Action Steps Sheet

SMART Goal: Repair my credit by raising my FICO score by 136 points to attain a score of 720 in 6 months.

#	Action Steps	Daily	Weekly	Monthly	Annually	Once
1	Request free credit reports from Equifax	☐	☐	☐	☒	☐
2	Request free credit reports from Experian	☐	☐	☐	☒	☐
3	Request free credit reports from TransUnion	☐	☐	☐	☒	☐
4	Review Experian credit reports for errors, inaccuracies, or outdated info	☐	☐	☒	☐	☐
5	Review Equifax credit reports for errors, inaccuracies, or outdated info	☐	☐	☒	☐	☐
6	Review TransUnion credit reports for errors, inaccuracies, or outdated info	☐	☐	☒	☐	☐

#	Action Steps	Daily	Weekly	Monthly	Annually	Once
7	Dispute any errors or inaccuracies on your credit reports	☐	☐	☒	☐	☐
8	Write detailed letters to credit bureaus explaining discrepancies	☐	☐	☒	☐	☐
9	Monitor progress of each credit bureau	☐	☒	☐	☐	☐
10	Record credit score	☐	☐	☒	☐	☐
11	Call Capital One to change due date to the 11th of each month	☐	☐	☐	☐	☒
12	Call Chase to change due date to the 11th of each month	☐	☐	☐	☐	☒
13	Call AMEX to change due date to the 11th of each month	☐	☐	☐	☐	☒
14	Call Walmart to change due date to the 25th of each month	☐	☐	☐	☐	☒
15	Call Kohl's to change due date to the 25th of each month	☐	☐	☐	☐	☒
16	Call Shell to change due date to the 25th of each month	☐	☐	☐	☐	☒
17	Call Amazon to change due date to the 25th of each month	☐	☐	☐	☐	☒
18	Pay all active bills, loans, credit card and mortgage payments early	☐	☐	☒	☐	☐
19	Negotiate better terms, such as lower interest or higher credit limit	☐	☐	☐	☒	☐
20	Make an additional $100 per month to Capital One or highest interest debt	☐	☐	☒	☐	☐
21	Open Credit Builder or Self account to save and rebuild credit	☐	☐	☐	☐	☒
22	Secure a secured credit card from Citibank	☐	☐	☐	☐	☒
23	Secure a secured credit card from Open Sky	☐	☐	☐	☐	☒
24	Become an authorized user on Joe's Discover Card	☐	☐	☐	☐	☒
25	Become an authorized user on Joe's B of A credit card	☐	☐	☐	☐	☒
26	Apply for new credit cards only after FICO score is over 610	☐	☐	☐	☒	☐
27	Celebrate reaching 618 FICO score	☐	☐	☐	☐	☒
28	Apply for new loans only after FICO is above 650	☐	☐	☐	☐	☒
29	Celebrate reaching 652 FICO score	☐	☐	☐	☐	☒

#	Action Steps	Daily	Weekly	Monthly	Annually	Once
30	Celebrate reaching 686 FICO score	☐	☐	☐	☐	☒
31	Celebrate reaching 720 FICO score	☐	☐	☐	☐	☒
32	Refinance mortgage (if not paid off)	☐	☐	☐	☐	☒

All done? Awesome! You now have your action steps listed, prioritized, and assigned a frequency. But this is not all that we need to do with our action steps. We also need to create a schedule for them. This will simplify the time management process later on.

STEP 4: Action Steps Schedule

Scheduling our action steps is akin to crafting a roadmap to our dreams, a compass that guides us through the labyrinth of possibilities. Just as a captain plots a course before embarking on a voyage, we meticulously arrange the moments of our days to accommodate the pursuit of our goals. The art of scheduling action steps grants us the gift of structure, transforming our aspirations into a series of intentional and purposeful movements. Each entry is a promise to us—a commitment to invest time in our growth, our passions, and our potential. As we allocate time to our ambitions, we build a bridge between where we stand and where we yearn to be. In the tapestry of our schedules, we weave the threads of dedication, discipline, and determination. Let us embrace this artistry of time, for it is through the canvas of our well-scheduled action steps that we paint the portrait of our own success, one vivid stroke at a time. The Action Steps Scheduler can be found on page 375 of your workbook, or you can create it in your notebook.

Action Steps Scheduler

#	Action Step	Start Date	Frequency	End Date
1	Request free credit reports from Equifax	8/15/2023	Annually	8/29/2023
2	Request free credit reports from Experian	8/15/2023	Annually	8/29/2023
3	Request free credit reports from TransUnion	8/15/2023	Annually	8/29/2023
4	Review Experian credit reports for errors, inaccuracies, or outdated info	8/30/2023	Annually	8/31/2023
5	Review Equifax credit reports for errors, inaccuracies, or outdated info	8/30/2023	Annually	8/31/2023
6	Review TransUnion credit reports for errors, inaccuracies, or outdated info	8/30/2023	Annually	8/31/2023

#	Action Step	Start Date	Frequency	End Date
7	Dispute any errors or inaccuracies on your credit reports	9/1/2023	Monthly	2/15/2024
8	Write detailed letters to credit bureaus explaining discrepancies	9/2/2023	Monthly	2/15/2024
9	Monitor progress of each credit bureau	9/7/2023	Weekly	2/15/2024
10	Record credit score	9/7/2023	Monthly	2/15/2024
11	Call Capital One to change due date to the 11th of each month	9/9/2023	Once	9/9/2023
12	Call Chase to change due date to the 11th of each month	9/9/2023	Once	9/9/2023
13	Call AMEX to change due date to the 11th of each month	9/9/2023	Once	9/9/2023
14	Call Walmart to change due date to the 25th of each month	9/16/2023	Once	9/16/2023
15	Call Kohl's to change due date to the 25th of each month	9/16/2023	Once	9/16/2023
16	Call Shell to change due date to the 25th of each month	9/16/2023	Once	9/16/2023
17	Call Amazon to change due date to the 25th of each month	9/16/2023	Once	9/16/2023
18	Pay all active bills, loans, credit card and mortgage payments early	10/1/2023	Monthly	2/15/2024
19	Negotiate better terms, such as lower interest or higher credit limit	10/15/2023	Annually	10/16/2023
20	Make an additional $100 per month to Capital One or highest interest debt	11/1/2023	Monthly	2/15/2024
21	Open Credit Builder or Self account to save and rebuild credit	11/1/2023	Once	11/8/2023
22	Secure a secured credit card from Citibank	11/1/2023	Once	11/16/2023
23	Secure a secured credit card from Open Sky	11/10/2023	Once	11/25/2023
24	Become an authorized user on Joe's Discover Card	11/15/2023	Once	11/25/2023
25	Become an authorized user on Joe's B of A credit card	11/15/2023	Once	11/25/2023
26	Apply for new credit cards only after FICO score is over 610	11/16/2023	Annually	11/16/2023
27	Celebrate reaching 618 FICO score	11/31/2023	Once	11/31/2023
28	Apply for new loans only after FICO is above 650	12/15/2023	Once	12/25/2023
29	Celebrate reaching 652 FICO score	12/31/2023	Once	12/31/2023
30	Celebrate reaching 686 FICO score	1/15/2024	Once	1/15/2024
31	Celebrate reaching 720 FICO score	2/15/2024	Once	2/15/2024
32	Refinance mortgage (if not paid off)	2/15/2024	Once	3/15/2024

Before we move on, review your Action Steps Scheduler to ensure that all the dates are aligned and make sense. This will take considerable time, but you need to do this for each goal that you have set. If you are like I was, you probably have well over a hundred goals set; in fact, I was close to two hundred when I finished setting my goals. Trust me, it is well worth doing if you want to achieve the goals you have set. Without these action steps, your goals will be all that much harder to fulfill and attain. I advise you not to move forward without completing each of the goals that you have set, because in the next chapter you will need to have the action steps to move forward. Once you have completed all, and I do mean all, you can move forward to start creating your milestones.

Tracking and Milestones

Embarking on a personal growth journey is like setting out on an epic road trip of self-discovery, where milestones become our cherished mile markers and tracking progress becomes the miles we proudly traverse. Just as mile markers reassure us that we're on the right path during a road trip, milestones affirm that we're advancing on our transformative quest. They remind us that every step, every effort, propels us forward, and just like the miles on a road trip, they reveal the exhilarating distance we've covered.

As we journey through personal growth, milestones act as signposts of our evolution, much like road signs that point us in the right direction. Each milestone is a testament to our resilience, courage, and unwavering commitment to self-improvement. These markers not only celebrate our achievements but also illuminate the trail of progress we've blazed. Tracking progress, much like counting miles on a road trip, allows us to see how far we've come and how much further we can go. It's like watching the odometer climb higher, reminding us that every action step is another mile etched into the map of our personal growth journey.

Just as a road trip becomes more exciting as the mileage increases, our personal growth journey becomes more exhilarating with each step of progress. Imagine each milestone as a scenic viewpoint during a road trip—a moment to pause, reflect, and take in the breathtaking vistas of our accomplishments. These milestones aren't just markers; they're vibrant snapshots of our transformation, capturing our dedication and hard work in a single frame. They urge us to stop, admire, and acknowledge the beauty of our journey.

Road trips are often filled with unexpected detours and diversions; just as personal growth journeys encounter unforeseen challenges. But like recalibrating a GPS, tracking our progress allows us to navigate these detours and keep moving forward. Each tracked step, much like each mile covered, reassures us that we're still making progress, even in the face of obstacles. The thrill of a road trip isn't solely in reaching the destination but relishing the experiences along the way. Similarly, personal growth is about embracing the journey, savoring each milestone, and delighting in the steps of progress.

Just as a road trip becomes a collection of stories, our personal growth journey becomes a tapestry woven with milestones—each one a tale of determination, growth, and self-discovery. Much like a road trip's final destination, the ultimate achievement of personal growth might feel far away at times. However, tracking progress shows us that every step is a mile toward that destination. It's a reminder that even the longest journeys are comprised of small, impactful moments, and each tracked action step is a testament to our commitment.

On a road trip, miles traveled become a source of pride, a testament to the distance you've conquered. Similarly, tracking progress ignites a sense of pride in your personal growth journey. Each step marked off, each milestone celebrated, reinforces your dedication and fuels your belief in your ability to create meaningful change.

So, fasten your seatbelt and navigate your personal growth journey with the compass of milestones and the odometer of progress tracking. Each milestone you reach is a mini-celebration, and each step you track is a testament to your dedication. Just as a road trip is an adventure of discovery, your personal growth journey is an expedition into the vast realm of your own potential, guided by the ever-present markers of milestones and progress.

Tracking Our Progress

Tracking the progress of our goals using action steps as the miles we've already traveled is like gazing at a map of our personal growth journey, tracing the winding paths of achievement and perseverance. Each action step completed becomes a milestone, a milepost of triumph that assures us we're moving forward. Just as a traveler marks the miles they've covered; we mark off action steps as a testament to our commitment and dedication.

Imagine each action step as a footprint on the sands of time, an indelible mark of progress that demonstrates our unwavering resolve. These footprints form a trail of determination, reminding us how far we've come, and propelling us toward the horizons of our dreams. With every action step taken, we leave a trail of inspiration for our future self to follow. Tracking progress through action steps is like unwrapping a gift with each accomplishment. Each marked step reveals the treasure of growth we've unlocked, reminding us that our journey is not only about the destination but also about the invaluable experiences gained along the way. Just as a traveler savors the diverse landscapes on a journey, we savor the richness of our personal growth experiences.

As we track the miles we've covered through action steps, we're not merely counting the steps; we're building a bridge between our aspirations and our reality. Each action step completed is a pillar of that bridge, sturdy and reliable, reminding us that with determination, we can cross over from where we once stood to where we envision ourselves. In the grand tapestry of our personal growth journey, tracking progress with action steps is like weaving a thread of accomplishment through the fabric of time. It's a testament to our resilience, a record of our efforts, and a source of inspiration for the future. With every mile covered through our action steps, we craft a narrative of empowerment, a story of triumph over challenges, and a legacy of continuous growth.

Milestones

In the captivating tapestry of our personal growth journey, milestones stand as shimmering threads that weave our story of transformation. Each milestone is a testament to our courage, resilience, and unwavering commitment to becoming the best version of ourselves. These milestones are not mere markers; they are the footprints of our progress, the echoes of our determination, and the steppingstones that pave the way to our aspirations. They are like beacons of light, guiding us through the terrain of self-discovery and empowerment. They remind us that our journey is not a race, but a deliberate and purposeful expedition towards fulfillment. With every milestone reached, we carve a path of achievement and mark our progress on the map of personal development.

Just as a gardener tends to their plants with care, nurturing their growth, milestones represent the blossoming of our efforts. Each milestone is a bud that unfolds into a vibrant flower, symbolizing the beauty and potential that reside within us. These milestones inspire us to embrace challenges, overcome obstacles, and stretch beyond our comfort zones, knowing that each step forward brings us closer to our dreams.

Milestones are the landmarks of our personal growth landscape, reminding us that every experience, whether triumphant or challenging, contributes to our evolution. They teach us that growth is not always linear, but a mosaic of moments that shape our character and expand our horizons. With each milestone achieved, we write a chapter in the book of our transformation, a chapter filled with determination, resilience, and the indomitable spirit of progress. In the symphony of our personal growth journey, milestones are the crescendos that mark our accomplishments. They fuel our motivation, inspire our actions, and remind us that we are architects of our destiny. As we celebrate each milestone, we acknowledge the strength within us, the progress we've made, and the boundless potential that lies ahead. With unwavering determination, we march forward, driven by the melody of milestones, towards a future illuminated by our growth, courage, and endless possibilities.

While there are many methods that can be used to determine milestones, I personally find that the simplest and easiest methods are the Quantified and the Qualified Methods. These are the ones I will be focusing on to make this simple.

Quantified and Qualified Milestones

In the exhilarating expedition of personal growth, quantifying and qualifying milestones serve as the rhythmic heartbeat that keeps us moving forward. Just as mile markers chart a traveler's progress, these quantified and qualified milestones navigate us through the intricate landscapes of self-discovery and transformation. Each milestone is a testament to our dedication, a reflection of our resilience, and tangible proof that our journey is not just a vague concept but a series of measurable triumphs.

Envision your personal growth journey as an open road, stretching ahead with milestones as bright guideposts leading the way. These markers are not merely numerical values; they are the embodiment of our passion, our persistence, and our unyielding commitment to growth. As we set and achieve quantified milestones, we weave a story of progress, a narrative of personal evolution that shapes the very essence of who we become.

Quantifying and qualifying milestones are like stars illuminating the night sky of your journey. They shine through the darkness of doubt and uncertainty, reminding you that every effort we invest, every step we take, propels us closer to the summit of our aspirations. With each milestone, you're not just measuring progress; you're manifesting your potential and carving our own path to greatness. As a traveler finds motivation in the sight of mile markers, draw inspiration from our quantified and qualified milestones. They are our allies, companions, and partners in progress. Each one represents a conquered challenge, a vanquished fear, and an achievement that testifies to our unbreakable spirit.

Quantified and qualified milestones are the threads that weave together the fabric of our personal growth journey. They form a tapestry of transformation, each thread representing an experience, a lesson, and a triumph that contributes to the masterpiece of your self-improvement. Just as a traveler cherishes the progress they've made, we need to embrace our quantified and qualified milestones with a sense of pride and accomplishment. They symbolize our dedication to personal growth and our commitment to becoming the best version of ourselves. These milestones are the compass that keeps us on track, guiding us through the twists and turns of our journey.

With each quantified and qualified milestone, we're not just reaching a checkpoint; we're crossing a threshold of potential. These markers are our steppingstones to greatness, guiding us toward the realization of our dreams and aspirations. They represent the culmination of our efforts, the embodiment of our growth, and the testament to our determination. So, let each quantified and qualified milestone remind us that our journey is not a random wander; it's a purposeful voyage toward self-discovery. Embrace these milestones as the pulse of our progress, the rhythm of our growth, and the embodiment of our transformation. With every milestone reached, we're not just quantifying and qualifying progress; we're embracing the extraordinary adventure of personal growth, guided by the unwavering light of our own inner milestones.

Quantified vs. Qualified Milestones

In the thrilling odyssey of personal growth, the distinction between quantified and qualified milestones becomes a compass that guides us through the dynamic landscape of transformation. Quantified milestones are the measurable checkpoints that dot our journey, each one representing a numerical achievement that we can track and celebrate. These milestones are like bright stars in the night sky, illuminating our progress with tangible markers that remind us of how far we've come. They provide us with clarity and direction, enabling us to gauge our advancement and stay motivated as we navigate the path of self-improvement.

On the other hand, qualified milestones are the qualitative gems that enrich our personal growth journey. These milestones represent the intangible, yet profound, shifts that occur within us. They capture the essence of personal development by reflecting changes in our mindset, attitudes, and emotional well-being. These milestones are like the changing colors of a sunset, painting our journey with depth and meaning. They remind us that growth isn't just about numbers; it's about the profound transformations that shape our character and shape our lives.

Quantified milestones serve as the foundation upon which we build our personal growth journey. They provide us with measurable targets that keep us accountable and focused. Just as a builder lays bricks one by one, quantified milestones allow us to construct our desired future step by step. These milestones are like the sturdy pillars that hold our aspirations high, giving us a tangible framework to track our progress and make adjustments along the way.

Qualified milestones, on the other hand, infuse our journey with soulful significance. They capture the nuances of personal growth that can't be measured by numbers alone. These milestones represent the breakthroughs, the aha moments, and the profound realizations that expand our horizons. Just as a painter adds layers of depth to a canvas, qualified milestones add layers of wisdom and insight to our personal growth journey. They remind us that personal development is a journey of inner transformation, where qualitative shifts lead to lasting change.

In essence, the interplay between quantified and qualified milestones creates a harmonious symphony of growth. They work hand in hand, with quantified milestones providing structure and measurable progress, while qualified milestones infuse our journey with depth and meaning. As we navigate the intricate dance between these two types of milestones, we embark on a truly holistic and enriching personal growth journey that encompasses both the tangible and the intangible, the measurable and the profound.

Using Qualified Milestone Method

The qualified milestone method is particularly effective when you want to measure and track qualitative or intangible aspects of your personal growth journey. This method focuses on the deeper, inner transformations and shifts that occur within you, which may not always be easily quantified by numerical metrics. Here are some scenarios where using the qualified milestone method can be valuable:

Mindset and Emotional Growth: If our personal growth journey involves cultivating a positive mindset, overcoming limiting beliefs, managing stress, or enhancing emotional intelligence, qualified milestones are ideal. These milestones allow us to assess and celebrate shifts in our perspective, resilience, and emotional well-being.

Self-Confidence and Self-Esteem: When our focus is on boosting self-confidence, self-esteem, and self-worth, qualified milestones help us gauge our progress through changes in our self-perception, self-assuredness, and self-compassion.

Interpersonal Skills and Relationships: If our personal growth goals involve improving communication, empathy, active listening, and building healthier relationships, qualified milestones enable us to measure our ability to connect with others on a deeper level.

Spiritual and Inner Development: For those of us seeking spiritual growth, inner peace, and a deeper connection with oneself, qualified milestones help us assess our progress in cultivating mindfulness, self-awareness, and a sense of purpose.

Creativity and Self-Expression: When working on creative pursuits, artistic endeavors, or self-expression, qualified milestones allow us to measure the evolution of our creative thinking, our ability to take risks, and the depth of our artistic exploration.

Personal Transformation and Identity: If our personal growth journey involves questioning and evolving our identity, values, and life purpose, qualified milestones help us measure our growth by tracking shifts in our sense of self, authenticity, and alignment with our values.

Adaptability and Resilience: For those of us navigating change, uncertainties, and challenges, qualified milestones help us assess our ability to adapt, bounce back from setbacks, and maintain a positive attitude in the face of adversity.

Inner Healing and Well-Being: If our focus is on inner healing, managing past traumas, or improving overall well-being, qualified milestones help us measure improvements in emotional healing, forgiveness, and the ability to let go of past pain.

Personal Values and Ethics: When aligning our actions with our values and ethical principles, qualified milestones allow us to evaluate our progress in making ethical choices, advocating for causes we believe in, and living in harmony with our values.

Lifelong Learning and Wisdom: If we're dedicated to continuous learning, personal growth, and acquiring wisdom, qualified milestones enable us to measure our depth of understanding, intellectual insights, and the integration of knowledge into our life.

In essence, the qualified milestone method is suitable whenever we seek to measure the qualitative, internal, and transformative aspects of our personal growth journey. It helps us acknowledge and celebrate the profound shifts, insights, and changes that occur within us as we evolve and develop into a better version of ourselves.

Using the Quantified Milestone Method

The quantified milestone method is most appropriate when we want to track and measure specific, tangible, and numerical achievements in our personal growth journey. This method involves setting clear, measurable targets that provide a concrete way to assess our progress. Here are some situations where using the quantified milestone method can be beneficial:

Skill Development: When we're learning a new skill or honing an existing one, quantified milestones can help us track the number of hours spent practicing, the proficiency level achieved, or the completion of specific skill-related tasks.

Educational Pursuits: If we're pursuing formal education, quantified milestones could involve completing a certain number of courses, earning specific grades, or obtaining certifications within a defined timeframe.

Physical Fitness and Health Goals: For health and fitness objectives, quantified milestones may include achieving a target weight, running a certain distance, lifting a particular amount of weight, or improving cardiovascular endurance.

Time Management and Productivity: When focusing on productivity and time management, quantified milestones could involve increasing the number of tasks completed per day, reducing procrastination time, or adhering to a specific schedule consistently. Because we have already assigned a start time and a deadline this method will be the most widely used.

Financial Objectives: For financial growth, quantified milestones might include saving a predetermined amount of money, paying off a certain portion of debt, or increasing your investment portfolio by a specific percentage.

Goal Attainment: When aiming to achieve personal or professional goals, quantified milestones can help us track the completion of specific steps or tasks related to our goals.

Networking and Social Connections: For expanding our network, quantified milestones could involve attending a certain number of networking events, making a specific number of new contacts, or participating in a set number of professional or social engagements.

Learning and Knowledge Acquisition: When seeking to broaden our knowledge, quantified milestones may involve reading a certain number of books, completing a specified amount of coursework, or attending a predetermined number of workshops or seminars.

Language Acquisition: If our goal is to learn a new language, quantified milestones could involve achieving a certain level of fluency, mastering a specific number of vocabulary words, or successfully holding conversations in the target language.

Career Progression: For career development, quantified milestones might include obtaining a promotion within a specific timeframe, achieving a certain performance metric, or contributing to a predetermined number of projects.

Volunteering and Community Engagement: When focusing on giving back, quantified milestones could involve volunteering for a set number of hours or participating in a specific number of community service projects.

Digital Presence and Branding: For online presence and personal branding, quantified milestones may include gaining a certain number of followers on social media, publishing a specific amount of content, or achieving a target level of engagement.

Travel and Exploration: If we're aiming to explore new places, quantified milestones might involve visiting a certain number of countries, experiencing a predetermined number of cultural activities, or embarking on a specific number of adventures.

In summary, the quantified milestone method is suitable when we want to track and measure concrete achievements and progress in areas that can be quantified with numbers or data. It provides a structured way to evaluate our growth and ensures that we can objectively assess our advancement toward specific goals.

Determining Qualified or Quantified Method

In this exercise, we will be focusing on our goals and not the action steps, as it will be less confusing and time-consuming than focusing on action steps. In fact, we have done most of the work already and at this point it is just a matter of transferring the data from one place to another. Turn to page 231 of your workbook or go to the first goal sheet you created in your notebook. We will be using the goal and the metrics or criteria from the question "What metrics or criteria will I use to track my achievements?" on the goal sheet. We will list the goal and then review the metrics or criteria to determine whether it is qualifying or quantifying method. I know that this exercise may take a considerable amount of time to complete, but it is a necessary step in achieving our goals, remember that the milestones feed our anticipation to reach our destination. It gives us the resilience, perseverance, and determination to continue on full speed ahead. It allows us to check off action steps as miles driven encouraging us to continue full speed ahead. On page 395 of your workbook you will find the Milestone Classification Form or create a copy of the form in your notebook from the example.

Milestone Classification Form

#	Goal	Qualifying	Quantifying
1	Repair my credit	☐	☒
2	Use a credit builder to increase my credit score	☐	☒
3	Open secure credit cards	☐	☒

#	Goal	Qualifying	Quantifying
4	Look for no money down deals	☐	☒
5	Use crowdfunding sites to raise money	☐	☒
6	Use other people's money	☐	☒
7	Find a capital partner	☐	☒
8	Do wholesale deals to build capital	☐	☒
9	Find successful real estate investors to talk to	☐	☒
10	Join a real estate investment club	☐	☒
11	Go to real estate seminars	☐	☒
12	Embrace failure as an opportunity for growth and learning	☒	☐
13	Challenge negative self-talk and replace it with positive affirmations	☒	☐
14	Focus on the process rather than solely on the end result	☒	☐
15	Practice being 15-minutes early for occasions	☐	☒
16	Schedule all occurrences to allow for travel time and incidents	☒	☐
17	Get the advice of people who have mastered time management	☐	☒
18	Learn to schedule everything	☒	☐
19	Use 15-minute intervals for time management instead of 30 minutes or hourly	☐	☒
20	Learn to prioritize	☒	☐
21	Create a to do list	☐	☒
22	Give start time and deadlines for what must be done	☒	☐

I am not going to go through all of my goals, by now you should be able determine which goals are quantified and which are qualified. The easy way to remember is that if it involves numbers or percentages, it is automatically quantified, but if it involves a decision or learning moment it is qualified. Continue this process until you have completely exhausted all of your goal sheets. Once you have completed all your goals we can move forward on monitoring and tracking our goals.

Tracking and Monitoring Your Goals

Imagine embarking on a thrilling road trip of personal growth, with each goal you set acting as a unique destination on your journey. Just as a seasoned traveler keeps a vigilant eye on the road signs and landmarks, monitoring and tracking your goals becomes your compass, ensuring you stay on course toward your desired destinations. Think of your goals as the vibrant cities you yearn to explore. Monitoring your progress is like checking the map to see how far you've come and how much closer you are to your destination. It's like observing the mile markers on the highway, each one representing a step forward and a triumph achieved. Tracking your goals is akin to the odometer on your dashboard, measuring the distance you've covered. With every milestone you pass, you gain a sense of accomplishment, much like reaching a rest stop where you pause to relish the progress you've made. Just as you adjust your speed to navigate winding roads or speed up on straightaways, monitoring your goals allows you to adapt your approach. If you encounter detours or unexpected obstacles, tracking your progress empowers you to make necessary adjustments and choose alternative routes.

As you track your goals, consider each one a checkpoint where you pause to refuel and recharge. Just like pulling into a gas station, monitoring your goals ensures you have the resources and strategies needed to continue your journey with renewed enthusiasm. Remember, every journey is unique, and so is your path of personal growth. Monitoring and tracking your goals offers you the chance to witness your evolution firsthand. Just as you celebrate arriving at a new city or landmark, celebrating your goal milestones fuels your motivation and reminds you of the progress you're making. In the same way that a road trip is a combination of scenic views and unexpected twists, your personal growth journey is a blend of successes and challenges. Monitoring and tracking your goals helps you appreciate the beautiful moments and navigate the hurdles with determination.

Consider each tracked goal as a story you collect along the way, a story that forms the narrative of your personal growth journey. Just as a road trip creates memories, tracking your goals allows you to create a tangible record of your achievements and experiences. And when you finally reach your ultimate destination, you'll look back at your tracked goals as a roadmap of your transformation. Just as a road trip leaves you with a sense of fulfillment and adventure, monitoring and tracking your goals infuses your personal growth journey with purpose and the joy of progress. So, fasten your seatbelt and embrace the exhilarating ride of monitoring and tracking your goals. With each goal achieved and milestone met, you're not just driving through life – you're steering your personal growth journey with intention, resilience, and an unwavering commitment to becoming the best version of yourself.

Method of Tracking

Tracking your goals is essential for maintaining focus, staying motivated, and ensuring your progress. There are various methods you can use to effectively track your goals:

Goal Journaling: Keep a dedicated journal where you write down your goals, action steps, and your progress. Regularly update your journal with notes, reflections, and milestones reached. Use journal prompts to reflect on your progress, setbacks, and lessons learned. Regular introspection can help you stay aligned with your goals.

Digital Apps and Tools: Use goal-tracking apps or software that allow you to input your goals, set deadlines, and track your progress. Some popular options include Trello, Asana, Todoist, and Evernote.

Spreadsheets: Create a spreadsheet using tools like Microsoft Excel or Google Sheets to list your goals, action steps, deadlines, and track your progress over time.

Vision Board: Create a visual representation of your goals using a vision board. Pin or display images, quotes, and symbols that represent your goals and regularly update it as you make progress.

Progress Photos: If your goals involve physical changes, such as fitness or weight loss, take regular photos to visually track your progress. Compare these photos over time to see the changes.

Calendar Reminders: Set up calendar reminders for specific action steps and deadlines related to your goals. This can help you allocate time and stay on track.

Regular Check-Ins: Schedule regular check-ins with yourself, a mentor, or an accountability partner to review your goals, discuss progress, and adjust your action steps as needed.

Progress Meetings: If you're working on goals with a team or group, hold regular progress meetings to share updates, discuss challenges, and celebrate achievements.

Daily Planners: Use daily planners that have dedicated sections for tracking goals, action steps, and progress. This can help you integrate goal tracking into your daily routine.

Mind Maps: Create visual mind maps that outline your goals, action steps, and the connections between them. Mind maps can help you see the bigger picture and identify areas for improvement.

Reward System: Establish a reward system where you treat yourself after reaching specific milestones. This can provide extra motivation to stay on track.

Social Accountability: Share your goals and progress on social media or with friends and family who can provide encouragement and hold you accountable.

Choose the tracking method that resonates with you the most and aligns with your preferences and lifestyle. The key is to regularly engage with your chosen method to ensure you're consistently tracking your goals and celebrating your achievements. As for me I use multiple methods:

Spreadsheet, because it will allow us to visually see our progress in real time. Reward system because it allows us to look forward to being rewarded for completing certain milestones. Calendar reminder, because it allows us to see everything we need to do and reminds us to get it done. Regular check-in because it allows us to share our progress with accountability partners, mentors, and coaches. Social accountability, because it allows us to share our progress with peers, allowing them to use our progress as a motivational tool. This is why we have the Life Progressors group page on Facebook. These are the same methods which I will be using throughout the rest of the book. If you haven't noticed I am a righteous user of spreadsheets, as you have seen throughout the book, every exercise contains some sort of spreadsheet for us to complete. They are an excellent tool to keep us on course in our personal growth journey, allowing us to better see and understand the route by which we are to travel. The reward system is an integral part of our milestones as it is through the rewards that we acknowledge certain achievements that we have made in our journey's progress. They are there not just as a gift, but as a message to encourage us to continue in our journey, that we may not become discouraged, overwhelmed, or feel as though there is no point to what we are achieving. The calendar reminders are used to remind us of the directions that we need to take before it is time to take them. They are like the little voice of the GPS which says continue straight for nine miles or turn left in one mile. They are not there to be ignored they are there to remind you of the impending actions that must be taken before it is time to take them. We will address the calendar reminders later in chapter 47 when we do our time management. Regular check-ins are utilized in order to let those we have entrusted with our travel plans know that we are still on the right course, that we are on schedule to arrive or ahead of schedule. Regular check-ins are what keep them informed of our whereabouts, but it also allows us the opportunity to give updates on our progress in our journey. And finally, social accountability is our way of communicating with fellow travelers where we are on our journey. It is much like having passengers in the car with us on our journey, we are giving them updates on our progress. It is not to brag or gloat, it is to help to encourage them as they travel along with us to know that we are going to reach our destination safely. By utilizing these five methods we not only help ourselves, but we encourage and give hope to others who are on the journey with us.

In our next exercise we will be utilizing the first two methods of tracking and monitoring, we will use the spreadsheet not just to have our goals organized, but as a visual aide to ignite a passion within, to exhilarate us to continue on the route that we are taking and give us the perseverance that we will need to push forward no matter what obstacles or challenges we may face. We will assign rewards for ourselves, just as a pit stop to take the time to enjoy the scenery along our journey that we may have a memory or tokens to share with others to say that I have been on this journey, I have made it past this location and here is the proof that I was there. It is much like stopping at a truck stop, rest area or a convenient store and buying a keychain, t-shirt or in my case a coffee mug. Our rewards are there as an everlasting memory to say that we have made it thus far in our journey and we are now moving along to our next stop or maybe even our final destination.

Remember when we did our goal setting, I told you we would get to the Tracking and Monitor Sheet of the page when we got to milestones, well this is it. Go back to your goal sheets or create it in your notebook from the example. In this exercise we will complete the Tracking and Monitoring section of our goal sheet, here we will be adding our milestones, checking the method by which we will be tracking our goals and the rewards we will receive each time we either reach a milestone or complete the goal. Depending on you, you may even decide to reward yourself in the beginning just because you started the goal. But before we start, let me say this your reward does not have to be anything big, it can be a small token. Your reward should in some way be associated with the goal you are striving to achieve. For example, if your goal is to buy a new car, your reward can be a new keychain or even something as small as one of those pine tree air fresheners or maybe even a new towel to dry the car, I'm sure you understand what I mean. Understand that the Tracking and Monitor Sheet section has ten milestones and ten rewards, you may not always use all of them, but they are there to allow you the opportunity to use as many as you need. A word of advice, having fewer milestones is better than many, to be honest, you should have somewhere around 4-6 milestones for each goal. Also, each milestone does not necessarily need to be rewarded, the rewards are solely given at your discretion.

In this example, I will use the quantifying method:

Tracking and Monitor Sheet				
Goal:	Repair my credit			
Method:	☐ Qualifying	☒ Quantifying	Metrics:	Every 34-point increase in credit score
Milestone 1:	Celebrate reaching 618 FICO score		Reward 1:	Charge a $5 Dunkin Donut gift card
Milestone 2:	Celebrate reaching 652 FICO score		Reward 2:	Apply for new loan
Milestone 3:	Celebrate reaching 686 FICO score		Reward 3:	Charge a $25 dinner on card for self
Milestone 4:	Celebrate reaching 720 FICO score		Reward 4:	Refinance home
Milestone 5:			Reward 5:	
Milestone 6:			Reward 6:	
Milestone 7:			Reward 7:	
Milestone 8:			Reward 8:	
Milestone 9:			Reward 9:	
Milestone 10:			Reward 10:	
Progress				

Tracking and Monitor Sheet

Before we continue any further, I want you to notice that there is a space under the word "progress." What we will do at this point is manually draw lines in the box for each milestone we have listed and then write in the milestone number or the value that we are going to use; you can even decide to do both, it is entirely up to you. I will use several methods to give you an idea of what I am talking about.

In this example I used the quantifying method, in the next I will use the qualifying method.

Tracking and Monitor Sheet				
Goal:	Repair my credit			
Method:	☐ Qualifying	☒ Quantifying	Metrics:	Every 34-point increase in credit score
Milestone 1:	Celebrate reaching 618 FICO score		Reward 1:	Charge a $5 Dunkin Donut gift card
Milestone 2:	Celebrate reaching 652 FICO score		Reward 2:	Apply for new loan
Milestone 3:	Celebrate reaching 686 FICO score		Reward 3:	Charge a $25 dinner on card for self
Milestone 4:	Celebrate reaching 720 FICO score		Reward 4:	Refinance home
Milestone 5:			Reward 5:	
Milestone 6:			Reward 6:	
Milestone 7:			Reward 7:	
Milestone 8:			Reward 8:	
Milestone 9:			Reward 9:	
Milestone 10:			Reward 10:	
Progress				
Milestone 1	652	Milestone 3 686	Milestone 4 720 FICO score	

Tracking and Monitor Sheet

Goal:	Learn to schedule everything.			
Method:	☒ Qualifying ☐ Quantifying		Metrics:	
Milestone 1:	Scheduled morning and evening routines for September	Reward 1:		
Milestone 2:	Scheduled daily drop off and pickups for September	Reward 2:		
Milestone 3:	Scheduled Daily Action Steps for month of September	Reward 3:		
Milestone 4:	Scheduled Recreation and activity time for family for September	Reward 4:		
Milestone 5:	Scheduled daily household chores for the month of September	Reward 5:		
Milestone 6:	Scheduled meetings and appointments for month of September	Reward 6:		
Milestone 7:	Scheduled events and outing for month of September	Reward 7:		
Milestone 8:	Scheduled to do list for month of September	Reward 8:		
Milestone 9:	Scheduled Birthdays and holidays for month of September	Reward 9:		
Milestone 10:	Scheduled work and study for the month of September	Reward 10:	Buy a new pen	

Progress									
Milestone 1	Milestone 2	Milestone 3	Milestone 4	Milestone 5	Milestone 6	Milestone 7	Milestone 8	Milestone 9	Milestone 10

Once you have completed all of your goals, you can track and monitor your progress by either crossing out what has been accomplished or by highlighting it, which is what I like to do because of how I feel. It is important to take the time to review and update your tracking and monitoring sheets daily. This will give you a sense of achievement and allow you to see that you are moving in the right direction. Tracking and monitoring your goals allows you to stay focused and motivated.

Staying Focused and Motivated

Embarking on the scenic route of personal development is akin to embarking on the road trip of a lifetime. As you navigate through the winding roads of growth, staying focused and motivated becomes your compass, guiding you toward the breathtaking vistas of self-discovery and transformation. Just as a skilled driver keeps their eyes on the road, keep your gaze fixed on your goals. The landmarks of your aspirations stand tall on the horizon, inspiring you to press on despite the twists and turns that may come your way.

Fuel your journey with the unwavering determination of a full tank of gas. Motivation acts as your premium fuel, propelling you forward even when the path gets challenging. Harness the power of your dreams, letting them accelerate your progress through every mile of your personal development expedition. Amidst the ever-changing landscape of life, distractions can be like tempting detours, pulling you away from your course. Stay focused, steering clear of these diversions, and keeping your compass set to your true north of growth and self-improvement.

Just as you savor the anticipation of reaching a beautiful destination, relish in the anticipation of your personal growth milestones. Visualize the sense of accomplishment that awaits you at each goal, and let that anticipation become the wind beneath your wings. The road may sometimes feel long, but remember that each step, no matter how small, takes you closer to your destination. Let your progress be your source of motivation, celebrating every milestone as a testament to your dedication and perseverance.

In the face of challenges and setbacks, channel the resilience of a seasoned traveler. Just as you navigate through storms and rough patches on the road, navigate through obstacles with unwavering resolve, knowing that each challenge is an opportunity for growth. Just as a road trip is best enjoyed with a supportive travel companion, surround yourself with a network of like-minded individuals who uplift and encourage you. Share your journey with those who understand the value of personal development, and let their companionship light your way. Remember, the journey of personal development is not just about reaching a destination—it's about the adventure itself. Embrace the joy of the journey, appreciating every lesson, experience, and transformation that comes your way.

Focus on the Goal

As you take the wheel on the journey of life, remember that your goals are the guiding stars that light up the path ahead. Just as a vigilant driver keeps their eyes on the road, maintaining unwavering focus on your goals ensures you stay on course toward your dreams. Imagine yourself behind the wheel, the road stretching out before you like a canvas of possibilities. Your goals are the milestones that mark your progress, and just like road signs, they provide clear direction, reminding you to stay true to your intended route. Distractions may arise like tempting scenic detours, but a dedicated driver knows that staying focused means resisting these diversions. Similarly, when you maintain your focus on your goals, you resist the allure of distractions that could veer you off your chosen path.

Think of your goals as the landmarks you're determined to reach. Each one represents a destination of achievement, and just like a driver keeps their eye on the upcoming landmark, keeping your focus on your goals propels you closer to realizing your aspirations. The road may wind and twist, but your steadfast focus ensures you navigate every curve with confidence. Like a driver maneuvering through challenging terrain, your focus empowers you to overcome obstacles and steer your journey toward success. Maintaining focus isn't just about looking straight ahead; it's also about staying attuned to the changing road and weather conditions. Similarly, focusing on your goals requires adaptability, allowing you to adjust your strategies while keeping your ultimate destination in sight.

Imagine the satisfaction of reaching your goals, each accomplishment a checkpoint along your journey. Just as a driver reaches their desired destination, you'll experience the fulfillment of achieving what you set out to accomplish when you maintain your focus. Even when the road gets tough and the journey seems long, a determined driver never loses sight of the road ahead. Likewise, maintaining your focus on your goals during challenging times empowers you to persevere and emerge stronger on the other side. As a driver stays alert to potential hazards, staying focused on your goals equips you to identify and mitigate obstacles that may come your way. Your focus serves as a shield, allowing you to navigate challenges with clarity and determination.

In the grand adventure of life, your goals are the ultimate destination you're working tirelessly to reach. Just as a driver's eyes are fixed on the road, maintaining your focus on your goals ensures you stay on track, steering your journey toward a future brimming with achievement, fulfillment, and endless possibilities. Ultimately, the road trip of personal development is a testament to your courage, determination, and commitment to becoming the best version of yourself. Stay focused on your path, stay motivated by your dreams, and let the road of growth lead you to a life enriched with purpose, fulfillment, and boundless possibilities.

Even Proverbs 4:25-27 forewarns us not only to stay focused but maintain our path. It states, "Let thine eyes look right on and let thine eyelids look straight before thee. Ponder the path of thy feet and let all thy ways be established. Turn not to the right hand nor to the left: remove thy foot from evil." It is easy to become distracted in our personal growth journey with all that is going on around us and within us. This is why it is ever so important to stay motivated along the way. This reminds me of a sermon I once heard preached by Pastor Floyd James at Greater Rock Missionary Baptist Church entitled "Keep your eye on the prize." He took his text from Philippians 3:14 where the Apostle Paul says, "I press toward the mark for the prize of the high calling of God in Christ Jesus." During his sermon he had three points and the first was to stay focused, he said the moment we lose focus we lose the desire to compete. His second point was, be persistent, because the moment you stop pressing is the moment you lose momentum and he used an analogy of a young boy's determination to press a cork into a hole in a dam that had sprung a leak, he said as long as the boy kept pressing on the cork the water stopped leaking. He stated that the boy knew the moment he released the pressure from the cork, the water would force the hole to get bigger and the dam would burst and the people in the village would drown. His third point was to stay motivated. He closed by stating as long as we are focused on God, persistent in being obedient and motivated to live righteously, we would receive our prize, which is eternal life in Heaven with Christ Jesus.

I realized late in life that the biggest problem that I was having with achieving my goals was staying focused. When we take our eyes off the prize, it is easy to prioritize other matters over our goals. Life will always be filled with the unexpected; there will always be something or someone that will shift our attention from the goal at hand. In today's world we are easily distracted by emails, social media, television, or personal and family issues. A road trip of personal growth is not always a journey paved with smooth roads. Just as unexpected detours can arise during an actual road trip, challenges can also surface along your path of self-discovery. It's during these moments of adversity that your ability to remain focused becomes a true testament to your resilience and determination. Imagine cruising down the highway of personal growth when suddenly, a roadblock appears. Instead of losing your way, embrace the challenge as an opportunity to recalibrate. Just as a navigator adjusts the route, you can adjust your approach, maintaining your focus on your ultimate destination.

Remember, even the most picturesque road trips have their share of bumps and potholes. Similarly, your personal growth journey might encounter setbacks. Stay focused on your goals, viewing these setbacks as valuable lessons that propel you even further when you overcome them. When faced with unexpected detours, summon the spirit of adventure that guides a road trip. Approach challenges with curiosity and adaptability, knowing that each twist in the road contributes to the richness of your experience. Stay focused on the exhilarating journey, even when the path takes unexpected turns. As rain clouds momentarily obscure the view on a road trip, challenges can cloud your perspective. Stay focused on your vision, just as a driver keeps their eyes on the road ahead. Your vision serves as your compass, guiding you even when the path is unclear.

A flat tire on a road trip doesn't signal the end of the journey—it's merely a temporary setback. Similarly, setbacks in your personal growth journey are not defeats; they're opportunities to practice perseverance. Stay focused on your goals, knowing that resilience is the key to navigating through adversity. Just as a road trip can encounter traffic jams, your personal growth journey might experience delays. Stay focused on your goals, even when progress seems slow. Use these moments to reflect, strategize, and recharge, knowing that the journey is as important as the destination. On a road trip, navigation tools guide you back on track when you take a wrong turn. In your personal growth journey, your values and goals serve as your internal compass. Stay focused on these guiding principles, allowing them to steer you in the right direction, even when things go wrong.

When a sudden storm disrupts a road trip, adaptability is key. Similarly, when challenges arise on your personal growth journey, stay focused on adapting your strategies rather than losing sight of your goals. Let flexibility and determination be your constant companions. Remember that a road trip's most memorable moments often stem from the unexpected. The same goes for your personal growth journey. Stay focused on embracing challenges as opportunities for growth, knowing that the difficulties you overcome will be woven into the fabric of your success story.

In the grand tapestry of personal growth, challenges and setbacks are not roadblocks; they are mere pauses on your journey. As you navigate through these moments with unwavering focus, you transform difficulties into steppingstones, ultimately arriving at your destination stronger, wiser, and more determined than ever before. Granted there may be some things that will take precedence over the goal at hand, but the key is to take care of it and continue to push towards the fulfillment of the goal and to never lose sight of the end result. In other words, we need to stay focused, persevere through obstacles and challenges, and stay motivated to complete the goal at hand. I know it sounds easy, but trust me, I know that it is easier said than done. The key is to always be motivated to continue to strive for the prize.

Maintain Motivation

Embarking on the exhilarating road trip of personal growth, every twist and turn offers an opportunity to fuel our motivation. Just as a road trip requires a steady supply of gas to keep moving forward, our personal growth journey thrives on the fuel of unwavering determination and inspiration. Imagine the road ahead as the uncharted path of our personal growth journey. Every mile we cover represents a step closer to becoming the best version of ourselves. Just as a traveler looks forward to reaching their destination, maintain our motivation by envisioning the incredible transformation awaiting us at the end of our journey.

Like a skilled navigator, we must remind ourselves of the milestones we've achieved. Celebrate each achievement as a checkpoint on your journey, similar to stopping at a scenic overlook to appreciate the progress we've made. Let these accomplishments reignite our motivation to keep driving forward. Consider motivation as the engine that propels us through challenges and uphill climbs. Just as a car's engine powers it up steep inclines, our motivation empowers us to overcome obstacles, even when the path seems daunting. Much like the joy of discovering hidden gems along the way, we uncover the hidden potential within ourselves. Allow these moments of self-discovery to reignite your motivation, reminding you of the incredible growth you're capable of achieving.

Remember that a road trip is not solely about reaching the destination—it's about the adventure itself. Similarly, our personal growth journey is a transformative adventure that's worth every effort. Keep your motivation alive by embracing the excitement of the journey and the growth it brings. As we pass through different landscapes, we should always maintain an open heart and open mind. Just as a traveler learns from the cultures they encounter, let every experience on our journey contribute to our personal growth. These lessons can reignite our motivation by reminding us of the profound impact this journey has on our life.

In the same way that a road trip is enriched by shared moments with travel companions, seek support and connection on our personal growth journey. Share your goals and progress with friends, mentors, or fellow travelers, allowing their encouragement to keep your motivation high. Visualize the destination of your personal growth journey with vivid clarity. Just as a traveler anticipates the beauty of their final stop, maintain your motivation by imagining the incredible sense of achievement and fulfillment that will come when you reach your goals. And just like a road trip is an experience that shapes our memories, our personal growth journey shapes our character and our future. Let the memories of your progress and accomplishments motivate you to continue, knowing that each step we take brings us closer to a life of purpose, growth, and endless possibilities.

Emily's Story

In the quaint town of Crestwood, nestled amidst rolling hills and winding roads, lived a young woman named Emily. She had always dreamed of pursuing a fulfilling career in the field of environmental conservation. Emily's journey began with excitement and enthusiasm, much like setting out on an adventurous road trip. As she pursued her studies and gained valuable insights, Emily encountered numerous challenges. The coursework was demanding, the competition was fierce, and the path ahead seemed steep. Doubts and moments of self-doubt crept in, threatening to derail her dreams. This was Emily's first crossroads, where her motivation was put to the test.

But Emily was not one to give up easily. She envisioned her goals with unwavering determination, much like a driver focusing on the distant horizon. She remembered the beauty of pristine forests and clean rivers, and she knew that her journey was a crucial part of creating that reality. Emily discovered the power of affirmations and began each day with positive declarations. These affirmations were her road signs, reminding her of her purpose and keeping her on track. She embraced mindfulness meditation, finding solace in its calming effect amidst the chaos of her studies and commitments. Through each challenge, Emily's motivation remained her constant companion. She built a support network of like-minded individuals—fellow students, mentors, and professors—who became her travel companions on this personal growth journey. Their encouragement was the fuel that propelled her forward, reminding her that she was not alone.

The journey wasn't without its setbacks. There were moments when she stumbled and encountered roadblocks. Emily faced the second crossroads, where maintaining her motivation seemed daunting. But she remembered a quote she had stumbled upon during a particularly trying day: "The journey of a thousand miles begins with a single step." Each step, no matter how small, was a step closer to her dreams. As Emily persisted, she started keeping a personal growth journal. She documented her progress, setbacks, and reflections. This journal became a map of her journey, capturing her growth and serving as a testament to her resilience. Just as a road trip leaves memories etched in photographs, her journal was a snapshot of her evolving self.

Emily's efforts soon bore fruit. She received recognition for her commitment to environmental conservation, and opportunities began to unfold before her like scenic vistas on a road trip. Each success, each accomplishment, was a milestone she celebrated with gratitude. Years passed, and Emily realized she had reached her destination. She was working in the field she had always dreamed of, making a tangible impact on the environment. Looking back, Emily marveled at her journey—a journey that had taught her that maintaining motivation was not about avoiding challenges, but about using them as steppingstones to growth.

Emily's story serves as a reminder that a personal growth journey is much like a road trip—full of unexpected turns, challenges, and breathtaking moments. It's about maintaining focus on your goals, even when the path seems unclear. And just as Emily's determination turned her dreams into reality, your journey too can be a testament to the power of motivation, perseverance, and the unwavering belief in the destination you're striving to reach. The story of Emily starts out like most of ours: we know what we want, in the beginning we are excited about receiving it, we are eager to obtain it, and we are driven to pursue it. Just like Emily, we all will face a crossroad, and it is at the crossroads that many of us are distracted by the choices that are before us or maybe it's an obstacle, a roadblock, a traffic jam, or a detour that requires us to have to take a detour. It is at the crossroad or during the detour that we have to decide. It is here that we begin to question whether the journey is worth taking. It is in this moment that we often lose our focus, it is in these times that we become depressed, fearful, or waver.

Emily's story should serve as a beacon of hope to us all. Her story is much like millions of other successful people throughout the world. Reflect on Emily's actions when she encountered her crossroad. Did she tuck tail and run, abandoning her dreams and aspirations? No. Did she pause? Yes, but only to motivate herself to continue forward in her journey. Often times along our journey, we have to stop and encourage ourselves. This reminds me of King David in I Samuel 30:6 when David was distressed because the people wanted to stone him. David could have easily given up and given in, but instead the verse says that David encouraged himself. That is what motivation is; it is simply encouraging yourself to continue on. Emily encouraged herself by envisioning the end result; she kept her eyes on the prize. Envisioning our goals continuously allows us to be encouraged to continue to move forward in our journey. Not only did she envision the goal, but she also affirmed it through her affirmations. This is why we have our affirmations; they are a tool to motivate us to continue to move forward.

According to her story, Emily then meditated. I know many of you are saying I am not about to sit down and cross my legs and start humming. That is not what it means to meditate; that is just a technique that helps some people to meditate. To meditate means to contemplate or reflect on. It means to have it continuously on or in your mind. Meditating helps us to have a clear understanding of what our goal is and gives us solid reasonings to pursue it. Through her meditation, Emily understood that she could not do it on her own, so she built a network of like-minded people to help her along the way.

Emily's story proves that we will have crossroads, setbacks, and challenges along the way, but not just one. Every path that we ponder upon will contain multiple challenges and obstacles. Understand that challenges and obstacles are not there to hurt us; in fact, most of the time they are there to help us. It is through the obstacles and challenges that we learn to grow, it is within them that we become stronger than we would have ever become. To prove this, Emily kept a journal of her journey, keeping a record of her obstacles, challenges, and setbacks. It was through this journal that she was able to not only track her growth and progress, but she was able to use it as a written testimony. In order for us to turn our dreams and desires into reality, we must have our focus fixed on the outcome and maintain our motivation on continual movement toward the achievement of our goal. Realize that we are often tested in our journey to prove our resilience, to build our self-esteem, to develop our creativity and adaptability.

Building Adaptability and Resilience

Life's journey, much like an adventurous road trip, is riddled with unpredictable twists and turns. The road ahead isn't always smooth; it tests our limits, challenges our resolve, and presents us with unanticipated obstacles. Just as a seasoned traveler prepares for unexpected detours, we must cultivate resilience and adaptability to navigate our personal growth journey successfully.

The truth of the matter is that along your life journey you will have to travel down some back roads, especially if you are trying to attain personal growth. It is when you encounter these back roads that you find yourself on some of the most treacherous, bumpiest, rockiest, and unpredictable terrains. These back roads are often filled with unforeseen twists and turns, they are never well lit, they are filled with the unknown and are usually the road that is less traveled.

Once my wife and I were in Rochester, New York, and we were leaving there headed to Detroit, Michigan, for a family reunion. Understand that we had never been on this journey before, so we were dependent on the GPS to give us directions to get there. After we inputted our destination, we were given the directions to get there. As we traveled, we followed the directions, starting out on the expressway, where there was plenty of traffic, the road was well lit, and it contained all the amenities. It was not long before we were directed to exit onto a two-lane highway. As we traveled down this two-lane highway, the lighting became non-existent. Here we were in unknown territory, struggling to see the road, filled with turns that you could not see until you were right on top of them. It was also filled with a lot of ups and downs, and I do mean ups and downs, with high hills and steep valleys, but I continued to drive. We were on this road for what seemed to be forever, but the truth is it was not even an hour and probably would have been less if I could see better and if I had known the road. During our journey down the two-lane highway, we passed two vehicles and never saw any vehicles behind us. It wasn't long before the GPS instructed us to turn right in 500 feet. When I turned, we were on another two-lane highway. It wasn't long before the highway turned into an unpaved road. At this point, I wondered if I was going the right way, and as soon as I thought it, my wife asked if I was sure we were going the right way. I told her it was the way the GPS said to go as we continued on our journey. Here we were, driving down a dirt road in the darkness of the night, not knowing where we were nor if we were on the right path, trusting that the GPS was taking us in the right direction. It was so dark that I drove for miles with my bright lights on, driving below the speed limit to ensure that I could safely maneuver the road ahead. All the while, I wondered if I was going the right way, was I on the right road, and was the GPS giving me good directions. I looked at the gas hand, and it was rapidly moving beyond the quarter of a tank and headed towards empty; it had been a while since I had seen a gas station. Now, I had a new worry, the fear of running out of gas in an unknown area, and to make matters worse, I had no cell service, and there was no shoulder to pull off on if I did run out of gas. As I continued to drive, the fear of running out of gas deepened, and I hoped and prayed that I would run into a gas station soon. As I looked at the GPS, I noticed I still had 28 miles left to travel on this road. I wondered if I should tell my wife about the issue that we would soon face, or should I keep it to myself and allow her to be spared the weight of worrying about the situation? I decided it was best to keep it to myself.

Then it happened: with three miles left on this isolated road, the fuel light popped on. Now I was really worried! As I continued to drive and pray, I contemplated what to do when I did run out of gas. All sorts of thoughts ran through my mind. I could see myself trying to explain to my wife why I had not told her we were running out of gas, and then us having to walk in the middle of the night on this dark, isolated road. I began to wonder how long we would have to walk, would we run into wild animals or even worse, people who would harm us? These are the thoughts that were running through my mind. My thoughts were interrupted by the GPS saying turn right in 500 feet. It took my attention off running out of gas to focus on where I would turn. Finally, we were off the unpaved road and onto another two-lane highway. Again, my thought went back to us running out of gas. Then the GPS instructed me to take a slight right in 1000 feet to enter onto the highway. As I entered the highway, I saw a sign which showed four gas stations at the next exit in two miles. This gave me a sense of ease, but I hoped that we could make it to the next exit before running out of gas. The closer I got, the more I worried, as the gas hand was now on E. The only thing that eased my mind was a sign that said right lane exit only. I exited the highway, and to the right was a Pilot truck stop. My mind was now at ease, my worries had subsided. As I pulled into the station, I breathed a huge sigh of relief. My wife noticed and asked me what that was for. I explained to her that the gas light had come on about eight miles ago when we were on the unpaved road. She looked at me and said, oh yeah, I saw that. She laughed and said she wasn't worried because she saw that we would be back on the highway in six miles and the next gas station was two miles away. I asked why she was not worried, and she said that when the light comes on, we have 25 miles before it actually runs out of gas. Here I was, worried to death, trying to spare her the need to worry, and she knew all along that everything would be alright. After filling up the car, we were back on the highway and soon arrived in Detroit.

This story later taught me some of life's most valuable lessons, especially in personal growth. We need to understand that personal growth is much like this road trip. It is filled with twists and turns, ups and downs, uncertainties, fears, and doubts, not to mention our motivation running low. The most important thing is to never stop driving, never stop moving forward, never give up and never give in. Another thing I learned from the journey is that it is okay to share your fears, doubts, and worries with others because they may know something that would eliminate them. It doesn't matter what obstacles and challenges you may face on your journey; what matters is that you keep driving towards your destination. Trust me, they will come, so it's important to be ready, prepare yourself and embrace the unpredictable.

Embrace the Unpredictable

Picture yourself cruising along a scenic highway, the sun illuminating the path before you. Suddenly, a detour sign appears, redirecting you onto an unfamiliar route. In life, detours manifest as setbacks, failures, or unforeseen circumstances. They are the true tests of our resilience. Instead of resisting these deviations, we must learn to embrace them.

Resilience is the armor that shields us from adversity. It's the unyielding spirit that allows us to bounce back from setbacks. Just as a well-prepared traveler faces unforeseen roadblocks, we must equip ourselves mentally, emotionally, and spiritually to handle the challenges that come our way.

Weathering the Storms

Imagine a sudden downpour during your road trip, obscuring your vision and dampening your spirits. Adapting to inclement weather requires a swift change in plans and a positive attitude. Similarly, life's storms—be they failures, disappointments, or unexpected changes—demand our ability to adapt. Adapting doesn't mean abandoning our goals; it means altering our strategies to suit the circumstances.

Adaptability is the compass that keeps us oriented when life takes unexpected turns. It's the willingness to adjust our course while maintaining our ultimate destination in sight. Just as a traveler finds alternative routes during road closures, our ability to adapt keeps us moving forward when faced with challenges.

Building Resilience

Resilience is not innate; it's a skill that can be cultivated through practice. Just as travelers train for endurance on a road trip, we can build resilience through self-care, mindfulness, and a growth mindset. Resilience is rooted in self-belief, reminding us that setbacks are temporary and can be overcome with determination.

Embrace failures as learning opportunities. Instead of succumbing to defeat, use setbacks as stepping stones toward growth. Remember, even the most well-planned road trips encounter bumps along the way. Likewise, our personal growth journey may encounter stumbling blocks, but each one presents a chance to rise stronger and wiser.

Harnessing Adaptability

Adaptability is a trait that empowers us to find opportunities in challenges. As a traveler adjusts their route to find scenic byways, we can adjust our strategies to capitalize on unexpected situations. Adaptability isn't about compromising our goals; it's about finding new paths to reach them.

Adaptability teaches us to relinquish control over the uncontrollable. Just as a traveler can't control the weather, we can't control every aspect of our personal growth journey. By learning to accept and adjust to the ebb and flow of life, we free ourselves from the burden of unrealistic expectations.

The Power of Perspective

Imagine you're driving through a dense forest. The road ahead may seem dark and intimidating, but the forest also holds the promise of discovery and hidden beauty. Similarly, challenges and setbacks on our personal growth journey offer hidden opportunities for growth and self-discovery.

Resilience and adaptability are the headlights that illuminate the darkness. Just as headlights guide you through the night, these qualities guide you through challenges. They give you the clarity and courage to keep moving forward even when the path seems unclear.

Thriving Through Turbulence

Road trips are never just about reaching a destination; they're about the journey itself—the landscapes, the experiences, and the growth along the way. In the same vein, our personal growth journey is about embracing the lessons and transformations that come from challenges. Resilience and adaptability are the vehicles that allow us to thrive amidst life's turbulence.

In the end, remember that both smooth roads and rugged terrains contribute to the richness of the journey. Just as a road trip becomes a collection of memories, our personal growth journey becomes a tapestry woven from resilience, adaptability, and the unwavering belief that every detour, every setback, is an opportunity to become stronger, wiser, and more resilient on the road to self-discovery, fulfillment, and achievement.

So remember along this personal growth journey, just like a road trip, you will have the unforeseen. No matter how well we plan, there will always be something that pops up out of nowhere that may cause us to have to adjust our plans. There will be accidents, there will be construction, and there will be some road closures, but no matter what, we must adapt our plan, shift our direction, or merely slowdown in order to overcome them. Being adaptive does not mean that we give up or abandon our dreams and aspirations. It means that we need to adapt to the current situation or circumstance. It means that we must remain resilient in our quest, keeping our focus on the end result. It is through these things that we truly evolve in our personal growth.

Just as a road trip takes you on unexpected routes, your personal growth journey is filled with uncharted adventures. Embrace the twists and turns, for they lead to experiences that shape your character and fuel your growth. On the road and in life, detours arise without warning. Embrace them as opportunities to explore new paths and uncover hidden gems. These unexpected moments often hold the most valuable lessons. Like a road trip's weather forecast, life's uncertainties can change in an instant. Embrace the dance with uncertainty, for within it lies the chance to develop resilience and the ability to thrive despite the unknown. Just as a sudden rainstorm can give way to a breathtaking rainbow, challenges can lead to remarkable growth. Embrace the storms in your personal growth journey, for they often precede moments of beauty and transformation. Just as a surfer adapts to changing waves, adapt to the waves of change in your journey. Embrace the unpredictability and let it sharpen your skills in staying focused and adaptable. Sometimes the scenic route takes us down unfamiliar roads. Embrace the road less traveled in your personal growth journey, as it may hold unique opportunities for self-discovery and growth.

In the same way a flat tire doesn't end a road trip, setbacks in your journey don't define your destination. Embrace setbacks as stepping stones to a higher level of resilience and determination. Just as discovering a hidden waterfall on a road trip brings joy, finding unexpected opportunities in your personal growth journey can fill your heart with excitement and satisfaction. As landscapes change during a road trip, so do the landscapes of your personal growth journey. Embrace change as a chance to evolve and transform into the best version of yourself. A road trip demands flexibility in adjusting plans. Embrace the same flexibility in your personal growth journey, allowing you to adapt and thrive in the face of unexpected challenges. Just as a road trip is about the journey as much as the destination, your personal growth journey is about the experiences, lessons, and growth you encounter along the way. Embrace every moment as part of your beautiful story.

Imagine stumbling upon a hidden café during a road trip. Embrace the thrill of discovering hidden talents, strengths, and passions within yourself as you journey toward personal growth. Memories of a road trip aren't only of smooth roads, but also the challenges. Embrace adversity as an opportunity to create memorable stories of triumph and resilience in your personal growth journey.

Just as a road trip takes you through varied landscapes, your personal growth journey involves navigating unknown terrain. Embrace the adventure of growth as you evolve through unexplored aspects of yourself. Embrace the uncertainty of your personal growth journey with the spirit of adventure. Just as facing a thrilling zip line brings both fear and excitement, so does stepping out of your comfort zone on your growth journey. Like discovering a breathtaking view during a road trip, embrace the moments of uncovering hidden strengths within yourself. These moments remind you of your resilience and power. Imagine capturing a stunning sunset on your road trip. Embrace the essence of resilience in your personal growth journey as you navigate through challenges and setbacks, knowing that every moment adds to your story. Just as a road trip might involve imperfect weather, embrace the imperfections in your personal growth journey. These moments teach you acceptance and resilience, making you stronger.

Just as a vehicle adapts to changing terrains, embrace the changes in your personal growth journey. Adaptation is a sign of strength and growth, enabling you to flourish amidst shifting circumstances. On a road trip, you navigate change with maps and GPS. Similarly, in your personal growth journey, embrace the role of a navigator, guiding yourself through life's changes with resilience, adaptability, and the unwavering belief in your destination.

In order for us to be resilient and adaptive, it's important to know what resources are available and required.

Part V
Recognizing Your Resources

Identifying the Resources in Life

A resource refers to a naturally occurring substance or asset that has potential value and utility for human beings. Resources can be categorized into various types, including natural resources (such as minerals, water, forests, and land) and human-made resources (like technology, knowledge, and infrastructure). Resources can exist in their natural state and might or might not be exploited or utilized for economic or practical purposes. A resource is a broader term that encompasses all types of assets that can be used or exploited for human benefit, whether they are tangible (like minerals) or intangible (like knowledge). Resources may or may not be traded or exchanged in markets. Some resources, like knowledge or a unique natural landscape, might not have a direct market value. Resources can vary widely in terms of quality, rarity, and uniqueness. They might not be easily interchangeable with other similar resources. Resources cover a broader spectrum of assets, including both tangible and intangible elements. They may or may not be the subject of trading or economic transactions. In summary, resources are a broader concept that encompasses various assets with potential value.

Life consists of many resources, but there are four major resources in life; it is through the proper utilization of these resources that achieving success becomes easy. Before I get into how to utilize them let me introduce these resources to you. The four major resources in life are: relationships, knowledge, money, and time. Every person on the planet has access to these resources. While they are not equally provided to each individual, they are all easily attainable once we learn how to access them. When we have an abundance of any one of these resources, we can succeed in whatever we desire to do, become, or achieve. The problem is that most of us focus on the one resource that carries the least value, but before I tell you which resource it is, I want you to do a quick exercise.

Prioritizing Resources

Here is what I want you to do: take a moment and prioritize the resources. Turn to page 399 of your workbook or write it in your notebook. All I need you to do is write each resource down in order of importance.

Resource Priority	
#	Resource
1	
2	
3	
4	

Okay, that was simple, wasn't it? First let me tell you, there really is no right or wrong answer; it is a matter of personal preference. While most people place money as the number one resource and most important, I place money as the number 4 resource and the least important. Understand the other three resources will automatically produce money. Before I get into that, I will give you my answer, so that you can better understand my perspective. Here is how I prioritize the four resources:

Resource Priority

Resource Priority	
#	Resource
1	Time
2	Knowledge
3	Relationships
4	Money

1. Time

2. Knowledge

3. Relationships

4. Money

Understand that my logic is far from the average thinker. I am what is considered a creative thinker. While the majority of people think inside the box and some think outside the box, there are a few who don't believe there is a box. For me, money is the least important of the four because the other three automatically produce money. Think about it: most people trade time for money, others trade knowledge for money, and relationships can produce money. But the vast majority of people see money as the top resource, and I understand why. They look at money as a means to have more time to do what they want to do, as a means to attain knowledge, and as a means to meet a higher quality of people. Here is where I have a problem with this philosophy: what happens when the money is lost? You no longer have the time to do what you want, and your friends soon depart. I have seen this happen in real life numerous times; I have even personally experienced it. Putting money ahead of all others is really a bad idea. My grandfather once asked me if I had a choice between a $1,000,000 or 1 million friends, which would I choose? Now mind you, I was only 11 or 12 at the time. My answer was to have 1 million friends. He asked me why, and I explained to him with a million friends, I can always ask each one of them for $5, and then I will have $5,000,000 and 1 million friends. For me, it was common sense. Of course, it was astounding to my grandfather, but it was the answer that he would have given me.

When it comes to prioritizing our resources, there are actually 24 different choices. Everyone will never choose the same answer, because everyone thinks differently, has different mindsets, and has different situations and circumstances. Also, we all have different beliefs. While some believe that having too much money is bad, others believe that you can never have enough money. But of all the resources, there is only one that is finite, and that is time.

Time as a Resource

Time is the most precious currency we possess. Unlike money, it cannot be earned or saved – only spent. Each moment that slips away is a reminder that time is finite, urging us to make the most of every opportunity and experience life to the fullest. The concept of "carpe diem" underscores the urgency of embracing the present moment. Time waits for no one, and each day that dawns brings about new possibilities. Seize the day with a fervor that turns mere existence into a vibrant and purposeful journey. Imagine time as the threads that weave the tapestry of your life. With each passing moment, you add colors, textures, and patterns that shape your story. The intricate design reflects the choices you make and the experiences you embrace. Time is the fuel that powers your aspirations. It provides the space to cultivate skills, build relationships, and chase your dreams. Cherish every tick of the clock, for it's a chance to invest in the future you envision.

The finite nature of time encourages us to live with intention and without regrets. Regret often stems from missed opportunities and unfulfilled dreams. Embrace the urgency of time, ensuring that you chase your goals and savor the experiences that matter most. Every day lived is another stroke on the canvas of your legacy. The way you spend your time shapes the impact you leave behind. Be mindful of the impression you create, for your legacy is the culmination of the moments you invest. Time teaches us the art of prioritization. When we recognize that time is limited, we become more discerning about how we allocate it. Distractions fade away, and we focus on what truly aligns with our values and aspirations.

Time's finiteness underscores the significance of the present moment. Rather than dwelling on the past or solely planning for the future, relish the gift of now. It's in these fleeting moments that life unfolds. Dreams remain unfulfilled until we infuse them with the energy of time. The clock's relentless movement reminds us that to make our dreams a reality, we must actively engage in the journey and consistently dedicate time to our pursuit. In a world that often rushes by, take a moment to appreciate the simple beauty of time ticking away. Each second is a chance to be grateful for the experiences, relationships, and growth that enrich your life's journey. Embrace the fleeting nature of time, and let it inspire you to live with purpose and passion.

Knowledge as a Resource

Imagine knowledge as an ever-flowing stream of wisdom, an infinite resource that springs eternal. Every moment presents an opportunity to tap into this boundless source, to quench your thirst for understanding, and to enrich your life's journey. Curiosity is the flame that keeps the torch of knowledge burning bright. It's a force that knows no bounds, propelling you to explore, question, and seek answers. Embrace your innate curiosity as the spark that ignites your quest for lifelong learning. Knowledge is the key that unlocks the doors of possibility. As you gather insights and skills, you open new avenues for personal and professional growth. The more you learn, the wider the spectrum of opportunities that beckon you forward. Just as the garden flourishes with care and attention, our minds thrive on the nourishment of knowledge. Each piece of information you absorb becomes a seed that, when cultivated, blossoms into new perspectives, innovative ideas, and profound insights. The journey of knowledge is not a sprint; it's a lifelong exploration. There are no finish lines, only milestones that mark your progress. Embrace the journey with excitement, knowing that every discovery brings you closer to the boundless frontiers of understanding.

Ignorance is like a veil that shrouds understanding. Knowledge is the light that pierces through the darkness, revealing the intricate patterns of the world around you. By seeking knowledge, you dispel ignorance, replacing it with awareness and enlightenment. Picture your life as a tapestry woven with threads of learning. Every experience, every book read, every lesson learned adds to the richness of this tapestry. As you continuously gather knowledge, your tapestry becomes a masterpiece that reflects the depth of your wisdom. Knowledge is the source of empowerment, giving you the tools to navigate life's challenges and seize its opportunities. With every bit of information, you acquire, you gain the ability to make informed decisions and shape your destiny. In the realm of knowledge, there are no dead ends or cul-de-sacs. It's a realm of infinite pathways, each leading to new discoveries. Embrace this boundless landscape as an invitation to explore, to grow, and to expand your horizons beyond imagination. The pursuit of knowledge leaves a lasting legacy that transcends generations. The insights you gather, the lessons you learn, and the wisdom you acquire become gifts that you can share with others. As you contribute to the reservoir of knowledge, you become part of an eternal chain of enlightenment, leaving an indelible mark on the world.

Relationships as a Resource

Relationships are the threads that weave the intricate tapestry of our lives. Each connection, whether fleeting or enduring, adds a unique hue to this vibrant masterpiece. Embrace the beauty of relationships as a resource that enriches your journey. Just as a tree draws strength from its roots, you too draw strength from the bonds you cultivate. Relationships provide a safety net of emotional support, encouragement, and companionship that empowers you to weather life's storms and reach new heights. Relationships serve as fertile ground for collaboration and growth. Through shared experiences and exchanges of ideas, you expand your horizons and tap into the collective wisdom of those around you. Embrace relationships as catalysts for personal and mutual development. The journey of life is marked by shared moments that become cherished memories. Relationships gift you with these moments – laughter, tears, milestones, and everyday adventures. Treasure these experiences as the true wealth that relationships bring. Your relationships mirror back the essence of who you are. They reflect your values, aspirations, and qualities. By surrounding yourself with positive and meaningful connections, you amplify your own positive traits and contribute to a network of support.

Relationships offer a unique window into the lives of others. The practice of empathy – stepping into someone else's shoes – deepens your understanding of the human experience. This empathy nurtures your own growth while fostering compassion and understanding. Within every relationship lies a treasure trove of shared wisdom. Conversations, disagreements, and moments of vulnerability offer opportunities to learn and gain insights from different perspectives. Embrace these interactions as a continuous source of personal enrichment. Emotions are the currency of relationships, exchanged through laughter, comfort, and understanding. The emotional resonance you experience in relationships is a priceless resource that uplifts your spirit, soothes your soul, and fuels your well-being. Relationships bridge gaps and dissolve barriers. They connect people from diverse backgrounds, cultures, and beliefs. Embrace this resource as a way to build bridges of understanding, promoting unity and celebrating the richness of human diversity. The relationships you cultivate are a legacy that echoes through time. The impact you make in the lives of others leaves a lasting imprint, influencing generations to come. Cherish the privilege of building connections that shape your story and contribute to the stories of others.

When it comes to relationships as a resource in your personal growth journey, imagine your personal growth journey as an exciting road trip, and relationships are the fellow travelers who share the ride. Just as a road trip becomes more enjoyable when shared with companions, your personal growth journey becomes enriched by the connections you build along the way. As you traverse the winding roads of self-discovery, the relationships you cultivate provide companionship and unwavering support. These connections are your travel buddies, cheering you on through challenges, offering encouragement, and celebrating your victories. Just as a road trip includes moments of bonding around a campfire, your personal growth journey involves sharing stories, experiences, and insights with your relationships. These shared narratives become the fabric of your growth, woven with the threads of connection. On a road trip, you encounter diverse landscapes and cultures. Similarly, the relationships you nurture expose you to a tapestry of perspectives and backgrounds. Embrace the opportunity to learn from these differences, broadening your horizons and fostering personal growth. In a road trip, you navigate crossroads and make collective decisions. Likewise, in your personal growth journey, your relationships play a role in shaping your choices. Engage in open discussions, seek advice, and let the insights from your companions guide you toward growth.

Road trips often come with unforeseen challenges and unexpected joys. Similarly, your relationships help you become better "travelers" in the journey of life. Through shared experiences, you learn resilience, adaptability, and the importance of navigating the unknown together. Just as a road trip includes milestones like reaching a scenic viewpoint, your personal growth journey is marked by achievements. Your relationships are there to celebrate these milestones with you, making your successes even more meaningful. During a road trip, you make rest stops to recharge and reconnect. Similarly, in your personal growth journey, take moments to reconnect with your relationships. These pauses provide an opportunity to reflect, share insights, and strengthen the bonds that contribute to your growth. A road trip encounters bumpy roads and smooth stretches alike. Likewise, your personal growth journey has its ups and downs. Your relationships act as shock absorbers, providing emotional stability and helping you navigate through life's rough patches. Just as a road trip leaves tire tracks on the pavement, your relationships leave footprints on each other's personal growth journeys. The connections you build shape not only your own journey but also the lives of those who accompany you. Embrace the beauty of relationships as an invaluable resource that propels your growth forward.

Money as a Resource

Money is the currency that unlocks a world of opportunities. Just as a key opens doors, financial resources grant you access to experiences, education, travel, and the chance to pursue your passions. Embrace money as a powerful tool that amplifies your ability to shape your destiny. Money serves as a vehicle for growth and learning. It provides you with the means to invest in books, courses, and experiences that expand your knowledge and skills. With financial resources at your disposal, you can continuously evolve and strive for mastery. Consider money as the fuel that propels your dreams into reality. Whether you aspire to launch a business, travel the world, or create art, financial resources provide the foundation upon which you can build your aspirations. Financial independence is synonymous with empowerment. Having money empowers you to make decisions aligned with your values, without being constrained by external limitations. It grants you the freedom to live life on your terms.

Money is not just about personal gain; it's a resource that enables you to make a positive impact on the world. With financial resources, you can support causes you believe in, contribute to charity, and create lasting change for those in need. Financial resources foster an environment where creativity and innovation can thrive. Just as an artist needs supplies to create a masterpiece, your ideas and ventures require financial support to flourish and transform the world around you. Financial stability acts as a safety net, providing peace of mind during challenging times. It offers security in the face of unexpected events and ensures that you can focus on your personal growth journey without constantly worrying about basic needs. View money as a legacy that transcends generations. By making wise financial choices and building wealth, you create opportunities for your loved ones and future generations. This legacy becomes a testament to your commitment to creating a brighter future.

Shift your mindset from scarcity to abundance. Recognize that money is a resource that can be attracted and managed through conscious choices. Approach financial decisions with intention and embrace the abundance that comes from a positive relationship with money. While money is a valuable resource, it's important to remember that true wealth encompasses well-being in all aspects of life. Balance your pursuit of financial growth with a focus on health, relationships, personal fulfillment, and a sense of purpose. The journey of personal growth is enriched when you view money as one of many tools that contribute to a fulfilling and meaningful life.

Understanding these four resources in life is the make-it-or-break-it factor when it comes to achieving our goals. Without having the right resources and the correct measure of them, we will always wind up wandering in a vast void of confusion. We can set an array of goals, but without making time to pursue them, we are simply dreaming of what we want to be, have, or do. But when we take inventory of our time, measuring it, monitoring it, and managing it properly, we give our goals the potential to become a reality. But making time for our goals is not enough. We also need to have the proper knowledge to fulfill our goals. Again, we can set our goals, but not having the knowledge to fulfill them leaves us battered, bruised, and confused trying to figure out what we need to do. But when we recognize the knowledge that we need to have and take the time to gain it, we make room for that goal to come to fruition. Many people say that knowledge is power, but the reality is just because we have the knowledge does not give us power. The fact is knowledge itself is not power, but it is the application and utilization of knowledge that is power. But the knowledge that we need does not necessarily have to be our own. Sometimes we can utilize the knowledge that others already possess. This is where your relationships play a factor in achieving your goals.

Our relationships can help us to achieve our goals. By having the right people in our circle, we can gain a lot of traction to attain our goals. These relationships can also give us that push that we need to stay motivated and focused on achieving our goals. Building the right team to assist us in our goal is an intricate part of getting to our destination. Imagine taking a 12-hour road trip alone. Because you are the only driver, it will require more than 12 hours because you will need to stop to take a break along the way. But when we have others with us, we are able to maintain our schedule because as we rest, they are driving, allowing us to gain more miles while we are taking a break. When we have the right relationships, we can build a strong team that will drive us forward in pursuing our goal. Our team may sometimes include professionals who need to be paid. This is where money plays a role in the fulfillment of goals. Know that pursuing your goals has a cost. I know that you have all heard the saying nothing in life is free. The truth is you will either pay on the front end or on the back end. This is why it is important to assess the cost of our goals. Creating goals without knowing the cost is much like building a house without assessing the cost before we start. Before I purchase a property, I assess the cost: how much will the closing cost be, how much will the repairs cost, how much will it cost to maintain the property? These are all the questions I need answered before I even submit an offer. Before we even start pursuing our goals, we need to know the cost. Every goal that we set has some type of cost attached to it, and it may not just be money. Sometimes it can be our time. Assigning a reward to our goal will have a cost.

Before I move to the next chapter, I would be doing you a disservice if I did not tell you about a new resource that is rapidly moving up the list of life's resources. It is a resource that saves time, gives knowledge, builds relationships, and creates money. What is it? It is technology. I refer to it as the fifth element.

Technology as a Resource

Technology is the newest frontier of human progress, propelling us into a future of boundless possibilities. Just as explorers venture into uncharted lands, you embark on a journey of discovery, harnessing the power of technology to shape your world and push the boundaries of what's achievable. In a world interconnected by technology, you're granted the ability to connect with individuals across the globe at the touch of a button. Embrace technology as a bridge that spans distances, fostering relationships and enabling collaboration on a global scale. It is the canvas on which your creativity and innovation come to life. Just as artists use new mediums to express their visions, you harness the digital tools at your disposal to bring your ideas, designs, and dreams into reality. Consider technology as an endless library of knowledge, available at your fingertips. With the internet as your guide, you can access information, learn new skills, and broaden your understanding in ways that were once unimaginable. It is reshaping industries and creating new pathways for success. Just as pioneers revolutionized transportation, communication, and more, you have the opportunity to innovate, disrupt, and lead within the evolving landscape of technology.

Technology has the power to tear down barriers and foster accessibility and inclusion. Through advancements in assistive technologies, you can ensure that everyone has the opportunity to participate, contribute, and thrive in the digital age. In a rapidly changing world, technology equips you with the agility to adapt and thrive. Embrace the transformative nature of technology, allowing it to be your compass as you navigate through the evolving landscapes of industries, trends, and opportunities. It has democratized entrepreneurship, enabling you to launch businesses, reach customers, and drive innovation with fewer barriers than ever before. Embrace technology as a launch pad for your entrepreneurial aspirations, where your ideas can take flight and change lives. It is a canvas for self-expression, allowing you to curate your online identity and share your voice with the world. Just as artists leave their mark on a canvas, you leave a digital footprint that contributes to the narrative of your journey. As technology reshapes the world, you have the potential to make a global impact from wherever you are. Embrace technology as a tool that empowers you to drive change, raise awareness, and inspire others to join you on the path of positive transformation. The journey is just beginning, and you're equipped with the latest resource that has the potential to shape the course of humanity's story.

You now know what the resources in life are, but remember, knowing is not power. It is the use of knowledge that gives us power. We all have access to these five resources, but yet we do not all utilize them in a way that is productive to fulfilling our dreams and aspirations. We need to exercise our knowledge of these resources in order to strengthen our power. When we utilize our resources, we empower ourselves to propel to new heights. Understanding how to use our resources creates an easier path and a smoother road for us to travel towards our destination of personal fulfillment. But before we can utilize these resources, we need to do two things: we need to take inventory of the resources that we already possess, and we need to know which resources we need to stock up on.

Knowing What Resources, You Have

Taking inventory of the five resources of life—time, knowledge, relationships, money, and technology—is an empowering exercise that highlights the abundance you already possess. Just as a treasure chest holds valuable gems, this inventory reveals the riches within your grasp. As you assess your resources, cultivate gratitude for what you have. Gratitude is the foundation upon which growth flourishes. Recognize that your current possession of these resources is a testament to the opportunities that await your diligent investment.

As you take inventory of your resources, align them with your purpose and goals. Reflect on whether your current investments are propelling you in the direction you desire. Adjust your strategies to ensure that your resources contribute to your ultimate aspirations. Celebrate your progress by acknowledging the milestones you've achieved, the relationships you've nurtured, and the knowledge you've gained. Celebrate these victories as steps along the path of personal growth.

Taking inventory isn't just a reflection of the past; it's a compass for the future. Use this reflection as a foundation for intentional goal achievement. Identify areas where you want to grow, strengthen relationships, deepen knowledge, manage finances, and leverage technology. With this blueprint, you embark on a journey where each resource becomes a steppingstone to achieving your aspirations.

Inventorying Your Time

Time is a precious commodity. Reflect on how you allocate it—whether for personal growth, relationships, learning, or leisure. Time is the only resource that is finite; we each only have 24 hours in a day. To inventory our time requires us to answer the question of how much time am I willing to commit to my personal growth. Most of our time is already consumed before we even commit to our personal growth, while there are only 24 hours in a day, the average person consumes 8 hours of it sleeping and another 8 hours working. This accounts for 16 hours of the day already accounted for each weekday, this only leaves 8 hours for other things. This does not allot for travel time to and from work, family time, leisure time, or anything else.

So, let's take a quick assessment of our time. Turn to page 399 of your workbook and complete the Time Inventory Worksheet or create it in your notebook from this example:

Time Inventory Worksheet							
Activity	Sunday	Monday	Tuesday	Wednesday	Thursday	Friday	Saturday
Sleeping	8	8	8	8	8	8	8
Personal Care/Hygiene	.75	.75	.75	.75	.75	.75	.75
Meal Preparation	1	1	1	1	1	1	1
Commute	.5	1	1	1	1	1	1
Work/School	0	8	8	8	8	8	0
Caring for Children or Family	4	2	2	2	2	2	4
Household Chores	0	.5	.5	.5	.5	.5	2
Total Time Utilized	14.25	21.25	21.25	21.25	21.25	21.25	16.75
Unallocated time	4.75	2.75	2.75	2.75	2.75	2.75	7.25

Notice this exercise does not include the time we spend on non-essential activities like watching TV, hobbies, leisure, socializing, entertaining, or exercise. The truth is that we don't have a lot of time. On average we only have about 2-5 hours of non-essential time on weekdays and 10-16 hours on weekends. Understanding that our time is so limited makes it even more precious. By optimizing your time management, you open the door to unlocking more moments for self-improvement and connection.

Inventorying Your Knowledge

Reflect on the knowledge you've acquired. Each piece of information, every lesson learned, contributes to your personal growth. Begin by setting aside time for self-reflection. Consider your educational background, work experiences, hobbies, and interests. Recall formal education, courses, workshops, seminars, and self-directed learning experiences you've undertaken. Note the skills and knowledge you gained from each. Think about the topics, skills, and subjects you feel confident and knowledgeable about.

Organize your knowledge into categories or areas of expertise. For example, you might have categories like "Professional Skills," "Hobbies and Interests," "Personal Development," and more. Within each category, list subtopics or specific subjects you have knowledge about. These can be as broad or as specific as you like. Next, assess your proficiency level for each subtopic. Rate yourself on a scale (e.g., beginner, intermediate, advanced) to gauge your level of expertise.

It took me quite a while to figure out how to inventory our knowledge. I realized that I needed to confine it to six categories: practical, professional, creative, technological, skills, and personal development. These are the areas which we will focus on as we take inventory of our knowledge.

Practical Knowledge

Practical knowledge encompasses the valuable skills and information that empower us to navigate the intricacies of daily life with confidence and competence. It's the hands-on understanding of tasks, procedures, and situations that are integral to our well-being and success. This type of knowledge fosters self-sufficiency, problem-solving, and a sense of empowerment, enabling us to tackle diverse situations and make informed decisions. Ultimately, it forms the foundation for a well-rounded and capable life, enhancing our ability to thrive in both ordinary and extraordinary circumstances.

Turn to page 400 of your workbook to the Practical Knowledge Form or create your list in your notebook using the following example:

Practical Knowledge Form				
#	Knowledge	Beginner	Intermediate	Advanced
1	Reading	☐	☐	☒

2	Writing	☐	☐	☒
3	Listening	☐	☐	☒
4	Communicating with others	☐	☐	☒
5	Speaking in public	☐	☐	☒
6	Solving mathematical	☐	☐	☒
7	Bookkeeping	☐	☐	☒
8	Accounting	☐	☒	☐
9	Critical thinking	☐	☐	☒
10	Cooking	☐	☐	☒
11	Meal preparation and planning	☐	☐	☒
12	Baking	☐	☐	☒
13	Grocery shopping	☐	☐	☒
14	Prioritizing tasks	☐	☐	☒
15	Setting goals	☐	☐	☒
16	Creating schedules and routines	☐	☒	☐
17	Managing distractions and staying focused	☐	☐	☒
18	Microsoft 365	☐	☐	☒
19	Email communication and digital etiquette	☐	☐	☒
20	Budgeting	☐	☐	☒
21	Saving for future goals	☐	☐	☒
22	Identifying challenges and obstacles	☐	☐	☒
23	Analyzing options and making decisions	☐	☐	☒
24	Sewing	☐	☐	☒
25	Reading and interpreting contracts	☐	☐	☒
26	Changing tires and oil	☐	☐	☒

Professional Knowledge

Professional knowledge signifies the specialized expertise and insights cultivated through education, training, and hands-on experience within a specific field or industry. This knowledge empowers individuals to make informed decisions, solve complex problems, and contribute innovatively to their respective fields. It not only propels personal growth but also strengthens the collective progress of industries and societies.

Turn to page 401 of your workbook to the Professional Knowledge Form or create your list in your notebook using the following example:

#	Knowledge	Beginner	Intermediate	Advanced
1	Analyze data	☐	☐	☒
2	Auditing financials	☐	☐	☒
3	Operating check encoder	☐	☐	☒
4	Operating check sorter	☐	☐	☒
5	Check fraud investigations	☐	☒	☐
6	Account balancing	☐	☐	☒
7	Creating debit entries	☐	☐	☒
8	Creating credit entries	☐	☐	☒
9	Clearing jam in check encoder	☐	☐	☒
10	Clearing jam in check sorter	☐	☐	☒
11	Identifying misread checks	☐	☐	☒
12	Supervising	☐	☐	☒
13	Delegating tasks	☐	☒	☐
14	Team motivation	☐	☐	☒
15	Conflict resolution	☐	☒	☐
16	Decision making	☐	☐	☒
17	Effective written and verbal communication skills	☐	☐	☒
18	Competence in crafting compelling presentations	☐	☒	☐
19	Proficiency in planning, executing, and monitoring projects.	☐	☐	☒
20	Assess challenges, identify root causes, and develop solutions.	☐	☐	☒
21	Approach problems from different angles and make informed decisions.	☐	☐	☒
22	Build professional networks and nurturing relationships.	☐	☐	☒
23	Establish partnerships, collaborations, and maintain client relationships.	☐	☐	☒

24	Effective negotiation, deal closing, and sales strategies.	☐	☐	☒
25	Knowledge of customer needs analysis and consultative selling approaches.	☐	☒	☐
26		☐	☐	☐

Skills Knowledge

Skills knowledge encapsulates the practical expertise and know-how required to perform specific tasks or activities effectively. This knowledge enables individuals to confidently execute tasks, address challenges, and seize opportunities.

Turn to page 402 of your workbook to the Skills Knowledge Form or create your list in your notebook using the following example:

Skills Knowledge Form				
#	Knowledge	Beginner	Intermediate	Advanced
1	Measuring and cutting lumber	☐	☐	☒
2	Building doll house and other thing with wood	☐	☐	☐
3	Installing dry wall	☐	☐	☒
4	Framing a room	☐	☐	☒
5	Patching walls	☐	☐	☒
6	Painting walls	☐	☐	☒
7	Cleaning gutters	☐	☐	☒
8	Mowing lawn	☐	☐	☒
9	Tilling garden	☐	☐	☒
10	Weeding	☐	☐	☒
11	Planting vegetables and flower	☐	☐	☒
12	Hanging pictures and mirrors	☐	☐	☒
13	Mounting televisions	☐	☐	☒
14	Installing surround sound	☐	☐	☒
15	Setting up VCR, DVD, cable, and streaming boxes	☐	☐	☒
16	Installing cable, phone, doorbell, and camera wiring	☐	☒	☐

#		Beginner	Intermediate	Advanced
17	Minor washing machine, dryer, refrigerator, freezer, and furnace repairs	☐	☐	☒
18	Installing vinyl, ceramic and laminate flooring	☐	☐	☒
19	Mixing, pouring and leveling concrete	☐	☒	☐
20	Installing and replacing light fixtures, receptacles, switches, and circuit breakers	☐	☐	☒
21	Installing and replacing faucets, shower fixtures, water lines, and drains	☐	☐	☒
22	Installing tubs, showers, toilets, and sinks	☐	☐	☒
23	Installing windows and doors	☐	☐	☒
24	Installing brake pads and rotors	☐	☐	☒
25	Install spark plugs, alternators, starters, power steering pumps, and radiators	☐	☐	☒
26	Installing and programming electric garage doors	☐	☐	☒

Creative Knowledge

Creative knowledge encompasses the imaginative insights, artistic sensibilities, and innovative thinking that fuel the creation of original ideas, artworks, and solutions. This unique knowledge ignites the spark of innovation and drives progress, fostering new perspectives, and reshaping the boundaries of what's possible.

Turn to page 403 of your workbook to the Creative Knowledge Form or create your list in your notebook using the following example:

Creative Knowledge Form				
#	Knowledge	Beginner	Intermediate	Advanced
1	Drawing	☒	☐	☐
2	Photography	☐	☒	☐
3	Graphic arts	☒	☐	☐
4	Writing non-fiction	☐	☒	☐
5	Writing poetry	☐	☒	☐
6	Writing speeches/sermons	☐	☐	☒
7	Storytelling	☒	☐	☐
8	Acting	☒	☐	☐
9	Singing	☒	☐	☐
10	Dance	☐	☒	☐
11	Modeling	☒	☐	☐

12	Interior design	☒	☐	☐
13	Developing innovative business ideas and concepts	☐	☐	☒
14	Creating unique value propositions and branding	☐	☐	☒
15	Woodworking	☐	☐	☒
16	Creative cooking and recipe development	☐	☒	☐
17	Architectural design	☐	☐	☒
18	Space planning	☐	☒	☐
19	Floral design	☒	☐	☐
20	House staging	☐	☒	☐
21	Web design	☐	☒	☐
22	Funnel creation	☒	☐	☐
23	Stimulating ideas through brainstorming and mind mapping	☐	☐	☒
24	Integrating ideas and approaches from various fields	☐	☐	☒
25	Combining knowledge to create unique solutions	☐	☐	☒

Technological Knowledge

Technological knowledge embodies the understanding and proficiency in harnessing the power of modern tools, systems, and digital advancements. This knowledge empowers problem-solving, efficiency gains, and innovation as individuals' leverage technology to streamline processes, enhance connectivity, and drive impactful change.

Turn to page 404 of your workbook to the Technological Knowledge Form or create your list in your notebook using the following example:

Technological Knowledge Form				
#	Knowledge	Beginner	Intermediate	Advanced
1	Program in C++, Java, dBase III, FoxPro, and FoxBASE	☐	☒	☐
2	Create websites with HTML, JavaScript, and CSS	☐	☒	☐
3	Creating and designing apps	☒	☐	☐
4	Setting up and maintaining computer networks.	☐	☒	☐
5	Network protocols, routing, and network security	☒	☐	☐
6	Designing, implementing, and managing databases	☒	☐	☐
7	Utilizing online marketing strategies to promote products and services	☐	☒	☐
8	Search engine optimization (SEO), social media marketing, and analytics.	☐	☒	☐
9	Providing technical support to users and troubleshooting issues	☐	☒	☐
10		☐	☐	☐

Personal Development Knowledge

Personal development knowledge encompasses the insights, strategies, and practices aimed at enhancing one's holistic growth and well-being. This knowledge empowers individuals to navigate life's challenges with resilience, foster meaningful relationships, and embrace continuous learning.

Turn to page 405 of your workbook to the Personal Development Knowledge Form or create your list in your notebook using the following example:

Personal Development Knowledge Form				
#	Knowledge	Beginner	Intermediate	Advanced
1	Understanding one's strengths, weaknesses, and emotions.	☐	☐	☒
2	Developing empathy, self-regulation, and social skills.	☐	☐	☒
3	Setting clear and achievable goals.	☐	☐	☒
4	Prioritizing tasks	☐	☐	☒
5	Managing time effectively	☐	☐	☒
6	Avoid procrastination	☐	☐	☒
7	Active listening	☐	☐	☒
8	Effective communication	☐	☐	☒
9	Conflict resolution	☐	☒	☐
10	Building and maintaining healthy relationships	☐	☐	☒

11	Fostering a growth mindset and cultivating positivity.	☐	☐	☒
12	Practicing gratitude, resilience, and mindfulness.	☐	☐	☒
13	Building self-assurance and a healthy self-image.	☐	☐	☒
14	Overcoming self-doubt and building self-esteem.	☐	☐	☒
15	Prioritizing self-care, wellness routines, and relaxation techniques.	☐	☒	☐
16	Budgeting, saving, and understanding personal finances	☐	☐	☒
17	Expanding professional networks and leveraging relationships	☐	☐	☒
18	Embracing a mindset of lifelong learning	☐	☐	☒
19	Seeking opportunities for self-improvement and skill enhancement	☐	☐	☒
20	Approaching challenges with fresh perspectives	☐	☐	☒
21	Developing leadership qualities and inspiring others	☐	☐	☒
22	Effective communication to influence and motivate.	☐	☐	☒
23	Embracing diversity and understanding different cultures	☐	☐	☒
24	Fostering inclusivity and cultural awareness	☐	☐	☒
25	Bouncing back from setbacks and embracing change	☐	☐	☒
26	Developing the ability to thrive in uncertain situations	☐	☐	☒

Review your knowledge inventory, think about how your knowledge can be applied in various contexts. Consider both personal and professional scenarios where your expertise can be valuable. Consider the relevance of your knowledge to your current goals, interests, and aspirations. Some knowledge may align closely with your objectives, while other knowledge may need updating or further exploration.

As you evaluate your knowledge, identify areas where you have limited or no expertise. These gaps represent potential areas for growth and learning. Based on your inventory, set goals for knowledge enhancement. Determine which areas you want to deepen, expand, or acquire new knowledge in. Develop a plan for acquiring new knowledge. This might involve enrolling in courses, reading books, attending workshops, or seeking mentorship from experts in the relevant field. Utilize resources such as online courses, libraries, educational websites, and communities to enhance your knowledge in identified areas.

Regularly review and update your knowledge inventory as you acquire new skills and expertise. This ongoing process ensures that you're aware of your strengths and continue to pursue growth opportunities. Taking inventory of your knowledge is a powerful way to not only recognize your current expertise but also chart a course for continuous learning and personal development. It empowers you to make intentional choices about how you invest your time and energy in the pursuit of knowledge and self-improvement. Acknowledge the wisdom you've gained and consider how you can continue to learn, adapt, and expand your understanding.

Inventorying Relationships

Relationships play a vital role in personal growth, acting as catalysts for learning, self-discovery, and holistic development. Interacting with people from different backgrounds, experiences, and viewpoints exposes you to diverse perspectives. This broadens your horizons and challenges your assumptions, leading to personal growth through expanded awareness. Positive relationships provide emotional support and encouragement during challenging times. Having a network that believes in you boosts your confidence and resilience, enabling you to overcome obstacles and grow. Trusted relationships offer honest feedback, helping you identify strengths and areas for improvement. Constructive criticism fosters self-awareness and guides your personal development journey. Each person you connect with brings unique knowledge and skills. By learning from their expertise, you gain new insights that contribute to your growth and broaden your skillset.

Building and maintaining relationships hones your communication. skills. Effective communication is crucial for personal and professional success and practicing it in relationships helps you articulate thoughts clearly. Challenges in relationships teach you conflict resolution and interpersonal skills. Learning to navigate disagreements fosters emotional intelligence and helps you maintain healthier connections. Engaging with others cultivates empathy and emotional intelligence. Understanding different emotions and perspectives enhances your social skills and enriches your emotional depth.

Meaningful relationships offer networking opportunities that can lead to personal and professional growth. Your connections can provide access to new opportunities, collaborations, and knowledge. Trustworthy relationships hold you accountable for your goals and actions. Sharing your aspirations with others encourages commitment and motivates you to progress. Celebrating milestones with others enhances your sense of accomplishment. Sharing successes with friends and loved ones reinforces positive feelings and encourages continued growth. Relationships expose you to role models and sources of inspiration. Learning from others' experiences and achievements can ignite your own aspirations. Building strong relationships contributes to your overall well-being. Positive connections reduce stress, boost happiness, and provide a sense of belonging. Conversations with others encourage introspection. Discussing goals, challenges, and experiences helps you reflect on your journey and refine your personal growth strategy. Relationships help you understand social norms and etiquette. This knowledge is essential for effective interaction in various situations. Connecting with people from diverse backgrounds enhances your cultural sensitivity and understanding, enabling you to thrive in an interconnected world.

In essence, relationships serve as a dynamic framework for personal growth. They provide opportunities for learning, collaboration, and self-improvement that can't be achieved in isolation. By nurturing healthy and meaningful connections, you create an environment conducive to continuous development and a fulfilling life journey.

Relationship Assessment

Taking inventory of your relationships involves assessing the quality, significance, and impact of the connections you have with others. This process can help you better understand the value of each relationship and make informed decisions about how to nurture and invest in them. Turn to page 406 in your workbook to the Relationship Assessment Form or create the form in your notebook from the example below. You may need to go through your contact list in your phone and your social media accounts to gain access to all your relationships. Completing this form will help you to evaluate your relationships and determine which relationships can help you in your personal growth journey, it will also help you to strengthen your relationships. You only need to complete a form for those who you are close to or engage with regularly.

Here is an example of the form, complete one for each relationship that you have:

Relationship Assessment Form

Name:		Renwick	Steven	Walker	
	Prefix	First	Middle	Last	Suffix

Category:	☒ Family	☐ Professional	☒ Close Friend	☐ Associate	☐ Social Media

Expertise:	1) Trucking	2) Real Estate	3) Taking Action

Briefly describe this relationship: We have been friends for over 45 years, became family when my uncle married his aunt. We have also partnered in several business ventures together. He is also my youngest son's god father.

Qualities:	☒ Positive	☒ Supportive	☒ Respectful	☒ Loyal	☒ Trustworthy
Contribute Positively:	☒ Always	☐ Often	☐ Seldom	☐ Never	

Reciprocity:	☒ Mutually Beneficial	☐ Giver	☐ Taker	☐ None

Reliable:	☒ Yes	☐ No	Keeps Promises:	☒ Yes	☐ No
Values Aligned:	☒ Yes	☐ No	Empathetic:	☒ Yes	☐ No

Interactions:	☐ Daily	☒ Weekly	☐ Monthly	☐ Annually	☐ On Occasions

Conversations:	☐ Small Talk	☒ Social	☒ Casual	☒ Intellectual	☒ Informative
	☒ Professional	☒ Networking	☐ Persuasive	☒ Educational	☐ Debate

Emotional Impact:	☒ Positive	☐ Neutral	☐ Negative	☐ Unsure
Support:	☒ Strong	☐ Moderate	☐ Minor	☐ Nonexistent

Relationship Needs Improvement:	☐ Yes	☒ No

If so, how can I improve this relationship?

Should the amount of interaction be increased in this relationship?			☐ Yes	☒ No
If yes, how often should it be?	☐ Daily	☐ Weekly	☐ Monthly	☐ Quarterly

What role can this person play in my personal growth journey?	☒ Accountability Partner		☒ Advisor
	☐ Coach	☒ Motivator	☒ Collaborator
	☐ Mentor	☒ Listener	☒ Role Model

Is this person a paid professional?	☐ Yes	☒ No

What additional resources can this person provide?	☒ Money	☒ Knowledge
	☒ Relationship	☐ Time
		☐ Technology

Additional Notes/Comments:

After taking inventory of your relationships as part of your personal growth journey, you gain valuable insights that can guide your actions and decisions. Completing this form for each relationship gives you a full understanding of the relationship as well as an outlook on how to strengthen it. Based on your assessment, identify which relationships are most important and valuable to you. Prioritize those that contribute positively to your growth and well-being. Invest time and effort in cultivating relationships that align with your personal growth goals. Focus on building deeper connections with individuals who support and uplift you. Use the information you've gathered to establish healthy boundaries in your relationships. Ensure that you allocate time and energy to relationships that enhance your life. If you've recognized that certain relationships

255

have played a significant role in your growth, express gratitude to those individuals for their support and positive influence. If you've identified toxic or negative relationships, consider setting boundaries or gradually distancing yourself from such influences. Your personal growth deserves a nurturing environment.

Inventorying Your Money

Reflect on your financial resources and how you manage them. Money is a tool that can amplify your aspirations. Evaluate your financial goals, allocate resources strategically, and seek opportunities to invest in your personal growth journey. Money plays a significant role in personal growth by providing the resources and opportunities necessary to enhance various aspects of your life. While personal growth encompasses more than just financial success, having a stable financial foundation can greatly facilitate your journey of self-improvement. Money enables you to invest in education, whether it's formal schooling, workshops, courses, or online learning. Education expands your knowledge, skills, and personal development. Financial resources allow you to acquire new skills and talents that contribute to your personal growth. You can attend classes, hire coaches, or buy materials for self-study. Money can provide access to quality healthcare, fitness programs, nutritious food, and wellness activities. Taking care of your physical and mental well-being is crucial for personal growth. Money facilitates attending conferences, workshops, and social events where you can meet like-minded individuals, mentors, and potential collaborators. Building a strong network contributes to personal growth. Financial resources give you the opportunity to pursue hobbies, creative projects, and passion-driven endeavors that nurture your personal development.

It can be used to fund entrepreneurial ventures, enabling you to turn innovative ideas into reality. Entrepreneurship fosters creativity, resilience, and personal growth. Financial stability can afford you the luxury of more time, as you may have the means to delegate tasks or reduce working hours. Time is a valuable resource for self-care, learning, and growth. Money can be invested in books, courses, workshops, and seminars that support your ongoing learning journey. Lifelong learning is a cornerstone of personal growth. Financial resources can be allocated for personal development tools, such as coaching, therapy, and self-help resources that contribute to self-awareness and growth. Having financial stability allows you to help others, whether through charitable contributions, mentoring, or assisting loved ones in their personal growth journeys. Financial stability reduces the stress associated with financial struggles, enabling you to focus more on your personal growth and self-improvement. Money provides the freedom to make choices aligned with your values and aspirations, whether it's pursuing a meaningful career, starting a business, or supporting causes you believe in. A stable financial foundation offers security and peace of mind, allowing you to concentrate on personal growth without constant financial worry.

While money is a tool that can enable personal growth, it's important to strike a balance and avoid equating financial success with overall well-being. True personal growth encompasses emotional intelligence, relationships, purpose, and overall life satisfaction. However, having financial stability can significantly enhance your ability to access opportunities, resources, and experiences that contribute to your holistic development.

Financial Assessment

Taking inventory of your money as a part of your personal growth journey can provide valuable insights and direction for achieving your aspirations. Reflect on your financial choices and spending patterns. Ensure that your money aligns with your values and long-term goals. This self-awareness enhances personal growth by promoting conscious decision-making. Money, much like time requires a lengthy and detailed conversation, to be honest money would require a lot more than time. This is why, as I told you before, I decided to write a separate book to deal with money and finances, called The Financial Positioning System. But here we will do a simple exercise that will allow us to take inventory of the money we currently have. Turn to page 416 of your workbook to the Financial Assessment Form or create the form in your notebook from the example below. In this exercise we are going to focus on our current financial situation. Simply place the last four numbers of the account, ticker symbol or any other way for you to identify the account in column two next to the type of account it is and then enter the current value of the account. Here is an example:

Financial Assessment Form		
Account type	Identifier	Value
Checking	1654	$87.02
	3617	$2,215.67
	1829	$1,587.14
Savings	1148	$1,200.00
	1297	$28,000.00
Certificate of Deposit		0.00
		0.00
Money Market		0.00
		0.00
Cryptocurrency	BTC	$129,287.18
	BCH	$19,018.00
	USDT	$999.50
	DOGE	$628.10
Stocks	PLTR	$145,300.00
	NOK	$38,000.00
	NVDA	$460,180.00
	CCEP	$63,480.00
Bonds		0.00
		0.00
Annuity	3718	$67,922.15
	1502	$28,762.89
		0.00

Mutual Funds		0.00
		0.00
Index Fund		0.00
		0.00
ETF's		0.00
		0.00
Commodities		0.00
		0.00
Precious Metals	GLD	$34,482.60
	SLV	$24,440.00
Retirement Accounts		
IRA	6675	$427,816.23
	6676	$872,716.91
		0.00
401K		0.00
		0.00
		0.00
403B		0.00
SEP	1107	$287,015.68
Total		$2,633,139.07

After taking inventory of your money for personal growth, you are equipped with a clear understanding of your financial resources and the potential avenues for enhancing your personal development. Use your financial inventory as a foundation for setting specific personal growth goals. Define what you want to achieve and how your financial resources can support those aspirations. Allocate a portion of your financial resources specifically for personal growth activities. This could include investments in education, experiences, skill development, and well-being.

Remember that personal growth is a holistic journey that encompasses various dimensions of your life. While financial resources can facilitate certain aspects of growth, they are just one component. Combining financial investments with emotional, intellectual, and relational growth will create a well-rounded and fulfilling personal development journey. Every goal that you set in your personal growth journey will have a financial requirement, even if it's just for your reward for completing the goal or maybe even to purchase the technology that you need.

Inventorying Your Technology

Consider the role technology plays in your life. It's a bridge to knowledge, connectivity, and innovation. Reflect on how you can leverage technology to enhance your learning, communication, and overall growth journey. Taking inventory of your technology for personal growth involves assessing your digital tools, devices, and online habits to ensure they align with your growth goals and promote a healthy digital lifestyle. Inventorying your technology is a three-step process that requires you to identify your devices and how you use them and then to identify the software that is installed on it and identify apps and websites that you use or access.

Device Inventory

Turn to page 418 of your workbook to the Device Assessment Form or create the form in your notebook from the example. Here we will begin by making a list of all the devices you own, including smartphones, tablets, laptops, desktop computers, e-readers, and smartwatches. List each item in column two. It's just that simple, here is the example:

Device Assessment Form		
#	Device Type	Usage
1	Acer Desktop	
2	Dell Desktop	
3	Dell 3593 Laptop	
4	Dell #### Laptop	
5	Dell #### Laptop	
6	Dell #### Tablet	
7	Dell #### Tablet	
8	Essential 1 Cellular Phone	
9	Samsung AG 21 Cellular Phone	
10		

See what I told you, it was simple, now that we have all your devices, it is time to reflect on how you use each device. Are they primarily used for productive activities, learning, or entertainment? Identify any patterns of excessive or unproductive use. Some Items may have multiple uses and that fine, list each use in column three.

Device Assessment Form		
#	Device Type	Usage
1	Acer Desktop	Business, entertainment, ministry, personal
2	Dell Desktop	Accounting, bookkeeping
3	Dell 3593 Laptop	Business, Learning, Writing
4	Dell 3609 Laptop	Real Estate

5	Dell 3609 Laptop	Ministry
6	Dell 3609 Laptop	Learning
7	Dell #### Tablet	Real estate
8	Dell #### Tablet	Personal
9	Essential 1 Cellular Phone	Communication, personal
10	Samsung AG 21 Cellular Phone	Communication, business

Next, we will look at what is inside the devices.

Software Inventory

Review the software and tools installed on each device. Identify which ones contribute positively to your personal growth and which ones may be distractions. Turn to page 419 in your workbook to the Software Assessment Form or create the form in your notebook from the example below. I am not going to list all of my software as it will be too lengthy, but I will give you enough to gain a general idea of how to list your software and apps. You do not have to list software that is used to control your device. Here is the example:

Software Assessment Form					
Device Name:	Dell 3593 Laptop				
#	Software Name	Type	Used	Contributes	
1	Microsoft Word	Word processor	☒	☒Positive	☐ Negative
2	Microsoft Excel	Spreadsheet	☒	☒Positive	☐ Negative
3	Microsoft PowerPoint	Presentation	☒	☒Positive	☐ Negative
4	Microsoft Outlook	Calendar, Mail, Contacts, Task Manager	☒	☒Positive	☐ Negative
5	Microsoft Access	Database	☒	☒Positive	☐ Negative
6	Microsoft Projects	Project management	☒	☒Positive	☐ Negative
7	Microsoft Edge	Web Browser	☐	☐Positive	☐ Negative
8	Microsoft Publisher	Desktop Publisher	☒	☒Positive	☐ Negative
9	Microsoft OneNote	Note taking	☒	☒Positive	☐ Negative
10	One Drive	Cloud Drive	☒	☒Positive	☐ Negative
11	Microsoft Defender	Anti-virus	☐	☐Positive	☐ Negative
12	QuickBooks	Accounting	☒	☒Positive	☐ Negative
13	Google Chrome	Web Browser	☒	☒Positive	☒ Negative
14	Google Docs	Word processor	☐	☐Positive	☐ Negative
15	Google Sheets	Spreadsheet	☐	☐Positive	☐ Negative
16	McAfee	Anti-virus	☒	☒Positive	☐ Negative
17	Paint	Graphic design	☐	☐Positive	☐ Negative
18	Notepad	Note taking	☐	☐Positive	☐ Negative
19	Skype	Communication	☐	☐Positive	☐ Negative

20	Snipping Tools	Screen shot tool	☒	☐Positive	☐ Negative
21	OBS	Video suite	☒	☒Positive	☐ Negative
22	Solitaire	Game	☒	☐Positive	☒ Negative
23	Sticky Notes	Note taking	☐	☐Positive	☐ Negative
24	Video editor	Video editor	☐	☐Positive	☐ Negative
25	Voice Recorder	Voice Recorder	☒	☒Positive	☐ Negative
			☐	☐Positive	☐ Negative

Complete a Software Assessment Form for each device that you own. Your devices and their software can be used to expedite your personal growth, if used correctly. The apps, contents, and websites that you utilize are also considered a part of your technological inventory.

Internet Inventory

In this exercise we will be using the Internet Assessment Form where we will list the app, content or website under column two "Content Name", the type of content it is in column three (i.e. app, website, podcast, etc.), how frequently you use them in column four (i.e. daily, weekly, monthly, etc.) and then determine whether it is a positive or negative contribution to your personal growth journey in column five "Contribute".

Turn to page 424 of your workbook to the Internet Assessment Form or create the form in your notebook from this example:

Internet Assessment Form			
#	Content Name	Type	Frequency	Contributes
1	YouVersion Bible	App	Daily	☒Positive ☐ Negative
2	Text	App	Daily	☒Positive ☐ Negative
3	Calendar	App	Daily	☒Positive ☐ Negative
4	Tasks	App	Daily	☒Positive ☐ Negative
5	Credit Karma	App	Weekly	☒Positive ☐ Negative
6	YouTube	Content	Daily	☒Positive ☐ Negative
7	Gmail	App	Daily	☒Positive ☐ Negative
8	Google Maps	App	Weekly	☐Positive ☐ Negative
9	Outlook	App	Daily	☒Positive ☒ Negative
10	Adobe Acrobat	App	Monthly	☒Positive ☐ Negative
11	T-Mobile Tuesday	App	Weekly	☒Positive ☐ Negative

12	Clubhouse	App	Daily	☒Positive ☐ Negative
13	My Chart Rush	App	Monthly	☒Positive ☐ Negative
14	My Library	App	Monthly	☐Positive ☐ Negative
15	Age of Origin	App	Daily	☐Positive ☒ Negative
16	Backgammon	App	Weekly	☐Positive ☒ Negative
17	Spades	App	Monthly	☐Positive ☒ Negative
18	Secret to Success	Podcast	Weekly	☒Positive ☐ Negative
19	Lurn	Content	Weekly	☒Positive ☐ Negative
20	CardoneU	Content	Weekly	☒Positive ☐ Negative
21	Master Mind	Content	Weekly	☒Positive ☐ Negative
22	ClickFunnels	Content	Weekly	☒Positive ☐ Negative
23	TikTok	Social Media	Daily	☒Positive ☒ Negative
24	Facebook	Social Media	Daily	☒Positive ☒ Negative
25	Instagram	Social Media	Weekly	☒Positive ☒ Negative
26	Openai.com	Website	Daily	☒Positive ☐ Negative

Complete your Internet Assessment Form. Once you have completed your internet assessment, we are done with taking inventory.

We now know every resource in life that we have, but that is just half the battle. In order to be successful you need to know what you need. To achieve our goals, we need to not only know what resources we are lacking but also figure out how we can get the resources that we need. Imagine setting a goal to own a new car, but you don't have a driver's license, you have no money saved to buy the car, and you can only shop for the car on Sunday when the dealership is closed. You have a knowledge issue, a money issue, and a time issue; in other words, there are three resources that you require: knowledge, money, and time. The only way to solve this problem is to determine exactly what you need.

Knowing What Resources You Need

Time Required

Determining the amount of time required to fulfill a goal in your personal growth journey depends on various factors, including the nature of the goal, your current skills and knowledge, your commitment level, and the resources available to you. First, mentally visualize the journey from where you are now to achieving your goal. This can help you set a realistic timeline. Consider the time required for research, learning, and acquiring the necessary knowledge or skills. Factor in online courses, books, workshops, and other learning resources. Allow time for practice and implementation of what you've learned. Practice is essential for skill development and mastery. Consider the frequency and consistency required to work on your goal. Regular practice and effort are crucial for steady progress. Allow time for experimentation and adjustments. Personal growth often involves trial and error as you refine your approach.

Be realistic about the time required. Set expectations that align with your current commitments and responsibilities. Personal growth isn't always linear. Be open to adjusting your timeline based on unexpected challenges or opportunities. As you make progress, periodically reevaluate your timeline. You might find that you're advancing faster or slower than anticipated. If your goal involves a complex skill or area of knowledge, seek advice from experts who can provide insights into the time needed for proficiency. Consider how much time you can realistically allocate to working on your goal each day or week. Effective time management is essential for consistent progress. Maintain motivation by reminding yourself of the benefits and rewards of achieving your goal. This positive outlook can impact your pace of progress. Realize that setbacks are a natural part of growth. Learn from them and adjust your timeline accordingly. Regularly reflect on your journey and the time you've spent. Adjust your plan as needed to stay on track. Know that personal growth is a dynamic process, and timelines can vary greatly depending on individual circumstances. The most important factor is your dedication, consistency, and willingness to put in the effort required to achieve your goal.

For the next exercise, we will take our action steps and assign time to each action step. Since we are only adding time to each action step, refer back to our action step scheduler in your workbook or notebook and assign time on the side of each action step. Here's an example of what I mean:

Action Steps Scheduler					
#	Action Step	Start Date	Frequency	End Date	
1	Request free credit reports from Equifax	8/15/2023	Annually	8/29/2023	10 mins
2	Request free credit reports from Experian	8/15/2023	Annually	8/29/2023	10 mins
3	Request free credit reports	8/15/2023	Annually	8/29/2023	10 mins

	from and TransUnion				30 mins
4	Review Experian credit reports for errors, inaccuracies, or outdated information.	8/30/2023	Annually	8/31/2023	30 mins
5	Review Equifax credit reports for errors, inaccuracies, or outdated information.	8/30/2023	Annually	8/31/2023	30 mins
6	Review TransUnion credit reports for errors, inaccuracies, or outdated information.	8/30/2023	Annually	8/31/2023	30 mins
7	Dispute any errors or inaccuracies on your credit reports.	9/1/2023	Monthly	2/15/2024	20 mins
8	Write detailed letters to the credit bureaus explaining the discrepancies and providing supporting documentation.	9/2/2023	Monthly	2/15/2024	45 mins
9	Monitor progress of each credit bureau.	9/7/2023	Weekly	2/15/2024	10 mins
10	Record credit score	9/7/2023	Monthly	2/15/2024	2 mins

					35 mins
11	Call Capital One to change due date to the 11th of each month (10 days after you receive your check).	9/9/2023	Once	9/9/2023	
12	Call Chase to change due date to the 11th of each month.	9/9/2023	Once	9/9/2023	35 mins
13	Call AMEX to change due date to the 11th of each month.	9/9/2023	Once	9/9/2023	35 mins
14	Call Walmart to change due date to the 25th of each month.	9/16/2023	Once	9/16/2023	35 mins
15	Call Kohl's to change due date to the 25th of each month.	9/16/2023	Once	9/16/2023	35 mins
16	Call Shell to change due date to the 25th of each month.	9/16/2023	Once	9/16/2023	35 mins
17	Call Amazon to change due date to the 25th of each month.	9/16/2023	Once	9/16/2023	35 mins
18	Pay all active bills, loans, credit card and mortgage payments at least 7-10 business days before due date.	10/1/2023	Monthly	2/15/2024	1 X 60 mins

265

19	Negotiate better terms, such as lower interest, higher credit limit or payment arrangement.	10/15/2023	Annually	10/16/2023	4.5 hrs. (45 mins per card)
20	Make an additional $100 per month to Capital One or the next highest interest credit card or debt until paid.	11/1/2023	Monthly	2/15/2024	2 mins
21	Open Credit Builder or Self account to save and rebuild credit.	11/1/2023	Once	11/8/2023	25 mins
22	Secure a secured credit card from Citibank	11/1/2023	Once	11/16/2023	20 mins
23	Secure a secured credit card from Open Sky	11/10/2023	Once	11/25/2023	20 mins
24	Become an Authorized User on Joe's Discover Card	11/15/2023	Once	11/25/2023	15 mins
25	Become an Authorized User on Joe's B of A credit card.	11/15/2023	Once	11/25/2023	15 mins
26	Apply for new credit cards only after FICO score is over 610.	11/16/2023	Annually	11/16/2023	20 mins

					25 mins
27	Celebrate reaching 618 FICO score	11/31/2023	Once	11/16/2023	
28	Apply for new loans only after FICO is above 650.	12/15/2023	Once	12/25/2023	40 mins
29	Celebrate reaching 652 FICO score	12/31/2023	Once	12/31/2023	0 mins
30	Celebrate reaching 686 FICO score	1/15/2024	Once	1/15/2024	45 mins
31	Celebrate reaching 720 FICO score	2/15/2024	Once	2/15/2024	60 mins
32	Refinance mortgage (if not paid off)	2/15/2024	Once	3/15/2024	0 mins

Add up all the time that you wrote and write the total at the bottom; this tells you approximately how much time you will spend achieving the goal that the action steps are for. Now complete the same process on each Action Step Scheduler. When you have completed them all, take the total from each page, which will give you the total amount of time that you will need to complete your personal growth journey. Doing this exercise will also come in handy when we start our time management.

Knowledge Needed

To achieve our goals, we sometimes need to learn new skills or gain new knowledge. Knowing what skills are needed in our personal growth journey is an important part of reaching our destination. Imagine going on a road trip and you don't know how to put gas in the car, you don't know how to read a fuel meter, or even worse, you don't know how to drive. Any one of these three will cause you to be delayed in reaching your destination or not reach it at all. This is why it is important to know what you need to know in order to achieve your goals.

In this exercise, we will categorize each action step as knowledge we either possess, need to attain, or will utilize from others. Possess means you already have the knowledge needed, attain means you are willing to learn the knowledge, and utilize means you will use someone else's knowledge. This helps us identify what we need to learn and who we can learn from. Turn to page 426 of your workbook to the Knowledge Assessment Form or use your notebook to create the Knowledge Assessment Form from this example:

Knowledge Assessment Form				
Goal:	Repair my credit			
#	**Action Step**	**Possess**	**Attain**	**Utilize**
1	Request free credit reports from Equifax	☒	☐	☐
2	Request free credit reports from Experian	☒	☐	☐
3	Request free credit reports from and TransUnion	☒	☐	☐
4	Review Experian credit reports for errors, inaccuracies, or outdated information.	☐	☒	☐
5	Review Equifax credit reports for errors, inaccuracies, or outdated information.	☐	☒	☐
6	Review TransUnion credit reports for errors, inaccuracies, or outdated information.	☐	☒	☐
7	Dispute any errors or inaccuracies on your credit reports.	☐	☒	☐
8	Write detailed letters to the credit bureaus explaining the discrepancies and providing supporting documentation.	☐	☒	☐
9	Monitor progress of each credit bureau.	☒	☐	☐
10	Record credit score	☒	☐	☐

11	Call Capital One to change due date to the 11th of each month (10 days after you receive your check).	☒	☐	☐
12	Call Chase to change due date to the 11th of each month.	☒	☐	☐
13	Call AMEX to change due date to the 11th of each month.	☒	☐	☐
14	Call Walmart to change due date to the 25th of each month.	☒	☐	☐
15	Call Kohl's to change due date to the 25th of each month.	☒	☐	☐
16	Call Shell to change due date to the 25th of each month.	☒	☐	☐
17	Call Amazon to change due date to the 25th of each month.	☒	☐	☐
18	Pay all active bills, loans, credit card and mortgage payments at least 7-10 business days before due date.	☒	☐	☐
19	Negotiate better terms, such as lower interest, higher credit limit or payment arrangement.	☐	☒	☐
20	Make an additional $100 per month to Capital One or the next highest interest credit card or debt until paid.	☒	☐	☐
21	Open Credit Builder or Self account to save and rebuild credit.	☒	☐	☐
22	Secure a secured credit card from Citibank	☒	☐	☐
23	Secure a secured credit card from Open Sky	☒	☐	☐
24	Become an Authorized User on Joe's Discover Card	☐	☐	☒
25	Become an Authorized User on Joe's B of A credit card.	☐	☐	☒
26	Apply for new credit cards only after FICO score is over 610.	☒	☐	☐
27	Celebrate reaching 618 FICO score	☒	☐	☐

28	Apply for new loans only after FICO is above 650.	☒	☐	☐
29	Celebrate reaching 652 FICO score	☒	☐	☐
30	Celebrate reaching 686 FICO score	☒	☐	☐
31	Celebrate reaching 720 FICO score	☒	☐	☐
32	Refinance mortgage (if not paid off)	☒	☐	☐
33		☐	☐	☐

Complete this form for each goal and its associated action steps. Next, we will move on to the Knowledge Acquisition Form, where we will list the things we need to learn in order to complete the action steps categorized as attain. Turn to page 444 of your workbook or create the form in your notebook from this example:

Knowledge Acquisition Form	
#	Things to Learn
1	Learn how to review credit reports for errors.
2	Learn how to review credit reports for inaccuracies.
3	Learn how to review credit reports for outdated information.
4	Learn how to dispute any errors or inaccuracies on credit reports.
5	Learn how to write detailed letters to the credit bureaus explaining the discrepancies.
6	Learn how to provide supporting documentation to the credit bureaus.
7	Learn how to negotiate better terms with creditors.

Once you've completed the Knowledge Assessment and Knowledge Acquisition forms, we can add the action steps categorized as attain to our goals and create the necessary action steps to achieve them. This process may take time, but it will make your personal growth journey easier to travel. These are what I call learning goals, and they're crucial for personal growth. Without them, we cannot attain the growth we are looking for.

Relationships Required

In the journey of personal growth, identifying the relationships we need is like choosing the threads that enrich the fabric of our experience. Just as a sculptor carefully selects each chisel stroke, we must discern the individuals who will contribute to our growth. These relationships are intentional alliances that align with our aspirations. Seek mentors whose wisdom resonates with your goals, friends who uplift and challenge you, and allies who share your passions.

Each relationship is a mirror reflecting different facets of our potential. Just as the sun's rays nourish the earth, the right relationships nurture our growth. Surround yourself with those who encourage your dreams, guide your decisions, and celebrate your achievements. By identifying these connections, we forge an alliance of growth—one that supports, motivates, and propels us forward.

As you embark on this journey, remember that identifying the relationships you need is not about quantity, but quality. It's about cultivating a garden of connections that nurtures your unique path. So be discerning, intentional, and open to the transformative power that these relationships hold. Together, they will help you cultivate a symphony of growth that resonates with your aspirations, filling your life with harmony and purpose.

In the next exercise, we will continue using the Knowledge Assessment Form, moving to the next column of the form, which is utilize. Here, we will use the Knowledge Utilization Form to list each action, the individual or entity needed, and the knowledge that will be utilized. The Knowledge Utilization Form helps us understand what knowledge we need to gain and who we can attain it from. This, in turn, helps us strengthen or build relationships with others that we may need to add to our team. Before we delve into team building, however, we need to finish identifying the resources we need.

Knowledge Utilization Form			
#	Action Step	Individual/Entity	Knowledge Utilized
1	Become an Authorized User on Joe's Discover Card	Joe Young	Card Authorization
2	Become an Authorized User on Joe's B of A credit card.	Joe Young	Card Authorization
3			

The Knowledge Utilization Form helps us identify what knowledge we need to gain and who we can attain it from. This, in turn, helps us build relationships with others that we may need to add to our team. Once we have identified the relationships we need, we can move on to assessing the financial cost of our personal growth journey.

Assess the Cost

As we embark on the journey of personal growth, it's essential to assess the financial cost not as an obstacle, but as an investment in our potential. This cost represents our commitment to growth, a commitment that speaks volumes about the value we place on our evolution. Remember, the cost of personal growth isn't just about the dollars spent; it's about the life-changing dividends received.

Each goal we have set has a cost associated with it, whether it is for the reward we give ourselves for reaching a milestone, the fuel we burn, the professionals we need to use, down to the paper we use to write on; it has a cost. Figuring in the cost of our personal growth is a matter of estimating what we think it will cost. In our next exercise, we will estimate how much each action will cost and total it up.

Action Steps Scheduler					
#	Action Step	Start Date	Frequency	End Date	
1	Request free credit reports from Equifax	8/15/2023	Annually	8/29/2023	10 mins $0.01
2	Request free credit reports from Experian	8/15/2023	Annually	8/29/2023	10 mins $0.01
3	Request free credit reports from and TransUnion	8/15/2023	Annually	8/29/2023	10 mins $0.01
4	Review Experian credit reports for errors, inaccuracies, or outdated information.	8/30/2023	Annually	8/31/2023	30 mins $0.00
5	Review Equifax credit reports for errors, inaccuracies, or outdated information.	8/30/2023	Annually	8/31/2023	30 mins $0.00
6	Review TransUnion credit reports for errors, inaccuracies, or outdated information.	8/30/2023	Annually	8/31/2023	30 mins $0.00
7	Dispute any errors or inaccuracies on your credit reports.	9/1/2023	Monthly	2/15/2024	20 mins $0.05
8	Write detailed letters to the credit bureaus explaining the discrepancies and providing supporting documentation.	9/2/2023	Monthly	2/15/2024	45 mins $7.30
9	Monitor progress of each credit bureau.	9/7/2023	Weekly	2/15/2024	10 mins $0.00
10	Record credit score	9/7/2023	Monthly	2/15/2024	2 mins $0.02

11	Call Capital One to change due date to the 11th of each month (10 days after you receive your check).	9/9/2023	Once	9/9/2023	35 mins $0.10
12	Call Chase to change due date to the 11th of each month.	9/9/2023	Once	9/9/2023	35 mins $0.10
13	Call AMEX to change due date to the 11th of each month.	9/9/2023	Once	9/9/2023	35 mins $0.10
14	Call Walmart to change due date to the 25th of each month.	9/16/2023	Once	9/16/2023	35 mins $0.10
15	Call Kohl's to change due date to the 25th of each month.	9/16/2023	Once	9/16/2023	35 mins $0.10
16	Call Shell to change due date to the 25th of each month.	9/16/2023	Once	9/16/2023	35 mins $0.10
17	Call Amazon to change due date to the 25th of each month.	9/16/2023	Once	9/16/2023	35 mins $0.10
18	Pay all active bills, loans, credit card and mortgage payments at least 7-10 business days before due date.	10/1/2023	Monthly	2/15/2024	1 X 60 mins $0.06
19	Negotiate better terms, such as lower interest, higher credit limit or payment arrangement.	10/15/2023	Annually	10/16/2023	270 mins (45 mins per card) $0.74

20	Make an additional $100 per month to Capital One or the next highest interest credit card or debt until paid.	11/1/2023	Monthly	2/15/2024	2 mins $100.00
21	Open Credit Builder or Self account to save and rebuild credit.	11/1/2023	Once	11/8/2023	25 mins $500.00
22	Secure a secured credit card from Citibank	11/1/2023	Once	11/16/2023	20 mins $500.00
23	Secure a secured credit card from Open Sky	11/10/2023	Once	11/25/2023	20 mins $500.00
24	Become an Authorized User on Joe's Discover Card	11/15/2023	Once	11/25/2023	15 mins $0.00
25	Become an Authorized User on Joe's B of A credit card.	11/15/2023	Once	11/25/2023	15 mins $0.00
26	Apply for new credit cards only after FICO score is over 610.	11/16/2023	Annually	11/16/2023	20 mins $0.05
27	Celebrate reaching 618 FICO score	11/31/2023	Once	11/16/2023	25 mins $5.74
28	Apply for new loans only after FICO is above 650.	12/15/2023	Once	12/25/2023	40 mins $1.28
29	Celebrate reaching 652 FICO score	12/31/2023	Once	12/31/2023	0 mins $0.00
30	Celebrate reaching 686 FICO score	1/15/2024	Once	1/15/2024	45 mins $36.15
31	Celebrate reaching 720 FICO score	2/15/2024	Once	2/15/2024	0 mins $0.00

32	Refinance mortgage (if not paid off)	2/15/2024	Once	3/15/2024	60 mins $750.00

Complete each Action Steps Scheduler for each goal. As you complete each of your Action Steps Scheduler, you will have an estimated cost for the goal it is associated with. By adding each of the Action Steps Scheduler, you will have an estimated cost of your personal growth journey. Once you are done with all of your Action Steps Scheduler, we can move on to our final resource, which is technology.

Technology Requirements

In the exhilarating journey of personal growth, accessing the necessary technology is like unlocking a treasure chest of boundless possibilities. Just as a painter selects the finest brushes to bring their canvas to life, we too must choose the right technological tools to illuminate our path forward. Technology is the amplifier of our efforts, the catalyst that accelerates our learning and connects us to a world of knowledge and innovation.

As we assess the technology required to achieve our growth goals, let us remember that these tools are bridges to our aspirations. They enable us to learn from the best minds, collaborate across boundaries, and harness information at our fingertips. Embrace technology not as a distraction, but as a compass guiding us toward our destination. Each app, platform, and device we incorporate becomes a pillar of support, strengthening our journey toward self-discovery and mastery.

While accessing technology may come with a learning curve, remember that every new skill acquired is a triumph in itself. Embrace the process with curiosity, adaptability, and a mindset eager to explore the uncharted territories of the digital landscape. With technology as your ally, you're not just stepping into the future; you're shaping it to match the contours of your dreams. So, as you navigate this exciting landscape, relish the opportunity to harness the power of technology in your personal growth journey, unlocking a realm of endless growth and boundless achievement.

Acquiring the necessary technology to achieve your goals in your personal growth journey involves a strategic approach to identifying, obtaining, and effectively utilizing the tools that will support your progress. Start by clearly defining the technology you need for your personal growth journey. Identify the specific tools, software, apps, or devices that align with your goals. Conduct thorough research to explore the options available. Look for technologies that cater to your needs, preferences, and learning style. Read reviews, watch demos, and gather insights from experts. While there may be a variety of tools available, focus on the essential ones that directly contribute to your goals. Prioritize tools that offer the features you require without overwhelming you.

In this next exercise, we will determine what technologies we need for each goal that we have set. This will require you to rewrite each goal you have set in the Technology Assessment Form; you will need to use your Goals Sheets to write your goals down and the Action Steps Scheduler to determine what technology you will need for each goal. Turn to page 447 of your workbook to the Technology Assessment Form or create one in your notebook from the example.

Technology Assessment Form					
#	Goal	Device/ Peripheral	Software	App	Website
1	Repair my credit	Dell 3593 Laptop Galaxy A71 5G	Microsoft Word Microsoft Excel Chrome	Credit Karma US Bank	Annualcreditreport.com Equifax.com Experian.com Transunion.com Self.inc Creditbuilder.com Citibank.com Opensky.com
2	Embrace failure as an opportunity for growth and learning	Dell 3593 Laptop	Chrome	Think Up Happify	Schoolofselfimage.com
3	To earn $100,000 per year as a Life Coach	Dell 3593 Laptop Video Camera Web Camera Black Magic Box Shure Microphone Shure sound board	OBS PowerPoint Chrome	TikTok Facebook Instagram Twitter	Clickfunnels.com Zoom.com Facebook.com Instagram.com Twitter.com
4	I live in a 15,000+ sq. ft. traditional style brick and cement home with three levels and an attic in	Dell 3593 Laptop Galaxy A71 5G Cannon 35mm Camera	Microsoft Excel Adobe Acrobat Adobe Sign Chrome	Redfin Realtor Zillow	Redfin.com Realtor.com Trulia.com Zillow.com

the suburbs of South Barrington on 10				
5				
6				

Integrate technology mindfully, ensuring that it enhances your growth without becoming a distraction or hindrance. While technology can be a powerful ally, remember that your commitment and efforts are essential. Stay focused on your goals and use technology as a supportive tool. By methodically integrating the selected technology tools into your personal growth plan, you're creating a tailored and effective approach that will propel you toward your goals with greater efficiency and success.

Getting the Resources You Need

Making Time

In the symphony of life's demands, increasing time for your personal growth journey is the harmonious melody of self-investment. Just as a skilled gardener tends to their plants, nurturing them to bloom, so must you tend to the garden of your aspirations. Recognize that time is your most valuable resource and dedicating it to your growth is an investment in your future self.

Start by auditing your daily routines. Just as a sculptor chisels away excess to unveil the masterpiece within, streamline activities that drain your time and energy. Set boundaries with distractions, creating sanctuaries for focused learning and reflection. Remember, it's not about adding more hours to the day; it's about utilizing the hours you have with intention.

Delegate tasks whenever possible. In delegation lies the art of effective time management. Release the belief that you must do everything yourself and welcome collaboration. Delegate routine tasks to free up your mental and physical space for activities that nourish your growth.

Practice the magic of saying "no." Just as a canvas gains depth with well-chosen brushstrokes, your journey thrives when you say no to commitments that don't align with your growth. Prioritize your goals and invest your time accordingly.

Design a mindful morning routine that sets the tone for the day. Just as the sunrise heralds a new beginning, cultivate habits that nurture your mind, body, and spirit. Engage in meditation, reading, exercise, or journaling to align yourself with purpose.

Use technology wisely. Just as the compass guides a traveler, apps and tools can direct your efforts. Utilize time management apps, learning platforms, and online resources to maximize your growth potential.

Celebrate progress. Each step forward is a triumph in your journey. Just as a hiker rejoices at the summit, acknowledge your achievements. Recognize that progress is a journey of many steps, and each one brings you closer to your aspirations.

Safeguard moments of solitude, as they are the canvas upon which your growth masterpiece is painted. Just as an artist finds inspiration in quiet contemplation, carve out time for introspection and self-discovery.

Set specific time blocks for learning and growth activities. Just as a composer arranges notes to create a beautiful melody, allocate chunks of time for reading, skill-building, and pursuing your passions.

Remember that self-care is not selfish; it's a key component of your growth journey. Just as the gardener waters their plants, nourish yourself physically and emotionally. Prioritize rest, exercise, and nourishing foods that fuel your energy.

Integrate learning into your daily life. Just as a river carves its path over time, weave learning into your routines. Listen to audiobooks during commutes, engage in discussions with peers, and turn mundane tasks into opportunities for growth.

In increasing time for your personal growth journey, you are reclaiming your power to shape your destiny. Each mindful decision, each prioritized hour, and each step you take propels you toward a future brimming with purpose, achievement, and the fulfillment of your most cherished dreams.

Consider what you do with your non-essential time. Do you remember earlier when we completed the Time Inventory sheet with the unallocated time that was left over? This is the time that we will be working with to take our personal growth journey. Currently, this time may be being utilized in an unproductive manner, more so for things that bring leisure or relaxation. There is a difference between being busy and being productive. Busyness consumes time but doesn't necessarily produce any results. Productivity consumes time and provides benefits. This is the difference between the average person and the successful person—successful people are productive.

In today's society, the average person spends three hours in front of a television each day. What is the benefit? They are entertained and have conversations they can share with other viewers. But is it really beneficial? Are they learning anything? Are they developing their minds? Are they increasing their income? More than likely, the answer is no to all of the above. Successful people, on the other hand, probably watch television three hours a week, which equates to about 26 minutes a day. That's a difference of two hours and 34 minutes. Successful people utilize this additional time to acquire knowledge, hone their skills, increase their self-awareness, and network with others. This is the difference between busy and productive. I will discuss this more in a later chapter.

Let's get productive and stop being busy. In other words, stop wasting your precious time making someone else productive by spending hours watching television. They call it a production for a reason. Here is what I want you to do: you know how many hours you need to fulfill your goals, and you know how many hours you have that are non-essential or unallocated. From those unallocated hours, decide how many you will use for your personal growth journey. It should be about 25% of your unallocated time. Using the Time Inventory example, there are 29.25 hours unallocated per week. Utilizing 25% of that time is 7.31 hours per week, which is a little over an hour per day. Now, let's say I wanted to work on four goals at one time, giving each of them the equivalent amount of time. I have 1 hour and 3 minutes or 63 minutes, which is 15.67 minutes per day per goal. Looking at my Action Step Scheduler for my goal of repairing my credit, the SMART goal is to repair my credit by raising my FICO score by 136 points to attain a score of 720 in six months. This goal requires 1059 minutes to achieve in 182 days, which is approximately 5.81 minutes per day required to achieve this goal. This goal frees up an additional 9.86 minutes that can be allocated to a goal that requires more time or a goal that is equal to be added.

While this may sound confusing to some, I have made it simpler for you to see. On page 450 of your workbook are several worksheets that can be used to calculate your minimum minutes per day per goal, your time per day for each goal, and a worksheet to determine the goals you can assign in the allotted time.

Daily Goal Time Requirement Worksheet

Goal	Duration in Days	Minutes Needed	Minutes per Day
Repair my credit	182	1059	5.81
Embrace failure as an opportunity for growth and learning	365	6000	16.44
I live in a 15,000+ sq. ft. traditional style brick and cement home with three levels and an attic in the suburbs of South Barrington on 10 acres	275	8000	29.09
Learn to schedule everything	1	10	10.00
Total			61.34

By completing the Daily Goal Time Requirement Worksheet, we now know exactly how much time each goal will require each day to be completed in the timeframe allotted. This worksheet now serves as a guide to determine which goals we will pursue based on the time we allocate to our personal growth. Determining the time we allocated to personal growth is determined by how we use our unallocated time. Turn to page 451 of your workbook or create the Unallocated Time Worksheet in your notebook. Using your Time Inventory Worksheet, add the total amount of unallocated time and multiply it by 60. This will give you your unallocated time for row a. Then determine what percentage of unallocated time you will use in row b. In row d, enter the number of days per week you will work on these goals. In row f, enter the number of goals you will work on. We decide how much of our unallocated time we spend toward our personal growth based on either a set number or a percentage. Here, let me give you an example:

Unallocated Time Worksheet

Unallocated Time	a	1755
Percentage to use for personal growth. (Minimum of 25% is suggested)	b	.25
Personal growth time (line a multiplied by line b)	c	438.75
Number of days per week	d	7
Minutes per day (line c divided by line d)	e	62.67
Number of goals to work on at one time	f	4
Minutes per day per goal	g	15.67

Once we have allocated time to our personal growth, we need to determine which goals we will pursue. This is a simple task. By using our Daily Goal Time Requirement Worksheet, we know exactly how much time each of our goals will require. By listing our goals and their minutes on the Goal Pursuit Worksheet, we are able to determine the goals we will pursue. This is also on page 451 of your workbook.

Goal Pursuit Worksheet

Goal	Available Minutes	Minutes per Day	Balance
Repair my credit	62.67	5.81	56.86
Embrace failure as an opportunity for growth and learning	56.86	16.44	40.42
I live in a 15,000+ sq. ft. traditional style brick and cement home with three levels and an attic in South Barrington on 10 acres	40.42	29.09	11.33
Learn to schedule everything	11.33	10.00	1.33

As you can see, the Goal Pursuit Worksheet is a balance sheet for how we spend our personal growth time. By knowing which goals we are pursuing, we are able to stay laser-focused. Understanding the amount of time we allocate for our personal growth is solely at our discretion, but the more we allocate, the more we have to spend, and the more we have to spend, the faster we achieve our goals.

Gaining time is more about taking control of our time. The better we control our time, the more productive we are. Many people say that we all only have 24 hours in a day; in fact, I have said it. While this is true, it is not fully correct. There is a way we can get more than 24 hours out of our day. It is a method that successful people use all the time. Would you like to know what it is? I was sure you would say yes. To be honest, there are two methods that we can use to gain more time. The first method is a simple one called delegating. By delegating tasks to others, we free up that time for ourselves, thereby adding to our 24 hours. Let me give you an example: it may take me thirty minutes to mow the lawn, but if I have my son do it, I just gained thirty minutes in my day. It's just that simple.

The second method is widely used all across the world by the rich. They can tally up to thousands of hours to their day through this technique, gaining more time and money at the same time. This method is called buying time.

Buying Time

Successful individuals understand that hiring others to work for them isn't just about tasks; it's about reclaiming precious hours to focus on what truly matters. By entrusting capable hands, they buy time to invest in strategic thinking and high-impact endeavors that propel their success forward.

In the realm of time management, the power of hiring lies in the concept of leverage. Successful people recognize that their time is a finite resource, while the potential for growth is limitless. By hiring experts and delegating tasks, they leverage collective skills and efforts to achieve more in less time.

Shifting from trading time for money to orchestrating a team is a hallmark of success. Leaders recognize that their value isn't solely in labor but in orchestrating a symphony of productivity. Through effective delegation, they buy time to focus on strategy, innovation, and building scalable systems.

The act of hiring others to work for you isn't just about freeing up time—it's an investment in your personal and professional growth. When you buy time, you're acquiring a commodity that can be redirected toward learning, networking, and expanding your horizons. Successful individuals understand that hiring team members isn't just about exchanging dollars for labor; it's about unlocking their potential. By leveraging diverse talents, they transcend the limits of their individual abilities and reach new heights.

While money is important, time is the most valuable currency. Successful people grasp that concept and make choices that prioritize their time. They delegate tasks that don't require their expertise, which in turn allows them to engage in more impactful endeavors.

Making the transition from trading time for money to hiring others is a strategic transformation. This shift marks a pivotal moment when your focus turns from the immediate to the long term. By buying time, you're investing in building an empire of productivity.

Time, once spent, is gone forever. Successful individuals acknowledge this reality and consciously choose to invest their time where it matters most. Hiring others to work for them is a way to maximize the use of their most precious asset. Just as a single spark ignites a wildfire, hiring others sparks a multiplication effect in your productivity. By exchanging money for their expertise, you ignite a chain reaction of efficiency, leading to exponential growth.

The true legacy of successful people isn't just in their wealth; it's in the impact they've made. By buying time and hiring others, they are freeing themselves to leave a lasting imprint on the world—transforming industries, inspiring others, and contributing to a brighter future. In the realm of time management and success, the distinction between exchanging time for money and exchanging money for time is transformative. By making strategic choices to hire capable individuals, you're not just gaining extra hours—you're unlocking a realm of possibilities that can redefine the trajectory of your personal and professional journey.

As a real estate investor, this was a lesson I had to learn the hard way. When I first started in real estate, I would manage my own properties, which meant I would spend 2-3 hours per week mowing grass. Those 2-3 hours each week allowed me to save $75 each week, but it took me a while to realize that I was wasting my time mowing lawns. It was actually a friend of mine who saw me mowing the lawn at one of my buildings and asked me why I was mowing the lawn. My response was I am saving money by mowing the lawn myself, so I don't have to pay someone else, and I am saving money. He laughed and asked me a question. He asked, "What if you paid someone to mow the lawn and used that time each week to work on real estate deals? How many deals would you be able to do in a year with the extra time?" I told him I could probably do about 2-3 deals in a year. "And how much do you make on a deal?" he asked. I said I usually make at least $10,000-$15,000 per deal. Then it hit me. Here I am saving less than $4,000 a year by cutting my grass when I could have paid someone to do it and earned at least $20,000. All I could say was okay, I get it. The next day, I hired a property manager and a landscaper. Sometimes when we think we are saving money, we are actually losing money.

Could you imagine if Mark Zuckerberg ran Facebook alone? Do you think he would make anywhere near the $1.4 billion he is making per day as a company? No. Instead, he started by hiring seven full-time employees. Those seven full-time employees added 56 hours to his day. But he didn't stop there. By 2008, he had 850 full-time employees, adding 6,800 hours to his day. By 2020, Facebook had 58,604 full-time employees, adding up to an additional 468,832 hours to his day. That is the power of buying time. We often hear people say that time is money, and this is true if you have the mindset of trading money for time. But successful people understand that money is time. This is why they exchange money for time. It's easy to trade time for money, but trading money for time requires knowledge.

Acquiring Knowledge

Gaining knowledge is a journey that begins with the simple act of embracing the quest for learning. Approach each day with an open heart and a curious mind, ready to absorb insights from the world around you. Every day is an opportunity to acquire new knowledge, and it can be gained through asking questions or researching new topics. I personally expand my knowledge each day by adding a new word to my vocabulary.

Curiosity is the compass that leads you on the path of knowledge. Cultivate this innate curiosity like a precious garden, allowing it to steer you toward questions, challenges, and subjects that ignite your interest. I know what you are thinking: curiosity killed the cat. But Danielle LaPorte says, "If knowledge is power, then curiosity is the muscle," and James Clear is quoted as saying, "Intelligence follows curiosity." Understand that our curiosity is there for us to gain knowledge, whether good or bad. Either way, we gain knowledge of what not to do or what we can.

To gain knowledge is to explore the unfamiliar. Venture beyond your comfort zone, embracing topics and ideas that challenge your current understanding. It's in these uncharted territories that you uncover the gems of insight that enrich your life.

Every experience, whether big or small, is an opportunity to gain knowledge. Approach each situation as a classroom, ready to extract lessons and wisdom from even the most mundane moments.

Experts and mentors are like beacons of knowledge, ready to illuminate your path. Seek guidance from those who have walked the road before you. Their insights and experiences can provide shortcuts to understanding that would take years to gain on your own.

Failure is not the end but a teacher on the journey of knowledge. Instead of shying away from mistakes, view them as valuable lessons. Through failure, you learn resilience, adaptability, and the importance of perseverance.

Books are windows into worlds of knowledge waiting to be explored. From ancient wisdom to modern insights, literature offers a treasure trove of perspectives. Additionally, online resources, courses, and podcasts provide limitless opportunities for self-guided learning.

Gaining knowledge is not limited to formal education. Active listening and keen observation are powerful tools. Engage in conversations, soak up the wisdom shared by others, and take note of the nuances in your surroundings.

True knowledge is not just theoretical; it's practical and applicable. Apply the insights you gain to your life, work, and relationships. Real magic happens when knowledge transforms into action, leading to growth and tangible results.

The pursuit of knowledge knows no age limits or boundaries. Embrace the mindset of lifelong learning, recognizing that every day presents an opportunity to gain wisdom. As you journey through life, remain committed to expanding your horizons and evolving through the continuous acquisition of knowledge.

Because we are living in the information age, knowledge is more freely and readily available. Internet search engines contain an array of information that can be accessed with the stroke of a few keys. In fact, our millennial generation is so addicted to it that their answer for everything is to Google it. But not only do we have search engines, in recent years the internet has been saturated with free community content, challenges, masterminds, and courses on various topics as an effort to gain followers, an audience, or subscribers. There are even apps that can be used to gain knowledge. The newest means of gaining information that is sweeping across the internet is Artificial Intelligence (AI). In fact, it is even being used in engine searches, websites, and apps now. Having access to knowledge is no longer an excuse for anyone. You already know what knowledge you need, so create a plan to get it.

Building Relationships

In the symphony of personal growth, relationships are the harmonious chords that elevate your journey. Just as each note contributes to a beautiful composition, every relationship you build adds depth, meaning, and resonance to your path of self-discovery. Imagine your personal growth journey as a garden of potential, and relationships are the seeds you plant. Nurture these seeds with care, attention, and authenticity. Over time, they grow into friendships that provide shade during challenges and blossoms of joy during triumphs. Every relationship you forge becomes a vessel for shared experiences. Through these interactions, you gain insights, perspectives, and wisdom that contribute to your personal growth. Embrace the journey of building relationships as a mutual path toward self-improvement.

Building relationships requires empathy – the ability to understand and share the feelings of others. This bridge of empathy enhances your personal growth journey. It allows you to connect on a deeper level, fostering mutual support, understanding, and emotional growth. As you weave the fabric of relationships, you create a network of collaboration and mutual growth. Just as a team collaborates to achieve greatness, your relationships offer opportunities to combine strengths, learn from each other, and collectively reach new heights.

In your personal growth journey, strangers can become allies. Approach new connections with an open heart and a willingness to learn. Each person you meet has a unique story to share, and these stories can inspire you to overcome challenges and broaden your perspective. Every relationship is a tapestry woven with threads of uniqueness. Embrace the diversity of individuals you connect with, as their differences provide opportunities to learn, grow, and challenge your own assumptions and beliefs.

Building relationships involves the art of active listening. By truly hearing the words and feelings of others, you create spaces of validation and understanding. Active listening not only strengthens your connections but also contributes to your own personal growth by enhancing your communication skills. Just as a diamond is formed under pressure, relationships can grow stronger through conflict. View disagreements as opportunities for growth, allowing you to learn effective communication, compromise, and problem-solving. By navigating conflicts with respect and empathy, you build relationships that withstand the tests of time.

Your personal growth journey is not just about your individual transformation; it's also about leaving a legacy of connection. The relationships you build become part of your story, creating a network of support, inspiration, and shared growth that echoes through time. Embrace the art of building relationships as a legacy that enriches both your life and the lives of those you touch.

Relationship Exercise

In this exercise, we will learn how to build strong, lasting relationships. Meeting new people is often daunting due to the fear of the unknown. But you will never know what a relationship can bring until you initiate it. Often, we see people daily but never speak to them. Speaking to someone costs nothing but can yield great benefits.

This exercise is more of a challenge: meet three new people each week. Here's how to do it:

1. Get the person's name.

2. Know what the person does for a living.

3. Exchange phone numbers with the person.

4. Get permission to contact them in the next week.

5. Complete a contact form for the person you meet.

Here is a simple script to help you meet new people:

Approach the person with a warm smile and friendly demeanor.

Start the conversation by introducing yourself: "Hi, I'm [Your Name]. How's your day going?"

Pay attention to their response and engage in some small talk to establish rapport. Show genuine interest in them: "It's great to meet new people. I'm making an effort to connect with new people and expand my circle. My goal is to meet around three new people each week and I'm hoping you are one of them."

"I'm always curious to learn about different backgrounds and interests of other people. By the way, I'm always fascinated by the diverse careers people have. What do you do for a living?"

Listen actively to their response and ask follow-up questions: "That sounds interesting! How did you get into that field?"

Share a bit about your own interests related to their field, if applicable: "I've always been curious about [related topic]. Have you ever explored that?"

Transition to their hobbies and interests: "Aside from work, what do you enjoy doing in your free time? Any hobbies or activities you're passionate about?"

If you share similar interests, mention it: "Oh, I'm a fan of [shared interest] too! How did you get into that?"

Express the desire to stay in touch: "It's been really great talking to you. I'd love to continue our conversation sometime. Would you be open to exchanging numbers?"

If they agree, you can say: "Awesome! Let me grab my phone. What's the best way to reach you?"

Thank them for the conversation: "Thank you for sharing your experiences with me. Looking forward to connecting again soon!"

Remember, the script is a guideline, and it's important to adapt it to the flow of the conversation and the context. Also, be respectful of the other person's comfort level and privacy when exchanging contact information. Let's complete the final requirement, the contact form. The contact form is a simple form, which will allow you to build a better relationship with others, not just the new people you meet, but also the ones you already know. In fact you should complete a contact form on everyone you know. Turn to page 452 of your workbook or create a contact form in your notebook.

Contact Form

It is important not to fill out the form in the presence of the person you just met. Complete the form when you are at home or in your office. Note: This person only becomes a contact or a relationship after you have completed the initial contact. Knowing a person's hobbies and goals is an important part of building your relationship. It gives you the opportunity to join in their hobbies if it is something that interests you, help them achieve their goals, or simply give you more to talk about. Constant follow-up also strengthens your relationship with others, so make it a habit to set aside a time slot each day just to reach out to others.

Here is an example of the contact form:

Contact Form

Name:					
	Prefix	First	Middle	Last	Suffix
Address:					
	Number	Direction	Street Name		
	City		State	Zip Code	
Contact Phone:	( ) -		( ) -		( ) -
	Mobile		Home		Work
Social Media:					
	Facebook		Twitter		Instagram
	LinkedIn		Skype		Other
When met:		Where met:			
Relationship:		Spouse Name:			
	Relationship Status		First	Middle	Last
Occupation:			Employer:		
Hobbies:					
	Hobby 1	Hobby 2	Hobby 3	Hobby 4	Hobby 5
	Hobby 6	Hobby 7	Hobby 8	Hobby 9	Hobby 10
Goals:					
	Goal 1	Goal 2	Goal 3	Goal 4	Goal 5

Communications Log

Date	Result	Conversation was about	Next Call

Meeting Log

Date	Result	Location	Next Meeting

By participating in this challenge, you will find it easy to meet new people and build new relationships. Just meeting three new people a week will allow you to meet over 150 people over

286

the course of a year. Building these relationships can also cause a ripple effect in your life that will cause you to meet other people through this new relationship you have formed. Just as a male and a female rabbit multiply, so will your relationships. I have found it helpful to keep a copy of the contact form and place them in a three-ring binder; it makes it easier to keep my contacts organized. I also schedule my next contact or meeting as soon as I make them. As you build more relationships, you may need to assign your next contact further apart. This does not mean that you will lose the relationship, it just means that you are not overwhelming yourself with just contacting people all day every day.

In fact, I have a friend named Marvin. We have been friends for almost 50 years. We met in grade school. He was in first grade, and I was in third grade. Marvin and I may talk to one another every 1-3 years. Yes, I said years. When we talk, we talk as if not much time has passed. We catch each other up on what has happened in our lives over the years and end our conversation with "I love you, bro." But the thing is, if we ever need something, we know that the other will be there without question. I tell you this so that you can understand that not all relationships require constant and consistent communication. The stronger the relationship, the less contact is required. You will find that each relationship is different. It all depends on the individual; some require daily, weekly, or monthly contact, while others may not require contact at all. But the important thing is to create relationships that can create an avenue for knowledge, help, and encouragement from both sides. Our relationships should enhance our personal growth journey. Our relationships should be valued; relationships are more valuable than money. Treat relationships like a precious jewel because, just like a jewel, our relationships only increase in value over the years. Expanding your relationships will also give you the opportunity to build a stronger support system.

Building Your Support System

A robust support system is like a safety net that catches you when you stumble. These are the individuals who understand your aspirations, fears, and dreams. They provide a safe space where you can express yourself openly and receive guidance without judgment. In your pursuit of personal growth, accountability is key. Your support system serves as a group of catalysts, gently nudging you to stay committed to your goals. They hold you accountable for the promises you make to yourself, driving you to persevere even in the face of obstacles.

Surrounding yourself with positivity is essential for growth. Your support system becomes the echoing chamber of positivity, reminding you of your strengths, applauding your achievements, and infusing you with the confidence needed to overcome challenges. Your support system offers a wealth of insights drawn from their own experiences. They become your mentors, sharing their wisdom, and offering guidance that helps you navigate the twists and turns of your personal growth journey.

The road to personal growth is not without setbacks, but your support system bolsters your resilience. Their encouragement and belief in you become the source of strength you draw from, helping you bounce back stronger and more determined than before. As you achieve milestones along your journey, your support system stands as your champions. They celebrate your victories as their own, magnifying your joy and reminding you that every step forward is worth acknowledging and applauding. Your support system serves as living examples of what's possible.

They inspire you through their own achievements, proving that growth is achievable and that the path you're on is well worth pursuing. Amid the distractions of life, your support system helps sharpen your focus. They remind you of your goals and encourage you to align your actions with your aspirations, ensuring that you stay on track even when the journey becomes challenging. Ultimately, your support system weaves the fabric of lifelong bonds. These are the relationships that endure, nourished by mutual growth and shared experiences. As you evolve, your support system remains by your side, a testament to the strength of connection and the importance of having a network that propels you toward the zenith of personal growth.

Your personal growth journey is a deeply personal and unique path that you embark upon to become the best version of yourself. While the people you choose to include in your journey will depend on your specific goals, needs, and preferences, there are some individuals who can play meaningful roles in your journey. For instance, having mentors and coaches who have expertise in your field of interest can provide invaluable guidance. They offer insights, share experiences, and provide constructive feedback to help you navigate challenges more effectively. Surrounding yourself with friends and family who support your growth is essential. They provide emotional support, understanding, and encouragement during your highs and lows, making your journey less daunting. Connecting with peers who share your aspirations can create a sense of camaraderie. Accountability partners can help keep you on track, as you mutually set goals, check in on each other's progress, and celebrate achievements. Engaging with individuals in your industry or field can broaden your perspective and offer opportunities for collaboration and learning. Networking connections provide insights into trends, challenges, and opportunities you might not be aware of.

Joining personal development groups, workshops, or online communities can expose you to diverse ideas, strategies, and experiences. These groups offer a platform for learning, sharing, and mutual support. Role models and inspirational figures, whether from history, literature, or your industry, can provide a source of motivation. Learning from their stories and accomplishments can inspire you to overcome obstacles and strive for greatness. Depending on your goals, subject matter experts in areas you're trying to improve can offer specialized knowledge and advice. Whether it's fitness, finance, creativity, or any other field, their expertise can help you make informed decisions. Engaging with thought leaders and influencers in your areas of interest through blogs, podcasts, social media, or other online platforms can provide ongoing inspiration, insights, and the latest trends. But above all, you are the most important part of your personal growth journey. Your self-awareness, commitment, and willingness to learn and adapt play a central role in your success. Your inner drive and dedication are the engines that propel your journey forward. Ultimately, those who are part of your personal growth journey should be individuals who uplift, challenge, and inspire you to become the best version of yourself. Selecting a combination of mentors, supporters, collaborators, and resources that align with your aspirations will enhance your journey's effectiveness and impact.

Grasping Technology

The choice of technology for your personal growth journey depends on your goals, preferences, and learning style. Utilize apps like task managers, calendar apps, and note-taking tools to organize your tasks, set goals, and track your progress. Online courses, webinars, and educational platforms offer a wealth of knowledge and skills to help you achieve personal growth milestones. E-books and audiobooks provide access to a vast library of personal development, self-help, and motivational content. Apps that offer guided meditation, relaxation techniques, and mindfulness exercises help reduce stress and enhance mental well-being. If your growth journey involves language acquisition, apps designed for language learning can be highly effective. When pursuing global opportunities, translation apps can assist in communication and understanding. Dedicated goal-tracking apps help you set, monitor, and celebrate your progress towards your personal growth objectives. Time tracking apps, Pomodoro timers, and time-blocking tools can help you manage your time efficiently.

Joining relevant online communities and forums allows you to connect with like-minded individuals, share insights, and seek advice. Listen to podcasts on personal development, success stories, and various areas of interest that align with your growth journey. Digital journaling apps offer a convenient way to reflect, document your thoughts, and track your personal growth journey. Video calls and virtual meetings enable you to connect with mentors, coaches, and peers, fostering learning and collaboration. Platforms like Coursera, Udemy, and LinkedIn Learning offer a wide range of courses to enhance your skills. Apps for fitness, nutrition tracking, and wellness routines contribute to your physical well-being. Professional networking platforms such as LinkedIn help you connect with mentors, colleagues, and peers in your field. For larger personal projects, project management tools help you plan, execute, and monitor progress effectively. Apps for budgeting, expense tracking, and investment management contribute to your financial growth. If data analysis is part of your journey, tools for data visualization and analysis can be invaluable. Apps for graphic design, drawing, and creative expression enhance your artistic skills. When used mindfully, social media platforms can offer access to valuable content, discussions, and connections.

Determine a budget for acquiring the technology you need. Consider both one-time costs and any ongoing subscription fees associated with the tools you're considering. Many technology tools offer free versions or trial periods. Take advantage of these opportunities to test the tools and determine if they're suitable for your needs. If a particular technology is crucial to your growth journey, don't hesitate to invest in it. Remember that investing in tools that enhance your learning, productivity, and organization can have a substantial long-term payoff. Ask peers, mentors, or experts in your field for recommendations on the best technology tools for your goals. Their insights can help you make informed decisions. Look for workshops, webinars, or online courses that provide guidance on using specific technology tools. Learning from experts can accelerate your mastery of the tools. Choose technology that can grow with you as your goals evolve. Tools that offer advanced features or the ability to customize your experience can be particularly valuable. Many technology providers offer tutorials, documentation, and support to help you make the most of their tools. Familiarize yourself with these resources to maximize your efficiency. Engage with peers who are using similar technology. Join online communities, forums, or social media groups where you can exchange insights, tips, and experiences. Develop a plan for integrating the chosen technology into your growth journey. Outline how you'll use the tools, when, and for what purpose.

Dedicate time to learning how to use technology effectively. Whether through online courses, tutorials, or trial and error, becoming proficient with the tools is essential. Regularly assess how the technology is impacting your growth journey. Are you making progress? Is the tool enhancing your productivity and learning? Be open to adjusting your technology choices if you find that certain tools aren't meeting your expectations. Flexibility is key to optimizing your growth journey. Consider how different technology tools can complement each other. For instance, using a time management app alongside a note-taking app can enhance your organization. Periodically reflect on your technology usage. Are there any tools you've outgrown? Are there new tools that align better with your evolving goals? As your needs change and your personal growth journey progresses, you might find that it's worth upgrading to more advanced versions of certain tools. Technology is constantly evolving. Stay curious and open to exploring new tools and trends that emerge in your field. By strategically acquiring and effectively utilizing technology, you can empower yourself to navigate your personal growth journey more efficiently and with greater impact.

Remember that the technology you choose should align with your goals, values, and learning preferences. Prioritize tools that enhance your learning, productivity, and overall growth, while being mindful of maintaining a healthy balance between technology use and meaningful real-world experiences. While technology is a tool to enhance your efforts, it is your commitment, dedication, and active participation that are the core factors of your growth.

By knowing the resources we need to have, we can now determine the mode by which we will be traveling.

Mode of Travel

Choosing the mode of travel on your personal growth journey is a deeply personal decision. It's important to remember that there is no one-size-fits-all approach, and what works for one person may not work for another. Your mode of travel is also dependent on the amount of each of the resources you have. Here are the modes of travel available to you in your personal growth journey:

1. **Walking** – This is a do-it-alone approach with limited knowledge, no money, no relationship, and time is not of importance. The slowest pace.

2. **Cycling** – This is a do-it-alone approach with some knowledge, limited money, no relationship, and time is a minor concern. A modest pace.

3. **Transit** – This involves some knowledge, budgeted money, an accountability partner, and an allotted time. A moderate pace.

4. **Car** – This involves trained knowledge, a little money to invest in yourself, an accountability partner, and monthly coaching on a scheduled time. A fast pace.

5. **Airplane** – This involves expert knowledge, money to invest, an accountability partner, coach, mentor, and a daily time schedule. The fastest pace.

Here is a more precise understanding of each mode:

Walking symbolizes a slow and solitary approach to personal growth. It suggests a journey where you're figuring things out as you go along, with limited resources and no external influences. Time is not a pressing concern, emphasizing the importance of taking things at your own pace. This is the worst mode of travel for personal growth and carries the lowest success rate.

Cycling represents a more deliberate, self-guided approach. You have some knowledge and resources at your disposal, and while you're still on your own, you're able to move at a modest pace. Time is a consideration, but it's not overly restrictive. This mode is chosen by those who want to grow but do not prioritize it, usually seeking free knowledge from community content. This mode rarely gets you to your destination due to burnout or loss of motivation.

Transit mode suggests a more structured approach to personal growth. You have knowledge and budgeted resources, and you're engaging with an accountability partner. There's a set schedule, indicating a level of commitment and consistency in your growth efforts. This mode is the most popular and carries an adequate success rate, requiring discipline and a dedicated accountability partner.

Car mode signifies a more accelerated and invested approach. You have specialized knowledge and are willing to invest financially in your personal growth. You're working closely with an accountability partner and receiving regular coaching. This approach implies a faster rate of progress and is suitable for those who are serious about changing their lives within a reasonable amount of time.

Airplane mode is the most intense and rapid approach to personal growth. It requires expert knowledge, significant financial investment, and involves close collaboration with an accountability partner, coach, and mentor. This mode is for the serious go-getter who wants to achieve success quickly, dedicating substantial time and money to their personal growth. It guarantees the highest rate of success.

These metaphors can help conceptualize the different approaches to your personal growth journey. There is no universally right or wrong approach, and what works best for one person may not work for another. The key is to choose a mode that aligns with your goals, resources, and preferences and to be consistent and committed to your journey.

Choose the mode by which you will travel. If you are choosing to travel by car or airplane and would like to have me as your coach, just send me an email at divineandrighteous@gmail.com with your contact information, and I will get in touch with you to schedule a consultation. My rates are affordable and dependent on your needs. For me, it is more important that you grow than it is for me to make money.

By understanding the resources needed, we can now determine how to effectively use them to achieve our personal growth goals.

Utilizing Your Resources

Utilizing Time for Personal Growth

Just as an exciting road trip begins with the ignition of the engine, your personal growth journey starts with a conscious decision to use time effectively. The road ahead is filled with opportunities to learn, evolve, and transform. Embrace this journey with enthusiasm, knowing that each moment counts toward your growth. Before embarking on a road trip, you plan your route to ensure a smooth journey. Similarly, outline your personal growth goals and milestones. Define the skills you want to acquire, the challenges you want to overcome, and the person you aim to become. This roadmap will keep you focused and motivated as you utilize time to your advantage. Just as a car requires fuel to keep moving, your personal growth journey thrives on knowledge. Invest time in learning, whether through reading, courses, or hands-on experiences. Like fuel propels a car forward, knowledge propels you toward your aspirations.

During a road trip, you make pit stops to rest and reflect. Similarly, allocate time for self-reflection on your personal growth journey. These moments of pause allow you to assess your progress, celebrate achievements, and adjust your course if needed. Road trips come with unexpected detours and roadblocks. Similarly, your personal growth journey may encounter obstacles and setbacks. Instead of letting them deter you, view them as opportunities to learn and grow. Adaptability and resilience are your greatest allies on this journey. A road trip isn't just about reaching the destination; it's about enjoying the journey itself. Likewise, your personal growth journey is enriched by the experiences you gather along the way. Savor every moment, relish the challenges, and celebrate the progress, for it's the journey that molds you.

During a road trip, you might take detours to explore captivating side roads. Similarly, allow yourself to explore new interests and avenues of personal growth. Sometimes, these detours lead to unexpected passions and insights that enhance your journey. Just as road trips often involve companionship, your personal growth journey can be enriched by meaningful relationships. Connect with mentors, peers, and like-minded individuals who inspire and support your growth. These connections provide encouragement and valuable insights as you utilize time for self-improvement. On a road trip, you periodically glance at the rearview mirror to admire the distance you've covered. Similarly, take moments to reflect on how far you've come on your personal growth journey. Acknowledge the milestones you've achieved and let them inspire you to continue utilizing time effectively. A road trip allows you to explore new horizons and experience the beauty of diverse landscapes. In your personal growth journey, each day presents a chance to venture into uncharted territories of self-discovery and advancement. As you navigate the road of time, remember that the growth you achieve becomes the scenery of the remarkable journey you create.

Utilizing Knowledge for Personal Growth

Just as a road trip begins with excitement and anticipation, your personal growth journey sets forth with the same fervor. Knowledge is your vehicle, propelling you forward on the winding roads of self-improvement. Embrace this expedition, armed with the understanding that every piece of information is fuel that drives your progress. Before embarking on a road trip, you map out your route to ensure a smooth voyage. Similarly, in your personal growth journey, chart a course by identifying areas of knowledge you wish to explore. Whether it's acquiring new skills, deepening your understanding, or broadening your perspectives, a well-planned path ensures you make the most of your expedition.

Just as a car requires fuel to keep moving, your personal growth journey thrives on insights. Knowledge is the fuel that powers your aspirations, propelling you toward your goals. Invest time in learning from books, mentors, experiences, and embrace the thrill of gaining new insights. A road trip comes with its share of challenges, from detours to unexpected obstacles. Likewise, your personal growth journey may have hurdles. The wisdom you've gathered serves as your GPS, guiding you through rough patches and helping you navigate the path ahead with confidence. A road trip often leads you to uncharted territories. Similarly, your personal growth journey will present you with unfamiliar concepts and ideas. Embrace these opportunities to expand your horizons, allowing each new piece of knowledge to broaden your perspective and enrich your understanding.

Road trips are dotted with hidden gems – picturesque landscapes and charming towns off the beaten path. In your journey of knowledge, every topic you explore is a hidden gem waiting to be discovered. Delve into subjects that intrigue you, unearthing valuable insights that add to the tapestry of your growth. During a road trip, you make stops to rest and take in the scenery. Similarly, allocate time for reflection on your personal growth journey. These pauses allow you to absorb the knowledge you've acquired, internalize its value, and apply it in meaningful ways. Road trips are often shared with companions, making the experience richer. In your pursuit of knowledge, connect with others who share your interests. Engage in discussions, exchange ideas, and learn from one another. The journey becomes more fulfilling when you are part of a community that values growth. A road trip exposes you to diverse landscapes and cultures. Likewise, seeking knowledge exposes you to diverse perspectives and viewpoints. Embrace this diversity as an opportunity to broaden your understanding, fostering empathy and a deeper connection with the world around you. A road trip takes you to new horizons and experiences. Similarly, knowledge is your compass to uncharted territories of self-discovery and enlightenment. As you navigate the road of learning, remember that each piece of knowledge becomes a landmark on your map of personal growth, guiding you toward the person you aspire to be.

Utilizing Relationships for Personal Growth

Just as a road trip is more enjoyable with companions, your relationships become your fellow travelers, accompanying you on this transformative voyage. As you navigate the twists and turns of your personal growth journey, your relationships become your navigational guides. Like road signs pointing the way, they offer insights, perspectives, and wisdom that help you make informed decisions. Imagine gathering around a campfire on your road trip, sharing stories, experiences, and laughter. Similarly, your relationships provide a platform for sharing insights, challenges, and triumphs. These conversations become the fire that fuels your personal growth. Just as travelers help carry each other's baggage on a road trip, your relationships support you in carrying the emotional baggage that may arise during your personal growth journey. They offer a safe space to vent, heal, and find solace.

Road trips have scenic stops where you pause to soak in the beauty around you. Your personal growth journey has milestones to celebrate. Your relationships stand with you at these checkpoints, celebrating your achievements and encouraging you to continue. A road trip isn't always smooth; storms may come. Similarly, your journey of growth may encounter challenges. Your relationships become the shelter that shields you from the storms, offering comfort, encouragement, and unwavering support. Just as you collect souvenirs on a road trip, your relationships provide you with souvenirs of wisdom and experiences. These insights become precious mementos that enrich your personal growth journey and stay with you forever. Road trips take you through changing landscapes, and your personal growth journey leads you through evolving phases. Your relationships are adaptable companions, changing with you, understanding your growth, and offering guidance as you transition.

Road trips are about making memories, and your personal growth journey is no different. Your relationships become part of the memories that shape your growth. Cherish these moments, for they become a mosaic of support in your journey. At the heart of a road trip lies the joy of connection, exploration, and shared experiences. Similarly, your personal growth journey is enriched by your relationships. Embrace the joy of connecting with others, for these connections are the milestones that mark your path to becoming the best version of yourself. Engage with friends or mentors who have shown genuine interest in your growth. Seek advice, feedback, and encouragement from those who align with your aspirations. Use the insights gained from your assessment to initiate open conversations with friends about your personal growth journey. Share your goals and aspirations to foster understanding. Collaborate with friends who are also on their personal growth journeys. Sharing experiences and challenges can lead to mutual growth and learning. Analyze patterns in your relationships. Are there consistent themes in the types of connections you've prioritized? Reflect on what these patterns reveal about your values and priorities.

As you continue to interact with people, be mindful of how those interactions align with your personal growth goals. Choose to engage in conversations and activities that contribute positively to your journey. Share your personal growth achievements and milestones with supportive friends. Celebrate your successes together and encourage each other's advancement. While taking inventory of existing relationships is important, remain open to forming new connections that align with your growth journey. Personal growth is an ongoing process. Regularly reassess your relationships to ensure they continue to align with your evolving aspirations. Prioritize self-care and well-being, as a strong foundation within yourself positively impacts how you engage with others. Remember that relationships are dynamic and can evolve over time. Your personal growth journey should be supported by connections that inspire, uplift, and contribute to your well-being. By using the insights from your inventory, you can curate a network of relationships that serve as pillars of strength in your pursuit of self-improvement and fulfillment.

Utilizing Money for Personal Growth

Picture your personal growth journey as an exhilarating road trip, and money is the fuel that propels you forward. Just as a car needs fuel to cover distance, your financial resources enable you to seize opportunities, explore uncharted territories, and expand the horizons of your personal growth. On a road trip, you choose your route wisely to ensure a smooth journey. Similarly, financial decisions are like the map you navigate to reach your goals. Allocate your resources strategically, investing in experiences, education, and tools that align with your growth aspirations.

As you embark on a road trip to explore new places, your financial resources allow you to explore new territories of knowledge, skills, and experiences. Whether it's investing in courses, workshops, or travel, money unlocks doors to personal growth that may have remained closed otherwise.

A road trip isn't without obstacles, and your personal growth journey may encounter challenges too. Financial resources act as your toolkit, enabling you to overcome roadblocks by seeking guidance, acquiring necessary resources, and seeking professional help when needed. Road trips are all about creating memorable experiences, and the same applies to your personal growth journey. Financial resources allow you to create experiences that become cherished memories, whether it's attending transformative retreats, participating in life-changing events, or exploring new passions. On a road trip, you adapt to changing weather conditions. Similarly, your financial flexibility enables you to adapt to evolving circumstances in your personal growth journey. It provides the freedom to pivot, experiment, and seize unexpected opportunities without being constrained.

Road trips require periodic stops for rest and rejuvenation. In your personal growth journey, financial resources provide you with the means to invest in self-care, wellness, and activities that recharge your mind, body, and spirit. A road trip is often more enjoyable when shared with others. Similarly, your financial resources can be shared to support others on their personal growth journeys. Whether it's contributing to a cause, mentoring, or providing resources, money can be a catalyst for shared growth. During a road trip, you capture moments of breathtaking beauty. In your personal growth journey, financial resources help capture the moments of transformation—whether through coaching, therapy, or transformative experiences—that shape you into the person you aspire to be. As you embark on this road trip of personal growth, remember that the journey itself is as important as the destination. Your financial resources not only help you reach milestones but also facilitate the experiences, growth, and self-discovery that make the journey truly meaningful and enriching. Just as a road trip is about embracing adventure, your utilization of money in your personal growth journey becomes a testament to your commitment to embracing the adventure of becoming the best version of yourself.

Utilizing Technology for Personal Growth

Imagine embarking on a road trip of personal growth with a backpack filled with advanced technological tools. Just as explorers set out with modern gear, you embark on your journey armed with technology that will empower and amplify your path of self-improvement. On a road trip, navigation is key, and technology becomes your GPS guiding you through uncharted territory. Similarly, in your personal growth journey, technology provides you with precision and direction, ensuring you're on the right track to achieve your goals. Technology becomes your map, charting your progress and milestones along the way. It keeps a digital record of your achievements, reminding you how far you've come and inspiring you to keep pushing forward.

Just as road trips bring people together across distances, technology connects you with mentors, peers, and resources across the globe. Online communities, virtual workshops, and video conferencing become your means of engaging with a diverse network of growth-minded individuals. During your road trip, you capture breathtaking landscapes. Similarly, technology allows you to capture moments of insight, reflection, and personal breakthroughs. Journaling apps, voice memos, or video diaries become your digital scrapbook of transformation. Technology turns your personal growth journey into a continuous learning experience. Podcasts, audiobooks, and online courses become your travel companions, providing knowledge and inspiration that fuel your journey of self-discovery.

On a road trip, weather conditions can change suddenly. Similarly, technology equips you to adapt to changing circumstances in your personal growth journey. Apps, tools, and online resources help you pivot, learn, and evolve as needed. Amidst the excitement of a road trip, moments of solitude are essential for reflection. Technology offers mindfulness apps, meditation guides, and self-care tools that enable you to stay connected with yourself, fostering self-awareness and inner growth. A road trip often presents unexpected challenges. In your personal growth journey, technology transforms challenge into opportunities. Online platforms for skill development, problem-solving apps, and virtual support groups become your toolkit for overcoming obstacles. Just as a road trip is an adventure, your journey of personal growth becomes a digital adventure with technology as your co-pilot. Embrace the power of technology as a partner in your journey, enhancing your capabilities, connecting you to a world of knowledge, and guiding you toward the destination of becoming the best version of yourself.

Utilizing Life's Resources for Personal Growth

Imagine your personal growth journey as a symphony, with time, knowledge, relationships, money, and technology as harmonious instruments. Just as a skilled conductor orchestrates a beautiful melody, utilizing these five resources in harmony accelerates your journey toward fulfillment and achievement. Time is the conductor that sets the tempo of your growth journey. When you allocate time purposefully, you gain the freedom to learn, connect, and innovate. Time becomes the canvas on which you paint your aspirations, ensuring that each stroke contributes to the masterpiece of your personal growth.

Knowledge acts as the guiding star on your road to fulfillment. Embrace learning as a journey itself, where the pursuit of knowledge equips you with the tools to overcome challenges, make informed decisions, and evolve into a wiser, more capable individual. Just as sunlight nurtures a garden, relationships nurture your personal growth journey. Cultivate connections that inspire, challenge, and support you. Through meaningful interactions, you gain insights, broaden your perspectives, and accelerate your progress by learning from the experiences of others. Money is the catalyst that propels your aspirations forward. It amplifies your ability to invest in self-improvement, access opportunities, and create experiences that expedite your growth journey. When used strategically, money fuels your ambitions and transforms them into tangible achievements.

Technology acts as the accelerator on your path of fulfillment. It empowers you to learn at your own pace, connect across borders, and leverage innovative tools for efficiency and effectiveness. Utilizing technology seamlessly integrates learning, collaboration, and progress into your daily life. By weaving these five resources together, you create a resilient framework that can weather the storms of challenges and setbacks. Just as a well-constructed structure can withstand external forces, your journey fortified by time, knowledge, relationships, money, and technology gains the resilience to adapt, evolve, and triumph. The synergy of these resources cultivates a growth mindset that propels you forward. Embrace challenges as opportunities, see setbacks as steppingstones, and view obstacles as chances to apply your knowledge, connect with your network, allocate resources effectively, and leverage technology for innovative solutions.

Imagine yourself as the captain of a ship, steering through uncharted waters toward your goals. With time, knowledge, relationships, money, and technology as your navigational tools, you chart a course with clarity, purpose, and determination, ensuring that every action moves you closer to your aspirations. As you harmonize time, knowledge, relationships, money, and technology, you create a symphony of fulfillment that resonates through your personal growth journey. Each resource contributes its unique melody, amplifying your potential, and propelling you toward a destination where your goals are achieved, your purpose is fulfilled, and your journey is a testament to the remarkable synergy of these five transformative forces.

Part VI

Estimated Time of Arrival

Your ETA

Just as a traveler eagerly anticipates reaching their destination, so should you anticipate your estimated time of arrival in your personal growth journey. Embrace every step of your transformation, for it's the journey that molds you into the person you aspire to be. Like a GPS recalculating the route when you take a detour, remember that setbacks and challenges are a natural part of personal growth. Trust that every experience, whether positive or negative, is contributing to your growth and leading you closer to your desired destination.

In a world of instant gratification, remember that personal growth is a gradual process. Stay patient and persistent, knowing that even small steps taken consistently can eventually cover great distances. Just as you would celebrate reaching a rest stop on a long journey, take time to acknowledge and celebrate your personal growth milestones. These moments serve as reminders of how far you've come and fuel your motivation to continue.

The estimated time of arrival is never fixed, and similarly, personal growth timelines can be unpredictable. Embrace the uncertainty and use it as an opportunity to adapt, learn, and evolve as you navigate the twists and turns of your journey. Sometimes, the most scenic routes are the ones that take unexpected turns. Similarly, detours in your personal growth journey can offer valuable lessons and perspectives. Embrace these detours as chances to learn and broaden your horizons.

Just as a traveler envisions the beauty of their destination, visualize the person you aspire to become. Keep this vision in your mind's eye, and let it guide you forward, even when the path seems challenging. A traveler doesn't turn back halfway through their journey; they keep moving forward. Apply this same dedication to your personal growth journey. Commit to your growth and remind yourself of your goals regularly.

Traveling companions make the journey more enjoyable. Surround yourself with supportive individuals who uplift and encourage your growth. Share your goals with them, and let their positivity propel you forward. Just as roads can change unexpectedly, your personal growth journey might take unexpected turns. Embrace these changes and view them as opportunities for new experiences. Flexibility in your approach will empower you to adapt and continue progressing.

Remember, the estimated time of arrival in personal growth is not fixed; it continuously changes. Enjoy the ride, learn from the experiences, and relish in the transformation you undergo as you journey toward becoming the best version of yourself. While traveling life's highway, time is our most precious resource. Just as a skilled conductor orchestrates a beautiful symphony, managing your time effectively allows you to harmonize your tasks and goals, creating a masterpiece of personal development.

Each day presents a fresh canvas for your growth, and effective time management ensures you make the most of it. By organizing your tasks, setting priorities, and allocating time wisely, you seize the opportunities for learning, progress, and transformation. Imagine a well-oiled machine running at peak efficiency – that's how your personal growth thrives with effective time management. By eliminating time-wasting activities and focusing on what truly matters, you fuel your progress and move closer to your goals.

Time management isn't just about maximizing productivity; it's about achieving balance and fulfillment. When you allocate time for self-care, learning, relationships, and pursuing passions, you create a holistic approach to personal growth that nurtures your overall well-being. The journey of personal growth is often marked by milestones – achievements that represent your progress. Effective time management allows you to set clear milestones, track your advancement, and celebrate your accomplishments along the way.

Time management is a powerful tool for cultivating discipline. Just as an athlete follows a rigorous training schedule, managing your time requires commitment and consistency, fostering self-discipline that extends to every aspect of your personal growth. Poor time management can lead to stress and a scattered focus, hindering your growth efforts. On the other hand, efficient time management reduces stress by providing a clear roadmap, allowing you to focus your energy on tasks that move you forward. Time management is an exercise in prioritization – a skill that empowers you to make conscious choices about where you invest your time. By aligning your activities with your goals, you take control of your personal growth trajectory.

Effective time management is a catalyst for forming lasting habits. Just as a river carves its path through consistent erosion, your habits shape your character and influence the direction of your personal growth journey. Your journey of personal growth isn't just for you; it leaves a legacy of impact on those around you. When you manage your time wisely, you model the value of intentional living and inspire others to embark on their paths of growth. In essence, time management is the compass that guides your personal growth voyage. It empowers you to navigate the waters of life with purpose, direction, and an unwavering commitment to becoming the best version of yourself.

The Importance of Prioritization

Understanding What is Urgent and Important

As you embark on your personal growth journey, one of the most vital compasses you can wield is the ability to differentiate between what is urgent and what is important in the realm of time management. These two concepts often intertwine, but grasping their distinctions can significantly impact the trajectory of your growth. Imagine your personal growth journey as a grand expedition through uncharted territories. Along this voyage, you encounter a continuous flow of tasks, challenges, and opportunities. In this dynamic landscape, tasks fall into two broad categories: the urgent and the important.

Urgency beckons your attention with its immediacy. These tasks are like sudden storms on your journey, demanding swift action to avoid setbacks. They are often externally imposed deadlines, crises, or pressing matters that require immediate resolution. Think of urgent tasks as the tempests that threaten to veer you off course if not managed promptly. On the other hand, importance is your true North star, guiding you towards your long-term goals and aspirations. Important tasks contribute directly to your personal growth, aligning with your values and driving you forward. They often don't have the urgency of a looming deadline but hold the promise of substantial rewards in the future.

The key to effective time management lies in your ability to strike a harmonious balance between the urgent and the important. Picture your time as a limited resource – a finite collection of hours to be invested wisely. When urgency overshadows importance, you risk constantly reacting to crises, leaving little room for the steady progress required for personal growth. Prioritizing the important tasks offers you a compass to navigate your journey. We already began by identifying our long-term goals – the peaks you wish to conquer – and then breaking them down into smaller action steps, manageable milestones. These milestones become your guideposts, allowing you to allocate your time and effort purposefully.

The Eisenhower Matrix: A Strategic Tool

To put this into practice, consider utilizing the Eisenhower Matrix, a time management tool that categorizes tasks based on their urgency and importance. Picture a four-quadrant grid:

1. Urgent and Important (Do First): These are goals that require immediate attention and directly contribute to your long-term growth and success. They are your top priorities and should be addressed promptly. These might include deadlines for important projects, health-related goals, or tasks that align with your core values.

2. Important but Not Urgent: These goals are significant for your personal growth but don't have an immediate deadline. They require planning and dedicated time to ensure consistent progress. Schedule these tasks into your calendar to make sure they are given the attention they deserve. Examples include skill development, relationship-building, and long-term planning. These tasks should be your focus. They align with your long-term goals and offer substantial benefits, but they don't demand immediate action.

3. Urgent but Not Important: These goals are tasks that demand your immediate attention but may not directly contribute to your personal growth. Evaluate whether these tasks can be delegated to someone else or minimized in their impact. They can often be distractions that divert your focus from more meaningful pursuits. These tasks often carry the illusion of importance due to their urgency, but they don't contribute directly to your growth. Delegate or minimize them if possible.

4. Neither Urgent nor Important: These goals are tasks that neither have urgency nor contribute significantly to your growth. They are timewasters and should be minimized or eliminated from your to-do list. Clearing out these tasks frees up valuable time and mental space for what truly matters.

Prioritizing Your Goals

Prioritizing your goals using the Eisenhower Matrix can be a powerful way to prioritize and manage your tasks based on their urgency and importance. The matrix consists of four quadrants, each representing a different category for your goals and tasks. In this exercise, we will begin by listing all our goals and tasks that we need to address. Assess each goal's urgency. Does it have a deadline or require immediate action? Determine the importance of each goal in relation to your long-term growth and overall well-being. Check the appropriate quadrant of the Eisenhower Matrix based on its urgency and importance for each goal or task into.

1. Quadrant 1 (Urgent and Important) tackle them first.

2. Quadrant 2 (Important but Not Urgent) schedule to ensure consistent progress.

3. Quadrant 3 (Urgent but Not Important) Consider delegating or minimizing tasks.

4. Quadrant 4 (Neither Urgent nor Important) Try to eliminate tasks.

Regularly review and update your goals and tasks in the Eisenhower Matrix as new priorities arise or circumstances change. Turn to page 462 of your workbook to the Goal Prioritization Worksheet or create it in your notebook from the example:

Goal Prioritization Worksheet

#	Goal	Quadrant 1	Quadrant 2	Quadrant 3	Quadrant 4
1	Repair my credit	☒	☐	☐	☐
2	Embrace failure as an opportunity for growth and learning	☐	☒	☐	☐
3	I get clarity from my wife after she has expressed her need, desires, and concerns	☐	☒	☐	☐

#	Goal	Quadrant 1	Quadrant 2	Quadrant 3	Quadrant 4
4	I earn $1000,000 per year as a life coach	☒	☐	☐	☐
5	I live in a 15,000+ sq. ft. traditional style brick and cement home in the suburbs	☐	☒	☐	☐
6	Learn to schedule everything	☒	☐	☐	☐

Remember, the goal of using the Eisenhower Matrix is to create a clear and structured way to manage your goals and tasks. It helps you allocate your time and energy effectively, ensuring that you're dedicating your efforts to what truly matters and aligns with your personal growth journey. Make sure that you categorize each of your goals, this will help later in your scheduling process.

Your ability to discern between urgency and importance is a key factor in your success and fulfillment. As you advance on your journey, remember that growth is a marathon, not a sprint. The ability to identify and prioritize the important over the urgent requires a growth mindset – one that values progress over perfection, resilience over reaction.

In conclusion, distinguishing between what is urgent and what is important is the cornerstone of effective time management on your personal growth journey. By nurturing this skill, you steer clear of distractions, navigate challenges, and chart a course that leads to lasting transformation. As you strive to become the best version of yourself, let the guiding principles of importance light your path through the ever-shifting landscape of urgency.

Balancing Time

In the grand theater of life, time takes center stage as both the stage and the spotlight. Balancing the myriad roles, just as a skilled dancer gracefully glides through various moves, mastering the art of time balance requires finesse, dedication, and a deep understanding of the rhythm of life.

Balancing time is not like placing items on a balancing scale or even that of a seesaw, think of it more like balancing a plate on a pencil. That is hard and requires not only a steady hand, but it requires a certain skill set. Imagine time as a pendulum that swings between the various facets of your life. On one end lies your personal growth journey – the path to becoming the best version of yourself. On the other end, there's the tapestry of life's responsibilities, including work, relationships, and self-care. The art of balancing time lies in ensuring that the pendulum swings harmoniously between these two realms.

Balancing time isn't about equal distribution but rather about orchestrating a symphony that resonates with your values and aspirations. Begin by acknowledging that personal growth is not an isolated pursuit; it intertwines with all aspects of your life. Reflect on your core values – the principles that guide your decisions. Align your personal growth goals with these values to ensure that your journey is woven into the fabric of your life. Just as a skilled dancer knows the boundaries of their stage, set clear boundaries for different areas of your life. Allocate dedicated time for work, family, personal growth, and relaxation. Self-care is the backbone of balance. Nurture your physical, mental, and emotional well-being. A well-rested, energized individual can navigate the demands of life and growth with resilience.

In a world of distractions, mastering focus is akin to mastering dance steps. Dedicate focused time to your personal growth tasks. Quality over quantity can lead to remarkable progress. Like a dance that adapts to the rhythm of the music, embrace flexibility in your schedule. Life is dynamic, and the ability to adjust your plans without losing sight of your goals is a valuable skill. Look for opportunities to merge personal growth with other areas of your life. Can you infuse learning into your work or incorporate mindfulness into your daily routines? Technology can be a double-edged sword. Use it to enhance your productivity and learning, but also establish tech-free zones to foster genuine connections.

Just as a dancer must decline some moves to maintain the flow of the routine, saying no to non-essential commitments is crucial. Guard your time fiercely. Just as applause fuels a dancer's passion, celebrate small wins in your personal growth journey. These moments of achievement motivate you to keep dancing forward. Like a dancer reviewing a recording of their performance, regularly reflect on your time balance. Are you nurturing both personal growth and life's responsibilities?

The dance of time balance isn't about perfection; it's about harmony. It's about recognizing that personal growth isn't a destination but a constant evolution that occurs alongside the multifaceted roles you play in life. As you progress on your journey, remember that finding equilibrium is a continuous practice – a practice that enriches your life and molds you into a well-rounded, fulfilled individual. In the end, the most captivating dance is the one that flows effortlessly, seamlessly blending grace and strength. As you choreograph the dance of time in your life, may it become a masterpiece of balance, where your personal growth journey and the symphony of life intertwine to create a captivating rhythm uniquely your own.

Hopefully, this has given you a better insight into time management. But before we get into the proper management of time, I want to discuss a few things that contribute to properly managing your time.

The to Do List

In the bustling landscape of modern life, the to-do list emerges as a beacon of organization and productivity. It's a tool that, when wielded with intention, can transform chaos into order and dreams into reality. In this chapter, we delve into the art of crafting a meaningful to-do list and harnessing its power for effective time.

Picture the to-do list as a blueprint for your day, a roadmap that guides you from dawn to dusk. It's a tangible representation of your intentions, ambitions, and commitments. However, creating a meaningful to-do list is an art that goes beyond scribbling down tasks haphazardly. It's about aligning your list with your goals, values, and personal growth aspirations.

Begin by gaining clarity about your short-term and long-term goals. With a clear vision, you can break these goals into smaller, actionable steps that become the building blocks of your to-do list. Each task on your list should contribute to your overall growth and purpose.

Not all tasks are created equally. The Eisenhower Matrix discussed earlier can be your guiding star here. Prioritize tasks based on their urgency and importance. Your to-do list should reflect a deliberate hierarchy that ensures your most important growth-related tasks take precedence.

While ambition is admirable, an overburdened to-do list can lead to overwhelm. Set realistic expectations for yourself. Focus on quality over quantity. A manageable list that you can realistically complete fosters a sense of accomplishment and motivates further progress. Though structure is essential, life often throws unexpected curveballs. Build flexibility into your to-do list. Allow room for spontaneous opportunities, necessary breaks, and adjustments. Adaptability is a hallmark of effective time management.

Large tasks can be daunting and discouraging. Break them down into smaller, manageable portions. This not only makes them less intimidating but also provides a sense of accomplishment as you tick off subtasks.

Time can slip away unnoticed, so set time limits for each task. This helps you maintain focus, prevent procrastination, and ensures that no single task consumes more time than necessary. Include routine tasks alongside growth-related activities. Incorporate daily practices that nurture your well-being, like exercise, meditation, or reading. A balanced to-do list acknowledges the importance of self-care in your personal growth journey.

Regularly review your to-do list, ideally the night before or early in the morning. Reflect on your accomplishments, adjust priorities if needed, and set the tone for the day ahead.

Celebrate each completed task as a step closer to your goals. This positive reinforcement not only boosts your motivation but also infuses positivity into your time management approach.

Life is a continuous journey, and sometimes tasks remain incomplete. Embrace the fact that not everything needs to be checked off your list every day. Carry unfinished tasks forward with grace and prioritize them the next day.

The to-do list may sound vaguely familiar and that is no coincidence because in the journey of personal growth our action steps are actually a to-do list, but it does not include all of our to-dos. This is why we need to have a to-do list outside of our personal growth journey.

The to-do list is more than a list; it's an instrument of empowerment. When thoughtfully crafted and diligently executed, it becomes a vehicle for propelling you towards your personal growth goals. It transforms time from a fleeting resource into a canvas for accomplishments and transformation. Remember, your to-do list is a tool to serve you, not the other way around. As you weave it into your daily routine, infuse it with intention and purpose. Let it be a guiding force that directs your actions towards a life of fulfillment and achievement, where your personal growth journey is nurtured and celebrated on the canvas of time.

Creating a to-do list is simple. Write down the things that you need to do each day and find time in your day to do them. The items on your to-do list are usually not urgent or important; they are just things we have to do, like mowing the lawn, picking up groceries, mopping the kitchen, taking out the trash, etc. Anything pertaining to your personal growth should not be on your to-do list.

Habits

In the rhythm of life, habits are the steady beat of the drum that keeps the tempo of our days, shaping our experiences and defining our outcomes. They are the small, seemingly mundane actions that hold the power to wield transformative influence over time. In this chapter, we delve into the profound impact of habits on your personal growth journey and how cultivating positive habits can propel you towards greatness.

Imagine habits as the architects of your destiny, quietly constructing the framework upon which your life unfolds. Just as a skilled artist wields a brush to create a masterpiece, the habits you cultivate paint the portrait of your character and shape the landscape of your future. Understanding their potency is the first step towards harnessing their potential for personal growth.

At the heart of every habit lies a loop: a cue, a routine, and a reward. The cue triggers your brain to initiate a routine, which is the behavior itself. The reward is the positive reinforcement that reinforces the habit. By understanding this loop, you can intentionally design and modify your habits to align with your growth goals.

Consistency is the compass that guides you towards your aspirations. Habits gain momentum through repetition. Just as a river carves a canyon over time, your consistent actions shape your character, skills, and trajectory. Certain habits, known as keystone habits, have the power to ripple positive effects across various areas of your life. For instance, exercising regularly not only improves your health but often leads to enhanced discipline, productivity, and self-confidence.

The beauty of habits lies in their simplicity. Small, consistent actions compound over time, yielding extraordinary results. The habit of reading a few pages daily accumulates into a library of knowledge, while the practice of journaling transforms into a chronicle of personal growth.

Cultivating habits transforms intentional actions into automatic responses. This automation conserves mental energy and willpower, allowing you to allocate cognitive resources to other areas of your growth journey.

Rituals are habits with a purposeful intent. They infuse your daily routine with meaning and intention, elevating ordinary actions into moments of mindfulness. From morning rituals that set the tone for the day to evening rituals that promote reflection and gratitude, positive rituals amplify your growth journey.

To replace or create habits, you must navigate the habit loop consciously. Identify the cue that triggers an unwanted habit and replace the routine with a positive action. Over time, the reward associated with the new routine reinforces the change.

Habit cultivation is a journey laden with successes and setbacks. Cultivate self-compassion on this journey. If a habit falters, view it as an opportunity to learn and adjust rather than a failure. As you journey through habit transformation, celebrate milestones. Whether it's a week of consistent practice or reaching a significant numerical goal, celebrate these markers as testaments to your dedication and growth.

Ultimately, your habits sculpt your identity. They shape the person you are and the person you're becoming. Intentionally crafting habits that align with your vision of greatness fuels a sense of purpose and empowers you to embody the qualities you admire.

In the tapestry of your personal growth journey, habits are the threads that weave success and transformation. As you cultivate positive habits, remember that you're not just altering your actions; you're sculpting the very essence of who you are. With intention, consistency, and a deep understanding of the habit loop, you're poised to unleash your potential and march confidently towards the greatness that lies within your grasp. But be forewarned, all habits are not as the one I have explained, the wrong habits can also distract and hinder us from achieving our goals.

Bad Habits

In the intricate tapestry of our lives, habits are the threads that either weave a masterpiece or unravel the fabric. Just as positive habits propel us towards our aspirations, bad habits have the power to cast a shadow over our potential for growth and fulfillment. In this chapter, we explore the profound impact of bad habits on personal growth and life in general, and how understanding and breaking these chains can lead us to a brighter future.

Bad habits often emerge from the comfort zones we create for ourselves. These habits promise immediate gratification or relief, masking their long-term consequences. Just as a river erodes the land it flows through, bad habits gradually erode our potential, stifling our personal growth and casting a cloud over our aspirations. They act as anchors that prevent us from sailing towards our goals. They breed stagnation, keeping us trapped in the confines of familiarity. As we indulge in these habits, we regress rather than progress, stuck in a cycle that thwarts our personal growth journey.

Every time we succumb to a bad habit, our self-confidence takes a hit. We see ourselves as lacking control, which can permeate other aspects of our lives. As the habit loop tightens its grip, self-doubt intensifies, hindering our courage to step into new territories.

These habits demand our attention and energy, often at the expense of our growth pursuits. This fragmented focus diverts us from our goals, rendering our dreams hazy and distant. We become passengers rather than drivers of our journey.

Discipline is the foundation of personal growth. Bad habits erode this foundation, weakening our ability to commit, persevere, and overcome challenges. Without discipline, our growth journey becomes a rudderless ship adrift on turbulent waters.

Many bad habits have a direct impact on our health and well-being. Whether it's poor dietary choices, lack of exercise, or negative coping mechanisms, these habits can lead to physical, mental, and emotional repercussions that hinder our ability to flourish.

Time is a finite resource, and bad habits are its thieves. Hours spent indulging in unproductive or harmful behaviors steal time that could be dedicated to personal growth pursuits, learning, and meaningful relationships.

They perpetuate negative thought and behavior patterns. They normalize complacency, procrastination, and instant gratification, eroding the values that underpin personal growth. These types of habits can strain relationships with loved ones. Whether it's the habit itself or the consequences it brings, these negative effects ripple into the connections that are crucial for our emotional well-being.

The more we indulge in bad habits, the more resistant we become to change. Breaking free from these chains requires immense effort and a willingness to face discomfort, which can deter us from pursuing personal growth.

Recognizing the detrimental effects of bad habits is the first step towards igniting transformation. Just as a butterfly emerges from a cocoon, you have the power to break free from the confines of destructive habits. The journey requires resilience, introspection, and a commitment to replacing bad habits with positive ones that align with your growth aspirations.

In the grand narrative of our lives, bad habits are the chapters that threaten to overshadow our potential for greatness. But every chapter can be rewritten. As you face the consequences of bad habits head-on, you seize control of your story. By replacing detrimental patterns with habits that foster growth, you transform yourself into the author of a narrative brimming with potential, resilience, and the triumph of personal growth.

Identifying Bad Habits

In the tapestry of personal growth, identifying and overcoming bad habits is an essential thread that paves the way to transformation. Just as a sculptor chips away at a block of stone to reveal a masterpiece, breaking the chains of bad habits requires intention, persistence, and a deep understanding of the forces that bind us. As we delve into the process of identifying bad habits and taking corrective measures to forge a path towards positive change, maintain an open mind, know that freedom is a matter of choice.

Understanding the Shackles

The first step to breaking bad habits is self-awareness. Reflect on your actions and routines. Identify habits that hinder our growth or well-being. Examine the triggers that initiate our bad habits. These cues could be emotional states, specific environments, or even certain times of the day. Analyze the patterns that surround your bad habits. What actions precede and follow them? Understand the consequences of these habits on your well-being and personal growth.

Okay, it is time to take a look at what holds us back from achieving our true potential. Turn to page 466 of your workbook to the Bad Habit Assessment Form or create it in your notebook from the example:

Bad Habit Assessment Form		
Habit	**Trigger**	**Consequences**
Playing Age of Origin	The need to compete with others	Lose a lot of time
Procrastination	Finding other things to do that are easier and less intimidating	I never get to complete the things that are urgent and important done.
Binge watching television	Start watching and can't stop	Lose a lot of time

Smoking	Stress prevention and addiction	Spend unnecessary money and cause future health problems

Breaking the Chains

Establish a strong intention to change. Clearly define the reasons you want to break the bad habit and how it aligns with your personal growth goals. Identify positive habits that can replace the negative ones. For instance, if you're trying to quit procrastination, replace it with a habit of setting specific time blocks for focused work. Overcoming bad habits can be overwhelming. Begin with small, manageable changes. Gradual progress builds momentum and boosts your confidence. Share your intention to break the bad habit with a friend, family member, or mentor. Their support and accountability can greatly enhance your efforts. Practice mindfulness to catch yourself in the act of engaging in the bad habit. Use moments of self-reflection to understand the triggers and underlying emotions. Alter your environment to reduce the cues that trigger the bad habit. For instance, if you're trying to cut down on unhealthy snacks, replace them with healthier options. Breaking bad habits can be challenging. Be kind to yourself, acknowledging that setbacks are part of the journey. Learn from them and move forward. Keep a journal or use habit-tracking apps to monitor your progress. Celebrate even the smallest victories. If a bad habit has a strong grip on you, consider seeking professional help, such as therapy or counseling, to address underlying issues.

Turn to page 467 of your workbook to the Habit Conversion Worksheet or create it in your notebook from the example:

Habit Conversion Worksheet		
Habit	**Replacement Habit**	**Benefit**
Playing Age of Origin	Take an educational course	Gain more knowledge
Procrastination	Have a just do it attitude	Achieve more goals and increase personal growth
Binge watching television	Watch motivational YouTube videos for an hour	Allows me to better manage time and get more done
Smoking	Eat veggie sticks	Saves money and increase health

Breaking the chains of bad habits is a journey of liberation. Just as a caterpillar transforms into a butterfly, your efforts to overcome negative patterns pave the way for a metamorphosis of the self. Each step you take, each decision to replace a detrimental habit with a positive one, contributes to the masterpiece of your personal growth.

Remember, the journey is not linear. It's a testament to your resilience and determination. As you navigate the process of change, you're rewriting the script of your life. The power to overcome bad habits and cultivate a life aligned with your aspirations is within your grasp, waiting to be claimed with every intentional choice you make.

Bridging Habits to Routines

Habits stand as the sturdy pillars that uphold our aspirations. Yet, it is the connection between habits and routines that constructs a seamless pathway towards lasting transformation. Just as a bridge connects two worlds, routines bridge the gap between intention and habit, fostering an environment where personal growth thrives. In this chapter, we begin by exploring the vital link between habits and routines and their significance in our journey of personal growth.

Imagine habits as the seeds of change planted deep within the soil of your daily life. These seeds, when nurtured, grow into towering trees of transformation. Just as a foundation supports a towering structure, habits support the framework of your personal growth journey.

Understand the habit loop – the cue, the routine, and the reward. Habits are formed when a specific cue triggers a routine that leads to a reward. This loop cements actions as automatic responses, laying the groundwork for habits. Initiate habits with small, achievable actions. Just as a stream is formed from tiny drops of water over time, our habits gain strength through consistent repetition. Start small to build momentum and prevent overwhelm. Consistency nourishes habits. Commit to performing the same action at the same time or in the same context daily. This consistency reinforces the neural pathways that make habits stick. Surround yourself with an environment that supports your desired habits. Set up your surroundings to reduce friction and make it easy to engage in your chosen actions.

Now, picture routines as the choreography of your day, a dance of intention that guides your actions. Just as a dancer follows the rhythm of music, routines establish a rhythm in your life that complements your growth journey.

Craft routines with intention. Align them with your personal growth goals. Every routine should contribute to your development, ensuring that your actions have purpose and meaning. Transform routines into rituals by infusing them with mindfulness and significance. Let your morning routine be a ritual that kick starts your day with positivity, or your evening routine a ritual that fosters gratitude and reflection. Create a flow in your day by sequencing routines logically. Transition seamlessly from one routine to another, reducing decision fatigue and optimizing your energy. Your routines should fit your lifestyle, not the other way around. Tailor your routines to accommodate your responsibilities and preferences, ensuring they're sustainable in the long run.

To bridge the gap between habits and routines is to create a symphony of consistent, intentional actions. Let habits take root within your routines, embedding them into the fabric of your daily life. Link your habits to specific points in your routines. Brushing your teeth can be the cue for practicing gratitude. Over time, these intertwined actions reinforce each other. Allocate time in your daily schedule for both routines and habit-related actions. Let your routines be the vessels that carry your habits towards transformation. Regularly review your routines and habits. Are they still aligned with your growth goals? Reflect on their impact and adjust as needed. Celebrate not only the successful formation of habits but also the integration of habits into routines. Each step forward is a triumph in your journey of self-improvement. While routines offer structure, be open to flexibility. Life is dynamic, and adapting routines to changing circumstances ensures that they remain effective and relevant.

In the grand narrative of personal growth, habits and routines are the co-authors that script your journey. As you intertwine the threads of habits into the rhythm of routines, you craft a masterpiece of lasting change. Recognize that while habits shape your character, routines shape your day. Together, they mold your future. Embrace the harmony between habits and routines as the gateway to an empowered life. Just as a bridge spans a chasm, this connection spans the distance between where you are and where you strive to be. The journey from intention to action, from action to habit, and from habit to routine is a testament to your dedication to becoming the best version of yourself.

Identifying Your Routines

Identifying your routines is akin to embarking on a journey of self-discovery. As you unravel the threads of your daily life, you gain insight into the patterns that shape your actions and experiences. This self-awareness becomes a cornerstone for your personal growth. Routines are the blueprint of your days, outlining the steps that guide you through life's labyrinth. By identifying these routines, you uncover the pathways that lead you towards your aspirations. With this awareness, you can consciously design your routines to align with your personal growth goals.

Your routines reflect your intentions. Each action, each choice you make, is a testament to your priorities. By identifying the routines that dominate your life, you gain a clear picture of where your energy is directed. This realization empowers you to make intentional choices that drive your growth.

By identifying and analyzing your daily habits, you unearth the seeds that hold the potential for lasting impact. Nurturing positive routines ensures that your growth journey is nurtured day by day. Your routines shape your identity. By identifying the actions that fill your days, you gain insight into the qualities you value and the roles you play. This understanding empowers you to curate routines that mold you into the person you aspire to be.

Identifying your routines is like discovering hidden pathways that lead to transformation. As you recognize the routines that hinder your growth, you open the door to change. By consciously modifying or replacing these routines, you pave the way for personal evolution.

Personal growth thrives on consistency, and routines provide the fertile ground for cultivating this consistency. By pinpointing your routines, you identify the pockets of time where you can plant the seeds of positive habits. These habits, when nurtured, blossom into remarkable changes.

Your routines are your daily rituals, and their impact is profound. By acknowledging their significance, you can transform mundane actions into meaningful moments. Intentionally infusing your routines with purpose elevates your personal growth journey.

Identifying your routines allows you to reclaim control over your time. By understanding where your hours are invested, you can realign your routines to ensure that they serve your growth goals. This deliberate allocation of time sets the stage for remarkable progress.

Your routines are the canvas upon which the brushstrokes of your personal growth are painted. By identifying these routines, you gain the power to reshape the canvas, adding new colors, textures, and dimensions. This artistic approach empowers you to craft a masterpiece of self-improvement.

We all have routines in our life; routines are like rituals we do them faithfully no matter what. They come in various sizes, often times we have names for them, like morning routine, morning ritual, exercise regiment and so many others, you know what I am talking about.

I have a stringent wake-up routine, it begins with me waking up at 4:30 in the morning giving God the glory for waking me up, thanking Him for the present of a new day, filled with His grace and mercies, then I pray that He will be my strength and my provider for the day, asking Him to be my guide, my counselor and my advisor throughout the day, requesting His protection for my family, my home, my friends and myself by building hedges around them and me, asking Him to deny any request that the devil may bring or ask permission for. After my wake-up routine, I go into my morning routine, which starts in the bathroom, first utilizing it if you know what I mean, then I wash-up or take a shower, brush my teeth, rinse my mouth, brush my hair and get dressed for the day, next I head straight for the kitchen and turn on my coffee pot, while waiting for it to boil, I smoke a cigarette (yes, I have bad habits, but not many), when the coffee pot whistles I make my morning coffee and sit on the enclosed porch and read my scriptures and daily word, recently as you can tell I have added researching and writing my book to this routine. My next routine is to bid my wife a good morning and give her a kiss, then speak to the children as they prepare to begin their day at school. Then I start my drop-off routine, first I drop the children off at school, sometimes this routine has a slight deviation, that is when I have to drop-off my Aunt Brenda at church after dropping the children at school, then I return home and drop my wife off at work and return home. As you can see from 4:30 – 8:00am all I do is routine.

I have a pick-up routine, routines for each day of the week, a church routine, an evening, and a bedtime routine. I am sure you got it by now, my life is filled with routines. Now that I have shared my routines it is time for you to share yours, what do you do in your day that is routine?

Turn to page 468 of your workbook to the Routine Worksheet or create it in your notebook from the example. In this exercise you will write the name of the routine, the time the routine starts, the purpose of the routine, list the activities performed in the routine and give the duration in minutes for the routine. Completing a Routine Worksheet for each routine we perform will help us in our time management later on. Here is the example:

Routine Worksheet				
Routine Name:	Wake-up Routine			
Routine Time:	4:30am	**Routine day(s):**		☐Sun. ☐ Mon. ☐Tue. ☐Wed. ☐Thur. ☐ Fri. ☐Sat.
	Routine Purpose:	Give God the glory, receive coverage and protection for my family, friends, and self		
Step	**Activity**			**Duration**
1	wake up			1
2	Give God the glory for waking me up			1
3	Thank God for the present of a new day, filled with His grace and mercies			1
4	Pray that He will be my strength and my provider for the day			1

5	Ask God to be my guide, my counselor, and my advisor throughout the day	1
6	Request God's protection for my family, my home, my friends, and myself	1
7	Request God to build hedges around them and me	1
8	Ask God to deny any request that the devil may bring or ask permission for	1
9	Get out of bed	1
10		

Once you have completed all your routines, we are ready to start creating our schedule.

Crafting a Transformative Schedule

In the orchestra of personal growth, creating a well-orchestrated schedule is akin to composing a symphony that harmonizes all aspects of your life. Just as a conductor blends different instruments to create beautiful music, crafting a schedule that weaves together sleep, work, exercise, routines, and action steps in your personal growth journey is an art that leads to transformative results. In this section, we delve into the transformative power of a thoughtfully designed schedule that nurtures every facet of your being.

Sleep: The Prelude to Success

Imagine sleep as the prelude that sets the tone for the entire composition. Adequate sleep is the foundation upon which your days are built. Prioritizing sleep ensures that you wake up refreshed, with the energy and clarity needed to tackle your personal growth pursuits. Develop a consistent sleep routine by aligning your sleep schedule with a regular wake-up time and bedtime. This helps regulate your body's internal clock, improving the quality of your sleep and potentially eliminating the need for an alarm clock. Create a relaxing bedtime ritual with calming activities such as reading, meditation, or gentle stretches. Design a sleep-friendly environment, ensuring your bedroom is dark, quiet, and at a comfortable temperature.

Work: Fueling Ambition

Work is the melody that carries your ambitions forward. Incorporating your professional responsibilities into your schedule allows you to nurture your career while progressing on your personal growth journey. Within your work schedule, prioritize tasks that align with your personal growth goals. Integrate growth-related responsibilities into your workday to foster synergy between the two. Segment your workday into focused blocks of time dedicated to specific tasks. This practice enhances productivity and prevents burnout by allowing periods of rest and recharge.

Exercise: Energizing the Soul

Exercise is the rhythm that infuses vitality into your days. Integrate physical activity into your schedule to rejuvenate your body and mind, fostering holistic well-being. Incorporate exercises that resonate with you, whether it's jogging, yoga, or dancing. Begin your day with exercise to invigorate your body and set a proactive tone. Morning exercise has been shown to boost mood and cognitive function.

Routines: Crafting Consistency

Routines are the harmonious chords that punctuate your day. Embed your daily rituals within your schedule, allowing them to guide your actions and foster mindfulness. Ensure your routines reflect your core values and personal growth aspirations. Let them be guiding lights that steer you towards your goals. Designate specific times for your routines, such as morning rituals that energize you or evening rituals that promote relaxation and reflection.

Action Steps: Navigating Growth

Action steps are the crescendos that amplify your personal growth symphony. These intentional actions propel you closer to your dreams, infusing your schedule with purpose. Within your schedule, allocate time for specific action steps related to your personal growth goals. Breaking tasks into smaller portions ensures steady progress. Consistently dedicating time to action steps reinforces their importance. Embrace persistence even on days when motivation wanes, knowing that each step counts.

Harmonizing Your Symphony

Crafting a transformative schedule is akin to composing a symphony that resonates with vitality, purpose, and balance. Just as the conductor harmonizes various instruments to create an enchanting melody, you harmonize sleep, work, exercise, routines, and action steps to create a life of holistic growth. Every note on your schedule carries the potential to create a harmonious masterpiece. By blending each element thoughtfully, you create a life that sings with accomplishment, well-being, and personal evolution. Embrace the power of a well-crafted schedule, and watch as it orchestrates your journey to greatness.

The Art of Mastering Time

In the tapestry of life, time is the most precious thread, weaving its way through our experiences, shaping our paths, and defining our destinies. In the context of personal growth, effective time management is the brush with which you paint the canvas of your aspirations. This chapter explores the art of mastering time as an essential tool in your personal growth journey. Time is the currency with which we pay for the moments that shape our lives. Just as a wise investor allocates resources strategically, effective time management allows you to invest in your personal growth pursuits with intention. Every tick of the clock is an opportunity to prioritize purpose. Allocate time to activities that align with your growth goals. Recognize that investing your time wisely is an investment in the person you aspire to become. Time management is the cornerstone of productivity. When you organize your day thoughtfully, you create pockets of focused effort that yield remarkable results. By dedicating time to learning, practicing, and reflecting, you amplify your personal growth journey.

Each day is a canvas awaiting the strokes of your intention. Design your schedule with purpose, allocating blocks of time for self-improvement. Just as an artist layers colors to create depth, layer your schedule with actions that enrich your growth. Routines are the rhythm of your days, setting the pace for your personal growth journey. Establish routines that become anchors for your development. Whether it's a morning ritual that kickstarts your day or an evening routine that fosters reflection, these rituals guide your actions. Allocate dedicated learning time within your schedule. Whether you're reading, attending courses, or engaging in skill-building activities, this time nourishes your mind and accelerates your growth. As you embark on your personal growth journey, you'll encounter numerous invitations and distractions. Embrace the power of saying "no" to commitments that don't align with your growth goals. This simple word safeguards your time for what truly matters.

Time management involves recognizing when to delegate tasks that don't directly contribute to your personal growth. By outsourcing or sharing responsibilities, you free up valuable time for pursuits that propel you forward. Allocate time for reflection, just as you might pause to admire a breathtaking view during a journey. Reflecting on your progress, setbacks, and learnings allows you to fine-tune your approach and make purposeful adjustments. Consistency is the heartbeat of effective time management. Small, intentional actions performed consistently compound over time, leading to significant progress. Embrace the power of the daily grind in nurturing your personal growth. As you manage your time, infuse each moment with mindfulness. Be fully present in your actions, whether it's reading a book, engaging in a growth activity, or simply taking a breather. Mindfulness enriches every experience. Just as an artist leaves behind a masterpiece, your management of time creates a legacy. The moments you invest in your personal growth journey shape not only your future but the impact you have on others and the world. Remember that time management isn't about rigid control; it's about embracing the journey. Personal growth is a voyage of discovery, and effective time management is the compass that ensures you sail in the right direction.

Harnessing Time's Potential

In the symphony of existence, time is the melody that carries us forward. Through skillful time management, you orchestrate the notes that compose your personal growth journey. Recognize that every tick of the clock is an opportunity, a reminder that the canvas of your life is painted one intentional stroke at a time. By mastering the art of time management, you sculpt the sculpture of your future, a testament to your dedication to growth, resilience, and the boundless possibilities that lie ahead. While the GPS gives us a time as to when we will arrive at our destination, it is through our time management that we discover our estimated time of arrival, our ETA in our personal growth. It is through our scheduling that we determine when we achieve our goals, and with proper time management, we can attain a general idea of when we will fulfill our goals.

Proper Time Management

Many of us have been disillusioned by the standard practices of managing by day planners that give us a preformatted range of time. We fill that as long as there is something written in each slot, we are managing our time precisely, but the truth is you are actually losing precious and valuable time each day. Let me give you an example of what I am talking about. This is Donald's Calendar:

Monday September 12, 2022

12 am	
5 am	
6 am	Wake up
7 am	
8 am	Work
9 am	Work
10 am	Work
11 am	Work
12 pm	Work
1 pm	Work
2 pm	Work
3 pm	Work
4 pm	Work
5 pm	
6 pm	Eat dinner

7 pm	NFL Post Game: Bears vs Packers	
8 pm	NFL Game: Bears vs Packers	
9 pm	NFL Game: Bears vs Packers	
10 pm	Go to bed	
11 pm	Sleep	

Notice that Donald's schedule has 8 items for the entire day. Is this all he will do on this day? I hope not! Do you see anything else wrong with his calendar? I want to see what you come up with. Here is what I see:

1. No Details – What does he do during his work time?
2. Blank Spaces – Is he idle all this time?
3. No Action steps – Does he have goals?
4. Missing Items – When does he groom? Does he read? Does he have a family? Does he have lunch or a break at work? If so, what does he do?
5. Too much time on one item – Does it take him an hour to wake up?
6. Too little time on one item – Does he only sleep an hour?

Did you get any of these? You may have even gotten something I didn't see, but you get the point. Do you schedule your time like Donald? Do you schedule your time at all? Your calendar should never have an hour interval. Thirty minutes is better, but fifteen minutes is optimal. Me personally, I prefer a fifteen-minute interval like Dennis uses.

Date: __08__/__15__/__2023__ **Day:** ☐Sun. ☐ Mon. ☒Tue. ☐Wed.

☐Thur. ☐ Fri. ☐Sat.

Time	Task	Urgency	Completed
8:45am	Respond to emails	1 2 3 4	☒
9:00am	Staff meeting	①② 3 4	☒
9:15am	Staff meeting	① 2 3 4	☒
9:30am	Work on presentation for Kia Motors	① 2 3 4	☒
11:45am	Work on presentation for Kia Motors	① 2 3 4	☒
12:00pm	Lunch / Listen to how to develop a winning attitude audiobook	1 ② 3 4	☒
12:15pm	Lunch / Apply for Amazon Master Card	1 ② 3 4	☒
12:30pm	Lunch / Call American Express to negotiate terms	1 ② 3 4	☒
12:45pm	Lunch / Listen to how to develop a winning attitude audiobook	1 ② 3 4	☒

Time	Activity	1 2 3 4	☑
1:00pm	Meeting with Reebok	① 2 3 4	☒
3:30pm	Meeting with Reebok	① 2 3 4	☒
3:45pm	Break / Read book of the week	① 2 3 4	☒
4:00pm	Check work emails and phone messages	1 ② 3 4	☒
4:15pm	Respond to work emails and phone calls	1 ② 3 4	☒
4:30pm	Respond to work emails and phone calls	1 ② 3 4	☒
4:45pm	Clean off desk	1 2 ③ 4	☒
5:00pm	Drive to work listening to how to develop a winning attitude audiobook	1 ② 3 4	☒
5:15pm	Drive to work listening to how to develop a winning attitude audiobook	1 ② 3 4	☒
5:30pm	Exercise Routine	1 ② 3 4	☒
5:45pm	Exercise Routine	1 ② 3 4	☒
6:00pm	Dinner with family	1 2 ③ 4	☒
6:15pm	Dinner with family	1 2 ③ 4	☒
6:30pm	Talk with wife about our day	1 2 ③ 4	☒
6:45pm	Talk with wife about our day	1 2 ③ 4	☒
7:00pm	Coaching call with Darryl / Email progress report for July	① 2 3 4	☒
7:15pm	Marketing agency training	1 ② 3 4	☐
7:30pm	Marketing agency training	1 ② 3 4	☐
7:45pm	Marketing agency training	1 ② 3 4	☐
8:00pm	Read bedtime story and say prayers with children	1 2 ③ 4	☐
8:15pm	Work on vision board	① 2 3 4	☐
8:30pm	Complete daily assessment	1 ② 3 4	☐
8:45pm	Read and discuss the Bible with wife	1 ② 3 4	☐
9:00pm	Read and discuss the Bible with wife / Pray	1 ② 3 4	☐
9:15pm	Bedtime routine / Turn on Meditational music	1 2 ③ 4	☐
9:30pm	Sleep	1 ② 3 4	☐
9:45pm	Sleep	1 ② 3 4	☐

Dennis uses the fifteen-minute method, which is the method I teach. He also uses color coding to categorize the things he does:

- Shades of blue are used for personal.

- Shades of yellow are used for spiritual growth.

- Shades of green are used for action steps towards his goals.

- Shades of orange are used for work.

- Shades of red are used for family time.

As you can see, Dennis is very detailed in what he has to do, and he uses his time wisely. For example, when he drives to work, he listens to an audiobook on self-development. During lunch, he also listens to his audiobook and makes phone calls, coding it as action steps towards his goals. He prioritizes his schedule and uses a checklist for items completed.

Now, I must be completely honest: Donald and Dennis are the same person. Before Dennis became a client, he was scheduling his time like Donald, but after learning the LPS methods, he blossomed. The scheduling method you see is the LPS scheduling method, which we have turned into a new daily planner that may be available for purchase by the time this book is available.

Understand that time management is where we allow our journey towards the fulfillment of our goals to become a reality. It is through time management that we will have our amenities along our journey. These amenities include such things as:

1. Family time
2. Meditation
3. Vacations
4. Dating
5. Dining out
6. Other entertainment

Time management is not only a critical part of achieving our goals, but it is also a crucial part of living a well-balanced and fulfilling life. Are you ready to live that type of life? If so, turn to page 473 of your workbook to the LPS Daily Calendar or create the Calendar in your notebook from the example above and plan out your day for tomorrow. I have included one LPS Daily Calendar in your workbook. It is a small part of the LPS Planner, which is sold separately and can be purchased online at www.[domainname.com]/planner for $9.95 in digital format or $19.95 in printed format for a 30-day planner.

Remember as you are scheduling your day, there are a few things that you need to keep in mind:

1. Make sure to include your routines.
2. Determine which goals you will start working on.
3. Include the action steps to start those goals in your schedule.
4. Make sure your day is well-balanced.

Reading this book has been nothing but a vehicle inspection up to this point. Once you have completed your schedule for tomorrow, your true journey begins. Once we know and understand who we are right now, know what our goals are, create action steps, utilize our resources, and take control of our time, it will be a much easier and smoother ride to reach our new destination in life. Now that you know what the LPS is and have a full understanding of how to use it, I hope it will help you to reach your destination in life. Safe travels and enjoy the journey.

But you need to know that true personal growth never ends; it is a series of destinations. Once you have completed one journey, there is always another one to be traveled and another one after that, and so on. Personal growth is much like a family vacation, allowing you to travel to new destinations each time, to experience more sceneries and build lasting memories that will last a lifetime. Just as we never grow tired of experiencing new adventures, we never grow tired of experiencing personal growth. Each time we reach our destination by achieving all our goals, we need to start planning for the next adventure.

While this may be the first time you have read this book, it will more than likely not be your last. Each time you reach your final destination in one of your personal growth journeys and begin a new personal growth adventure, you may need to refer back to it to begin your next personal growth journey. Just as we will never see the entire world and experience every scene, culture, or inhabitant of it, we will never reach our full potential in life. But know that we will complete several personal growth journeys throughout our lifetime, each time arriving at our destination being better, stronger, smarter, and more resilient than we have ever been.

Part VII
You have Arrived

"You Have Arrived"

"You have arrived." These three words from a GPS bring a sense of accomplishment and relief, signaling that we've reached our destination safely and can now enjoy the benefits of our journey.

Imagine your personal growth journey as a long and rewarding road trip. The miles you've traveled, the challenges you've overcome, and the dreams you've pursued have all brought you to this moment. Just as a GPS announces, "You have arrived at your destination," it's time to pause, reflect, and celebrate your remarkable journey.

As you stand at the intersection of your goals and dreams, take a moment to look back on the path you've traversed. Just as a GPS reviews your route, consider the twists, turns, and detours that brought you here. Each challenge, setback, and triumph has contributed to the person you've become. Celebrate your progress, no matter how small or significant. Each step forward, each lesson learned, and each goal achieved is a testament to your dedication and resilience.

Express gratitude for the journey itself. Just as a road trip is as much about the experiences along the way as it is about the destination, your personal growth journey is enriched by the moments, relationships, and lessons you've encountered. Recognize the transformative power of your journey. Much like a road trip allows you to explore new landscapes, your personal growth journey has expanded the horizons of your potential, pushing you beyond your comfort zone.

While it's essential to celebrate how far you've come, it's equally important to acknowledge that personal growth is an ongoing process. Just as a GPS recalculates your route if you choose a new destination, consider what lies ahead in your continued journey. Set new goals and aspirations for yourself. Just as a traveler might decide to visit new places, identify areas of growth and self-improvement that excite you. Embrace the adaptability and resilience you've developed. Personal growth isn't just about reaching a destination; it's about evolving continuously and rising to new challenges.

Just as a road trip can lead to meaningful encounters and shared experiences, consider how your personal growth journey can benefit others. Share your knowledge, support, and insights with those who may be on their own paths to growth.

"You have arrived at your destination" is a moment of triumph, but it's also a reminder that every destination is a stepping stone to the next. As you celebrate this milestone in your personal growth journey, savor the victory, reflect on your progress, and embrace the possibilities that lie ahead. Take time to reflect on your achievements. Express gratitude for the resources, support, and opportunities that have enabled your growth. Celebrate not only the destination but the joy you've found in the journey itself. Just as a road trip is an adventure, so too is your path of personal growth. As you pause to celebrate, refocus your purpose. Set new goals and intentions and embark on the next leg of your journey with enthusiasm and determination. Consider sharing your personal growth story with others. Just as a traveler might inspire someone to explore new places, your journey can inspire others to pursue their own growth and self-discovery.

You Have Arrived, but the Journey Continues

In the grand tapestry of life, personal growth is the road trip of a lifetime. "You have arrived at your destination" is not the end; it's a checkpoint along the way. Embrace this moment as a testament to your commitment, your resilience, and your unwavering belief in the limitless potential of your own growth. With this milestone as a launching point, continue to navigate the remarkable journey that is your life, ever eager to discover the new horizons that await you. Just as there will always be another road trip to a new unseen destination, there will always be another personal growth journey.

The Joy of Being Your Traveling Companion

It is with a heart brimming with gratitude that I extend my deepest thanks to each one of you. Being a part of your personal growth journey through the Life Progression System has been an incredible privilege and honor. Your dedication, resilience, and unwavering commitment to self-improvement have inspired me beyond measure. Remember that personal growth is a lifelong adventure, and I'm immensely proud of the strides you've taken so far. As you continue to chart your path towards success and fulfillment, know that I'm here, cheering you on, and believing in your limitless potential. Together, we'll keep exploring the incredible possibilities that life offers. Thank you for allowing me to be a part of your journey.

My Letter to You

If you have made it this far, I want you to pause for a moment.

Take a breath.

Finishing this book is not a small accomplishment. It means you are not content with drifting. It means something inside of you refuses to settle. It means you believe—whether quietly or boldly—that your life can be more structured, more disciplined, more impactful, and more intentional.

And you are right.

The Life Progression System was never meant to simply be read. It was meant to be lived. Every chapter, every assessment, every exercise was designed to move you from awareness to execution. From confusion to clarity. From reaction to design.

But here is the truth: no system works unless the person using it commits to it.

Your progress from this point forward will not depend on your talent. It will not depend on your past. It will not depend on what others think about you. It will depend on your willingness to be disciplined when no one is watching. To execute when it is inconvenient. To remain consistent when motivation fades.

You already possess everything necessary to move forward.

You have the ability to change your beliefs.
You have the power to set goals.
You have the strength to take action.
You have the resources to grow.
You have the authority to design your future.

Do not return to autopilot.

Do not allow old habits to reclaim new territory.

You are not here by accident. You are not reading this by coincidence. The desire for growth that stirred you to pick up this book is evidence that you are meant for intentional living—not accidental outcomes.

Your family needs your discipline.
Your community needs your structure.
Your future needs your consistency.
Your legacy needs your courage.

From this day forward, live on purpose.

Let your goals be written.
Let your habits be measured.
Let your time be guarded.
Let your resources be stewarded.
Let your progress be visible.

This is your life. Design it carefully.

And remember—progress is not a moment. It is a system.

Now go build.

With conviction and belief in your greatness,

Rev. Darryl Bass

The 90-Day Life Reset

From Awareness to Alignment to Acceleration

Transformation does not happen by accident.
It happens by design.

The next 90 days are not just another quarter of your life. They are a reset. A recalibration. A deliberate interruption of old patterns and a structured installation of new ones.

This 90-Day Life Reset is broken into three phases:

- **Phase I: Awareness (Days 1–30)**
- **Phase II: Alignment (Days 31–60)**
- **Phase III: Acceleration (Days 61–90)**

Each phase builds upon the previous one. Do not rush. Do not skip. Systems require sequence.

Phase I: Awareness (Days 1–30)

"Know Where You Are"

You cannot correct what you refuse to confront.

The first 30 days are about clarity—not change. You are observing, assessing, identifying, and documenting.

During This Phase You Will:

- Complete a full self-assessment (beliefs, strengths, weaknesses)
- Identify and write down all current fears
- Define your current financial position (income, debt, savings, obligations)
- Audit your daily habits
- Track how you spend your time
- Document your emotional triggers
- Clarify your values and non-negotiables

No major lifestyle changes yet.
No dramatic overhauls.
Just radical honesty.

Weekly Focus:

Week 1: Identity & Beliefs
Week 2: Habits & Time
Week 3: Financial Reality
Week 4: Emotional & Behavioral Patterns

At the end of 30 days, you should clearly know:

- Who you are today
- What is helping you
- What is hurting you
- What must change

Clarity removes confusion. Confusion delays progress.

Phase II: Alignment (Days 31–60)

"Correct the Misalignment"

Now that you know where you are, we begin realignment.

In this phase, you align:

- Identity with goals
- Beliefs with vision
- Habits with outcomes
- Spending with priorities
- Time with purpose

During This Phase You Will:

- Rewrite limiting beliefs
- Establish 3–5 major 12-month goals
- Create weekly action steps for each goal
- Implement a structured daily schedule
- Begin eliminating one destructive habit
- Begin building one empowering habit
- Create a basic financial plan (income allocation system)

This is where discipline begins.

You are no longer observing. You are restructuring.

Weekly Focus:

Week 5: Goal Architecture
Week 6: Habit Installation
Week 7: Financial Structure
Week 8: Time & Execution Systems

By Day 60, your life should feel more intentional, more organized, and more directed.

Phase III: Acceleration (Days 61–90)

"Execute with Precision"

This phase is about momentum.

You now:

- Execute consistently
- Track measurable progress
- Adjust without quitting
- Strengthen discipline
- Eliminate distractions

During This Phase You Will:

- Review goals weekly
- Measure financial progress
- Strengthen new habits
- Increase productivity
- Eliminate one more major weakness
- Leverage one major strength intentionally

You are no longer restarting.
You are accelerating.

Weekly Focus:

Week 9: Performance Tracking
Week 10: Resource Optimization
Week 11: Strength Leverage
Week 12: System Refinement & Commitment Renewal

The 90-Day Declaration

At the end of 90 days, you will not be perfect.
But you will not be the same.

You will:

- Think differently
- Spend differently
- Act differently
- Prioritize differently
- Plan differently

The Life Progression System works—but only for those who work it.

These 90 days are not about motivation.
They are about installation.

And once discipline is installed, progress becomes predictable.

Personal Commitment Contract

This is not a symbolic exercise.
This is a declaration of discipline.

I understand that progress does not happen by accident.
It happens by design, structure, and execution.

By signing this agreement, I acknowledge that my life will only change to the degree that I change.

Personal Declaration

I, _____, choose to commit to living intentionally.

I acknowledge that:

• My current results are a reflection of my current habits.
• My future results will be determined by my daily decisions.
• My beliefs shape my actions.
• My actions shape my outcomes.
• My discipline determines my destiny.

I accept full responsibility for my growth, development, and progress.

My 90-Day Commitments

For the next 90 days, I commit to:

☐ Completing all Life Progression exercises honestly
☐ Writing down my goals clearly and specifically
☐ Tracking my habits consistently
☐ Guarding my time intentionally
☐ Eliminating at least one destructive habit
☐ Installing at least one empowering habit
☐ Reviewing my goals weekly
☐ Taking action daily, even when I do not feel motivated

I understand that motivation is temporary, but discipline builds momentum.

My Vision Statement

The version of myself I am committed to becoming is:

_____

_____

_____

_____

My Top 3 Goals for the Next 12 Months

1. _____
2. _____
3. _____

Consequence & Accountability

If I break this commitment through neglect, procrastination, or excuse-making, I will:

(Define a real consequence that reinforces discipline.)

My accountability partner (optional): _____

Final Declaration

I am not waiting for permission.
I am not waiting for perfect conditions.
I am not waiting for motivation.

I am building structure.
I am building discipline.
I am building legacy.

Beginning today, I choose progress over excuses.

Signed: _____

Date: _____

Witness (optional): _____

Appendix A

List of Fears

In the journey of personal growth, various fears may arise, hindering our progress and self-discovery. Here is an extensive and detailed list of fears that one may encounter along the path to personal development:

1. **Fear of Failure:** The fear of not meeting expectations, making mistakes, or not achieving desired outcomes can deter us from taking risks and pursuing our goals.

2. **Fear of Rejection:** The fear of being unaccepted or rejected by others can hold us back from expressing ourselves authentically and forming meaningful connections.

3. **Fear of Success:** The fear of success can stem from concerns about handling increased responsibilities or fears of how success might change our relationships and identity.

4. **Fear of Change:** The fear of the unknown and uncertainty that accompanies change can make us resistant to stepping out of our comfort zones.

5. **Fear of Judgment:** The fear of being judged or criticized by others can prevent us from expressing our opinions and staying true to ourselves.

6. **Fear of Vulnerability:** The fear of being emotionally exposed or hurt can lead us to build emotional barriers, inhibiting genuine connections with others.

7. **Fear of Uncertainty:** The fear of not knowing what the future holds can create anxiety and impede us from making decisions and taking action.

8. **Fear of Abandonment:** The fear of being left or abandoned can affect our ability to trust and maintain healthy relationships.

9. **Fear of Success and Not Sustaining It:** The fear of achieving success only to lose it later can hinder our efforts to fully embrace accomplishments.

10. **Fear of Confrontation:** The fear of conflict or difficult conversations can prevent us from addressing issues and resolving conflicts effectively.

11. **Fear of Loneliness:** The fear of being alone can lead us to stay in unhealthy relationships or avoid solitude, hindering self-discovery.

12. **Fear of Inadequacy:** The fear of not being good enough or capable enough can erode our self-confidence and self-esteem.

13. Fear of Abandoning Comfort: The fear of leaving behind the familiar and stepping into the unknown can stifle personal growth.

14. Fear of Making Decisions: The fear of making the wrong choice can lead to indecisiveness and missed opportunities.

15. Fear of Being Authentic: The fear of showing our true selves to the world can result in living a life that feels unfulfilling and inauthentic.

16. Fear of Being Vulnerable in Relationships: The fear of getting hurt or betrayed can make us build walls around our hearts, hindering emotional intimacy.

17. Fear of Public Speaking: The fear of speaking in front of a group can limit our ability to share our ideas and influence others positively.

18. Fear of Criticism: The fear of receiving negative feedback can discourage us from taking risks and expressing our creativity.

19. Fear of Not Being Good Enough: The fear of not measuring up to societal standards or others' expectations can hold us back from pursuing our passions.

20. Fear of Missing Out (FOMO): The fear of missing out on experiences or opportunities can lead to constant comparison and dissatisfaction.

21. Fear of Trusting Others: The fear of being betrayed or taken advantage of can make it challenging to build trusting relationships.

22. Fear of Disappointing Others: The fear of letting others down can prevent us from setting boundaries and prioritizing our own needs.

23. Fear of Critiquing Our Beliefs: The fear of challenging our long-held beliefs can impede personal growth and self-awareness.

24. Fear of Not Living Up to Our Potential: The fear of not reaching our full potential can create pressure and inhibit us from taking risks.

25. Fear of Financial Insecurity: The fear of not having enough money to meet our needs can lead to anxiety and excessive worry.

26. Fear of Missing Opportunities: The fear of missing out on chances for growth and success can lead to constant restlessness and discontent.

27. Fear of Being Unworthy of Love: The fear of not being lovable or deserving of love can impact our ability to form healthy relationships.

28. Fear of Letting Go: The fear of releasing attachments to the past can hinder our ability to embrace change and move forward.

29. Fear of Being Alone with Our Thoughts: The fear of self-reflection and introspection can prevent us from understanding ourselves better.

30. Fear of Standing Out: The fear of being different or standing out from the crowd can hinder self-expression and authenticity.

31. Fear of Being Vulnerable in Creative Pursuits: The fear of criticism or rejection can hold us back from expressing our creativity fully.

32. Fear of Being Unsuccessful: The fear of not achieving our goals or measuring up to others' achievements can create self-doubt.

33. Fear of Emotional Pain: The fear of experiencing emotional pain or heartache can lead to emotional avoidance and detachment.

34. Fear of Not Being Respected: The fear of not being respected or valued can affect our self-worth and assertiveness.

35. Fear of Confronting Past Traumas: The fear of revisiting past traumas can hinder the healing process and personal growth.

36. Fear of Being Vulnerable with Ourselves: The fear of facing our own insecurities and vulnerabilities can inhibit self-acceptance.

37. Fear of Taking Responsibility: The fear of taking ownership of our actions and choices can lead to blaming others or external circumstances.

38. Fear of Letting Go of Control: The fear of surrendering control can prevent us from embracing uncertainty and new experiences.

39. Fear of Letting Others Down: The fear of disappointing others can lead to people-pleasing and prioritizing others' needs over our own.

40. Fear of Being a Burden: The fear of burdening others with our problems or emotions can inhibit seeking support and connection.

41. Fear of Losing Independence: The fear of depending on others can make us reluctant to seek help or collaborate with others.

42. Fear of Being Different: The fear of not fitting in or being judged for our uniqueness can suppress individuality and self-expression.

43. Fear of Making Mistakes: The fear of making errors or being imperfect can create a fear of failure and hinder taking action.

44. Fear of Not Being Enough for Others: The fear of not meeting others' expectations can lead to seeking external validation and approval.

45. Fear of Being Rejected by Our Own Self: The fear of not accepting ourselves fully can result in self-rejection and low self-esteem.

46. Fear of Not Living Authentically: The fear of living a life that doesn't align with our true values and passions can lead to inner conflict.

47. Fear of Success and Its Responsibilities: The fear of the responsibilities that come with success can lead to self-sabotage.

48. Fear of Being Alone in Adversity: The fear of facing challenges alone can deter us from pursuing our goals.

49. Fear of Losing Control of Emotions: The fear of being overwhelmed by emotions can lead to emotional suppression.

50. Fear of Failure and Its Impact on Self-Worth: The fear of failure affecting our sense of self-worth can lead to a fear of trying new things.

51. Fear of Not Being Loved for Who We Are: The fear of not being accepted and loved for our authentic selves can affect our relationships.

52. Fear of Change and Its Unpredictability: The fear of the unknown aspects of change can lead to resistance and stagnation.

53. Fear of Being Betrayed: The fear of being betrayed by others can impact our ability to trust and form deep connections.

54. Fear of Being Ignored or Overlooked: The fear of being overlooked or not being seen can lead to seeking external validation.

55. Fear of Not Meeting Societal Expectations: The fear of not conforming to societal norms can create pressure to fit in.

56. Fear of the Future and Its Uncertainty: The fear of the unknown future can lead to anxiety and worry.

57. Fear of Being Judged for Our Choices: The fear of judgment for our decisions can prevent us from following our hearts.

58. Fear of Losing Loved Ones: The fear of losing loved ones can lead to anxiety and clinginess.

59. Fear of Not Finding Purpose or Meaning: The fear of not finding our life's purpose can create existential angst.

60. Fear of Being Unseen: The fear of not being recognized or acknowledged can impact our self-esteem.

61. Fear of Letting Go of Negative Habits: The fear of breaking free from negative habits can lead to resistance to change.

62. Fear of Not Being Good Enough for Our Goals: The fear of not being capable enough to achieve our goals can hinder progress.

63. Fear of Being Vulnerable in Intimate Relationships: The fear of emotional intimacy can affect our ability to form deep connections.

64. Fear of Not Being Respected for Our Boundaries: The fear of not being respected when setting boundaries can lead to people-pleasing.

65. Fear of Losing Connection with Loved Ones: The fear of losing connections with family or friends can create emotional attachment.

66. Fear of Being Judged by Peers: The fear of judgment from peers can impact our ability to express ourselves authentically.

67. Fear of Failure and Its Impact on Others: The fear of failing and disappointing others can hinder taking risks.

68. Fear of Not Being in Control of Our Lives: The fear of not having control can lead to anxiety and stress.

69. Fear of Not Being Appreciated: The fear of not receiving appreciation can affect our self-esteem.

70. Fear of Not Being Taken Seriously: The fear of not being heard or valued can affect assertiveness.

71. Fear of Being Overlooked for Opportunities: The fear of missing out on opportunities can lead to restlessness.

72. Fear of Being Stagnant: The fear of not growing or evolving can create a sense of complacency.

73. Fear of Being Alone with Our Thoughts: The fear of self-reflection can hinder self-awareness.

74. Fear of Disappointing Our Role Models: The fear of not living up to the expectations of our role models can create pressure.

75. Fear of Betraying Our Values: The fear of compromising our values can lead to inner conflict.

76. Fear of Losing Our Identity: The fear of losing our sense of self can create resistance to change.

77. Fear of Being Vulnerable in Friendship: The fear of rejection in friendships can affect trust-building.

78. Fear of Not Making a Difference: The fear of not having an impact on others can create a sense of purposelessness.

79. Fear of Not Finding Contentment: The fear of not finding happiness and contentment can create restlessness.

80. Fear of Being Out of Our Comfort Zones: The fear of discomfort can hinder personal growth.

81. Fear of Not Being Taken Care of: The fear of not being provided for can lead to a dependence on others.

82. Fear of Not Having Control Over Our Emotions: The fear of being overwhelmed by emotions can create emotional suppression.

83. Fear of Not Meeting Others' Expectations: The fear of not measuring up to others' standards can create self-doubt.

84. Fear of Not Living Up to Our Potential: The fear of not reaching our full potential can create pressure.

85. Fear of Being Disconnected from Others: The fear of losing connection with loved ones can lead to emotional attachment.

86. Fear of Being Alone in Adversity: The fear of facing challenges alone can deter us from pursuing our goals.

87. Fear of Losing Control of Emotions: The fear of being overwhelmed by emotions can lead to emotional suppression.

88. Fear of Failure and Its Impact on Self-Worth: The fear of failure affecting our sense of self-worth can lead to a fear of trying new things.

89. Fear of Not Being Loved for Who We Are: The fear of not being accepted and loved for our authentic selves can affect our relationships.

90. Fear of Change and Its Unpredictability: The fear of the unknown aspects of change can lead to resistance and stagnation.

91. Fear of Being Betrayed: The fear of being betrayed by others can impact our ability to trust and form deep connections.

92. Fear of Being Ignored or Overlooked: The fear of being overlooked or not being seen can lead to seeking external validation.

93. Fear of Not Meeting Societal Expectations: The fear of not conforming to societal norms can create pressure to fit in.

94. Fear of the Future and Its Uncertainty: The fear of the unknown future can lead to anxiety and worry.

95. Fear of Being Judged for Our Choices: The fear of judgment for our decisions can prevent us from following our hearts.

96. Fear of Losing Loved Ones: The fear of losing loved ones can lead to anxiety and clinginess.

97. Fear of Not Finding Purpose or Meaning: The fear of not finding our life's purpose can create existential angst.

98. Fear of Being Unseen: The fear of not being recognized or acknowledged can impact our self-esteem.

99. Fear of Letting Go of Negative Habits: The fear of breaking free from negative habits can lead to resistance to change.

100. Fear of Not Being Good Enough for Our Goals: The fear of not being capable enough to achieve our goals can hinder progress.

Appendix B - List of Morals

Here is an extensive list of morals that encompasses a wide range of values and principles:

Honesty	Open-mindedness	Family values	Love
Authenticity	Community service	Faith	Truthfulness
Flexibility	Environmental consciousness	Hope	Thoughtfulness
Mindfulness	Social responsibility	Resourcefulness	Consistency
Prudence	Constructive criticism	Initiative	Unity
Balance	Personal growth	Adaptability	Dignity
Cooperation	Caring for others	Accountability	Serenity
Gratitude	Moral responsibility	Ethical conduct	Creativity
Responsibility	Respect for elders	Excellence	Modesty
Accountability	Respect for authority	Honor	Curiosity
Fairness	Self-respect	Authenticity	Dependability
Justice	Respect for animals	Moral courage	Peacekeeping
Trustworthiness	Mindful communication	Wisdom	Restraint
Loyalty	Healthy boundaries	Knowledge	Temperance
Generosity	Inner peace	Education	Hopefulness
Patience	Harmony	Self-confidence	Self-reflection
Perseverance	Respect for diversity	Self-care	Conscientiousness
Humility	Cultural sensitivity	Graciousness	Moderation
Courage	Tolerance	Teamwork	Acceptance
Nonviolence	Equality	Social justice	Selflessness
Empowerment	Independence	Self-discipline	Humor

Remember, this is not an exhaustive list, and individual morals can vary based on personal beliefs, cultural backgrounds, and life experiences. Choose the morals that resonate with you and align with your values and consider how you can embody them in your daily life.

Appendix C - Grooming Tasks

Bathing and Showering	Haircare
Full-body cleansing Using soap or body wash Scrubbing or exfoliating the body Washing and conditioning hair	Shampooing Conditioning Brushing or combing Haircut or trim Styling Coloring or dyeing
Skincare	**Oral Hygiene**
Cleansing Exfoliating Moisturizing Applying sunscreen Treating acne or blemishes Using anti-aging products Applying serums or toners	Brushing teeth Flossing Using mouthwash Cleaning the tongue Dental check-ups and cleanings
Fragrance and Perfume	**Hand Care**
Applying deodorant Using perfume or cologne Applying scented body lotion	Washing hands Moisturizing hands Cleaning and trimming fingernails
Nail Care	**Facial Grooming**
Trimming nails Filing nails Buffing nails Applying nail polish Caring for cuticles	Shaving or trimming facial hair Waxing or threading Eyebrow maintenance Cleansing and moisturizing the face
Nose Care	**Ear Care**
Nasal hygiene Trimming nose hairs	Cleaning ears Earwax removal Hearing aid maintenance
Foot Care	**Makeup Application**
Washing and scrubbing feet Trimming toenails Moisturizing Wearing clean socks and shoes Treating foot conditions	Foundation Concealer Eyeshadow Eyeliner Mascara Lipstick or lip gloss Blush Setting spray

Body Hair Removal	Intimate Grooming
Shaving Waxing Laser hair removal Depilatory creams Trimming or grooming body hair	Pubic hair grooming (shaving, waxing, trimming) Feminine hygiene products (for women) Genital care and cleanliness
Men's Grooming	**Hair Extensions and Weaves**
Beard care Mustache grooming Shaving routine Aftershave application	Cleaning and maintaining hair extensions. Treating the scalp underneath
General Hygiene	**Dental Appliances**
Regular handwashing throughout the day Bathing or showering as needed. Changing clothes and undergarments regularly Proper disposal of personal hygiene waste	Cleaning braces or retainers Denture care (if applicable)
Eye Care	**Personal Scent Management**
Using eye drops Cleaning and disinfecting contact lenses Eyebrow and eyelash grooming	Using deodorant or antiperspirant Managing body odor
Grooming Accessories Care	**Specialized Skincare**
Cleaning and maintaining grooming tools. Replacing or cleaning toothbrushes and loofahs	Treating skin conditions Applying medicated creams or ointments Skin allergy management
Grooming for Special Occasions	**Tattoo and Body Art Care**
Preparing for weddings, parties, or formal events Hairstyling and makeup for special occasions	Cleaning and moisturizing tattoos Sunscreen protection for tattoos
Skin Protection	
Applying skincare products to protect against pollution or harsh weather conditions.	

Appendix D

Exercises

Cardiovascular and Full-Body Exercises:

1. **Running:** Jogging, sprinting, long-distance running.
2. **Cycling:** Road cycling, mountain biking, stationary bike.
3. **Swimming:** Freestyle, breaststroke, butterfly, backstroke.
4. **Jumping Jacks:** A full-body exercise involving jumping while extending the arms and legs.
5. **Burpees:** A high-intensity exercise combining squats, push-ups, and jumps.
6. **Rowing:** Using a rowing machine to work the upper and lower body.
7. **Jump Rope:** Skipping rope for cardio and agility.
8. **High-Intensity Interval Training (HIIT):** Alternating between short bursts of intense exercise and rest.

Strength Training Exercises:

Upper Body:

9. **Push-Ups:** Chest and triceps.
10. **Pull-Ups/Chin-Ups:** Back and biceps.
11. **Bench Press:** Chest and triceps.
12. **Dumbbell Rows:** Back and biceps.
13. **Bicep Curls:** Biceps.
14. **Triceps Dips:** Triceps.
15. **Overhead Shoulder Press:** Shoulders and triceps.
16. **Push Press:** Shoulders and triceps.
17. **Lateral Raises:** Shoulder isolation.
18. **Front Raises:** Anterior shoulder isolation.
19. **Lateral Pulldowns:** Latissimus dorsi.
20. **Face Pulls:** Upper back and rear deltoids.

Lower Body:

21. **Squats:** Quadriceps, hamstrings, and glutes.
22. **Deadlifts:** Glutes, hamstrings, lower back, and traps.
23. **Lunges:** Quadriceps, hamstrings, and glutes.
24. **Leg Press:** Quadriceps, hamstrings, and glutes.
25. **Calf Raises:** Calves.
26. **Step-Ups:** Quadriceps, hamstrings, and glutes.
27. **Glute Bridges:** Glutes and lower back.
28. **Romanian Deadlifts:** Hamstrings and lower back.
29. **Hamstring Curls:** Hamstrings.

Core:

30. **Crunches:** Rectus abdominis.
31. **Planks:** Core muscles.
32. **Russian Twists:** Oblique.
33. **Bicycle Crunches:** Oblique.
34. **Leg Raises:** Lower abs.
35. **Sit-Ups:** Core muscles.
36. **Ab Wheel Rollouts:** Core muscles.
37. **Hanging Leg Raises:** Core muscles and hip flexors.

Flexibility and Mobility:

38. **Yoga:** Various poses and flows to improve flexibility and balance.
39. **Pilates:** Core-focused exercises for strength and flexibility.
40. **Static Stretching:** Stretching to improve flexibility and range of motion.
41. **Dynamic Stretching:** Stretching with movement, often used in warm-up routines.
42. **Foam Rolling:** Self-myofascial release to reduce muscle tightness.

Balance and Stability:

43. **Bosu Ball Exercises:** Using a Bosu ball for balance challenges.
44. **Stability Ball Exercises:** Core and balance work.
45. **Single-Leg Exercises:** Lunges, squats, and deadlifts on one leg.

Functional Exercises:

46. **Kettlebell Swings:** Full-body exercise.
47. **Medicine Ball Throws:** Core and explosive power.
48. **Battle Ropes:** Full-body workout for endurance and strength.

Sports-Specific Exercises:

49. **Basketball Drills:** Dribbling, shooting, and agility drills.
50. **Soccer Drills:** Passing, shooting, and agility drills.
51. **Tennis Drills:** Serve practice, volleying, and footwork.
52. **Golf Swing Drills:** Swing mechanics and core stability exercises.

Mind-Body Exercises:

53. **Tai Chi:** Slow, flowing movements for balance and relaxation.
54. **Qi Gong:** Breath and movement exercises for health and vitality.
55. **Meditation:** Mental relaxation and stress reduction.

Group Fitness Classes:

56. **Zumba:** Dance-based cardio workout.
57. **Spinning:** Indoor cycling classes.
58. **Aerobics:** High-energy group fitness classes.

Other Books by Rev. Darryl Bass

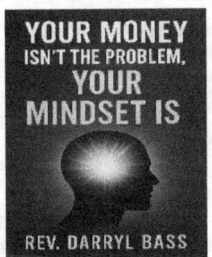

Your Money Isn't the Problem, Your Mindset Is

A transformational work that challenges limiting financial beliefs and redefines wealth from the inside out, empowering readers to align their identity with abundance and responsibility.

This Is Why You're Broke

A bold and unapologetic examination of the habits, beliefs, and financial behaviors that keep people trapped in cycles of struggle. This book confronts uncomfortable truths and replaces excuses with execution, helping readers shift from reactive spending to strategic wealth building.

Healing Your Financial Trauma

This book addresses the psychological and emotional roots of money struggles, helping readers break cycles, confront financial pain, and rebuild confidence and stability.

The Financial Identity Shift

A mindset-and-behavior reset that helps readers align who they are with how they handle money, transforming financial habits through identity-based discipline.

The Life Progression System Workbook

A comprehensive blueprint for intentional living, The Life Progression System guides readers through structured personal growth, goal alignment, mindset transformation, and legacy building. It equips individuals with practical tools to move from drifting through life to deliberately designing it.

Financial Progression System

This book provides a step-by-step roadmap to financial stability and long-term wealth building. It teaches readers how to increase income, eliminate debt, build credit, create savings systems, and establish generational financial security.

Borrowed Futures

A wake-up call about the hidden costs of debt and financial shortcuts, showing readers how to escape debt cycles and build futures without financial bondage.

Life Insurance: The Gift of Life After Life

More than a policy explanation, this book reframes life insurance as a strategic wealth-building and legacy-protection tool. It educates families on how to use life insurance for income replacement, debt protection, estate planning, generational wealth transfer, and financial leverage.

The Debt Eliminator

Coming 2026

What if 2026 was the year everything changed?

What if this was the year you stopped surviving… and started building?
The year you stopped juggling bills… and started creating wealth?
The year debt stopped controlling your decisions?

The **Debt Eliminator** is not another budgeting class.
It is a structured financial transformation system designed to help individuals and families break free from consumer debt, rebuild financial confidence, and establish a foundation for long-term wealth.

This course was built for hardworking people who are tired of living paycheck to paycheck. It was created for families who want stability, not stress. It was designed for individuals who know they are capable of more—but need a system that works.

What the Debt Eliminator Will Teach You:

• How to eliminate consumer debt strategically and aggressively
• How to increase income without adding overwhelm
• How to rebuild and optimize your credit profile
• How to build savings while eliminating debt
• How to structure emergency funds and protection plans
• How to shift your financial identity from borrower to builder
• How to create systems that prevent debt from returning

This is not theory.
This is execution.

Through step-by-step modules, implementation tools, accountability structure, and real-life application, you will learn how to take control of your money instead of letting it control you.

Imagine waking up without financial anxiety.
Imagine having a plan.
Imagine watching your balances decrease and your confidence increase.
Imagine positioning your household for ownership, investing, and generational legacy.

The Debt Eliminator is more than a course.
It is a movement toward financial clarity, discipline, and freedom.

Get ready to break cycles.
Get ready to build stability.
Get ready to eliminate debt—permanently.

The Debt Eliminator — Launching 2026.

Join our waiting list Today!
https://savingssolution.org/join

The Financial Freedom Revolution Tour

Launching 2026

This is not a seminar.
This is not a motivational rally.
This is a financial awakening.

The **Financial Freedom Revolution Tour** is a live, high-impact experience designed to ignite transformation in individuals, families, entrepreneurs, and communities ready to break financial cycles and build generational stability.

For too long, people have been working harder but falling further behind. Income rises. Expenses rise. Stress rises. Yet true financial progress feels out of reach.

The Revolution changes that.

This national tour brings together powerful teaching, real strategy, live coaching, and structured execution plans that move attendees from confusion to clarity—and from debt to disciplined wealth-building.

What You'll Experience:

• A clear roadmap to financial stability and long-term wealth
• Step-by-step strategies for eliminating consumer debt
• Income growth frameworks and entrepreneurship positioning
• Credit optimization and financial leverage strategies
• Protection planning and legacy-building principles
• Live financial assessments and actionable implementation steps
• A mindset shift from survival thinking to ownership thinking

This is not inspiration without structure.
This is strategy with accountability.

The Financial Freedom Revolution Tour is built for families who want peace instead of pressure. For entrepreneurs who want profit with structure. For leaders who understand that financial stability is the foundation for community impact.

Imagine thousands gathered in one space—learning, planning, committing to real change.
Imagine leaving with a clear blueprint instead of just excitement.
Imagine knowing exactly what steps to take the next day.

This is more than an event.
It is a declaration that debt cycles end here.
It is a call to financial responsibility, ownership, and generational leadership.

Cities across the country will host this movement in 2026.

Seats will fill.
Lives will shift.
Legacies will be built.

The Financial Freedom Revolution Tour — Coming 2026.

This is the year you stop reacting to money
...and start commanding it.

The revolution begins with one decision.
https://savingssolution.org/tour

Follow on Social Media

Facebook

https://www.facebook.com/LPSCoach

Twitter

https://twitter.com/LPS_Coach

Instagram

https://www.instagram.com/lps_coach/

YouTube

https://www.youtube.com/@life_progression_system

TikTok

https://www.tiktok.com/@debt_annihilator

LinkedIn

https://www.linkedin.com/in/lpscoach/

www.ingramcontent.com/pod-product-compliance
Lightning Source LLC
Chambersburg PA
CBHW081715220526
45468CB00008B/1850